SS∂/9⁹⁸

The Litigious Athenian

Ancient Society and History

MATTHEW R. CHRIST

The Litigious Athenian

The Johns Hopkins University Press
Baltimore and London

© 1998 The Johns Hopkins University Press
All rights reserved. Published 1998
Printed in the United States of America on acid-free paper
9 8 7 6 5 4 3 2 1

The Johns Hopkins University Press
2715 North Charles Street
Baltimore, Maryland 21218-4363
The Johns Hopkins Press Ltd., London
www.press.jhu.edu

Library of Congress Cataloging-in-Publication Data will be found at the end of this book.
A catalog record for this book is available from the British Library.

ISBN 0-8018-5863-1

To Robert I. Christ, 1927–1995

Contents

Acknowledgments   ix

Abbreviations   xi

Introduction
Litigiousness, Ancient and Modern   1

One
Litigation in Democratic Athens   14

Two
The Invention of Sykophancy:
Idea and Ideology   48

Three
Litigation and Class Conflict   72

Four
Public Suits and Volunteer Prosecutors   118

Five
Private Quarrels and Public Disputes: Quarrelsomeness
and Community Ideals   160

Contents

Six
Beyond the Letter of the Law   193

Conclusion   225

Notes   229

Select Bibliography   277

Index of Ancient Citations   297

General Index   308

Acknowledgments

A fellowship from the American Council of Learned Societies and a research grant from Indiana University in 1994–95 made it possible for me to do much of the work for this book. While on leave in Washington, D.C., during that year, I benefited from access to the library at the Center for Hellenic Studies, and appreciated the hospitality of the Center's directors, Kurt Raaflaub and Deborah Boedeker; Raymond and Dorothy Goodman generously provided me with a peaceful garret and an endless supply of coffee. I am grateful to my colleagues, Cynthia Bannon, James Franklin, William Hansen, and Eleanor Leach, for their kindness and support; to Adele Scafuro for sharing with me the proofs of her forthcoming book; and to Douglas Armato and Brian MacDonald at the Johns Hopkins University Press. I wish to extend special thanks to Edward Harris, Steven Johnstone, S. Douglas Olson, and the press's anonymous reader for their helpful criticisms of earlier versions of this manuscript. I am deeply indebted to Sophia Goodman for her support and patience.

Abbreviations

Abbreviated references to ancient authors and works are based primarily on those used in the ninth edition of *A Greek-English Lexicon*, edited by H. G. Liddell, R. Scott, and H. S. Jones (Oxford, 1940). In citing orations, I use the enumeration found in the Loeb editions; Ober ([1989] 341–48) provides a convenient catalog that lists and dates the extant orations. Where the attribution of an oration to an author has been challenged, I do not bracket the author's name. Unless otherwise noted, citations of comic fragments are from *Poetae Comici Graeci*, edited by R. Kassel and C. Austin (Berlin, 1983–95). Abbreviations of periodicals cited in the bibliography follow the system of *L'Année philologique*. Translations are adapted from the Loeb editions for most authors, and from Sommerstein's editions for Aristophanes.

The Litigious Athenian

Introduction

Litigiousness, Ancient and Modern

> You Athenians do nothing but judge lawsuits.
> —Aristophanes (*Pax* 505)
>
> Americans are the most litigious nation in human history.
> —Judge L. Forer ([1975] 133)

Over the past several decades many American and foreign observers have come to embrace the idea that litigation is out of control in the United States. This concern crops up regularly in the popular press, in political debate, and in scholarly circles. Alarming titles appear with regularity: *The Litigious Society; The Litigation Explosion; A Nation under Lawyers*.[1] The current fervor over "hyperlexis" in the United States recalls for the classicist the animated discussion of legal excess and abuse in the world's first democracy, classical Athens (508–322 B.C.).[2]

There are numerous similarities between the ancient and modern discussions. For example, ancient writers sometimes depict the pursuit of litigation as a disease (Dem. 55.30) or manifestation of madness (Dem. 48.56);[3] according to modern psychologists, for "litigious paranoids" the pursuit of litigation really is pathological.[4] The Athenian comic poet Aristophanes caricatures Athenians as addicts to jury service, who would gladly judge suits at home if they could (*V.* 764–1008). With the advent of the court channel on cable television, Americans are now able to play judge in their own living rooms; even teens can join in the fun with *Teen Court TV*.[5] Aristophanes proposed exporting legal tricksters from Athens to neighboring Boeotia in exchange for valuable Boeotian produce (*Ach.* 898–905). Columnist Russell Baker suggests that one might export U.S. lawyers to Japan in exchange for Japanese cars, and thus remedy the U.S. trade deficit with Japan.[6]

If these similarities invite the conclusion that there is nothing new under the sun, however, closer comparison of the ancient and modern situations brings out striking differences. For example, in the United States complaints concerning litigiousness are often directed against professional practitioners of law. Friedman comments on the poor reputation of lawyers:

> In some ways it is easy to understand why people dislike lawyers. The ordinary person goes to a lawyer only in times of serious trouble. Nobody likes morticians either. These professions batten off human misery. But at least the public does not accuse morticians of creating death. Lawyers, on the other hand, are widely suspected of stirring up demand for their product, making trouble in the interest of fees.[7]

In Athens, by contrast, legal self-help was the norm and there were no lawyers, that is, no professional class of legal experts who represented clients in and out of court. Although concerns over professionalism enter into the Athenian discussion of litigation in a variety of ways, these do not center on "lawyers."

To understand the Athenian discussion of litigation, one must appreciate the specific circumstances in which it arose. In classical Athens, litigation came to occupy center stage under the emerging democracy. Law, litigation, and popular courts—that is, large courts composed of average citizens—took on new and expanded roles in the fifth century B.C. and had a profound impact on public and private life within the city. Citizens in large numbers came into direct contact with the democracy's expanding "legal system,"[8] as litigants, advocates, witnesses, jurors, and spectators.[9] Lawcourts dotted the urban landscape (cf. Ar. *Nu.* 206–8). Laws and decrees, inscribed on stone slabs or building walls, were visible throughout the city. These changes came about with the consent of the Athenian people: a majority vote of the democratic Assembly introduced most of these changes and could at any point have reversed or modified them. But as long as democratic rule prevailed, the Athenian people did not alter the basic institutions that gave law and litigation this prominence. In fact, Athenians took great pride in their legal institutions, and the city's encomiasts went so far as to credit Athens with the invention of law and its promulgation among the Greeks (Isoc. 4.39–40; cf. Lys. 2.18–19; Dem. 24.210). More humble testimony to civic pride in legal institutions is provided by the discovery of jurors' bronze identification plaques in Athenian graves.[10]

This does not mean, however, that Athenians were entirely comfortable with the role of litigation in their society. In fact, to all appearances Athenians discussed legal excess and abuse frequently, intensely, and in a variety of social settings from the private dinner parties of the rich to the public settings of the courts, Assembly, Council, and Theater of Dionysus. Numerous concerns are expressed in contemporary sources. Lawsuits destroy social relations: private disputes should be resolved outside of court, not in ugly public legal battles. Politicians trump up suits against their rivals for personal gain and advancement rather than to serve the public interest. Litigants with legal experience and intimate knowledge of the law harass honest Athenians. Dirty tricks of all sorts abound, including the use of legal blackmail and false witnesses. Legal tricksters, pejoratively labeled "sykophants" (their devious activity is "sykophancy"), rule the day, and decent, peaceable men suffer at their hands.[11] Jurors are willing to support even the most dubious and fraudulent of claims.

Although these complaints could be interpreted as evidence of a legal crisis in Athens, they must not be taken entirely at face value. This book argues that the ongoing Athenian discussion of legal excess and abuse allows the modern observer to inquire into an intriguing facet of classical Athens: how Athenians conceived of, and responded to, problematic aspects of their personal and collective legal experience. Because litigation in Athens was closely linked to many aspects of life within the city, the discussion of legal excess and abuse gives us access to Athenian attitudes not only toward litigation, but also more generally toward the proper conduct of public and private life within the democracy. At issue in the ongoing discussion are basic cultural values concerning competition, aggression, and wiliness. No modern study has attempted to explore in detail the Athenian discussion of legal excess and abuse in these terms. In filling this gap, this book seeks both to illuminate the ancient context and to contribute to the growing body of scholarship concerning perceptions of litigation in diverse societies.

Two basic problems can hinder the evaluation of the ancient evidence: the nature of the ancient sources and modern preconceptions concerning litigiousness.

Our knowledge of Athenian litigation derives not from court records or archival material, but for the most part from the contemporary literary record. Most relevant are the extant comedies of Aristophanes, which date from 425 to 388 B.C.; some one hundred forensic orations preserved in their entirety or in significant fragments, ranging in date from the 420s to 322 B.C.;[12] and the works of prose writers of the fourth century B.C., especially Xenophon, Isocrates, Plato, and Aristotle.

These sources are difficult to interpret because they reflect biases of various kinds. For example, all of their authors were men, and male assumptions about gender permeate them. Furthermore, these writers were all in some sense members of the elite. They were highly educated and, because education required leisure and wealth, all must have been at least moderately well-off. The privileges these authors enjoyed set them apart from average Athenians and affected their outlooks on litigation. For conservative authors like Xenophon, Isocrates, Plato, and Aristotle, who were critical of the Athenian democracy, political bias went hand in hand with class bias, profoundly shaping their commentary on the democratic legal system.

Forensic oratory presents numerous additional obstacles to interpretation.[13] First, forensic orations are patently partisan representations of legal contests, and the veracity of statements in them cannot normally be tested, since opposing speeches are rarely extant; often little is known concerning the identities of the litigants, the facts of the case, and the court's verdict. Furthermore, because logographers, the professional speech writers who provided litigants with orations, most likely revised these speeches before publishing them, the speeches as transmitted may not always accurately reflect litigants' arguments in court.[14] The process of publication and transmission has also obscured important information that might help in the evaluation of litigants' claims. The surviving speeches indicate where a litigant paused for the reading out of witness testimony, but they do not normally include the deposition. Similarly, they mark where laws were read in support of litigants' claims but often do not include the text of the laws cited, and when laws are included, scholars frequently suspect that they have been inserted by later editors. The evaluation of litigants' legal claims is all the more difficult because no complete collection of Athenian laws or rules of procedure survives. When detailed information concerning laws and procedural rules appears centuries after the classical period in lexica and scholia, it should be regarded with skepticism.[15]

Modern interpreters must also be aware that the corpus of forensic orations was selected by ancient editors who were more interested in rhetorical style than in transmitting to later generations an accurate picture of what kinds of suits were most prevalent in Athens.[16] Forensic orations, moreover, give us access primarily to conflicts that reached court, although sometimes they allude to those that were settled out of court. Information concerning the presumably large number of conflicts that did not reach the courts is thus very limited.

Another obstacle to the study of Athenian litigation is that the surviving sources are distributed irregularly over time. Because most of the sources date from the period ca. 430–322 B.C., it is difficult to assess the Athenian reaction to the dramatic legal changes that occurred in the decades immediately following the reform of the popular courts in 462 B.C. When the sources speak of legal excess and abuse, they are probably not reacting so much to a revolution in progress as to its aftermath. Even for the period 430–322 B.C., the ancient record is checkered. For the early years, Aristophanes' comedies provide a disproportionate amount of information. For the later years, forensic orations are the primary source, although some decades, especially the 370s and 360s B.C., are poorly represented.[17]

Although these features of the ancient sources make it difficult to answer many basic questions concerning litigation in Athens, they present less of an obstacle to the study of social attitudes toward litigation. In fact, some of the biases that frustrate research concerning details of law and litigation make the surviving sources rich repositories of information concerning the prejudices and assumptions of their authors and the audiences for whom they tailored their views. Furthermore, the irregular distribution of source material over time poses less of a problem for the study of attitudes toward litigation than for inquiry into the development of legal rules and institutions.[18] Although ideally the sources would allow us to track the vacillations in social attitudes which must have occurred from time to time, there is good reason to believe that basic Athenian concerns about litigation did not change dramatically during the period 430–322 B.C. The areas of concern and manner of expression are remarkably consistent throughout this period. The static nature of the discussion reflects, first, the stability of democratic legal institutions during this period. Second, even where innovation occurred—for example, in the form of new legal actions—Athenian audiences evaluated excess and abuse of these in the same basic terms in which they assessed the use of other, older actions. Because of the continuity of the Athenian discussion of legal excess and abuse during the period 430–322 B.C., this book will treat the period as a historic epoch within which it is legitimate to draw on sources of different dates. Furthermore, material will for the most part be arranged topically rather than chronologically in the view that more is gained than lost by this arrangement.

To make sense of the Athenian discussion of litigation, one must come to terms not only with the problems inherent in the ancient sources but also with modern preconceptions. Political and ideological assumptions strongly color the modern interpretation of the ancient discussion. Much early scholarship on Athenian litigation, as on Athenian democracy in general, accepts at face value ancient conservative perspectives.[19] This is conspicuous, for example, in Lofberg's *Sycophancy in Athens* (1917), which has served throughout

Introduction

most of this century as the standard work on the abuse of litigation in Athens:

> Pay for the service [on juries] made it possible for the poorer and more undesirable to act as jurors. The result was that the courts grew to be gatherings of the idle and less competent who enjoyed the flattering respect of the litigants and the sense of importance that their authority gave them . . . . In such a soil the business of the sycophant grew apace . . . Sycophancy was the inevitable disease of democracy.[20]

Lofberg's failure to appreciate the prejudices of the ancient critics of the Athenian courts, whom he cites in support of these criticisms, profoundly affects his assessment of litigation in Athens.[21] Many scholars have followed Lofberg, embracing his view that Athens suffered from a legal crisis of great proportions and that the city's democratic constitution was to blame for this.[22]

More recently, scholars have become increasingly aware of the conservative bias of many ancient sources and have reevaluated their complaints about the democracy and litigation within it in this light.[23] Although this scholarly trend has been salutary in its liberation of modern interpretations of the Athenian democracy from the jaundiced perspectives of its ancient critics, there is some risk that the ideological pendulum may swing too far. Skepticism toward elite complaints of abuse and excess has led Osborne, for example, to argue: "Sykophantic allegations were an important democratic mechanism of social regulation; by them the rich were prevented from using their wealth in an anti-social way, and were also prevented from withdrawing their means from public service."[24] While Osborne is right to point to class dimensions of the discussion of sykophancy in Athens, this picture of extreme class polarization over sykophancy and the idea that "sykophants had a structural part to play in democracy"[25] do not do justice to the complexity of the ancient situation.[26] First, the rich of Athens were not uniformly in need of prodding by sykophantic accusers to participate in civic life. Second, the Athenian people were not entirely unsympathetic to the legal situation of the wealthy. For example, the city's laws, which came into existence with popular approval, gave members of the elite numerous footholds for pursuing their complaints of legal excess and abuse (see Chapter 1). Furthermore, wealthy litigants assumed that their complaints about sykophancy might sway juries composed of average citizens (Chapter 3).

It is not surprising that the twentieth-century debate concerning litigation in the Athenian courts displays ideological bias. The discussion of legal excess and abuse in modern societies involves controversial political and cultural questions concerning the proper role of law in society, and it is naturally difficult for scholars to set these aside in evaluating the ancient situation. The modern discussion of litigiousness is worth considering closely. First, this can make us more self-conscious about the assumptions that we, as moderns, may bring to the Athenian material. Second, recent scholarship assessing the modern discussion can make us aware of facets of the Athenian discussion that we might otherwise miss.

Legal anthropologists have called attention to the ideological character of the discussion of legal excess and abuse in the late twentieth-century United States. Galanter's work on the supposed litigiousness of American society has been seminal. The title of one of Galanter's articles (1983) conveys his skepticism: "Reading the Landscape of Disputes: What We Know and Don't Know (and Think We Know) about Our Allegedly Contentious and Litigious Society." In this and other articles, Galanter draws attention to the alarmist tone and tendentious nature of the discussion of litigiousness in the United States. Galanter argues that frequently those who complain about litigiousness in the United States do so on the basis of haphazard impressions. Conspicuous individual cases or certain types of cases, especially tort suits, have an undue impact on the public's perceptions of litigation.[27] Furthermore, even if it is true that certain types of suits are on the rise, those who decry "hyperlexis" often seem to take for granted that litigation per se is an evil, because, for example, it reflects the level of contentiousness within a society. This ignores the fact that rising levels of litigation may be due more to an increasing readiness on the part of disputants to resolve conflicts in formal, rather than informal, settings.[28] Galanter argues that litigation levels may also rise because outsiders, who were previously barred from seeking legal remedies by structural impediments, have gained access to the system.[29] In this case, a high level of litigation is an indication not so much of contentiousness as of improved access to social justice. Those who complain of litigiousness in these circumstances may do so because their vested interests are threatened. Galanter goes so far as to label the "litigation explosion" an item of elite folklore.[30]

Although one need not take as optimistic a view of the role of litigation in society as Galanter does, his assessment of the basic nature of the discussion of litigiousness in American society is cogent.[31] This discussion is grounded less in neutral observation of the legal system than in value-laden assumptions concerning the proper role of litigation in society. That "litigiousness" is a lightning rod for controversy and for the expression of conflicting ideological perspectives is strikingly evident in the political arena. For example, while Republicans seeking to reform the rules governing tort suits decry what they perceive as unbridled litigiousness, Democrats emphasize the importance of access to relief for those who have suffered injury at the hands of irresponsible individuals or corporations: the Republican's tort reform bill is thus the Democrat's "Drunk Drivers' Protection Act."[32] Behind the political rhetoric and catchwords lie fundamentally different views concerning the purposes of litigation and the courts within a democratic society.

Other scholars, building on Galanter's work, have studied how the idea of "litigiousness" comes into play within various American communities and have begun to develop a framework for understanding the ideas, concerns, and tensions that are embedded in the discussion.[33] Engel, for example, who has studied concerns about litigation in a rural county in Illinois, concludes: "The differentiation of legitimate and illegitimate legal claims was part of a more general process of comparing and distinguishing that which was legitimately of the community and that which was to be condemned, shunned, or banished from it."[34] Engel notes in particular how members of the community studied used the categories of "insiders and outsiders" to differentiate between proper and improper uses of law: insiders appropriately sue in pursuit of their contractual rights, outsiders inappropriately press tort claims.[35] Greenhouse points to similar features of the discussion of litigiousness in a Baptist community located in a suburb of a southern U.S. city. Residents of this community engaged in a discourse characterized by "the creation and reproduction of generic categories of others, sometimes named, sometimes not, whose social predations are served by their allegedly inappropriate use of courts." She suggests that "to the extent that Americans worry about litigiousness, they share with Hopewell's Baptists a cultural vision that reveals at once a cultural model of society and a portrait of its enemies."[36] Viewed in this light, the American discussion of litigiousness can be taken as "cultural self-representation of American society."[37]

It is not only in the appeal to categories of self and other, however, that the American discussion of litigiousness reveals itself as a discourse about the nature of community. Frequently, the discussion takes the form of a critique of the situation in the United States relative "to some better past or some more favored place":[38] if only Americans could return to a golden past or emulate the model of some distant utopia, they could regain the sense of community they have lost.

Persons complaining of American litigiousness often contrast the current situation in which litigation has "exploded" with a vague past in which recourse to litigation was less frequent. Historians of the colonial period, however, have discovered that litigation rates at this time may well have been higher than those in the late twentieth century.[39] Similarly, the decline of the "once noble profession of law" is regularly lamented.[40] But were lawyers ever noble? As Judge Richard Posner cynically remarks, "The clock cannot be turned back, especially to a time that never existed."[41] Those appealing to a better past, however, are not so much making verifiable historical claims as they are commenting on what they perceive to be deficiencies of the status quo. In so doing, they "recall and reaffirm an untainted world that exist[s] nowhere but in their imaginations."[42]

Ideal alternatives to the current situation in the United States are sometimes sought in other contemporary societies, most conspicuously in Japan. It is commonplace for those who complain of American litigiousness to point to Japan as a society in which litigation has its proper place, and to exalt it as a model for the United States.

They assert, moreover, that the Japanese are more able to compete in world markets because they are not hindered, as their American competitors are, by litigation at home. Those who view Japan in these ideal terms fail to appreciate, however, the potentially negative consequences of limited access to courts in Japan. Galanter argues, for example, that "the low rate of litigation in Japan evidences not the preferences of the population, but deliberate policy choices by political elites."[43]

The prominence of rhetoric, image, unsubstantiated generalization, and polemic in the American discussion of excess and abuse in litigation should alert one to the possibility that in other societies too such discussion may not be a straightforward reflection of a historical problem or crisis, but rather part of a discourse about complex aspects of legal experience. Engel astutely observes:

> Criticism of what is seen as an overuse of law and legal institutions often reveals less about the quantity of litigation at any given time than about the interests being asserted or protected through litigation and the kinds of individuals or groups involved in cases that the courts are asked to resolve. Periodic concerns over litigation as a "problem" in particular societies or historical eras can thus draw our attention to important underlying conflicts in cultural values and changes or tensions in the structure of social relationships.[44]

Similarly, Galanter suggests that "[d]isputes and knowledge about disputes are kindred social constructions. Just as patterns of disputes may reveal something of the changing contours of the social world, so may patterns of social knowledge about disputes."[45]

"Litigiousness," therefore, is not so much something that can be measured—although one can attempt to compile statistics on litigation rates and use them to support or refute assertions concerning litigiousness—as it is an evaluative and value-laden concept that reveals as much about those making claims concerning it as about patterns of litigation within a society. As Greenhouse observes, "litigiousness" can thus be viewed as "an element of the semiotics of social experience."[46]

The scholarly analysis of litigiousness as an element of discourse within the United States can enrich our understanding of the Athenian discussion of litigation. I argue that the Athenian discussion of legal excess and abuse, like the modern discussion, is given to polemic, abstraction, utopianism, and ideological manipulation. It resembles the modern discussion, moreover, in its manipulation of categories of self and other in the denigration of supposed legal tricksters. All of this suggests that in Athens, too, the discussion of legal excess and abuse constitutes a complex and multifaceted discourse concerning society, community, and culture. At the same time, to assimilate the Athenian experience too readily to a modern one risks obscuring its most distinctive features. The Athenian discussion must be examined in its own terms. For example, despite the title of this book, I avoid the use of the word "litigious" in my analysis of the ancient material, because it is a vague and loaded term in the modern discussion and can therefore create confusion when transplanted to the ancient setting.[47] To be sure, Athenians frequently applied the root *sukophant-* to devious legal behavior, but its usage does not correspond precisely to that of "litigious" and its cognates in the modern discussion. Furthermore, because words of the root *sukophant-* are loaded and imprecise terms in their own right in the ancient context, one must be careful in using them as terms in modern analysis of the ancient situation. In general, therefore, I prefer to characterize the ancient discussion as one concerning "legal excess and abuse." This phrase conveys broadly the range of concerns expressed in the ancient discussion: it subsumes not only complaints of "sykophancy" but also concerns about litigation that do not happen to fall precisely within the philological field of *sukophant-*.

In the chapters that follow, I attempt first to place the Athenian discussion of legal excess and abuse within its cultural and historical context by considering litigation under the Athenian democracy (508–322 B.C.) (Chapter 1). I then look at the imagery and terms of the discussion, and argue that they convey a great deal about its social meaning and significance; of particular interest is the way Athenians often envision devious legal behavior as the province of the sykophant, who is presented as an absolute outsider and enemy of society (Chapter 2). Behind the appealing idea that Athenians unanimously condemn legal chicanery as vividly embodied in the

Introduction

figure of the sykophant, however, lies a more complex reality. Embedded in the Athenian discussion are fundamental tensions over the proper place of law and litigation in the private and public lives of citizens under the democracy. For example, when elite Athenians spoke of legal excess and abuse, they often blamed the Athenian people for encouraging litigation in the popular courts (Chapter 3). Members of all classes, however, were ambivalent about aspects of litigation. When Athenians discussed legal excess and abuse, they expressed concerns about the appropriateness of private individuals volunteering to bring public prosecutions on behalf of the city (Chapter 4); the role of conflict and dispute within the Athenian community (Chapter 5); and the role of laws and legal expertise within an ideally egalitarian society (Chapter 6).

One

Litigation in Democratic Athens

During the shadowy, but critical, period ca. 508–430 B.C., dramatic changes took place in Athenian political and legal institutions. Over a period of some two generations after the founding of the democracy under Cleisthenes (508/7 B.C.),[1] the Athenian people (*dēmos*) wrested power from the hands of a narrow elite and moved toward realizing the ideal of equality in relation to the laws (*isonomia*),[2] at least for the fully enfranchised male minority that dominated civic life. A critical juncture in this process was the transfer in 462 B.C. of most of the judicial powers of the Council of the Areopagus, an aristocratic bastion composed of former chief magistrates, to popular courts (*dikastēria*) composed of large numbers of citizens. Although the details of this transfer, initiated by a certain Ephialtes, are elusive, it is clear that the popular courts gained jurisdiction over the vast majority of suits, while the Areopagus retained control over, most notably, cases involving intentional homicide and wounding.[3] Sometime in the next decade Pericles introduced pay for jurors and thus ensured that even less well-off Athenians could afford to serve on juries ([Arist.] *AP* 27.3–5; cf. Arist. *Pol.* 1274a8–9).

As the Athenian empire expanded after the Ephialtic reforms, several factors worked together to bring litigants before the popular courts in increasing numbers.[4] The popular courts had jurisdiction over suits against subjects alleged to have violated imperial regulations, as well as over some types of disputes between Athenian citizens and subjects.[5] As Athens became the trading center of the Aegean, and as trade increased, so too must have legal disputes arising in connection with it. Empire fostered litigation in yet another way. As the revenues of empire flowed into Athens and were distributed among citizens in various forms, including pay for service on juries, Athenians came to guard citizenship rights more jealously and therefore passed Pericles' restrictive citizenship law in 451/0 B.C.[6] This law allowed for prosecution of persons exercising citizens' rights illegally, and, if the testimony of late sources can be believed, gave rise in 445/4 B.C. to many suits against supposed noncitizens in connection with a grain distribution to which only citizens were entitled (Philoch. *FGrH* 328 F 119; Plu. *Per.* 37.3–4; cf. Ar. *V.* 717–18).[7]

At the same time, democratic reforms created many new opportunities for litigation. From at least the 450s B.C., an active democratic Assembly passed numerous decrees that bore the force of laws, and this expanded body of rules created new footholds for litigation (cf. Ar. fr. 226).[8] Furthermore, the democracy entrusted the city's administration to large numbers of magistrates and councilmen, each of whom could be prosecuted for malefaction. Any citizen could act as volunteer prosecutor and bring charges against these officeholders or others alleged to have harmed the city. Aspiring politicians in particular took advantage of this opportunity and sought to advance their reputations and political careers by initiating public prosecutions. Indeed, volunteer prosecution soon became the favorite instrument of a new breed of politicians who presented themselves as the watchdogs of the people.[9]

To attribute responsibility for Athens's increasing litigation to a few aggressive politicians, as Aristophanes' comedies might lead one to do, however, would be a mistake. Private citizens who were not politically ambitious must have contributed significantly to the rise in litigation. The popular courts, meeting regularly and with several panels available each day, made public adjudication accessible to private disputants to an extent unmatched in earlier times, and disputants, for a variety of reasons, availed themselves of this option.

During this period, the formal study and practice of oratory came into their own in Athens. The ability to speak effectively was critical for success in addressing the Assembly, Council, and courts, where litigants were required to represent themselves. To be trained in public speaking, some Athenians turned to sophists, self-proclaimed experts in all facets of human knowledge, who congregated in Athens from the mid-fifth century B.C. in part to capitalize on the demand for instruction in speaking. For a price the sophists taught their pupils, usually wealthy young men, the art of rhetoric, or, as some put it more cynically, how to make the weaker argument appear the stronger (Ar. *Nu.* 112–15). Although the sophists did not cause the Athenian legal revolution, they helped fuel it, and their teachings gave legal argumentation much of the shape it was to exhibit through the end of the fourth century B.C.[10] Probably also in this period logographers began providing clients with written speeches to memorize and present in court.[11]

Because the period 462–430 B.C. is poorly documented, it is difficult to assess contemporary reactions to the altered role of the popular courts and rising litigation within them. Beginning in the 420s, the literary record becomes fuller, due largely to the survival of many of Aristophanes' comedies. Because these comedies take for granted the centrality of the courts in Athens and considerable litigation within them, it is reasonable to infer that the Athenian legal revolution was by now substantially complete. At the same time, Aristophanes' persistent treatment of litigation and its abuse in his comedies of the 420s suggests that his audience, to whose concerns and interests he presumably adapted his material, was still coming to terms with the results of legal changes that had taken place over the previous decades. Aristophanes and other comic writers, in fact, dramatize the recent and controversial nature of the changes in question by representing the young and the old at odds over them (see Chapter 3).

While it is undeniable that litigation rose in the period following the Ephialtic reforms, one should not assume that Athenians had become more contentious and disputatious. Although conservative critics of the democracy in the fourth century asserted (Isoc. 7.51) or implied (X. *Mem.* 3.5.16–17) that this was so, they read the past to suit their own negative views of litigation under the democracy. As scholars have observed in other historical contexts, rising litigation in public courts may well make contention more conspicuous in a society, but this does not necessarily mean that basic attitudes toward conflict have changed.[12] To be sure, the relative ease with which personal conflicts could be taken to court in Athens after the Ephialtic reforms must have altered how individuals acted once they were involved in disputes.[13] One may doubt, however, that the availability of the popular courts encouraged them to enter into disputes in the first place.[14] Although the spectacle of ongoing litigation in Athens and the involvement of large numbers of citizens in it as litigants or jurors prompted the city's critics to assert that Athenians were overly fond of litigation (cf. Th. 1.77.1), other Greeks may have been equally or more contentious. For example, while Sparta did not have an extensive court system,[15] its citizens were known to strive contentiously with one another in pursuit of honor and prestige (Pl. *R.* 545a2–3).

In assessing the social significance of rising litigation in Athens, one must also keep in mind that litigation, whatever its effect on individual relationships, can benefit a society in ways that may not be immediately obvious. For example, Greenhouse points out that

> it is possible to imagine circumstances under which rising rates of litigation would indicate the increasing integration of society, not the reverse. When law-aversion stems from a rejection of judicial institutions and the state that they represent, rising law use may signal a positive accommodation to or acceptance of the social system. The law is a basis and means of social participation, quite apart from its potential effect of permanently damaging private relationships.[16]

This may well apply to the Athenian situation. When elite litigants in considerable numbers brought their suits before popular courts composed of average citizens, they acknowledged the authority of the demos and its legal institutions (see Chapter 3). In this case, rising litigation in Athens may actually have encouraged the integration of society and thus social stability.

Legal Institutions and Rules

The legal institutions and rules that emerged in the mid-fifth century remained relatively stable until the fall of the democracy in 322 B.C., and the legal innovations and rule changes that occurred within this period should be viewed as modifications of existing institutions rather than as evidence of significant evolution.[17] This section sketches out some basic features of the popular courts, laws and law making, and rules governing litigation throughout the period 430–322 B.C.

THE POPULAR COURTS

The Athenian democracy relied on direct and wide participation in governance and administration of the city by adult, male citizens, who probably numbered about thirty thousand of perhaps three hundred thousand residents of Attica.[18] All citizens were eligible to attend the Assembly (*ekklēsia*), where they could listen to and join in debate on any matter of public interest, and vote on decrees proposed. The difficulties involved in convening large numbers of citizens, however, prompted Athenians to entrust oversight of the daily administration of the city to the Council (*boulē*), a body composed of five hundred citizens, fifty chosen annually by lot from each of the ten tribes into which Cleisthenes had divided the citizenry in 508/7 B.C. The Council drafted decrees to be considered by the Assembly, received foreign embassies, and oversaw the city's magistrates.[19] Some seven hundred magistrates were chosen by lot each year to carry out functions ranging from the organization of festivals to the supervision of public sanitation.[20] The most important of the magistrates were the nine archons (six of whom were designated "lawgivers" [*thesmothetai*]) whose administrative responsibilities included supervision of the courts ([Arist.] *AP* 55–59). Because councilmen and magistrates received pay for their services, any citizen could in theory afford to serve the city in these capacities.[21]

Although Athenians relied on the lot for selection of magistrates and councilmen, they did not trust blindly in the citizens selected.[22] For example, both groups were subject to review (*dokimasia*) before they entered office so as to determine whether they met the formal qualifications for office and were suitable for it, and both underwent scrutiny (*euthunai*) when they left office to ensure that they had conducted their duties properly. The Athenian people did not, moreover, rely on these randomly selected amateurs for political leadership and advice, but looked instead to generals (*stratēgoi*) and orators (*rhētores*) for expert advice and leadership from year to year. The ten generals, unlike other city officials, were annually elected and could serve any number of times. Through repeated election as general, an individual could exercise considerable sway over the Athenian people, as for example Pericles did. Generals were subject, however, to annual *euthunai* and could be, and often were, impeached through the legal action of *eisangelia* during their terms. Equally important as leaders and advisers were orators, who, although they held no official position, gained public prominence and political power by regularly addressing the Assembly and bringing suits before the courts. At any given time, the number of *rhētores* was small, perhaps twenty or so.[23] Although orators, unlike generals, did not undergo *euthunai,* from at least 415 B.C. (And. 1.17) they were frequently subject to indictment for proposing illegal decrees through the legal action known as *graphē paranomōn*. While in the fifth century the same persons tended to serve as generals and *rhētores,* in the fourth century different groups of persons tended to fill these two roles.[24]

The most distinctive feature of democratic rule was the popular courts.[25] Each year six thousand male citizens at least thirty years old were selected by lot from volunteers to serve as the pool of prospective jurors (*dikastai*). On designated court days (between 150 and 200 in the course of a year), juries ranging in size from several hundred to occasionally several thousand members were empaneled from eligible citizens who appeared for service.[26] From the 420s to the 320s B.C., jurors were paid three obols (half a drachma) for a day's service. This represented about half of the wage of a skilled worker in the late fifth century, but only about a quarter of a skilled worker's wage by the late fourth century.[27] Juries were in all likelihood dominated by more or less average citizens who had the strongest motivation to seek out this wage.[28]

Popular juries possessed enormous power due to their wide jurisdiction and absolute authority. They not only judged a wide range of disputes between private citizens, but also played a critical role in the political life of the city because of their jurisdiction over suits against magistrates, generals, and orators. In the fourth century, moreover, panels of jurors were involved in law making. Jurors were not, however, ordinarily involved in judging common criminals, who, if caught red-handed, were punished summarily by police magistrates known as the Eleven and the public slaves who assisted them.[29] The popular courts also did not judge homicide suits, which were under the jurisdiction of the Areopagus and special homicide courts.[30]

Although magistrates convened courts, they exercised no control over the course of a trial. At the end of a trial, which lasted at most a single day, the jury gave its verdict without formal deliberation.[31] There was no appeal from this verdict, and Athenian jurors were not accountable for their rulings: they were distinct from most other agents of the city in that they were not subject to *euthunai* (cf. Ar. V. 587). Although I refer to Athenian *dikastai* throughout this study as "jurors," it is important to realize that they had more power than jurors in the modern United States do, and performed some tasks that are delegated to a judge in the modern context. If one must choose between "juror" and "judge" as a translation of *dikastēs,* however, the former is in my view preferable, since the *dikastēs* was one of many on a panel, an amateur, and played an essentially passive role at trial.[32]

The popular courts did not so much constitute a separate judicial branch as miniature bodies of the assembled demos.[33] The way litigants addressed jurors assumes this relationship between the Assembly and the courts: they attribute to "you"—that is, the jurors before them—actions of the demos in the Assembly.[34] Indeed, since the jurors who manned the courts were a considerable subset of the citizens likely to attend the Assembly, court was not held on days when the Assembly met (Dem. 24.80). The overlap of persons serving on the courts with those attending meetings of the Assembly meant that the two institutions, though formally distinct, would never quarrel over constitutional prerogatives.[35] There was no reason, in fact, why the Assembly could not hold trials, and on occasion it did, as did the Council also.[36] Practical considerations, in particular the requirement of six thousand for a quorum, were probably more important than constitutional principles in keeping the Assembly from assuming a more active judicial role.

LAWS AND LAW MAKING

Throughout most of the fifth century B.C., Athenians lived under laws attributed to Draco and Solon and the decrees of the Assembly, which had the force of law.[37] The situation was a rather confusing one by the end of the century.[38] Laws and decrees, inscribed on stone slabs (*stēlai*), were scattered throughout the city. Decrees were numerous, since the Assembly had been active over a period of several decades in passing them. Some laws were written in archaic language. At the end of the fifth century, therefore, Athenians took measures to impose a degree of order on this situation.[39]

First, during the period 410–399 B.C. Athenians acted to collect and revise the laws already in existence. This involved the removal of archaisms from laws, although some clearly remained in the fourth century (Lys. 10.15–20).[40] Initially public posting of the laws in a central location may have been a goal, but, if so, this does not appear to have been carried through.[41] Instead, it was determined that a copy of all laws and decrees should be placed henceforth in an archive, the Metroön, located in the agora.[42] In addition, sometime between 403 and 399 B.C., Athenians charged the *thesmothetai* with reviewing the laws regularly and reporting contradictions and inconsistencies to the people (Aesch. 3.38–40).

Second, during the period 403–399 B.C. Athenians altered the way that laws would be made in the future. Decrees of the Assembly no longer had the force of law. Instead, laws came into being through an extended, public process that culminated in the "trial" of the proposed law by a specially convened popular court of lawmakers (*nomothetai*). While any citizen could initiate the lawmaking procedure by proposing a new law in the Assembly, he had first to win the repeal of any existing law that it contradicted. If he failed to do so, he was liable to indictment by a *graphē nomon mē epitēdeion theinai*.⁴³ Likewise, anyone who sought to propose a decree that was in conflict with an existing law had to win repeal of this law before proceeding, or risk indictment through a *graphē paranomōn*.⁴⁴ These measures thus gave laws greater authority than decrees and, by reforming the procedure for making laws, effectively limited the number of new laws passed.⁴⁵

Taken together, these reforms suggest that laws and law making were of great concern to Athenians during the period 410–399 B.C. The historical context in which these reforms were instituted suggests that the Athenian demos was seeking, first and foremost, to protect itself from oligarchic enemies, who twice took power during this period—the Four Hundred in 411 B.C., and the Thirty in 404/3 B.C. In both cases, confusion about what the city's laws actually were and the ease of making new laws, even ones altering the city's constitution, enabled the oligarchs to achieve their goals.⁴⁶

Some scholars, however, have argued on the basis of these reforms, particularly those concerning law making, that Athenians placed themselves under the "rule of law" at this time and "popular sovereignty" thus yielded to the "sovereignty of law." Other scholars have in my view successfully refuted this position, arguing that the demos did not cede authority to the laws at this time, but rather retained complete control over them.⁴⁷ Members of the demos served as *nomothetai* for ratifying laws and as *thesmothetai* for reviewing laws, and there was no law that the demos could not alter. Before and after the reforms, moreover, jurors selected from the people at large interpreted and applied the laws. Therefore, as Ober argues, "there is no reason to suppose that these changes abrogated the ultimate authority of the demos."⁴⁸ These reforms are best viewed as practical measures designed to ensure that the laws serve the interests of the demos more effectively rather than to redefine the relationship between the demos and the laws.

Advocates of the "rule of law" theory point to the common claim of fourth-century litigants that the laws are authoritative (*kurioi*) as evidence of the sovereignty of the laws.⁴⁹ When litigants made these claims, however, they were not offering constitutional analysis but appealing to an uncontroversial precept of popular ideology: under democracy the laws—made and interpreted by members of the demos—were indeed authoritative.[50] When Demosthenes tells the jurors in his suit against Meidias, "the laws are strong through you and you through the laws" (21.224), he articulates an important truth about the relation between the demos and the laws: the demos gave the laws whatever strength they had and the laws in turn—as enforced by the people—preserved the authority of the demos.[51] While Demosthenes stops short of saying the demos is the law, he leaves no doubt that law serves the demos and not vice versa.[52]

Several features of Athenian legal regulation are noteworthy. First, laws—and, in the fifth century, decrees bearing the force of law—came into being as ad hoc accretions to the body of existing regulation and not as attempts to fill in methodically gaps in a legal system.[53] For this reason, the body of known Athenian laws can seem rather incoherent to the modern eye.

Second, Athenians were reluctant to regulate the private sphere through legislation.[54] A fundamental democratic ideal in Athens was that citizens were free and autonomous in their private lives. Athenians contrasted the situation in their city with that of Sparta, where rigid rules severely constrained private life (Th. 2.39.4). While Athenians did not formulate a "Bill of Rights" protecting personal freedoms, they were reluctant to pass laws infringing on individual autonomy or to endorse the use of existing laws in such a way as to bring about state intrusion into private life. For example, while the city did regulate the transmission of family property, in most family matters the decision of the man who was in authority (*kurios*) over a household was final.[55] Furthermore, Athenian laws tended to steer clear of questions of private morality. For example, the laws had little to say about consensual sexual activity, including prostitution and homosexual relations. Generally, social pressure, especially in the form of gossip, rather than laws regulated sexual behavior, and only when sexual activity was thought to threaten the city was prosecution likely.[56]

Third, Athenian laws tended to make offenses actionable without defining them precisely.⁵⁷ Although Athens was like other ancient societies in framing laws in this way, in Athens democratic principles may help explain why the city did not employ experts to draft legislation more precisely. Vague laws left interpretation to the discretion of popular juries and thus ensured that a democratic body would have the last word on the enforcement of them (cf. [Arist.] *AP* 9.2). If the laws were more specific, this might make them more complicated and give expert litigants an unfair advantage over average citizens (Dem. 20.93).⁵⁸ Because laws were drafted in this way, it was incumbent on a prosecutor to show how his opponent's actions fit popular understandings of the terms of the law in question. Thus, as D. Cohen observes, "the only applicable definitions of offenses were those residing in the collective consciousness of the community."⁵⁹

Although the Athenian democracy has left us no formal statement of a democratic political theory that would explain the rationale behind the design of the popular courts and the laws sketched out here, the democratic principles at stake are illuminated by the criticisms of opponents of the democracy.⁶⁰ Plato and Aristotle are both critical of the wide discretion of popular juries and therefore argue that if such juries are to exist at all, their discretion should be limited by precise laws drafted by experts. Plato asserts that when the democratic rabble dominates the courts, the lawmaker should fix nearly everything in advance, dealing himself "with most cases by express legislation, if indeed one ever legislates at all for a state of that sort" (*Lg.* 876b1–c3).⁶¹ Aristotle is less extreme than Plato on the subject of democratic courts. He concedes that many judges are more difficult to corrupt than few (*Pol.* 1286a35–40), but nonetheless concurs with Plato's view that precise laws, framed by an expert lawmaker, should limit judicial discretion: it is easier, after all, to find a single expert competent to design good and precise laws than a large number capable of framing or judging them (*Rh.* 1354a32–b1).⁶² While both philosophers acknowledge that no lawmaker can anticipate all possible circumstances in laws (Pl. *Lg.* 875e2–876a6; Arist. *Pol.* 1282b1–6), both place confidence in expert lawmakers—projections of themselves—to design and craft laws with precision (*akribeia*).⁶³ To judge by the detailed legislation Plato sets forth in the *Laws*, he is especially optimistic that a law code can subsume a multitude of human circumstances, and he suggests, in fact, that what one generation of lawmakers fails to achieve in precision, the next generation can seek to rectify (769d1–e2).⁶⁴ Aristotle, on the other hand, is more pragmatic: because there are inherent gaps between law and human circumstances, men must fill in those gaps by issuing judgments with fairness (*epieikeia*) (*EN* 1137a31–1138a3).⁶⁵ It is not only in their preference for precision in laws that Plato and Aristotle diverge from democratic practice, but also in their view of the proper scope of law within society. Both propose that laws should regulate the private sphere to a high degree. As D. Cohen observes, their schemes for regulating society entail "the complete collapse of the public/private dichotomy."⁶⁶

The contrast between democratic practice and conservative theory is thus dramatic. The Athenian demos reserved law making as the prerogative of the people rather than of individual experts. The people preferred vague laws, open to interpretation by democratic juries, to specific laws that might restrict judicial discretion. They chose not to restrict individual freedoms by a proliferation of the sort of laws concerning private life that conservatives, like Plato and Aristotle, advocated. Thus, although no theoretical statement of the democratic principles underlying Athenian legal institutions survives, the choices that Athenians made in designing them are consistent with a democratic view of the proper place of law in society.

LITIGATION: RULES AND PARAMETERS

The ability to litigate was a privilege enjoyed and exercised primarily by male citizens, although in some cases, a foreigner (*xenos*) or a resident alien (metic) could initiate an action and pursue it in his own person.⁶⁷ Athenian women and children were dependent on male relatives to represent their legal interests in court.⁶⁸ Although slaves were not entirely without legal protection, they could not sue on their own behalf.⁶⁹ The low status of slaves is evident, moreover, in the fact that a litigant could offer up his slaves for torture so as to confirm the veracity of his statements, or challenge his opponent to do the same with his slaves.⁷⁰

Athenians distinguished two kinds of suits, private and public. In a private suit (*dikē*), normally only a person who claimed to have suffered some wrong directly could prosecute, whereas in a public suit—for example, an indictment (*graphē*) or impeachment (*eisangelia*)—any willing party could volunteer to prosecute.[71] This distinction does not correspond to the modern one between civil and criminal suits: private suits in Athens could arise in connection with what moderns would label crimes, and public suits did not necessarily involve crimes in the modern sense.[72] Because of this lack of correspondence between the modern and ancient classifications, I designate all charging parties in Athenian suits public or private as "prosecutors," rather than using "prosecutor" exclusively of public suits, and "plaintiff" of private suits.[73]

In fact, an aggrieved party in Athens could sometimes choose between bringing a private or public suit.[74] When prosecutors had a choice of actions, however, the decision to lodge a public rather than a private suit was significant. Public suits were generally more conspicuous than private ones, since litigants were allotted more time to present their cases and these suits were heard by larger juries.[75] In addition, public suits involved greater risks for both defendant and prosecutor. Whereas the defendant who was found guilty in a private suit in most cases only paid a fine to the prosecutor,[76] a defendant convicted in a public suit might be subject to a fine (normally payable to the state),[77] exile, or even death. The prosecutor of a public action who dropped his suit or received less than one-fifth of the jurors' votes had to pay the huge penalty of a thousand drachmas and was subject to partial disfranchisement (*atimia*). It was necessary, therefore, for a prosecutor choosing between a public and private action to decide how much personal risk he was willing to assume and what sort of penalty he wished to inflict upon his opponent (Dem 22.25–27).

A prosecutor had to exercise self-help, or "private initiative," at all stages of litigation—in apprehension, investigation, and prosecution.[78] To bring his suit before a popular court, a prosecutor generally first had to confront his opponent in person before witnesses and issue him an oral summons to appear on a given day before the magistrate responsible for the charge in question.[79]

When that day arrived, the prosecutor, in the presence of the defendant, presented the magistrate with his complaint—in writing by the early fourth century[80]—and the accused indicated his response. The magistrate then set a date for a preliminary hearing (*anakrisis*) at which he could interrogate the parties so as to bring out the details of the dispute. After the *anakrisis,* public suits went directly before a popular court. Most private suits, however, came before magistrates known as deme judges who could resolve on their own authority at the *anakrisis* claims up to ten drachmas.[81] Before 400/399 B.C., the deme judges referred cases involving greater sums directly to a popular court; from this date, they sent these cases to a public arbitrator, an Athenian citizen in his sixtieth year, who was to rule on the dispute.[82] Although either party could appeal the arbitrator's decision before a popular court, the evidence adducible in court was limited to the laws, witness testimony, and other evidence that had been presented before the arbitrator. After ca. 380 B.C., each litigant was required to submit these items in written form at arbitration,[83] at the conclusion of which each litigant's documents were sealed in a separate jar (*echinos*); the two jars, entrusted to tribal officials before trial, were opened up in court ([Arist.] *AP* 53.2–3).[84] The requirement that documents be produced at public arbitration made this a serious alternative to trial, because the arbitrator's decision could take into account all the written documentation that might be cited at a public trial. This process also gave litigants ample time, if the arbitration failed, to consider before trial how to respond to claims based on the documents placed in the *echinos*.[85]

At trial, litigants were required to speak on their own behalf but could deliver speeches purchased from logographers. If they wished, however, they could yield part, and in exceptional cases all, of their allotted time to one or more friends or family members to speak as advocates (*sunēgoroi*) on their behalf.[86] Speeches were timed by a water clock (*klepsudra*), which in private suits, but probably not in public ones, was stopped for the reading out of laws and witness testimony.[87] In the fourth century, witness testimony was read by a clerk from statements taken in advance, and witnesses were present in court only to swear to the veracity of their statements. During his own speech a litigant could ask his opponent questions and require an answer,[88] but there was no formal cross-examination of litigants. Although speakers swore to keep to the point ([Arist.] *AP* 67.1) and were to observe rules governing the use of "hearsay," in practice there were few constraints on them.[89]

After the litigants presented their cases (prosecutors spoke first), the jury voted immediately. Secret ballot was the rule probably from the mid-fifth century.[90] The verdict was determined by a majority of votes, and in the case of a tie the defendant was acquitted. If the defendant was found guilty, his penalty was in some cases set in advance by law; in other cases (and in most private suits), however, there was no fixed penalty and the jury chose between alternate penalties urged by opposing litigants in supplementary speeches.[91] In most cases, the penalty was monetary, but it could take the form of *atimia,* exile, or death.[92] It was uncommon for free citizens to suffer physical punishment or humiliation upon conviction, and imprisonment was not ordinarily an option.[93] Whereas in some public suits the magistrate who had convened the court was responsible for the enforcement of the verdict, in private suits enforcement regularly fell upon the prosecutor. When enforcement was in private hands, often only an additional lawsuit, for example, a suit for ejection (*dikē exoulēs*), could compel a reluctant defendant to comply with the verdict.[94]

Athenians were conscious that litigation could be abused and discouraged this in three ways.

1. *Court Fees.* Litigants were often required to pay court fees in advance of trial: useful to the city as a source of revenue, these fees also were deterrents to frivolous or false suits. In many public suits the prosecutor had to pay a deposit (*parastasis*)—the amount is not known—which was probably returned to him if he was successful ([Arist.] *AP* 59.3).[95] In some private suits, both litigants were required to pay in advance a fee (*prutaneia*), and after the verdict the loser was supposed to reimburse the winner for his fee. The amount of the fee was based on the amount at issue in the case—three drachmas per litigant in disputes concerning one hundred to one thousand drachmas, thirty drachmas per litigant in disputes con-

cerning more than a thousand drachmas—and the revenue raised went toward jurors' wages (Poll. 8.38; Dem. 47.64; [X.] *Ath.* 1.16).[96] Although these fees were not huge, litigants had to take them into account in reckoning the risks of engaging in litigation.

2. *Statutory Penalties.* Unsuccessful prosecutors were liable to statutory penalties in two sets of circumstances. First, in most public suits a prosecutor who either dropped a suit before it came to court or received less than one-fifth of a jury's vote was subject to a penalty of a thousand drachmas, payable to the state, and to partial *atimia*.[97] This *atimia* may have prevented him in the future from bringing any public action or perhaps only the type in which he had failed. Until he paid his fine, moreover, he was also subject to *atimia* as a state debtor.[98] Second, in some private suits a prosecutor who failed to receive one-fifth of the votes cast had to pay his opponent the *epōbelia,* a sum equal to one-sixth of the value of his claim.[99]

While Harrison labels these penalties "automatic," this is somewhat misleading.[100] These penalties were automatic only in the sense that they applied automatically by law under the circumstances specified. As a practical matter, however, they were not automatic, since enforcement, which depended on private initiative, was haphazard.

The statutory penalties that applied in public suits do not seem to have been enforced very regularly. Prosecutors could drop public actions with relative impunity, especially if by arrangement with the defendant; if both parties agreed to let the matter slide, it was unlikely that anyone would protest the rule violation.[101] One tactic a prosecutor who wished to drop his suit could take was to feign illness and thereby postpone the hearing of the suit indefinitely (Dem. 58.43). Likewise, a prosecutor who pursued a suit to trial and failed to win one-fifth of the votes did not necessarily suffer the statutory penalties.[102] If he did not pay the large fine within a given period, he would be designated a state debtor, and his name would be publicly recorded and posted by city officials. In general, however, Athenians were lax about the collection of state debts (cf. Dem. 25.85–91), and only a further legal action (*apographē*), dependent on private initiative, would force the payment.[103] Theoretically, the unsuccessful prosecutor was also subject to *atimia,* but until someone challenged him through a separate legal action (*endeixis*) he was free to exercise his civic rights.[104]

It was probably even more difficult to enforce the payment of the *epōbelia*, since it was due to a private person rather than to the state (Dem. 47.64). Just as litigants in private suits might encounter difficulties in collecting fines awarded by a court, so too might they have trouble collecting the *epōbelia*. Only in suits involving trade (*dikai emporikai*) was a prosecutor owing the *epōbelia* imprisoned until payment of it, presumably because these suits regularly involved non-Athenians who might flee the city to avoid payment.[105] The problem of nonpayment could perhaps have been avoided by requiring prosecutors to deposit a sum equal to the *epōbelia* with the court in advance of the trial. In fact, a prosecutor of certain types of actions was required to deposit with the court in advance a sum (*parakatabolē*) that he forfeited to his opponent in the event of his failure.[106] No such practice, however, was ever instituted in the case of the *epōbelia*.

3. *Legal Actions against Abuse*. Violations of rules governing litigation and the legal process were susceptible to a wide range of legal actions. All of these actions, however, required private initiative.

Persons falsely attesting that an individual had been served with a summons were liable to indictment for false summons (*graphē pseudoklēteias*). In some private suits from ca. 400 B.C. on, a defendant could lodge a protest in the form of a *paragraphē* at the *anakrisis* that the suit against him violated procedural rules, and in this case his protest took priority and had to be judged by a court before his opponent's suit could proceed. A litigant could bring suit against an opponent's witness for false testimony (*dikē pseudomarturiōn*), provided that he had formally challenged the testimony in question at trial before a verdict was given ([Arist.] *AP* 68.4); in some cases, at least, a successful false-witness suit could force the rehearing of the initial dispute.[107] A litigant who suborned a witness was subject to a private suit for using illegal devices (*dikē kakotechniōn*).[108] If a witness failed to appear on a litigant's behalf after promising to do so, he could be sued through a private suit (*dikē lipomarturiou*).[109] A litigant paying money to a supporting speaker (*sunēgoros*) could be prosecuted (Dem. 46.26). A litigant citing a nonexistent law was subject to prosecution (Dem. 26.24). Certain slanderous statements made in the course of a trial, such as the false claim that a man had killed his own father (Lys. 10.1–2), were actionable through a *dikē kakēgorias*. Abuse of legal self-help at any phase of the legal process was actionable. For example, illegal restraint of an individual could be punished through a *graphē adikōs heirchthēnai* (cf. Dem. 59.66),[110] and use of excessive force in distraining on property could lead to a suit alleging assault (*dikē aikeias*) (Dem. 47.45, with 34–38).

Arbitrators and magistrates associated with the courts were subject to prosecution for bribery or other malfeasance through a variety of actions.[111] Moreover, it was illegal for an individual to bribe jurors and for jurors to accept bribes.[112] A person engaging in bribery in connection with a trial involving a charge of impersonating a citizen (*graphē xenias*) was subject to a special indictment, a *graphē dōroxenias*.[113]

In addition to these actions against particular kinds of abuses, others were available for the prosecution of the vague crime of sykophancy.[114] In his *Antidosis* (354/3 B.C.), Isocrates asserts that Athenians in the time of Solon

> made the laws concerning sykophants more harsh than those concerning other criminals; for, while they placed judgment of the greatest crimes in the hands of a single one of the courts, against sykophants they instituted indictments [*graphas*] before the *thesmothetai*, impeachments [*eisangelias*] before the Council, and censures [*probolas*] before the Assembly, believing that those who plied this trade exceeded all other forms of villainy. (15.313–14)

Although Isocrates' assertion that these three measures originated in the distant past is probably false, his statement that there are various ways to take action against sykophants is true for his day. There is corroboration outside of Isocrates for the existence of both the *graphē sukophantias* ([Arist.] *AP* 59.3)[115] and the *probolē*—a vote of censure that in itself carried no legal penalty—against sykophants ([Arist.] *AP* 43.5). No evidence outside of Isocrates confirms the existence of an *eisangelia* against sykophants, but Isocrates' accuracy in the first two cases may be reason to believe that

31

he is accurate here as well.[116] Indeed, other actions may also have been available against putative sykophants.[117] No indisputable evidence survives, however, of any actions against sykophants actually being used.[118]

Charges of legal abuse were themselves subject to abuse and were therefore discouraged in a variety of ways.[119] For example, a prosecutor bringing an indictment for sykophancy (*graphē sukophantias*) or for falsely attesting to a summons (*graphē pseudoklēteias*) had to pay a deposit in advance (*parastasis*) ([Arist.] *AP* 59.3). Prosecutors charging their opponents with legal abuse were also susceptible to the statutory penalties sketched out earlier where they pertained and could themselves be sued on any number of grounds for legal abuse. So too a witness in a false-witness suit could himself be charged with false witness.[120] In some cases, moreover, Athenians specified limits in connection with charges of abuse. In the case of the *probolē* against sykophants, for example, only three citizens and three metics could be charged annually with sykophancy ([Arist.] *AP* 43.5).[121] Furthermore, it was only after a man was convicted three times of giving false witness (And. 1.74; Hyp. 2.12) or of falsely testifying that a summons had been presented (And. 1.74) that he incurred a penalty of *atimia*.[122]

Litigation and Adjudication in Practice

The preceding survey of legal institutions and rules provides a groundwork for understanding Athenian litigation, but fundamental questions remain about litigation in its social context. Who litigated in Athens? Why did they do so? How did litigants compete against one another? What role did jurors play, and on what basis did they cast their votes? How much litigation was there in Athens?

WHO LITIGATED IN ATHENS?

The powerful and wealthy in Athenian society figured prominently as litigants in the courts. To be sure, the surviving record may give a skewed impression of the sociology of Athenian litigation, since the forensic speeches that constitute the bulk of the ancient evidence were composed for well-off litigants. Nonetheless, it is probable that elite Athenians, that is, the top 5 to 10 percent of citizens by wealth, constituted a "litigating class" that was disproportionately active in the courts.[123] While many Athenians may have become involved in litigation at some point in their lives, the wealthy were far more likely than average Athenians to appear frequently in court for three reasons.

First, the circumstances of wealthy men increased the likelihood of their engaging in litigation. Their wealth made them more likely than average Athenians to become involved in disputes over property and questions of inheritance and to be victims of false suits.[124] Moreover, because those with leisure, money, and education were disproportionately involved in public life as *rhētores* and generals, the wealthy were more likely than other citizens to appear as volunteer prosecutors or defendants in public suits. Even wealthy men who were not active in politics could find themselves involved in litigation in connection with their performance of compulsory public services (liturgies), including the maintenance and supervision of a warship (the trierarchy) or the patronage of a chorus for one of the city's many festivals (the *chorēgia*).[125]

Second, the wealthy were in a much better position than average citizens to initiate and pursue suits. Men of means were best able to exercise the self-help that was required at all stages of litigation. They could afford to study oratory in anticipation of litigation, to purchase speeches from logographers for use at trial, to pay court fees and risk the statutory penalties that applied to failed prosecutions, and to manipulate the legal process in a variety of ways.[126]

Third, Athenian legal institutions privileged legal conflicts among the rich and powerful in several ways. As noted previously, small-scale disputes involving sums of ten drachmas or less were decided on the authority of deme judges. Among private suits that reached court, those involving large sums were allowed more court time than suits concerning smaller sums ([Arist.] *AP* 67.2), which tended to favor wealthier disputants.[127] Public actions, in which the rich were more active than other citizens, were allotted an entire day—more time than was allotted to any private suit ([Arist.] *AP* 67.1).

The advantages of the wealthy in litigation and their greater access to the courts existed in tension with democratic egalitarian ideals. Athenians cherished the ideal of equality in relation to the laws (*isonomia*) and no doubt found appealing the ideal expressed by Euripides' Theseus that, "when laws have been written down, the weak man and the wealthy one have an equal legal case" (*Supp.* 433–34).[128] In reality, however, an average citizen was in a poor position to compete at law with a wealthy man (cf. Dem. 21.112). Likewise, although Athenians could idealize volunteer prosecution as a democratic institution that was available to "anyone who wished" (*ho boulomenos*) to undertake it, the wealthy were best able to do so.

It is intriguing that the Athenian demos tolerated this inequality in the democracy's legal institutions. This is consistent, however, with its accommodation elsewhere of differences in status and privileges among citizens.[129] Athenian democracy did not entail the elimination of social and economic differences among citizens, and, if differences were to be allowed, it was inevitable that some citizens would enjoy privileges that others did not. Two considerations may have made average Athenians accept the legal advantages enjoyed by the rich. First, because elite Athenians were most likely to engage in legal contests with their peers, their advantages in litigation did not normally pose a direct threat to average Athenians. Second, because the demos controlled the popular courts, average Athenians could be relatively confident that wealthy prosecutors could not use their power to win grossly unfair verdicts against them.

WHY DID ATHENIANS LITIGATE?

Athenians engaged in litigation to pursue financial and political interests, and often simultaneously to preserve or enhance their reputations. These motivations are difficult to separate from one another, since wealth and political power enhanced reputation, and reputation, though valued for its own sake, was also a means to wealth and political power. If these motivations were intimately connected with one another, however, litigants in their forensic speeches tended to downplay their financial and political objectives, and to emphasize the extent to which their personal honor was at stake. This tendency suggests that Athenian audiences were more comfortable with the defense of manly honor than with the naked pursuit of financial and political ends.

The institutional setting of litigation reflected and reinforced the importance of reputation within it. A defining feature of Hellenic culture was its tendency to foster public competitions that tested excellence (*aretē*) in fixed circumstances and under formal rules. Athletic games, poetic contests, and even military encounters were envisioned as forms of contest (*agōn*). These contests were games of high risk (*kindunos*): at stake for competitors was not only a tangible and immediate prize, but also reputation and status within the community.[130] Athenians viewed a legal trial as a contest that was akin to these other forms of *agōn*:[131] it was a high-stakes competition before the public—as represented by large panels of jurors and bystanders—in which the victor won prestige, while the loser incurred shame.[132]

Prestige and reputation emerged as concerns in Athenian lawsuits in different ways and to varying degrees. Personal honor (*timē*) was explicitly at issue, for example, in prosecutions for slander or gross insult (*hubris*). Even when prosecutions did not take these forms, slights to manhood and prestige were often woven into their fabric. Prosecutors in a variety of suits, public and private, openly acknowledged that they were seeking vengeance (*timōria*) on the defendants for slights to themselves or their families. Consistent with the importance of *timē* in Athenian trials is the fact that in most private suits (and some public ones), when the verdict was against the defendant, the trial entered a second phase involving *timēsis*, an evaluation of alternative penalties offered by prosecutor and defendant. Furthermore, in public suits, one penalty available was *atimia*, "dishonor," which took the form of a deprivation of civic rights.[133]

Although reputation and honor must have mattered to litigants of all socioeconomic backgrounds, elite litigants may have been especially sensitive to the evaluation of their reputations in public trials. Traditionally in Greek society, aristocrats had been under pressure to validate their claims to privileges as "gentlemen" by proving their excellence in conspicuous public competitions. This pattern of status competition continued under the Athenian democracy, but often in new arenas, including the popular courts.[134]

Because most jurors were of lower social status than elite litigants and were perhaps envious of their privileged status, the pressures on elite litigants as they competed against one another for prestige were even greater.[135]

The undeniable importance of prestige concerns in Athenian litigation has led some scholars to view litigation in Athens primarily in terms of status competition.[136] This model has some appeal but should not be pressed too far. First, while Athenian litigants emphasize honor as a concern in their forensic speeches, concrete political and financial interests often lurk in the background. Second, although Athenians address prestige concerns in their lawsuits more openly than litigants in modern Western democracies do, the difference between modern and ancient contexts can be overemphasized: arguably, most modern litigants also see their personal reputations and honor on the line in litigation.[137]

HOW DID LITIGANTS PLAY THE GAME?

Legal competition was intense. Rivals sometimes cursed their opponents by name on lead curse tablets, or appealed to the gods through judicial prayers for divine assistance and vengeance.[138] Violence in the course of self-help during the legal process was probably common. Because of the high emotions involved, a pending lawsuit could even be cited as a possible motive for murder (Ant. 2.1.5–8; cf. Lys. 1.44). This intensity reflects the high stakes of trial and the risks inherent in it (cf. Isoc. 18.9–10); it was for good reason that "trial" was synonymous with "risk" (*kindunos*).

If litigation was inherently risky, however, intelligent gamesmanship could make the gamble a favorable one.[139] To all appearances, Athenian litigants recognized this, and in pursuit of victory were ready to resort to tactics that were in tension or direct conflict with the rules governing litigation. A possible indication that devious practices were widespread is that, as noted previously, many rules and actions were directly or indirectly concerned with abuse of the legal process. Lofberg infers from this that "[i]n spite of the numerous methods of meeting the evil sycophancy flourished and the very fact that many different means of combatting it were necessary shows that none of them were very successful."[140] Some caution must be exercised here, however: the number of measures against abuse is better testimony to the diverse forms that abuse could take than to actual levels of unscrupulous behavior.

Another rough indication that devious behavior was not uncommon is that litigants regularly accuse one another and supporters of a variety of dirty tricks, including the blackmailing of opponents with the threat of false charges, cheating, lying, and fabricating documents.[141] Individual allegations are impossible to verify now and must also have been difficult to evaluate at the time. As a group, however, these complaints of abuse are telling. Many may well be true, and those that are false are significant for two reasons: they are presumably based on real abuses that juries would find credible; and false allegations themselves constitute evidence of unscrupulous behavior, namely, brazen lying at trial about an opponent's legal behavior.

The conspicuous place given to complaints of gross abuse in forensic oratory, however, should not make us miss more subtle ways in which the practice of litigation diverged from ideals of proper legal behavior. Three basic divergences may be identified.

First, Athenians tended to view litigation ideally as a contest between two litigants acting for the most part on their own against one another.[142] While litigants were allowed the support of friends and family members in various capacities—for example, as witness to a summons, witness at trial, or supporting speaker (*sunēgoros*)—this support was to be offered spontaneously out of friendship and was not to supplant the role of the litigant as principal. In reality, networks of friends and supporters played a large role in litigation.[143] This gap between ideal and practice is sometimes exploited when litigants insist that they are acting by themselves, while their opponents are acting in collusion with others as participants in a plot or conspiracy (Ant. 5.25; And. 1.132; Is. 9.26; Dem 35.27).

Second, Athenians envisioned litigation, especially when it involved private persons, ideally as a contest between amateurs. A litigant's conspicuous display of legal knowledge or slick speaking at trial was thus cause for suspicion (see Chapter 6). The ideal of amateurism, however, clashed with the reality that professionalism entered into the process in several ways. Some litigants were themselves quite experienced in legal matters. Many, however, were not, and these turned to logographers, who for a price advised them on how to present their cases and provided them with prepared speeches. Thus, while it is true that Athens had no class of professional lawyers, it did have a class of expert logographers, whose activities overlapped in some respects with those of modern lawyers.[144] Although the practice of consulting a logographer was common and violated no law, logographers were easy targets for criticism—for example, on the grounds that they cared for money rather than the truth (Pl. Com. fr. 110; cf. [Arist.] *Rh. Al.*1444b3–7)[145]—and persons who had recourse to them did well to suppress this information at trial. It was also best for a litigant to disguise the fact that he was using a written speech, whether his own or one provided by a logographer, since a popular audience would perceive this as inconsistent with amateurism (cf. Thphr. *Char.* 6.8; [Arist.] *Rh. Al.* 1444a18–28).

Third, Athenians viewed litigation ideally as free of the influence of money, although the rich could and did use their wealth to manipulate the legal process. Demosthenes thus complains of the wealthy Meidias: "[The rich] are given whatever dates they wish for undergoing trial, and their offenses are stale and cold when they come before you; but the rest of us, if anything happens to us, are each tried when fresh. They have witnesses ready and advocates [*sunēgoroi*] all prepared against us" (21.112). In the same speech, Demosthenes offers the further complaint that Meidias has used his wealth to hire a legal agent to bring false charges against him (21.103).[146] Demosthenes' own wealth does not stop him from exploiting popular concern over these options of the rich in litigation.

A common way litigants protest violations of the ideals sketched here is by asserting that their opponents have "prepared" (*paraskeuaz-* and related forms) a suit against them. They apply this image to the formation of groups of legal conspirators (Dem. 40.9), preparation in advance of expert arguments and speeches (Dem. 30.3), and devious furnishing of witnesses (Dem. 29.28) and *sunēgoroi* (Aesch. 1.193). By contrast, litigants portray themselves as totally "unprepared" in the face of such machinations (Dem.

40.30). One litigant goes so far as to call upon the jury to assist him and thus even out the disparity between him and his deviously prepared opponent (Dem. 44.15).

Although jurors were presumably not naive about how litigation actually worked, the frequency with which litigants appeal to ideals of proper legal behavior and complain of legal abuse suggests that jurors were receptive to these claims. Because these complaints are an integral part of forensic oratory in Athens, legal debate sometimes seems to be as much about what constitutes fair play in the legal process as about the particular matters at stake in the suit. This unusual feature of Athenian forensic oratory makes it an especially rich source for the study of attitudes toward the proper use of litigation.[147]

To the extent that litigants acted unscrupulously in pursuing their suits, they did not manifest any characteristic "dishonesty of the Athenians,"[148] but acted like litigants in other places and times in viewing law and litigation as instruments in their struggles against one another.[149] The temptation for litigants in Athens to break formal or informal rules was no doubt heightened by their ability to escape detection or even punishment if they were found out.[150] From the perspective of individual litigants, moreover, sharp practices were justifiable: litigants naturally thought their own causes just (cf. Ant. 3.4.1) and believed that their opponents were acting unscrupulously. A similar disregard for social rules and high valuation of personal interests made elite Athenians conceal their wealth so as to reduce or avoid the burden of financial obligations to the city.[151] In each case it was incumbent on individuals addressing popular audiences to suppress their own subversion of social rules, while exposing their enemies' antisocial practices.[152]

WHAT ROLE DID JURORS PLAY?

One role jurors played was that of spectators in the legal theater. If a trial was a dangerous contest for litigants, it was potentially entertaining drama, tragedy or comedy, for jurors.[153] Several aspects of trials could make them interesting: the element of intense contest, the spectacle of the rich and powerful at each other's throats, and the free exchange of slanders concerning male prostitution, the beating of parents, theft from shrines, and embezzlement of public funds. Add to all of this the incentive of a daily wage of three obols, and it is no surprise that Athenians lined up to serve in the courts (cf. Ar. *V.* 230–47, 505) and that annual and daily lotteries were therefore necessary to determine who would serve. Even in the fourth century B.C., when the wages of skilled workers rose while the juror's wage remained fixed,[154] Athenians apparently continued to show up in sufficient numbers to man the courts. By contrast, it was more difficult to induce Athenians to attend the Assembly (cf. Ar. *Ach.* 17–22), whose business was ordinarily less interesting; this may be why in the fourth century a wage of one drachma (six obols) was offered as an enticement to attendance there.[155]

Jurors were not mere spectators, however, since unlike theater audiences they determined the outcome of the drama played out before them. As noted earlier, jurors reached their decisions without formal deliberation. To be sure, jurors could exchange views with those seated near them during the course of the trial and chat about the case as they waited to cast their votes; some standing around must have been necessary, since jurors stepped forward to cast their votes one by one and panels were large.[156] Moreover, jurors with strong opinions could shout out and interrupt litigants and thereby influence other jurors.[157] Individual jurors nonetheless had to cast their votes based primarily on their own perceptions of the case.

According to what criteria did jurors cast their votes? The surviving forensic orations suggest that jurors were receptive to arguments based on a variety of factors that moderns would label both legal and extralegal.[158] Facts and laws clearly mattered. Litigants devote much of their allotted time to advancing their versions of the facts and to proving these to be more truthful than those of their opponents. Litigants also cite and discuss laws and, when they do so, treat them as if they deserve special consideration; they take for granted that legality matters and thus regularly protest abuses of the legal process. In fact, jurors swore an oath when they took office to enforce the written laws. In practice, however, jurors were not constrained to apply the law, much less the letter of the law, and there is excellent reason to believe that they exercised their broad discretion freely. Jurors' understandings of community norms and ultimately their sense of what was right (*to dikaion*) determined how and even whether they applied laws (see Chapter 6).

Jurors were free to consider a wide variety of factors in conjunction with, or in lieu of, laws and factual claims in reaching their determination of what was right. While this may be true to some degree in any jury system, in Athens litigants were not only allowed, but indeed expected, to address "extralegal" considerations. First, Athenian litigants regularly compare and contrast their reputations within the community as good family members, neighbors, and citizens. They do so not simply to support their credibility as speakers, but as if jurors should take character into account independently when reaching a verdict.[159] In keeping with this emphasis on character is the role of witness testimony at trial: litigants introduce this not only to support factual claims but also to show that men of good character within the community endorse them personally.[160] Second, litigants regularly assert that jurors should support them because this is in keeping with the city's best interests.[161] Litigants stop short of suggesting, however, that jurors should ignore concerns of fairness altogether: a vote in their favor, they insist is compatible with justice *and* the city's advantage. Litigants could, moreover, criticize their opponents for making base appeals to jurors' self-interest (Lys. 27.1; Hyp. 4.32), or complain of an opponent's introduction of public charges into a private suit, on the grounds that "charges involving the public interest have nothing to do with private suits" (Isoc. 16.3). How much the city's interests should be taken into account in a particular trial was thus open to debate.

Arguments based on character and the city's interests come into play simultaneously when elite litigants assert that they are good citizens who have spent money generously on the city through liturgies and payment of the war tax (*eisphora*). Some litigants quite unabashedly assert that because they have done the city favors of this sort, jurors are obliged to show gratitude (*charis*) by voting for them.[162] They point out that it is in the city's interest to reward its benefactors and thus to encourage this kind of behavior. Such appeals to past benefaction were, however, susceptible to criticism by opponents and not entirely uncontroversial.[163]

That "extralegal" arguments were allowed in Athenian courts has drawn much criticism, especially among earlier generations of scholars. For example, Maine protests that "questions of pure law were constantly argued on every consideration which could possibly influence the mind of the judges."[164] Similarly, Lofberg observes that "a startling amount of all kinds of irrelevant matter was brought into nearly every case."[165] In particular, moderns have been uncomfortable, as S. Todd points out, with the "politicization" of the Athenian courts.[166]

It is undeniable that law and politics overlapped in Athens, and more conspicuously than they do in modern Western democracies.[167] After all, the popular courts were responsible for hearing charges against public persons and thus played an integral role in the city's political life. Indeed, when politicians and generals appeared as litigants, the courts served as a forum for the registration of the public's satisfaction or dissatisfaction with leaders and their policies. Jurors were able to express their political views not only through their verdicts at the end of a trial but also through their shouts and cries at key points during it. The political role of the courts was not, however, limited to their oversight of prominent public persons. Through their verdicts jurors could reward or punish wealthy men for their behavior as citizens, for example, in carrying out liturgies and paying the war tax, and thus exert control over the civic behavior of Athens's elite.

The political dimensions of Athenian litigation do not, however, warrant the conclusion that "politics and law were at Athens ultimately indistinguishable."[168] Athenian discomfort with numerous aspects of the "politicization" of adjudication provides the best explanation for why litigants do not appeal to the city's interests over concerns of justice but rather as compatible with them: jurors believed that courts should, first and foremost, dispense justice and were uncomfortable with the explicit subordination of what was fair in a particular case to collective political interests and expedience. While jurors no doubt were conscious of the welfare of the city in issuing verdicts, they were not so radicalized as to dispense openly with traditional ideas of justice. Even in trials involving public figures, legal and factual claims are conspicuous: these were not merely, or not only, "political" trials in which a segment of the populace expressed its political opinions, but contests played out within a distinctly legal framework. Moreover, Athenians were well aware that politicians could twist the laws and abuse legal institutions, like volunteer prosecution, for their own political gain, and viewed this as misuse of the popular courts.

How fair were the Athenian courts by modern Western standards?[169] The popular courts could be harsh and vindictive in their judgment of the rich and powerful. One of Aristophanes' characters thus compares the juror's power in the realm of the courts with that of Zeus (V. 619–20),[170] remarking on the pleasure members of the demos take in deciding the fates of the high and mighty (V. 548–58, 625–26). In particular, Athenian jurors had a record of blaming their generals for losses and condemning them at trial. While some generals no doubt deserved censure, others were held accountable for failures for which they were not directly responsible. Furthermore, Socrates' condemnation to death on a charge of impiety in 399 B.C. is hardly a bright moment in the history of the Athenian courts. Despite such episodes, the popular courts were far from kangaroo courts: litigants had the opportunity to attempt to win jurors over to their side, and the outcome of contests was not predetermined. Although trials frequently had political undercurrents, not every trial in Athens was a "political" trial.[171] It is important, moreover, to put the excesses of Athenian juries in perspective: when the Thirty took power briefly in 404/3 B.C., they were far more vicious and capricious in their administration of justice than the popular courts ever were.[172]

HOW MUCH LITIGATION WAS THERE IN ATHENS?

Legal historians studying modern societies are able to gather from a variety of sources data that allow them to track litigation levels over time and thereby to identify shifting patterns of legal behavior. In the absence of court records or any similar documentation for Athens, it is impossible to measure Athenian litigation levels in this way. The complaints of some contemporaries that Athenians are too fond of lawsuits or that the courts are always hearing cases do not lend themselves to quantitative analysis. Nonetheless, one thing at least seems certain: the number of lawsuits reaching court did not climb steadily through the classical period. Although the number of lawsuits coming before the courts must have risen dramatically in the first generation after the reform of the popular courts (462–430 B.C.) for the reasons discussed, during the period 430–322 B.C. Athenian court capacity does not appear to have expanded significantly, which suggests that lawsuits reaching court did not continue to climb.

Various constraints on court capacity were left unaltered over the life of the democracy. For example, the number of court days each year probably did not exceed two hundred.[173] The number of jurors available for service each year remained at six thousand; only a portion of these showed up for service on any given day, and these persons were allotted to a small number of large panels, rather than numerous smaller panels. The number of juries empaneled each day may have depended on the number of court facilities available. Unfortunately our knowledge of court buildings in the agora and elsewhere is insufficient to establish how much court space was available at any given time.[174] Besides, Athenians were comfortable in holding court in buildings not specifically designated for court use, for example, in the Odeion, which also served as a theater, or the Stoa Poikilē.[175] Even ancient references to new courts may be evidence not of expansion but of the maintenance of court capacity, since new buildings may simply have replaced earlier ones: this was probably the case, for example, with the new consolidated court complex raised ca. 340 B.C.[176]

The capacity of the Athenian court system was flexible insofar as the number of juries empaneled on a given day could be adjusted in response to demand, but the constraints noted here meant that this flexibility was limited and that the courts could not accommodate a steadily rising number of suits. Because of these limitations on court capacity, the question arises whether there was often a backlog of suits and thus delay in adjudication. The Old Oligarch, the anonymous author of a pamphlet (420s B.C.?) that is critical of the democracy, remarks that a person may sometimes have to wait a year to negotiate with the Council or the Assembly ([X.] *Ath.* 3.1), and attributes this delay to a number of factors, including the large numbers of trials held in the city (3.2). He asserts that "the adjudicating has to go on throughout the year, since not even now when they do adjudicate throughout the year can they stop all the wrongdoers because there are so many" (3.6). Although some have taken these passages to constitute claims about court delay,[177] the Old Oligarch speaks in the first case not of court delay, but rather of delays in the Assembly and Council arising because the Athenians are busy judging cases; and in the second case he is probably just taking a snipe at the supposed license granted to misbehavior within the democracy (cf. 1.10) without claiming anything about delays.

At times, Athenians may have been concerned that private suits were causing, or might lead to, court congestion. This could explain why in 453/2 B.C. Athenians established deme judges and gave them the authority to decide suits involving small sums; and why in 400/399 B.C. they required litigants in most private suits to submit to public arbitration before appearing before a popular court. These reforms, however, may have been prompted not so much by concern over court congestion as by interest in avoiding costly adjudication for small-scale disputes.[178] Although the courts may have had the capacity to hear these suits, the public may have regarded their use as too expensive.[179]

Evidence of court congestion may also be sought in the designation of certain private suits, including those involving trade (*dikē emporikē*) and assault (*dikē aikeias*), as monthly suits (*dikai emmēnoi*) starting in the mid-fourth century B.C. Although scholars dispute what "monthly" meant in this context—that they were filed monthly, heard within a month of filing, or perhaps both—most agree that this classification was intended to expedite adjudication.[180] The speedy adjudication of suits involving trade was important to the city, especially since it was dependent on the import of grain by traders. The expedited trial of assault suits may reflect the view that assault on citizens was an especially serious matter that should be swiftly punished.[181] One may infer from this special classification, however, only that Athenians thought it desirable that some suits be heard *more quickly* than others, not that most cases faced lengthy court delays.

Where there was delay in bringing a suit to court, this may well have been the result not of court congestion but of pretrial maneuvering on the part of one or both litigants.[182] E. Cohen argues that one way monthly suits expedited litigation was by exempting litigants from pretrial arbitration, where such delay might occur.[183]

While the Athenian courts were not, as far as we can tell, so congested as to cause long delays in hearing suits, they were probably always relatively busy.[184] Because of the many possible sources of litigation, private and public, there was little risk that daily court sessions would be entirely suspended due to a dearth of business. At the same time, however, there was no guarantee on any given day that there would be so many suits ready for trial that all prospective jurors would be empaneled. Contemporary critics of the courts go so far as to claim that politicians curry favor with jurors by bringing false suits that keep the courts busy and thus ensure that jurors receive their daily stipend (see Chapter 3). While this is no doubt an exaggeration, jurors may well have appreciated the efforts of volunteer prosecutors, who, in pursuing the city's alleged enemies, simultaneously provided jurors with their wage.

If these arguments concerning litigation levels in Athens are correct, Athenians did not witness a continuing rise in suits reaching the courts during the period 430–322 B.C. It is possible that suits initiated but not reaching court were on the rise, because from 400/399 B.C. suits could be diverted to public arbitration and many parties settled here. But here, as with suits reaching court, one may infer from the stability of institutional structures that there was no constant climb: as far as we know, the number of public arbitrators, which was fixed in 400/399, sufficed until the end of the democracy in 322.[185]

Whatever the actual level of litigation in Athens at any given time, individuals may have believed, based on their personal experience and perceptions, that Athens was teeming with litigation and that the situation was out of hand. For example, when the conservative Isocrates lost an *antidosis* suit to a rival, he viewed this as evidence of the decadence of his times and looked back wistfully to an earlier, less contentious—and less democratic—era (15.313–15; cf. 7.51). But Athenian concerns over litigation tend to focus not so much on the overall level of litigation as on the abuse of litigation in particular circumstances—this is to say, less on the quantity of litigation and more on its quality. This reflects the fact that the ancient sources derive largely from the courts, where abuses arising in particular circumstances are naturally of more interest to litigants than historical trends. While Athenian complaints concerning abuse most commonly center on litigants and their supporters, they extend to the role of jurors in the popular courts, and to the role of law, legal argument, and legal expertise in litigation. Before considering these dimensions of the ancient discussion, however, it is worth looking closely first at the curious form the discussion itself takes.

Two

The Invention of Sykophancy: Idea and Ideology

Athenians expressed their concerns about litigation hyperbolically and colorfully. These features of the ancient discussion are an integral part of it, not mere rhetorical embellishments to be stripped away and discarded in a quest for the facts concealed beneath them. They convey the energy and emotion with which Athenians voiced their legal concerns, while also providing evidence of how Athenians conceived of the social significance of legal excess and abuse. Especially revealing is the way Athenians characterized persons who grossly abused litigation as "sykophants" and their activity as "sykophancy."[1] Sykophancy constituted a negative social category, founded upon the notion that Athenian society consisted of insiders and outsiders and that it was critical for Athenians to distinguish sharply between these. The idea of sykophancy was a powerful and flexible imaginative vehicle through which Athenians communicated with one another about legal excess and abuse. It was both an element in the invective wielded by individuals against one another and a part of Athenian discourse about civic identity.

Word, Concept, Social Idea: Imagining the Other

What did Athenians mean when they spoke of sykophancy? This question can be answered to some extent through philological analysis.

How and why words based on the root *sukophant-* came to be applied in Athens to legal excess and abuse is a complete mystery. Harvey summarizes well the results of some twenty-five hundred years of speculation on the question: "Ancient etymologies are unconvincing and mutually contradictory . . . Modern efforts are no happier."[2] To judge by the puns classical Athenians made on the root, they viewed it as a compound of *sukon* ("fig") and *phainein* ("to reveal").[3] Later, ancient scholars speculated directly on the question. The Atthidographer Istros (late third century B.C.), for example, asserted that there was once a prohibition on the export of figs from Attica, and those who informed against violators of the ban were dubbed "sykophants," that is, "fig revealers" (*FGrH* 334 F 12).[4] Although this explanation is not preposterous, it is suspect, since writers of local history such as Istros regularly invented circumstances in early Attica to explain later terms and institutions. From the nineteenth century, modern scholars have exercised their ingenuity to explain the etymology of *sukophant-*, but to no avail:[5] the fig, like the olive, has a wide range of cultural associations, agricultural, ritual, mythical, and sexual ("fig" was slang for "genitals"), and *sukophant-* may incorporate any of these meanings.[6]

Whatever the etymology and origins of *sukophant-*, it almost certainly came into vogue sometime in the mid-fifth century B.C. in conjunction with the rise of the popular courts.[7] It may have been a completely new coinage, or an older word applied in a new context.[8] Once in use, it remained popular throughout the fourth century B.C.[9] Although some writers came to apply *sukophant-* metaphorically in the sense of "quibble" outside of legal contexts (Pl. *R.* 340d1–341a9),[10] most classical usages appear in the context of the discussion of legal excess or abuse, and here there is no observable shift in usage.[11] Only after the classical period did *sukophant-* come to be applied to a parasite and flatterer, as in modern English.[12]

In a useful recent study of words based on *sukophant-*, D. Harvey argues that the sykophant typically engages in one or more of the following activities: (1) He seeks to make money by (a) blackmailing individuals with the threat of a legal prosecution; (b) bringing suits of the variety in which the prosecutor received a share of the fine; (c) prosecuting people for a fee. (2) He levels false charges. (3) He engages in sophistical quibbling. (4) He makes slanderous attacks. (5) He frequently takes people to court. (6) He acts after the event and rakes up old charges. (7) He is a fluent speaker.[13] Two further points should be emphasized. First, prosecutors of *all* kinds could be denounced as sykophants. Although scholars have often associated *sukophant-* exclusively with the abuse of volunteer prosecution of public actions,[14] in fact, as Osborne has observed, *sukophant-* is commonly wielded against prosecutors of private actions as well.[15] Second, while *sukophant-* is most commonly applied to the prosecutor of a suit, it could be extended to include those supporting him, for example, *sunēgoroi* (Dem. 51.16; cf. Theopomp. Hist. *FGrH* 115 F 110) and witnesses (Isoc. 18.55–56).[16] In addition, Athenians cast the slur of sykophancy on sophists and putative sophists on the grounds that they armed unscrupulous litigants for the courts (cf. Pl. *Lg.* 937d6–938c5).[17] Thus, "sykophancy" is best viewed as a flexible vehicle for condemning almost any form of unscrupulous behavior by legal actors and those assisting them.[18]

While the allegation of sykophancy involved factual claims concerning a wide range of legal abuses, at the same time it was an emotive charge imbued with rich social meaning. One indication of this is that a myriad of "negative value-words" crop up in connection with sykophancy. Harvey lists some seventy of these words and argues persuasively on this basis that for Athenians sykophancy was an unambiguously negative moral category.[19] One may go further than this: the sykophant is not only absolutely "bad" and a magnet for terms drawn from a well-established tradition of Greek invective, but also in public discourse—that is, oratory and comedy presented before a wide public—recognizably an anti-Athenian.[20]

Athenians conceive of the sykophant as an "other" and emphasize his alterity in a number of ways.[21] They attribute to him traits that are diametrically opposed to those ideally displayed by good

Athenian citizens: for example, in treating others savagely (he is a "beast"), he rejects the Athenian democratic ideal of tolerance and kindness (*praotēs*).[22] Athenians equate the sykophant with a variety of social outsiders including common criminals and barbarians,[23] and label him a "common enemy."[24] They characterize his enterprise as one that lies outside normal social categories designating work.

Athenians further stress the sykophant's alterity by depicting him as a source of restless and destructive energy that threatens to upset the equilibrium of the city and the peace of its inhabitants. Edmunds aptly describes sykophancy as "a fundamental mode of 'disturbance.'"[25] The sykophant bustles about (*perieimi*) the city in pursuit of victims[26] and never desists from his sykophantic activity;[27] he is a meddlesome troublemaker (*polupragmōn*) and busybody (*periergos*);[28] he disturbs (*tarattō*), confuses (*kukaō*), and shakes down (*seiō*)—that is, blackmails—his victims;[29] though himself an outsider and civic imposter, he forces legitimate members of society to leave the city in exile;[30] he twists, turns, and upsets (*strephō*) everything in pursuit of his goals.[31] Authors characterize the sykophant as a restless force not only through imagery, but also syntactically: they pile up active verbs and participles, miming on the rhetorical level the sykophant's breathless energy. "I/They (?) shook down, demanded money, threatened and sykophanted again" (Ar. fr. 228). "You harass him, you prosecute, you sykophant" (Dem. 36.52).[32]

Athenians applied to the sykophant the strongest language of social disapproval they could muster, namely, the vocabulary of religious pollution. As Burkert observes, "To belong to a group is to conform to its standard of purity; the reprobate, the outsider, and the rebel are unclean."[33] The sykophant is polluted, unclean, and accursed,[34] and the city should therefore cleanse (*kathairō*) itself of his corrupting presence.[35] When Athenians represented the sykophant in these terms, they drew on the deeply ingrained Hellenic idea that a city should purify itself by casting out impure elements. In fact, Athenians, like other Greeks, engaged in ritual expulsion of scapegoats (*pharmakoi*). Once a year during the festival of the Thargelia, Athenians cleansed the city by abusing and driving out two unfortunate citizens who had been designated as scapegoats; one of these wore black (dried) figs, one white (dried) figs.[36] As Parker observes, "It is tempting to try to connect the sykophant (fig shower) directly with the fig-wearing scapegoat: but how?"[37] The sykophant, however, need not be linked directly to scapegoat ritual to be a product of the same kind of thinking that inspired it.

That contemporaries viewed the sykophant as a scapegoat of sorts is evident from a variety of sources. For example, the Thirty (404/3 B.C.) exploited the popular idea that the sykophant was a polluted outsider, when they executed democratic opponents on the pretext that they were cleansing the city of sykophants (Lys. 12.5; cf. X. *HG* 2.3.12; [Arist.] *AP* 35.3). Other ancient sources, which may well have drawn their inspiration from the Athenian characterization of sykophants, also appeal to the idea that the sykophant is a public enemy who should be expelled from a city. For example, the historian Theopompus (late fourth century B.C.) claims that Philip of Macedon founded a city, Poneropolis ("City of the Wicked"), into which he sent "men denounced for their wickedness—sykophants, bearers of false testimony, advocates [*sunēgorous*], and other villains up to a number of two thousand" (*FGrH* 115 F 110).[38] The outcast status of the sykophant is also the basis of a peculiar tale related by Diodorus Siculus (first century B.C.) concerning the panhellenic colony of Thurii, which was founded in 444/3 B.C. with the help of Athens (D.S. 12.10):

> [Charondas][39] ordained that men who had been found guilty of sykophancy should go about crowned with tamarisk, so that they might show to all their fellow citizens that they had won first prize for villainy. As a consequence certain men who had been judged guilty of this charge, being unable to bear their great disgrace, voluntarily removed themselves from life. When this took place, every man who had made a practice of sykophancy was banished from the city and the government enjoyed a blessed life free from this evil. (12.12.2)

This tale claims that the Thurians eliminated sykophancy altogether from their city by requiring sykophants to wear a physical sign of their marginalized status. The Thurian sykophants resemble ritual scapegoats in Athens in wearing a vegetal token signifying their marginality, although Diodorus does not suggest that in Thurii the marking of sykophants was actually part of a ritual of expulsion.[40]

A few examples from Aristophanes' comedies (425–388 B.C.) and the Demosthenic oration *Against Aristogeiton* I (324 B.C.) illustrate how authors working in different genres and active at different times consistently portray the sykophant as a hated and polluted outsider. This similarity can be taken as further evidence of what Dover describes as the "essential continuity between the theatrical audiences of Aristophanes and the juries and assemblies addressed by Demosthenes."[41]

Three of Aristophanes' comedies contain scenes in which sykophants make extended appearances. In *Acharnians* (425 B.C.), Aristophanes twice brings onstage marketplace predators who seek to denounce through the legal procedure of *phasis* the import of goods from enemy lands in wartime (818–29, 908–58).[42] In *Birds* (414 B.C.), the comic poet introduces a legal carpetbagger who travels around harassing members of Athens's subject states (1410–69). In *Wealth* (388 B.C.), Aristophanes presents a sykophant who acts as a free-lance volunteer prosecutor wherever he wishes (850–958). The characters involved are not so much individuals as variations on a familiar type.[43] These sykophants variously attack the weak and vulnerable (*Ach.* 818–29; *Av.* 1430–31), invent false charges (*Pl.* 945–50; cf. *Av.* 1451–61),[44] and meddle in others' affairs (*Pl.* 913). Aristophanes emphasizes their status as social outsiders by portraying them as practitioners of a pseudocraft (*Av.* 1423, 1430–35; *Pl.* 902–6) and as pseudocitizens (*Ach.* 517–19, 725–26).[45]

The structure of Aristophanes' sykophant scenes strongly reinforces the idea that the sykophant is an unwelcome outsider. In each case a sykophant appears onstage, is mocked, and is then expelled from the stage. This process of intrusion and expulsion dramatizes the status of the sykophant as an outsider who must be shunned. While sykophants are by no means the only undesirable characters driven off the stage in Aristophanic comedy, Aristophanes appears to take particular pleasure in inventing bizarre punishments that suit these peculiar figures.

In the second sykophant scene in *Acharnians*, for example, Dikaiopolis disposes of the intruder in a curious way: he packs him up as if he were a pot (904–5, 926–28) and exports him. The sykophant's transformation into a pot involves several steps: Dikaiopolis gags his mouth (926), binds him (927, 952), and apparently hangs him upside down (944–45). In this way, the sykophant's restless and disruptive energy is literally contained and this inverter of norms is himself appropriately turned upside down. The resulting sykophant-pot, however, retains some of the traits of its raw material: it is good for stirring up suits as well as mixing up trouble (936–39). Dikaiopolis gulls a trader from Thebes into accepting the sykophant-pot in exchange for Boeotian delicacies (926–58). An Athenian audience could take pleasure in this fantasy, not only because Dikaiopolis thus discovers a means of getting rid of the city's surplus sykophants, but also because he sets them loose against Athens's hostile neighbor, Thebes.

In *Birds*, Peisetairos threatens to work a different kind of transformation on the listless sykophant he encounters. When the sykophant characterizes himself as a top (1460–61) whirling back and forth in a circle (cf. 1425, 1455–56, 1459) between the islands of the empire and the courts in Athens, Peisetairos seizes upon the image and threatens to whip him like a top (1461–65) if he does not take off on his own. Peisetairos thus bestows a punishment that fits his twisted perversion of justice (*strepsodikopanourgia*: 1468).

A different but equally strange punishment is prepared for the sykophant in *Wealth*. Carion and Dikaios abuse the intruding sykophant by stripping him (926–34) and then dressing him in the ragged clothing (*tribōnion*: 935) that Dikaios had intended to dedicate to Wealth for rescuing him from poverty.[46] This abuse takes the form of a mock ritual: Carion envisions the placement of rags on the sykophant as an act of dedication (938);[47] he then threatens to nail Dikaios's shoes to the sykophant's forehead "as if to a wild-olive tree" (943)—according to a scholiast, this plays on a form of dedication to divinities. The sykophant prudently flees before this dedication is completed. That he is put to flight in this way is fitting: although he labels his interlocutors unclean (870) and corrupt (893), he is himself an enemy of the god Wealth—he threatens to sue him (858–59; cf. *Pax* 107–8)—and is therefore an especially worthy object for abuse that takes the form of a ritual.

Aristophanes' campaign against sykophants is, however, by no means limited to attacks on generic representatives of the craft. Often he denounces particular individuals as sykophants, especially politicians (cf. *Pl.* 30–31) who had frequent recourse to the courts. Nowhere is Aristophanes more brutal in his comic abuse than when he casts his personal enemy, the popular and successful politician Cleon, in the role of sykophant extraordinaire.[48]

Throughout *Knights* (424 B.C.), for example, Aristophanes portrays Cleon as a restless sykophant (esp. *Eq.* 437), who agitates and confounds the city with the false charges that he stirs up.[49] Cleon's comic stand-in, Paphlagon—a barbarian name that conveys his status as an outsider—is a slave of Demos, a personification of the Athenian people. Paphlagon makes a trade (*technē*) of blackmailing his fellow slaves (other politicians): he "demands money from them, confounds them, seeks bribes," and if they refuse to pay him off, slanders them before their easily duped master (63–70). Paphlagon squeezes potential victims as if they were figs (a punning allusion to sykophancy) in order to select the best targets for his blackmail, and preys especially on vulnerable peaceful types (*apragmones*) (259–65). Although he claims to keep the city's treasury full "by putting the screws on some men, and throttling and blackmailing others" (775), in fact he seeks only to glut his own appetite, when for example he gobbles down the choicest bits from the scrutinies (*euthunai*) of officeholders (824–26). The sykophantic Paphlagon/Cleon, like the figures in Aristophanes' discrete sykophant scenes, is ultimately expelled: he is relegated to the periphery of the city to sell sausages at the city's gates (1397–1401) as befits a scapegoat (*pharmakos*: 1405). A coarse Sausage-seller is the agent who brings this about, defeating Paphlagon at his own game of false charges and thereby displacing him as Demos's favorite.

It is fair to infer from Aristophanes' lambasting of sykophants throughout his career that he and his audiences delighted in this abuse. The first parabasis of *Wasps* (422 B.C.) explicitly addresses the poet's relation to this kind of material, and suggests that attacking sykophants is fundamental to his comic persona. The chorus praises Aristophanes because in a comedy of the previous year he had "attacked the agues and the fevers, who by night strangled fathers and choked grandfathers, and who lay down on the beds of the peaceable folk [*apragmosin*] among you and stuck together affidavits, summonses and depositions, so that many jumped up in terror to go to the polemarch" (1037–42).⁵⁰ Although the comedy alluded to is no longer extant,⁵¹ the chorus's description suggests that sykophants figured prominently in it: while it does not actually use the word "sykophant," its characterization of the offending creatures as legal aggressors against peaceable folk (cf. *Eq.* 261) makes the identification secure.⁵² After lauding Aristophanes for his efforts against these sykophantic outsiders (the polemarch was the magistrate with whom one registered complaints against metics),⁵³ the chorus proceeds to hail Aristophanes as a "purifier [*kathartēn*] of this land, warding off evil from it" (1043). In so doing, it casts the comic poet as a Heraclean figure who heroically purges the city of sykophants through his comedy.⁵⁴

Nearly a century after Aristophanes first launched his assault on sykophants, the idea of sykophancy was still vital. Striking testimony to this is found in a forensic oration, Demosthenes 25: *Against Aristogeiton I,* that portrays the *rhētōr* Aristogeiton as a consummate sykophant. This prosecution speech and its companion, Demosthenes 26: *Against Aristogeiton II,* were presented by Aristogeiton's political enemies, who brought an *endeixis* against him in 324 B.C. alleging that he was not entitled to exercise the rights of an Athenian citizen since he had become a state debtor.⁵⁵ Although some scholars doubt that Demosthenes wrote either speech, the grounds for doubting his authorship are not compelling and both speeches are, in any event, almost certainly genuine products of late classical Attic oratory and thus legitimate sources concerning contemporary ideas.⁵⁶

In his prosecution, Demosthenes objects not so much to Aristogeiton's illegal appropriation of civic privileges—he concedes that the city was often lenient in enforcing restrictions on state debtors (25.85–86)—as to his sykophantic abuse of them. The speech derives much of its power from its appeal to an Athenian audience's disdain for sykophants. It draws extensively on, and plays creatively with, the traditional imagery associated with sykophancy.

Demosthenes portrays Aristogeiton as a classic sykophantic outsider: he is "thrice-accursed, the common foe, the universal enemy" (25.82). Like sykophants elsewhere, Aristogeiton is a savage beast (25.40, 52, 96) and an enemy of common human decency (*philanthrōpia*: 25.87). He engages in a pseudocareer, in which he sows not crops but lawsuits (25.82; cf. 25.51). He is a hyperactive force of malice. He darts here and there like a snake or scorpion, as he seeks out victims for blackmail in the agora (25.52). Even after the current suit was initiated, Aristogeiton "did not let up bellowing, acting the sykophant, and threatening" (25.49); instead, he harassed the magistrates by "assaulting them, making demands, exacting money from them" (25.50). In short, Aristogeiton sees fit "to do all things—to make accusations, give speeches, slander, malign, demand the death penalty, impeach, calumniate" (25.94). Like his sykophantic forebears in Aristophanes, Aristogeiton threatens to throw the civic order into confusion through his noxious hyperactivity. He thinks he can overturn the laws with his false charges (25.28; cf. 25.32); he attempts to "upset, undermine, and overthrow" civic harmony (25.90). In fact, Aristogeiton is ready to turn the whole universe upside down, since, though disfranchised and thus barred from prosecuting, he threatens legitimate citizens with his lawsuits (25.74–75; cf. 25.47).[57]

Throughout *Against Aristogeiton I,* vivid anecdotes illustrate Aristogeiton's sykophantic opposition to, and inversion of, normal social relations. For example, Aristogeiton brought suit against those who paid for his father's funeral, and was himself sued by his brother when he attempted to have his half-sister sold off (25.54–55). Because Aristogeiton treats his own family members and friends in this way, it comes as no surprise that he is also aggressive and abusive in his relations with the larger family of Athenian citizens (cf. 25.87–90).

Aristogeiton's status as sykophant is encapsulated in the dramatic tale that Demosthenes relates about his escapades in the city's jail while a state debtor:

> Before Aristogeiton left jail, a man of Tanagra was thrown in until he could find bail. With him he brought a document [*grammateion*]. Aristogeiton approached him and, while chatting on some topic or other, stole his *grammateion*; but when the man blamed him for the theft and made a fuss about it, saying that no one else could have taken it, Aristogeiton was so shameless that he tried to strike the fellow. But the Tanagran, a fresh-caught fish, was getting the better of the defendant, who was thoroughly pickled since he had been in jail a long time. So when it came to this, Aristogeiton bit off the other man's nose. At this point, the victim in his distress abandoned the search for his *grammateion*. The other prisoners, however, later found it in a chest of which the defendant possessed the key. After that, the inmates of the jail voted not to share fire or light, drink or food with him, not to receive anything from him, not to give him anything. To prove the truth of my statements, please call the man whose nose this monster bit off and swallowed. (25.60–62)

After narrating this grisly tale,[58] Demosthenes poses a climactic, rhetorical question: "Is [Aristogeiton] not impious, savage [*ōmos*], and unclean? Is he not a sykophant?" (25.63).

Although this tale of cannibalism is set within the walls of the city's jail, it clearly has significance for society at large. Aristogeiton's cannibalistic attack on a fellow inmate—arising perhaps from his pursuit of written evidence that he might use to blackmail or prosecute the Tanagran or someone else (cf. 25.50)—enacts an old Greek metaphor for utter savagery, "to eat someone raw" (e.g., Hom. *Il.* 4.35), and is the natural analogue to Aristogeiton's savage (*ōmos*: 25.83–84), sykophantic behavior against fellow citizens.[59] In fact, to encourage the analogy, Demosthenes depicts jailhouse society as a mirror image of Athenian society. When Aristogeiton's fellow inmates observe his gross inhumanity, they pass a resolution—a copy of which Demosthenes claims to have (25.62)—that designates Aristogeiton as a social outcast within the jail. Although this is hardly credible, since neither democratic procedure nor record keeping were presumably practiced among the inmates of Athens's jail, it offers the jurors a model to emulate: by voting against Aristogeiton, they too can render him an outcast. In case his audience misses the analogy, Demosthenes addresses the relationship between the jail and Athenian society in the moral he draws from his tale: if social outcasts themselves view Aristogeiton as untouchable (*ameiktos*: 25.63; cf. 25.58; Isoc. 15.300), surely decent Athenian citizens should refuse to have contact with him.[60]

Consistent with this portrayal of Aristogeiton as a sykophantic outcast is Demosthenes' exhortation near the end of his speech: "Just as physicians, when they detect a cancer or an ulcer or some other incurable evil, cauterize it or cut it away, so you must all unite in sending this monster beyond the frontier, in casting him out of the city, in destroying him" (25.95). Thus, just as Aristophanes takes it on himself to purge the city of sykophants, so too Demosthenes poses as the city's protector in identifying the sykophant, Aristogeiton, and in urging his expulsion.

Making Sykophants: Social Labeling

The preceding analysis argues that Athenians envisioned the sykophant as a consummate outsider and enemy of society. But no individual was a sykophant until a hostile party labeled him one (cf. X. *HG* 2.3.12; Men. *Georg.* fr. 1 Sandbach), and for the designation to stick and thus do any harm, the labeler had to persuade an audience to join in bestowing it.[61] The social dynamics of the process by which individuals "became" sykophants is of some interest.

Athenian audiences seem to have been highly susceptible to the kind of thinking that viewed society in terms of insiders and outsiders: they were acutely conscious of, and arguably even insecure about, their group identity, and this encouraged a scapegoat mentality.[62] Persons addressing popular audiences exploit and perpetuate this view of society when they present themselves as representatives of the community seeking to expose common enemies to the public eye. Comic poets, for example, invite their audiences to join in deriding a variety of social misfits paraded across the stage, and thus to assert their solidarity against these outsiders.[63] Similarly, in court litigants regularly pose as exposers of public enemies. One litigant prosecuting an opponent for assault thus asserts:

> It would indeed have been best, if only some other sign [*sēmeion*] were borne by villainous men, that we might punish them before any citizen

has been injured by them. But since it is impossible to perceive who such men are before victims have suffered at their hands, at any rate as soon as they are recognized, it is everyone's duty to hate them and regard them as common enemies. (Isoc. 20.14)

Adjudication, in this view, is an opportunity for the public exposure of social outsiders: because public enemies, unlike the tamarisk-crowned Thurian sykophants of Diodorus's tale (D.S. 12.12.2), do not bear a physical emblem of their depravity, it is necessary to mark them out as outsiders through prosecution before the public.

The designation of certain individuals as sykophants in public contexts can be viewed as a particular example of this general Athenian tendency to imagine society in terms of insiders and outsiders. The manner in which the label "sykophant" is imposed, however, takes a special form that reflects the status of the sykophant as a recognizable social type. It was incumbent on the labeler to convince his listeners that the individual targeted was a living example of the social type with which they were already familiar; this entailed matching up the supposed traits of the individual in question with those that audiences associated with the social type. This made the creation of a sykophant very much a cooperative social enterprise in the public arena.

The labeler's task was greatly facilitated by the fact that Athenian audiences were well acquainted with this social type and on the lookout for allusions to it. For example, when comic writers pun on *sukophant-*, they rely on their listeners to catch the wordplay without explanation. Consider the following exchange in Eubulus's *Olbia* (mid-fourth century B.C.):

> A: For all things will be sold together in the same place in Athens: figs [*suka*]
> B: summoners
> A: grapes, turnips, pears, apples
> B: witnesses
> A: roses, medlars, haggis, honeycombs, chick-peas
> B: lawsuits
> A: milk, pudding, myrtle berries
> B: allotment machines for juries

A: hyacinth, lambs
B: water clocks, laws, indictments.

(fr. 74)

Character A's reference to the sale of figs elicits from Character B a chain of associations that are all connected with the venal sykophant and his legal milieu. Eubulus takes for granted that, even though he does not use the word "sykophant," his audience needs no explanation of Character B's free associations, since "figs" will evoke similar associations for them.[64] Just as Athenians were attuned to puns on *sukophant-*, so too were they on the lookout for the negative traits that indicated a sykophant was before them. The mention of a few sykophantic traits was sufficient to alert an audience that the allegation of sykophancy was lurking. Some labelers, in fact, actively engage their audiences in the process of labeling by attributing familiar sykophantic traits to their targets and then encouraging their audiences to join them in inferring from these signs that an individual is a sykophant.

This process is perhaps most conspicuous on the comic stage, where it takes a playful and teasing form. In his sykophant scenes in *Birds* and *Wealth,* Aristophanes brings onstage an unnamed stranger and only gradually unveils him as a sykophant.[65] Although this postponement of identification is common with characters other than sykophants, this has a special dimension in the case of sykophants.[66] Because the title of sykophant—unlike that of poet, farmer, or surveyor—is a hostile and controversial designation, Aristophanes goes out of his way to demonstrate to his audience that the character onstage in fact deserves to be called a sykophant. This revelation of a sykophant draws both the characters onstage and the audience offstage into the social game of labeling sykophants.

In *Birds,* telltale signs of sykophancy prepare the audience for the disclosure of the stranger's identity. His ragged dress (1416–17, 1421) provides Aristophanes' audience with an indication, even before he speaks, that he is desperately impoverished. While sykophants are sometimes characterized as poor men,[67] others are also depicted in this way (e.g., the poet at 935–51), and the audience must therefore await further clues before identifying this ragged figure. A hint is provided by the stranger's opening words: "What birds are these, who—though they are poor[68]—are well-plumed?" (1410). Like both sykophants in *Acharnians* (818, 910), this stranger opens with an aggressive question. Apparently he sees an opportunity for prosecution or legal blackmail against the birds, who—he reasons comically—must have some illicit source of wealth, since they are luxuriantly plumed despite their lack of resources.[69] Peisetairos expresses immediate misgivings ("this is no trivial evil we've roused up": 1412; cf. *Ach.* 829), but gives no indication yet that he recognizes what is before him. The intruder's impatient repetition of words (1411, with 1415; 1420) provides a further hint that he is a member of the restless and hyperactive class of sykophants. Finally, the puzzle is solved, as the intruder himself comically discloses his identity as "an island-hopping summoner, a sykophant . . . and a trouble-seeker" (1422–24).[70]

In *Wealth*, Aristophanes teases his audience by drawing out the identification of the sykophant-stranger for over twenty lines.[71] When the intruder—ragged like the sykophant in *Birds*[72]—absurdly threatens to make Wealth blind again "if lawsuits have any force" (858–59), he provides an excellent initial clue to his trade. Dikaios, however, only infers that a man "of bad stamp" (862; cf. 957; *Ach.* 517) is before him. The intruder's next words also hint at his identity: he falsely claims that Wealth had promised to make "all of us rich straightaway, if he should regain his sight" (864–66).[73] The claim that Wealth has violated a public promise calls to mind the serious charge of deceiving the demos ([Arist.] *AP* 43.5). When Carion learns that the ragged figure before him has suffered financial ruin under the new order, where good men are rich and bad men poor, he hazards a guess that his interlocutor is a rascal or thief (869). Only after the intruder falsely accuses Carion and Dikaios of stealing his money (870–71; cf. 890–95), however, does Carion finally identify him as a sykophant (873). The postponement of this labeling allows Aristophanes' audience to play detective and, moreover, to accept the label imposed, since it has witnessed the behavior that justifies this.

Athenian litigants exposing their opponents as "manifest sykophants" usually are more direct than this.[74] Too much was at stake for them to engage in the kind of teasing postponement that Aristophanes does, and therefore they tend to label their opponents as sykophants early in their speeches and to reiterate the claim periodically.[75] Litigants too, however, had to justify their imposition of the label, and this required matching up an opponent's behavior with the public's prior understanding of the sykophantic type. This process is especially salient when a litigant relates an anecdote illustrating his opponent's unscrupulous behavior, and then draws from it the conclusion that his opponent is indeed a sykophant, as Demosthenes does at the end of his colorful narrative of Aristogeiton's behavior in jail (25.63). So too a client of Isocrates first relates at length how his opponent Callimachus was exposed as a false witness in a homicide case when the supposed victim was produced in court (18.52–54),[76] and then asks, "Who would be able to find a more flagrant manifestation [*paradeigma*] of wrongdoing, sykophancy, and villainy?" (18.55).

When litigants and comic writers in their different ways involved their audiences in the identification of sykophants, they acknowledged and exploited the social nature of the designation. In both the courts and the comic theater, audience participation in the imposition of the label sykophant may well have gone beyond tacit approval of the claim and extended to shouted verbal support of it. In both settings, audiences were free to voice their opinions aloud (cf. Pl. *Lg*. 876b3–5) and they appear to have exercised that freedom regularly.[77] Thus, members of Aristophanes' audience who recognized from the clues provided that an intruding stranger was a sykophant could share that knowledge with other members of the audience. Similarly, jurors and bystanders at court were free to cry out against a "manifest sykophant." When a litigant asked, "Is my opponent not a sykophant?" (Dem. 25.63; cf. Isoc. 18.55), he may well have intended to elicit just such audience support for his claim.

A Real Profession?

It should be evident from the preceding discussion that the combination "real" and "sykophant" is an oxymoron. The sykophant is a social type and an individual's identity as a sykophant an imposed one.[78] This identification could be disputed in advance of its hostile application: for example, a prosecutor might open his speech by insisting that he was *not* a sykophant (Dem. 53.1; cf. Ar. *Pax* 191). Furthermore, a party denounced as a sykophant could turn the allegation back against the accusing party and thus participate in a game of sykophant hot-potato.[79] Although effective labeling of an individual as a sykophant might lead to some consensus that he *really* was a sykophant, in most cases this identification was probably evanescent. To be sure, according to Isocrates, the names of persons facing prosecution for sykophancy were posted publicly on notice boards (*sanides*) (15.237). But such prosecutions appear to have been rare (see Chapter 1), and this type of posting in any event was only temporary (by contrast, the names of traitors were inscribed in stone: Lyc. 1.124–26).[80] Arguably, a prosecutor's conspicuous loss of a suit, especially if he won less than one-fifth of the votes cast in a public suit and therefore incurred the normal statutory penalties, might make him more susceptible to the claim in later suits that he was a sykophant. But even in such cases it was incumbent on his opponent to convince a jury, which was not necessarily familiar with the alleged sykophant's record, that he had misused the courts in the past. This was not a simple matter: normally written evidence of a verdict was unavailable,[81] and therefore a litigant seeking to document an opponent's history of sykophancy had to bring forward witnesses to the outcomes of earlier suits (Isoc. 18.54).[82]

The manner in which hostile parties talk about sykophants has led many scholars to assume, however, that sykophants constituted not (or not merely) a conceptual class, but a (sub)sociological one—*the* sykophants, who practiced sykophancy as a profession.[83] This represents an overly literal interpretation of metaphorical language in the ancient sources. First, although some sources refer to sykophants as a class (*genos*),[84] this term can be applied to actual social groupings or to persons assumed to share common traits, and it seems clear that those complaining about the "class" of sykophants are appealing to the latter idea. Another indication that we are dealing with a conceptual class is, as Osborne observes, the role of abstraction in the discussion: classical authors tend to use the abstract noun *sukophantia* and verb *sukophanteō*, rather than the personal noun *sukophantēs*.[85]

Second, while ancient authors often characterize sykophancy as a job (*ergon*), trade (*technē*), or a living (*zēn ek tou sukophantein; bios*),[86] it is clear that they are employing vivid metaphors that convey the idea that an individual is a habitual abuser of litigation and profits from it. Most scholars have recognized that one ought not to take literally the assertion that workshops (*ergastēria*) of sykophants have conspired against a litigant, but many have not appreciated fully the poetic color of these other figures.[87] In fact, these figures appear first in the playful banter of Aristophanic dialogue and may indeed have been coined originally for the comic stage.

In Aristophanes' *Birds* (414 B.C.), for example, Peisetairos wittily construes sykophancy as a trade (*technē*) or job (*ergon*) that its practitioners perversely choose over respectable work.[88] When an intruder appears onstage and identifies himself as a sykophant, Peisetairos remarks ironically, "How fortunate you are in your trade [*technēs*]" (1423), and inquires incredulously:

> *Peisetairos:* Do you really work [*ergazei*] this job [*ergon*]—tell me, do you, a young man, act as sykophant against foreigners?
> *Sykophant:* What do you want me to do? I don't know how to dig.[89]
> *Peisetairos:* Great Zeus, there are other honest jobs [*erga*] from which a strong fellow like you could live [*diazēn*] justly without weaving suits—lawsuits, that is [*dikorrhaphein*].[90]
>
> (1430–35)

Later, when Peisetairos invites the sykophant to turn to traditional work (*ergon nomimon:* 1450), the sykophant rejects the suggestion on the absurd ground that his living (*bios*) is a hereditary one and to give it up would be to shame his family (1451–52). Much of this scene's humor derives from its exploration of the metaphor that men practice sykophancy as a deviant and even hereditary career: if sykophancy were in fact recognized as a real profession, there would be little point to this excursus.[91]

Likewise, when speakers in the courts cast sykophancy as a trade or career, they are employing colorful metaphors. Jurors, like members of Aristophanes' audience, did not have to believe that sykophancy was a profession to find this imagery compelling.[92] Just as they understood that a litigant was employing a figure of speech if he accused a man of being "by trade an adulterer" (Lys. 1.16), so too they would not have taken literally the application of the figure to sykophants. In fact, this figure is consistent with other metaphors of art and artifice that litigants use when decrying manipulation of the legal process. Litigants complain that their opponents use devices (*mēchanaomai*) (Ant. 5.25; Lys. 1.28; Is. 11.36; Dem. 22.35), fashion (*plattō*) suits (Dem. 52.12; cf. 18.121; 45.42), and fabricate (*para-* or *kataskeuazō*) charges (And. 1.132; Dem. 21.103); the designer of such schemes can be said to be their architect (Dem. 40.32; 56.11).[93] These metaphors find their natural culmination in the protest that the abuse of litigation has become a *technē* in the hands of sykophantic opponents.

It is easy to confuse social types with real social groups in studying an ancient society, since often social types are vividly depicted and information about social groupings is vague. Similar confusion has arisen about the status of "peaceful men" (*apragmones*), who are often treated in the sources as victims of sykophants.[94] Carter assumes that *apragmones* were an identifiable group of persons, namely, disillusioned elite Athenians who withdrew from civic life starting in the late fifth century.[95] But other scholars have argued persuasively that no single group had exclusive claim to the social ideal of quietude, and that it is a mistake therefore to take the term *apragmones* as a designation for a social grouping.[96]

Just as the search for a real class of *apragmones* is bound to fail, so too is one for an actual class of sykophants.[97] In fact, the status of each class as a social type is confirmed by the complementary role of the two in forensic oratory.[98] Litigants tend to divide the world into *apragmones* (themselves and by implication their sympathetic audiences), and sykophants (their opponents and those supporting them) (Dem. 58.65). The *apragmōn* minds his own business and avoids legal trouble; the sykophant is meddlesome (*polupragmōn*) and seeks out lawsuits. The *apragmōn* is unfamiliar with the courts and legal argument; the sykophant is intimately familiar with the city's legal apparatus and with legal subtleties.[99]

While Harvey recognizes the rhetorical nature of the allegation of sykophancy, he nonetheless argues in favor of the view that there were professional sykophants. He cites numerous references in oratory and comedy to large sums paid to putative sykophants, and argues on this basis that individuals could make sufficient money "to live off sykophancy."[100] There are numerous objections to this. First, allegations of particular acts of sykophancy are inherently suspect, and all the more so are allegations of lifetime patterns of legal abuse.[101] Second, it is hard to believe that illicit litigation was a predictable source of income for anyone, and Harvey acknowledges as much.[102] Third, for the elite litigants against whom the slander of "living off sykophancy" is leveled in our sources, whatever profits they made from litigation were surely not the basis of their subsistence. Fourth, the persons most likely to be labeled career sykophants in our sources are *rhētores,* who frequently brought prosecutions: their "sykophancy" arose in connection with their carrying out recognized public roles, and it is misleading therefore to speak of them as if they possessed a separate and distinct identity as professional sykophants.

Sykophancy and Civic Ideology

The general appeal of the idea of the sykophant to Athenian audiences can be explained, as suggested earlier, by the attraction of Athenians, like members of many societies, to a model of society in which insiders and outsiders are sharply delineated. But why were Athenians attracted to the application of this idea in connection with litigation and the courts? The impetus to create such a model arose from the need to reconcile the problematic role of litigation within the city with civic ideals. The idea of sykophancy was very much a part of Athenian civic ideology.

One attraction of the idea of the sykophant to Athenians was that it allowed them to distance their city from criticisms leveled against it in connection with litigation and the popular courts. Athens's critics, internal and external, asserted that because the democracy embraced and encouraged litigation, the city was full of sykophants (cf. Theopomp. Hist. *FGrH* 115 F 281).[103] In particular, they alleged that popular juries endorsed legal harassment of vulnerable Athenians and non-Athenians—men from subject states under the empire[104] and foreigners visiting Athens.[105] These critics may even have originally "invented" the idea of sykophancy as a vehicle for railing at democratic excesses.[106] If they did, however, Athenians took the idea of sykophancy and appropriated it as a part of their civic ideology.

Athenians insisted that it was unfair for others to characterize them as "overly fond of litigation" (*philodikein*) (Th. 1.77.1),[107] and, in keeping with this, foisted blame for legal abuse and excess off onto a minority of "sykophants." In Athenian public discourse, in fact, this distinction between the majority of good Athenians and a minority of sykophants is sometimes made explicitly. Aristophanes' Dikaiopolis, for example, blames the Peloponnesian War on sykophantic outsiders: "For men among us (I am not talking about the city as a whole; remember this, that I am not speaking of the city), in any case, rascally fellows, ill-struck, worthless, ill-coined, spurious fellows kept crying out as sykophants against Megarian cloaks" (*Ach*. 515–19).[108] In the courts too, litigants distinguish between exceptional sykophantic individuals and the majority of citizens. One of Lysias's clients thus attributes to his audience a reluctance to share in the blame for the actions of a few sykophants: "you considered it monstrous that the crimes of the few should be spread over the whole city" (25.19). Similarly, Demosthenes protests in his prosecution of the sykophantic Aristogeiton "how much shame and ill-repute are brought upon the city by these beasts" (25.8).

This scapegoating of sykophants for negative behavior that the city's critics associated with democratic Athens suggests that the Athenian discussion of sykophancy is very much tied up with the city's self-presentation. In recent years, scholars have explored how the funeral orations given annually in honor of the city's war dead helped generate and promulgate an ideal image of the city and its citizens. These patriotic celebrations of "Athenianism" enshrined Athenian ideals of good citizenship through their praise of the city's war dead who had made the absolute sacrifice for the benefit of their city.[109] If the city's encomiasts provided models of ideal citizen behavior in funeral oratory, however, negative models were also useful for articulating and reflecting on what it meant to be a good citizen. Hunter has noted the relative neglect of these negative models in the study of Athenian ideology, and well observes, "The competing stereotypes of the good and the bad citizen . . . are part of an ideology of citizenship."[110] The sykophant, who manifestly inverts the ideals of good citizenship in his legal behavior, may be viewed as a prime example of Hunter's stereotypical bad citizen. Whether Athenians embraced the positive ideals of citizenship articulated in funeral oratory, or rejected the inversion of these ideals in the figure of the sykophant, they affirmed their shared values.

The complementary relationship of these positive and negative models of civic behavior is evident in the writings of Isocrates, a fourth-century orator, educator, pamphleteer, and political conservative. In a remarkable passage in his *Antidosis* (354/3 B.C.), Isocrates juxtaposes the ideals of Athenian funeral oratory with the negative model of sykophancy, so as to spur Athenians on to protect the city's good name and thus to advance its claim to hegemony over the other Hellenes:

> I think that you [members of the jury] are not unaware that while some of the Hellenes are hostile to you, others are extremely friendly, and rest their hopes of rescue upon you. These say that Athens is the only true city, the others being mere villages, and that it deserves to be termed the capital of Hellas both because of its size and because of the resources that it furnishes to others, and most of all because of the character of its inhabitants; for they say that no people are more kindly or more sociable, and a man could not find any people with whom to spend all his days on friendlier terms. Indeed, so extravagant are they in their praise that they do not even hesitate to say that they would rather suffer injury at the hands of an Athenian than benefit through the savagery of people from another city [i.e., the Lacedaimonians]. There are, on the other hand, those who scoff at this praise, and, dwelling upon the cruelty and villainy of sykophants, accuse the entire city of being hostile and harsh. It is therefore the duty of intelligent jurors to kill those responsible for these criticisms on the grounds that they bring great shame upon the city, and to honor those who are responsible in some degree for the praise given to it. (15.299–301)

On the one hand, Isocrates attributes to admiring Hellenes an ideal vision of the city that closely resembles the praise of the city found in Attic funeral orations: Athens stands alone among the Hellenes, is a benefactor of them, is a furnisher of resources, and its people are outstanding in their character.[111] On the other hand, Isocrates asserts, some dismiss this praise because they judge the city by its sykophants and conclude on this basis that the entire city shares the nature of sykophants. Thus, he suggests, Athenians must not only affirm the positive ideals of funeral oratory, but also reject the inversion of these by sykophants, if they are to preserve and advance the city's good reputation. Although Isocrates' dream of a new Athenian empire founded on the city's high repute thus maintained is his own hobbyhorse, his manipulation of Athenian ideals to advance his program is based on an intimate familiarity with civic ideology.

If the idea of sykophancy was important to the city's defense of its reputation in the Greek world, it could also help foster unity at home. Again, an analogy may be drawn with the Attic funeral orations. Scholars have noted that the Attic funeral orations present Athenians with an ideal image of their city as united and harmonious, while suppressing the real social, economic, and political tensions among citizens.[112] So too, when Athenians appealed to the idea of sykophancy in public discourse, they worked to suppress division and tension in the interest of fostering unity. When Athenians publicly condemned sykophants and sykophancy, they asserted their unity and solidarity as a people against legal excess and abuse in its most extreme form: although the line between proper and improper uses of litigation was ill defined, the sykophant overstepped that line so clearly that all Athenians could unanimously condemn the extreme behavior he embodied. Athenians would have agreed with Aristotle's assertion, "everyone hates a sykophant" (*Rh.* 1382a7), and herein lay much of the appeal of the idea of sykophancy within Athenian ideology.[113]

Behind the Athenian consensus that sykophancy was bad and un-Athenian, however, lay numerous unresolved tensions concerning legal institutions and litigation. What were sufficient and proper protections for the wealthy against sykophantic prosecutions?

When was the pursuit of volunteer prosecution appropriate? How could litigation, especially among those enjoying close social bonds, be reconciled with social ideals of cooperation? What role should laws and legal expertise play in the course of litigation and adjudication? The following chapters consider how Athenians addressed these problematic questions.

Three

Litigation and Class Conflict

Concerns over legal excess and abuse figured prominently in the worst episode of civil strife in the history of democratic Athens. When the oligarchic Thirty, supported largely by members of the leisure class, came into power in 404 B.C., they made legal "reform" a central part of their program.[1] The Thirty put on trial and condemned their democratic enemies, who had been active in the courts in prosecuting their social betters, on the grounds that they were thus purging the city of sykophants (X. *HG* 2.3.12; cf. [Arist.] *AP* 35.3; Lys. 12.5);[2] eventually they condemned some fifteen hundred citizens, probably on the same pretext.[3] Furthermore, the Thirty altered inheritance laws "in order that there might be no leeway for sykophants" ([Arist.] *AP* 35.2). Indeed, the Thirty went even further in their war on sykophancy by suppressing the popular courts that, in the view of conservatives, empowered and sustained sykophants.[4] If in the eyes of the Thirty and their supporters the whole democratic legal apparatus was sykophantic, those who suffered at the far more capricious justice meted out in 404 B.C. labeled the Thirty as "scoundrels and sykophants" (Lys. 12.5) and even worse than sykophants (X. *HG* 2.3.22).[5]

While it was only in the democracy's darkest hour that class violence erupted in Athens, the legal concerns subsumed under "sykophancy" that played a part in this violence affected interclass relations significantly throughout the period 430–322 B.C. It is against this backdrop of ongoing tension that the frequent discussion of sykophancy in elite sources should be situated. This chapter explores how class differences in Athens shape the discussion of legal excess and abuse in these sources. First, it considers what "class" means in an Athenian context and sketches out some of the class dimensions of concerns over litigation. Second, it examines how the predominantly elite sources address the subject of legal excess and abuse. Although elite authors express concerns that share much in common with one another, they advance a variety of perspectives and adapt their criticisms to the audiences they are addressing.

Class and the Perception of Legal Excess and Abuse

To understand the diversity of Athenian perspectives on legal abuse and excess, one must appreciate the socioeconomic differences that distinguished Athenians from one another and helped shape their points of view. Although Athens and its environs had perhaps three hundred thousand inhabitants in the classical period, only about thirty thousand adult, male Athenians enjoyed full civic privileges.[6] Within this select group some were sufficiently wealthy that they did not have to work to support themselves and their families. While the wealthiest members of this "leisure class" were required to carry out costly liturgies and pay the irregularly imposed *eisphora*, less wealthy members were liable only to the *eisphora*. This leisure class probably did not number more than a few thousand and thus constituted somewhere between 5 and 10 percent of the citizen body.[7] Although the composition of this group changed over time, its members never constituted more than a small part of the citizen body. Besides wealth, a distinguished bloodline or an advanced education could set an Athenian apart from his fellow citizens, but wealth was the primary determinant of elite status, and those with other elite attributes were normally also well-off.[8] Contemporaries were conscious of the disparity between members of the leisure class and the majority of citizens, and commonly characterized the former as "rich," the latter as "poor."[9] While there were many gradations of wealth among the majority of less well-off citizens, Athenians did not divide the majority into, for example, a middle and lower class.[10] Ober has argued therefore that it is not anachronistic to speak of Athenian class divisions in terms of "masses" and "elite."[11]

Class relations were generally stable in democratic Athens. Only twice did class tensions contribute to civil upheaval, once in 411 B.C., when the oligarchic Four Hundred took power, and again in 404 B.C., when the Thirty did so; on both occasions Athenian society was under exceptional pressure due to the Peloponnesian War. As scholars frequently point out, Athens' experience of stability is remarkable, especially when compared with the ongoing class warfare that plagued other Greek city-states particularly in the fourth century B.C. Numerous explanations for Athens' relative tranquillity have been offered. First, the majority, though politically dominant, did not attempt to place all citizens at the same economic level, which kept the wealthy from leaguing together to protect their property interests. Instead, the wealthy were allowed to contribute "voluntarily" to the city through liturgies and other forms of civic benevolence, for which they received public gratitude (*charis*) and prestige. Furthermore, throughout the entire classical period, Athenians, rich and poor alike, had a common interest in preserving the citizenship privileges that set them apart from other inhabitants of Attica; under the fifth-century Athenian empire, the benefits to all classes from maintaining the city's dominance abroad provided an additional incentive for cooperation. Athenians, moreover, appear to have been especially successful in fostering a sense of common identity through their shared rituals and civic ideology.

Athens's relatively good class relations, however, were achieved in the face of real tensions and divergent class interests. Although the members of its leisure class were diverse in their political outlooks and loyalties, they shared a number of concerns as men of wealth interested in protecting their property and status. For example, they had a common interest in preserving their fortunes for themselves and their heirs, and therefore as a matter of course concealed their wealth from their fellow citizens to prevent its depletion through liturgies and the *eisphora*.¹² While for opponents of the democracy this concealment of wealth was politically as well as financially motivated, for elite supporters of the democracy concealment was a practical means by which to protect their fortunes. By concealing his wealth, a rich man could discourage his economic peers from attempting to transfer their civic obligations to him through the legal procedure of *antidosis*.¹³ Concealment also gave a wealthy man the option to choose when it was financially convenient and politically advantageous to volunteer to undertake a liturgy.

So too men of wealth had concerns in common about litigation, since they were, willing or not, frequent participants in it, and their reputations and fortunes were at risk. The pressures and uncertainties of arguing a case before popular juries made litigation a frightening prospect for some members of the elite. Consider, for example, how one of Isocrates' clients characterizes the pressures that his opponent brought to bear on him to settle their suit before trial:

> Some of his friends approached me and advised me to settle the dispute with him, and not deliberately to risk defamation and great financial loss, even if I had the greatest confidence in my case. They went on to say that many decisions in the courts turn out contrary to expectation, and that chance rather than justice determined the issue in your courts. Consequently, they asserted, it was in my interest to be freed of serious charges by paying a petty sum, rather than by paying nothing to run such great risks. Why need I relate to you all the details? They omitted none of the arguments which are customarily urged in such cases. In any event, I was finally persuaded (for I will tell you the whole truth) to give him two hundred drachmas. (18.9–10)

While this litigant may well be exaggerating when he proceeds to characterize the payment to which he agreed as sykophantic extortion (18.10),¹⁴ he presents a plausible picture of the concerns a wealthy man might have about litigation and his readiness to pay money to avoid it.¹⁵

Although complaints of sykophantic blackmail in elite sources are difficult to evaluate in individual cases, as in the episode just described, taken as a group they point to the ambiguous position of the city's elite in relation to litigation and the popular courts.[16] On the one hand, timid members of the elite were probably vulnerable, as is often claimed in elite sources, to blackmail by false accusers, who threatened to pursue lawsuits against them unless they paid extortion.[17] On the other hand, wealthy men who were guilty of the charges threatened against them, or of other misdeeds (e.g., liturgy avoidance) that might be exposed at trial, had far more reason to pay off their accusers.[18] Thus Isocrates asserts that sykophants "advertise their powers in their attacks upon men who have done no wrong, and so get more money from those who are clearly guilty" (15.24).[19] Especially when the amount demanded by a blackmailer was trifling by the standards of the rich—and members of the elite often characterize it as such[20]—the temptation must have been great for a guilty rich man to pay off an accuser. Litigants often accuse one another of guilty payoffs and obviously deem the charge to be a credible one.[21] One of Lysias's wealthy clients even acknowledges that this would be a natural option for a man of his class: had he been guilty of the charges against him, he would have been forced to buy off the prosecution (7.21).[22] A late anecdote concerning the fourth-century politician Lycurgus alleges that when he was legitimately accused in the Assembly of having bought off sykophants, he quipped, "At any rate, I have only been caught giving out money, not taking it" ([Plu.] *Mor.* 842a7–b2; cf. Plu. *Mor.* 541f2–6; *Comp. Nic. et Crass.* 1.3). Although this anecdote may well be apocryphal (contrast Ael. *VH* 13.24.1–5), the cavalier attitude attributed to Lycurgus is probably typical of men of wealth in Athens: to pay a bribe to protect one's private interests was a prerogative of wealth and hardly shocking.[23]

Thus, members of Athens's leisure class were not only in a vulnerable position as potential litigants but also in an excellent position to circumvent the city's legal system. The public was presumably well aware that wealth gave rich men advantages in litigation and that, as one of Lysias's clients points out, "the wealthy purchase with their money escape from [legal] dangers [*kindunous*]" (24.17).[24] This probably made average Athenians less sympathetic to complaints of sykophantic harassment than they might otherwise have been. A wealthy man had many advantages in and out of court, and might reasonably be expected to use his own resources to deal with any threats arising in connection with his enviable status. If his complaints were valid ones, moreover, he was free to bring a lawsuit against his harasser through any of the many actions available for pursuing such claims.

While elite sources surely exaggerate the vulnerability of the wealthy in litigation, the concerns raised are of considerable historical interest.[25] After all, the perceptions and misperceptions behind these concerns were real ones that could affect the behavior of members of the leisure class, as they did conspicuously in the episode of the Thirty discussed at this chapter's opening. Furthermore, the elite representation of legal excess and abuse provides an opportunity to explore how elite Athenians conceived of, and voiced their concerns about, litigation.

The elite sources in question can be divided into two categories, based on the audiences to whom they were directed.

1. *Works Addressed Primarily to the Reading Public.* Some works were circulated among an audience of private readers, rather than presented to the public at large. This reading audience probably consisted primarily of elite Athenians and other well-off Greeks, who had the leisure and money to acquire a high degree of literacy,[26] could afford to purchase texts, and had time to read them. Works that fall into this category include the antidemocratic treatise attributed to the Old Oligarch, the writings of Xenophon, Plato, and Aristotle, and Isocrates' political "pamphlets."

2. *Works Performed before the Public.* Two types of works are best viewed as examples of public discourse: (a) orations written by members of the elite primarily for the use of elite speakers in the popular assemblies and courts; and (b) comedies composed by elite writers for mass audiences. While these works were eventually circulated among private readers, they were initially designed for public presentation and this profoundly shapes their form.

Dividing the sources into these categories allows us not only to take into account the conventions of different genres, but also to distinguish the discussion of legal excess and abuse that takes place primarily among members of the elite (in works of the first category) from that involving elite communication with the public at large (in works of the second category). The treatment of legal excess and abuse as a class issue varies considerably between these two groups.

Sykophancy, Democrats, and Oligarchs

The most critical comments concerning legal excess and abuse under the democracy are found in the works of elite writers addressing their reading peers.[27] This can be explained in two ways. First, this communication was relatively private and therefore well suited to the voicing of criticism of the democracy that was not welcome before large popular audiences. Second, the authors of these works were, to varying degrees, marginalized observers of the democracy and thus especially critical of it. If these authors were atypical members of the elite, however, they broached issues that, as we shall see, were of concern to a wide spectrum of Athens's elite. It is likely, moreover, that these elite writers helped mold the outlooks of the elite readership they reached (the extent of circulation of their works is unknown), even when their peers were not inclined to accept the political extremism they sometimes express.

Elite writers addressing their peers tend to identify legal excess and abuse closely with democracy and to assess the situation in class-hostile terms. They assert that gentlemen are victimized in and out of the courts by sykophants who are *ponēroi*, a term that for them conveys the idea both of low social standing ("poor") and of base moral character ("villainous").[28] Furthermore, they suggest that average Athenians—sometimes designated collectively as the demos[29]—who dominate the popular courts, favor sykophants out of envy of the rich and a desire to preserve their source of wages as jurors. Sykophancy thus emerges in elite writers as a tool of the masses against men of the upper class, and as an expression of class polarization and antagonism. Whereas in public discourse in Athens elite speakers invoke the category of sykophants to designate persons outside of the Athenian family, these elite writers tend to draw the dividing lines between insiders and outsiders very differently: gentlemen are oppressed insiders, and their democratic enemies—a category in some cases extended to include all of those outside the upper class—are sykophantic outsiders.

There is much that is tendentious about the representation of legal excess and abuse in these stark socioeconomic terms. For example, because litigation was more likely to involve social or at least economic equals than men at opposite ends of the socioeconomic spectrum, the dichotomy drawn between gentlemen and *ponēroi* accusers is misleading.[30] Furthermore, when elite writers rail at popular courts for favoring sykophants, they may in many cases simply be expressing resentment at the fact that socially inferior jurors have it in their power to humiliate and ruin them.[31] Consider, for example, the ire of Isocrates, who, when he lost an *antidosis* suit to another wealthy man, railed at length in his pamphlet, *Antidosis,* against the demos for supporting base sykophants.[32] With these reservations in mind, let us consider first how elite writers use the idea of sykophancy to criticize the democratic constitution in its various facets, and then explore how they treat sykophancy as an intrusion on an aristocratic life-style.

SYKOPHANCY AND THE DEMOCRATIC CONSTITUTION

Early evidence of a class-hostile view of sykophancy is found in the short treatise of the Old Oligarch (420s B.C.?). Although the Old Oligarch holds the democratic mob in disdain ([X.] *Ath.* 2.10), he emphasizes that members of the demos have acted intelligently, if cynically, in arranging civic affairs so as to preserve their power. They monopolize law making, since, if they allowed the best men to make the laws, this would lead to their own enslavement (1.9); and in the popular courts, they "are not so much concerned with justice as with their own advantage" (1.13). In support of the latter claim, the Old Oligarch asserts that

> in regard to the allies, the Athenian people sail out and engage in sykophancy against them, as they are said to do; they hate the aristocrats [*chrēstous*], since they realize that the ruler is necessarily hated by the ruled and that if the rich [*plousioi*] and aristocratic men in the cities are strong, the rule of the people at Athens will last for a very short time. This is why they disfranchise the aristocrats, take away their money, expel and kill them, whereas they promote the interests of the lower

class [ponērous]. The Athenian aristocrats protect their opposite numbers in the allied cities, since they realize that it is to their advantage always to protect the better sort in the cities. (1.14)

Under the fifth-century Athenian empire, the complaint that Athenian sykophants exploit the jurisdiction of the popular courts over suits involving subjects is commonplace.[33] The Old Oligarch, however, attributes this behavior not merely to individuals, but to the entire demos,[34] which he vividly depicts as sailing out en masse to bring sykophantic charges against non-Athenian aristocrats. Presumably in his view this figure of speech is justified, because the demos, serving as jurors, supports unscrupulous prosecutors and is thus complicit in their sykophancy.

According to the Old Oligarch, when elements of the demos support sykophancy against gentlemen from subject states, they cynically advance their financial interests as well as their political ones. For example, "from litigant's court fees [prutaneiōn] they take their dikastic wage through the year" (1.16).[35] Furthermore, they reap profit, because litigants arriving in Athens from allied states must pay a 1 percent tax on arrival in the Piraeus and rent lodgings, animals, and slaves from Athenians (1.17). The demos, however, reaps other, less concrete benefits from its judicial power over gentlemen from subject states: "each of the allies is compelled to flatter the Athenian populace," and "in the courts he is obliged to entreat whoever comes in and to grasp him by the hand. In this way the allies have become the slaves of the Athenian people" (1.18).

While the Old Oligarch focuses his attention on the legal plight of aristocrats from subject states in the late fifth century, some aristocrats in Athens in this same period felt equally strongly about democratic sykophancy. This is abundantly clear in the program of the Thirty (404/3 B.C.), as noted earlier, to purge the city of sykophancy. Xenophon, who was probably a supporter of the Thirty initially,[36] provides an account of their actions that betrays his own aristocratic bias on the subject:

First, they arrested and brought to trial for their lives those persons whom all knew to have lived off sykophancy under the democracy and to have been offensive to the gentlemen [kalois k'agathois]; and the

Council gladly condemned them, and the rest of the citizens—at least all who thought that they were not of the same sort themselves—were not displeased. (*HG* 2.3.12)

Xenophon draws on class-hostile terms reminiscent of those of the Old Oligarch, when he speaks of sykophants under the democracy as harassers of gentlemen (cf. [Arist.] *AP* 35.3).[37] Indeed, because Xenophon approves of the initial purge of democratic riffraff, he exaggerates the public's support for it: the Council's verdict against these persons is hardly evidence of a wide consensus, since the Thirty handpicked its members (*HG* 2.3.11).[38] Where Xenophon disapproves of the Thirty's purge, however, is in their extension of the label sykophant ultimately to gentlemen, like Theramenes, who shared in their rule (*HG* 2.3.38).

In the fourth-century conservative philosophical analysis and critique of constitutions, democracy is closely associated with sykophancy. Although philosophers do not normally mention Athens by name in this connection, the identification of sykophancy with Athenian democracy was so pervasive that generalizations about sykophancy and democracy must have been inspired largely by it.[39] For example, it was probably the episode of the Thirty that inspired Plato to generalize that when demagogues bring sykophantic charges against the rich, their victims naturally league together against the demos (*R*. 565b5–c4; cf. Arist. *Pol*. 1304b19–24).

Anaximenes of Lampsacus (ca. 380–320 B.C.) takes for granted the general association of sykophancy with democracy when he advises on how to prevent strife between rich and poor in a democracy: he suggests that the laws should ensure that "the multitude devote itself not to sykophancy but rather to honest work" ([Arist.] *Rh. Al*. 1424a31–32), as if this were not at all the natural inclination of the democratic mob. When Plato and Aristotle talk about the ideal construction of legal systems, it is clear that they are seeking to avoid what they perceive as abuses under democracy. Both advocate limiting the discretion of jurors through precise laws, and thus presumably their ability to accede to sykophantic claims (see Chapter 1). Plato proposes direct and harsh measures against legal abuse in the *Laws*: those found guilty of bringing suits often (*poludikein*) for money ought to be executed if they are citizens, or banished if foreigners (938a7–938c5). The interest of the Aristotelian school in penalties for sykophancy is suggested by a fragment that cites a law of Cyrene providing for the punishment and disfranchisement of persons bringing multiple suits (*poludikoi*) (Arist. fr. 611.18 Rose). So too Theophrastus in his *Laws* appears to have taken interest in measures relating to legal excess and abuse (fr. 4a,b Sz-M). One may suspect that these philosophers, who were to varying degrees critical of the Athenian democracy, took more than an academic interest in measures that might protect men of their class from legal abuse.

THE PLIGHT OF GENTLEMEN: PARADISE LOST

At the roots of elite complaints about sykophancy in Athens lie basic concerns about the situation of members of the elite under the democracy. This is vaguely conveyed by the common protest in elite authors that "life is difficult" for men of their class because of sykophancy (X. *Mem.* 2.9.1; Isoc. fr. 11 Mathieu; Arist. fr. 667 Rose; cf. Thphr. *Char.* 26.5). Most obviously, litigation and the abuse of it threatened the property and power of the elite. Less obviously, litigation presented a challenge to an ideal aristocratic way of life, grounded in autonomy and self-sufficiency, and to aristocratic values. The manner in which elite authors express this dimension of their legal concerns provides a tantalizing glimpse into aristocratic mentalité under the democracy.

There is often a wistful quality to the elite commentary on abuse of litigation under the democracy. Conservative writers in the fourth century idealize the undemocratic past as a time when social harmony was widespread and litigation less prevalent. For example, Isocrates asserts that before the democratic reforms of Ephialtes, when Athens was still under the sway of the elite Areopagus, the city was not "teeming with lawsuits," but rather "her citizens lived in harmony [*hēsuchian*] with each other and at peace with mankind" (7.51); in this ideal past, few laws were needed (7.39–42) and sykophants were not tolerated (15.313–15; Dem. 25.97).[40] Xenophon likewise views litigation as a symptom of social disintegration under the democracy: his younger Pericles laments the growth of strife and enmity in Athens, and how Athenians of all men "most often bring suit against one another, and prefer to make profit [*kerdainein*] of one another so than by mutual service" (*Mem.* 3.5.16–17).[41] The notion that the current situation in Athens represents an inversion of an ideal one is also conveyed by a quip attributed to Aristotle: "it is troublesome to spend time in Athens, for there pear grows upon pear, and fig upon fig" (fr. 667 Rose). This enigmatic assertion must mean, as the commentators who preserve it suggest, that life in Athens is unpleasant because of the superabundance of sykophants.[42] The allusion to Homer's description of the paradisal gardens of Phaeacia, where "pear grows upon pear . . . and fig upon fig" (*Od.* 7.120–21), is pointed: Athens's bumper crop of sykophants is anything but a feature of paradise for gentlemen who spend time there.[43]

Consistent with the way elite writers characterize the contemporary Athenian situation as a gross deviation from the way things should be or once were is their representation of litigation as an incursion on an ideal aristocratic life-style. They depict the democratic courts in general and the sykophant in particular as threats to the ideal that a gentleman should be self-sufficient (*autarkēs*), autonomous, and free to live his life in peace, secure from threats to his person and property.

While it is clear how litigation might threaten a wealthy man's sense of peace and security, it is less obvious how this might infringe on his self-sufficiency and autonomy. Elite writers assert that there is something fundamentally servile and demeaning in a gentleman's dependence on the verdict of a popular court. Plato's Socrates, for example, asks if it is not shameful

> when a man not only wastes the better part of his life in the courts as defendant or prosecutor, but also from vulgarity is led to pride himself on this very thing, as a man clever at wrongdoing and adept at twisting, turning, maneuvering, wriggling, and thereby evading conviction; and he does all of this for trifles and worthless things, because he does not know how much nobler and better it is to arrange his life so as to have no need of a drowsy juryman. (*R.* 405b6–c6)

The inveterate litigant described here acts in utter contradiction to aristocratic ideals not only in turning from athleticism to legal wrestling,[44] but also in sacrificing his autonomy to the will of an inattentive juror.[45] Such dependence is, according to elite writers, tantamount to slavery ([X.] *Ath.* 1.18; X. *Smp.* 4.32; Pl. *Tht.* 172c3–173b3).

Three brief narratives in Xenophon's works illustrate well aristocratic perspectives on the threat democratic sykophancy poses to a gentleman's ideal life-style and self-sufficiency (*Smp.* 4.29–33; *Oec.* 11.21–25; *Mem.* 2.9.1–8).[46] Although these three narratives pose as historical accounts involving real persons, fact and fiction coalesce in them. Each describes how an aristocratic protagonist confronts a topsy-turvy world in which democratic sykophants threaten his way of life, and attempts to set that world aright again either by transforming himself or those around him.

One of Xenophon's narratives is set at a late fifth-century symposium (*Smp.* 4.29–33; cf. 3.9). Long a key aristocratic institution in Greece, the symposium persisted in democratic Athens and provided a setting in which elite Athenians could confirm social and political bonds with one another and discuss matters of mutual concern.[47] That sykophancy should appear in this context as a subject of conversation is credible, since here, if anywhere, a rich man might expect to find sympathetic ears for his complaints.[48] In this literary setting, Xenophon's Charmides describes in ironic terms to his fellow symposiasts how his transformation from a rich man into a poor one has actually improved his situation: he is now secure from a variety of threats to himself and his property, and free from his former slavery to the city (4.29).[49] Charmides notes, for example, how as a rich man, "I was constantly fawning on sykophants, knowing that I was more likely to suffer injury than to inflict it on them" (4.30).[50] Now that he has lost his wealth, however, this and other worries have disappeared: "I am trusted by the city, and no longer do I endure threats, but rather now threaten others" (4.31). The rich, he explains, are obsequious to him now: they get up from their seats when he is present and stand out of his way on the road (4.31); and thus, he asserts, "Now I am like a despot; then I was clearly a slave" (4.32). Charmides notes, furthermore, that he no longer worries about the city or bad luck depriving him of his wealth, but rather "I am always expecting to get my hands on something" (4.32). When Callias interjects that Charmides no doubt prays therefore that he may never be rich again, Charmides replies, "On the contrary, I hazard the danger boldly, if I have any expectation of getting my hands on *something* from *somewhere*" (4.33).

Although the historical Charmides, like other Athenians, probably suffered financially during the Peloponnesian War,[51] this tale of his conversion into an avid democrat is fictional: indeed, he served under the Thirty and died fighting for them (X. *HG* 2.4.19). Xenophon's Charmides playfully hints that he has overcome his difficulties with sykophants by becoming a sykophant himself. At first glance, one might suppose that Charmides merely imagines himself transformed into the aristocrat's vision of an average member of the demos who eagerly *takes* a wage (cf. [X.] *Ath.* 1.13) and, when serving as juror, relishes his tyrannical power over wealthy litigants (cf. Ar. *V.* 620–30).[52] There are several clues, however, that Charmides envisions himself, alternatively or in addition, in the more conspicuous and active role of a sykophant: the transformed Charmides sykophantically exploits the public's trust (4.31; cf. Dem. 58.29), threatens others (4.31; cf. Ar. fr. 228; Dem. 25.49), and eagerly seeks financial gain (4.32, 33; cf. Is. 11.31).[53]

Charmides' pretended metamorphosis into an aggressive democratic sykophant might well amuse his fellow symposiasts. First, Charmides is an especially unlikely candidate for this conversion: elsewhere Xenophon's Socrates urges a reluctant and bashful Charmides to enter politics (*Mem.* 3.7).[54] Second, Charmides' solution to the wealthy man's problem with sykophants and the demos—"if you can't beat 'em, join 'em"—is darkly humorous: it suggests that there is no way for an aristocrat to escape democratic sykophancy short of abandoning his wealth and turning into a sykophant himself.[55]

In his *Oeconomicus,* Xenophon portrays a different aristocratic response to sykophancy. Xenophon's Socrates reports how Ischomachus found himself a constant target of sykophants due to his wealth and success (11.21) and therefore took to practicing oratory at home so that he might be ready to defend himself against malicious accusers.[56] He would, for example, argue mock cases against one of his household slaves, pretend to assist at the prosecution of a general, and play at defending a man who is unjustly blamed or accusing one who is unjustly honored (11.23–24). Initially, Ischomachus appears to be a paragon of aristocratic self-sufficiency in his practice of oratory at home and a model for wealthy Athenians who are harassed by sykophantic prosecutors. There is something humorous, however, about a mock home court, and in fact comic writers exploited this very scenario (Ar. *V.* 764–1008; Men. *Epiklēros* Test. K-T).[57] Xenophon is not oblivious to these comic overtones, to judge by the way his Ischomachus elaborates on the scene:

> "I have often been singled out before now, Socrates, and judged[58] in cases involving punishment or fines."
> "By whom, Ischomachus?" I [Socrates] asked; "I am in the dark about that."
> "By my wife," Ischomachus replied.
> "And how do you fare in the contest of litigation?" said I.
> "When it is in my interest to speak the truth, pretty well. But when lying is called for, Socrates, by Zeus, I cannot make the weaker argument appear the stronger."
> I retorted, "Perhaps, Ischomachus, you cannot make what is false into the truth." (11.25)

The fact that Ischomachus's own wife sometimes rules against him is amusing and adds welcome color to Xenophon's portrayal of the relations between the two. But Ischomachus's failure to persuade even his own wife in cases "when lying is called for" makes one wonder how he would fare if dragged before a popular court by a sykophantic prosecutor who has no scruples about telling lies. Although Ischomachus's inability to tell lies earns him Socrates' commendation, this would surely impede him in actual litigation. What begins as a tale of aristocratic resourcefulness against sykophancy thus turns out to be, like the Charmides' tale, a comment on the gap that separates a gentleman from a sykophant.

Xenophon's most intriguing portrayal of elite ingenuity in the face of sykophancy is found in his *Memorabilia* (2.9.1–8):

> I remember that Socrates once heard Crito say that life in Athens was difficult for a man who wanted to mind his own business [*ta heautou prattein*].

Litigation and Class Conflict

"For now," Crito explained, "certain persons are bringing suit against me, not because I have done them any wrong, but because they think that I would sooner pay money than have legal trouble [*pragmata*]."

"Tell me, Crito," Socrates said, "do you keep dogs to fend the wolves from your sheep?"

"Certainly," replied Crito, "because it pays me better to keep them than not to."

"Then would you not also keep a man who may be willing and able to fend off from you those attempting to injure you?"

"I would gladly do so," Crito replied, "were I not afraid that he might turn on me."

Despite Crito's misgivings, Xenophon recounts, they discovered a certain Archedemus, a poor but decent man who happened to be "quite adept at speaking and acting" and who often "said it was a cinch to put the pinch on sykophants."[59] Crito shared the products of his fields with Archedemus, invited him to sacrifices, and was generally solicitous toward him. In gratitude Archedemus ferreted out the crime of a sykophant who was threatening Crito and brought a public suit against him; only when this sykophant dropped his charges against Crito and gave him money, would Archedemus let him off.

> Now when Archedemus had carried out this and other similar enterprises, many of Crito's friends begged him to make Archedemus their protector, just as when a shepherd has a good dog, the other shepherds want to place their flocks near his, in order to enjoy the use of his dog. Archedemus was glad to oblige [*echarizeto*] Crito, and so not only Crito but his friends as well lived in peace [*hēsuchiai*].

Whenever Archedemus's enemies accused him of being a lackey (*kolax*), he replied that there was nothing shameful in making friends of gentlemen (*chrēstoi*) by accepting and returning their favors, and thereby to fall out with base men (*ponēroi*). "From this time on," Xenophon concludes his happy tale, "Archedemus was one of Crito's friends and was held in esteem by Crito's other friends."

Xenophon's Archedemus is plausibly identified with the democratic politician of the same name who was active in the late fifth and early fourth centuries, most notably in indicting the general Erasinides after the battle of Arginusae (X. *HG* 1.7.2).[60] Contemporary sources apply to him the same slanders used against other popular politicians.[61] Although this popular democrat seems an unlikely member of Crito's aristocratic circle, Lysias (14.25) also links Archedemus to the Socratic circle (as the supposed lover of the younger Alcibiades) and it is thus possible that Archedemus performed legal favors of some kind for Crito. But if the tale has some basis in reality, Xenophon has surely taken liberties in casting Crito and Archedemus in the roles of patron and dependent client, respectively. While some poor Athenians must have found themselves dependent on their wealthy neighbors,[62] Archedemus, whom Xenophon labels elsewhere "the leader of the demos" (*HG* 1.7.2), is an unlikely candidate for this utter subservience. Why then has Xenophon cast Archedemus in this role?

First, this advances a fanciful aristocratic view of social relations. The idea of lower-class dependence upon upper-class largesse would appeal to men of Xenophon's ilk, especially in this extreme case in which a powerful democrat humbly and appreciatively receives handouts from the rich. Furthermore, it would tickle an aristocrat's fancy to imagine a democratic politician embracing the role of "watchdog" of gentlemen, since democratic politicians commonly boasted that they were watchdogs of the demos (see Chapter 4). This transformation is doubly amusing since Archedemus's name can be taken to mean "ruler of the demos," and in the course of the story, he indeed becomes the rich man's tool against unruly elements within the demos. Like Charmides' ironic tale, therefore, this anecdote plays with the ideas of inversion and social transformation. Whereas Charmides claims to have solved his difficulties with malicious prosecutors by joining the demos and becoming a sykophant, the *apragmōn* Crito solves his problems by transforming a member of the demos—and an avid and powerful democrat at that—into a friend of the wealthy and superweapon against sykophants.[63] The seduction of Archedemus is so complete, in fact, that he not only learns to serve his social betters, but also comes to embrace aristocratic social doctrine in rejecting the company of the "base" in favor of that of "gentlemen."

The aristocratic slant of this fantasy is also evident in its emphasis on the ideal of friendship. It is critical to Xenophon that Crito not pay money directly to Archedemus for his services. To pay a wage (*misthos*) to a legal agent would not only be to risk the appearance of hiring a sykophant,[64] but also to enter into the value system of a debased world where money, rather than gratitude (*charis*), governs social relations.[65] Xenophon therefore represents Archedemus's wage simply as the friendship of good men. What Xenophon's Crito has done therefore is to overcome a new world problem, sykophancy under the democracy, with an old world solution, the strong bonds of aristocratic *philia*.

On the surface the Archedemus tale is more optimistic than the Charmides and Ischomachus tales concerning the ability of an aristocrat to overcome his sykophantic antagonists. It suggests that a self-sufficient aristocrat, like Crito, can find his way out of difficulties with sykophants by exercising his ingenuity and taking advantage of his superior status and wealth.[66] But Crito's success takes place in a fictional world where aristocratic power has not been eroded by democratic values and institutions, and where the promise of aristocratic *philia* is enough to turn a watchdog of the demos into a protector of the rich. Viewed in this way, the Archedemus tale becomes an aristocratic daydream of power and control that evokes a world that once was, but offers no real hope to the aristocrat disenchanted with litigation under the democracy.

Some elements of elite writers' treatment of legal excess and abuse would probably appeal only to harsh critics of the Athenian democracy among the reading elite. For example, probably few elite Athenians would have embraced the extreme position, suggested by Xenophon's tales discussed here, that an aristocrat should be left completely alone by the city and its legal apparatus. Other elements of elite writers' commentary on sykophancy, however, were of potentially wider appeal, in particular, the ideal that a man should be allowed to live free of legal harassment. Wealthy Athenians did not have to be oligarchs to find this attractive. Indeed, when elite Athenians, representing in all likelihood a variety of political orientations, addressed popular audiences, they appealed to this very ideal. In so doing, moreover, they took for granted that the average

Athenians in their audiences might be ready to accept this ideal as one that all peace-loving men, regardless of class, could embrace.

Sykophancy in Public Discourse: Mediating Class Differences

When elite Athenians address popular audiences through public orations and comic dramas, they raise many of the same concerns about legal excess and abuse expressed by elite writers. They tend, however, to adapt their criticisms of litigation and the courts under the democracy to the sensitivities of popular audiences so as to avoid alienating them. Their generally conciliatory, but at times pointed, treatment of sykophancy provides an opportunity to examine how elite Athenians communicated with mass audiences over a tense class issue.

SYKOPHANCY IN THE ATTIC ORATORS

Elite speakers were in a vulnerable position when they addressed the topic of sykophancy in public settings, most commonly in the popular courts. Jurors could easily construe their criticisms of sykophancy as an attack on the administration of the courts by the demos and respond with a hostile verdict. Elite litigants therefore tend to approach the subject tactfully. While they complain that in general jurors are too soft on sykophancy, they express hope that the jury before them will recognize sykophancy as a threat to Athenians of all classes, and therefore take action against it.[67] Their conciliatory approach to this potentially divisive class issue is evident in their treatment of (1) the attitude of the demos toward sykophancy; (2) the identity of sykophants; and (3) the identity of the victims of sykophants.

The Demos and Sykophancy

For a litigant to accuse the Athenian people of sykophancy, as the Old Oligarch does ([X.] *Ath.* 1.14), was unacceptable. One of Lysias's clients, in the course of presenting an impeachment before the Assembly, slanders his opponent, the general Ergocles, by attributing this extreme criticism to him: when the people in Assembly decreed that Ergocles and his fellow commanders should return home to undergo their scrutiny (*euthunai*), "Ergocles said that there you were at your sykophancy and hankering after the ancient laws" (28.5). Only an enemy of the demos would characterize the democratic *euthunai* in this way, the speaker suggests, and he proceeds in fact to charge that Ergocles and his cronies had oligarchic aspirations (28.6–7).

While elite litigants stop short of accusing the demos of sykophancy, they enjoy considerable latitude in advancing the critical position that the people tolerate sykophancy.[68] Some litigants approach the matter very delicately. For example, one litigant attributes to the demos a hatred of sykophants (Ant. 5.78), but nonetheless expresses concern that the jury may favor his sykophantic opponents (5.80). One of Lysias's clients goes somewhat further than this, when he implies that the demos could be viewed as responsible for the actions of sykophants: he praises his uncle, Diognetus, because, although the slander of sykophants forced him into exile in the late years of the Peloponnesian War, he did not harm the masses (*plēthos*) during that time or when he returned to the city (18.9). The implication is that, while Diognetus might well have been angry at the demos for allowing sykophants to attack him, he magnanimously held no grudge against them.

Often, however, elite litigants are more confrontational and rebuke the demos openly for accommodating sykophants. Epichares, for example, asserts, "You alone, I think, are able to endure the villainy of these [sykophants], while no one else of the Hellenes does this" (Dem. 58.38), and places blame squarely on the demos for tolerating sykophancy, since "you have all these [sykophants] under your control" (58.55). As he approaches his peroration, Epichares' criticism reaches a climax: "You have never punished any [sykophant] in the way his villainy deserves, but you put up with their saying that the safety of the demos comes from those who bring indictments and play the sykophant; but there is no class more pernicious than such men" (58.63). Epichares prudently tempers his harsh words, however, with a generous explanation as to why the demos act in this way. Like so many speakers chastising the Athenian people, Epichares attributes their error to traits that would be admirable in other circumstances, easygoing indulgence (*rhaithumia*: 58.63) and gentleness (*praotēs*: 58.55). Thus, while his criticism is pointed, it is ostensibly friendly and designed to rouse jurors to action in their own interest.

Likewise, Demosthenes expresses concern that jurors may, because of their "easy good nature" (*euētheia*), be overly sympathetic toward his sykophantic opponent, Aristogeiton, and therefore take personal offense at the prosecution: "I am afraid that . . . we who think we are prosecuting Aristogeiton may be found to be accusing you" (25.12). In the same speech, however, Demosthenes hints that jurors might favor Aristogeiton for less admirable reasons, from some motive "which none would care to confess, but which your votes will betray" (25.7).

Other litigants are less oblique than Demosthenes and express concern that jurors will sympathize with sykophantic prosecutors, since the false convictions they win bolster state finances (Lys. 19.11; 30.22) and ensure that jurors receive their wages.[69] While litigants treat this supposed collusion more delicately than conservative critics of the democracy do, they take a cynical view of the role of financial self-interest in jurors' determinations of verdicts. For example, when one of Lysias's clients opens his prosecution of Epicrates and his associates on a charge involving bribery, he condemns them for the way they win unjust verdicts in the courts by asserting that "unless you make the convictions they demand, your receipt of wages [*misthophora*] will come to a halt" (27.1). The speaker himself, however, takes for granted that jurors will consider what is profitable to them, when he points out that in the present case jurors get no profit, only shame: his sykophantic opponents do not share with the public the bribes they receive from persons guilty of crimes against the state (27.1–2; cf. Ar. *V.* 673–79).

Hyperides, acting as *sunēgoros* for the defendant Euxenippus, deals masterfully with this sensitive subject. He protests that the prosecutor has emphasized to the jury that Euxenippus, a contractor for state mines, is rich:

> It has surely nothing to do with this case whether he is a man of large means or small, and to raise the matter is malicious and implies an unfair assumption regarding the jury, namely that they would base their

verdict on some consideration other than the matter at issue and the question whether the man on trial does you wrong or not. (4.32)

The speaker insists that no matter how much money sykophants promise to bring into the treasury, the Athenian people stand above any temptation to rule unfairly against wealthy defendants (4.32–36).[70] Significantly, however, he does not rely too heavily on jurors' sense of fairness: he estimates that the demos profit far more in the long-term from the regular source of revenue that contractors for mines, like Euxenippus, provide to the city than from the short-term and dishonest profits that result from favoring sykophantic suits against them (4.36–37). Thus, he maintains, it is possible for jurors to act in accordance with justice *and* without doing any harm to their own self-interest.

The idea that jurors have more to gain from protecting the fortunes of the wealthy than from supporting their sykophantic harassers is commonplace in forensic oratory. For example, the banker Phormio's advocate insists that not only would it be shameful for the Athenian people to allow sykophants to take away the property of decent men like Phormio, but also that this wealth "is far more useful to you while it remains in his possession," since he uses it to help persons in need (Dem. 36.58). Wealthy litigants emphasize in particular that they use their wealth to benefit their fellow citizens by performing liturgies: it is not only just that the people return this favor (*charis*) by supporting them against sykophants in the courts, but also advantageous, since the people have a vested interest in protecting the fortunes of their benefactors.[71] There is, moreover, an implicit threat in such arguments that, if the city does not honor its debt of *charis* to the wealthy and instead abandons them to sykophants, wealthy men may cut back on the extravagance of the liturgies they perform, or shirk these altogether.[72]

The city's elite have other options too, if they receive no relief from sykophancy: Andocides asserts that men in his situation may "choose between buying off sykophants or fleeing and quitting Athens as fast as they can" (1.105; cf. Ant. 5.80). Although a mass exodus of the wealthy was not a real threat, the suggestion that the rich might pay off their accusers and thus circumvent the democratic courts was presumably quite credible. While these various reminders of the power of men of property within the city have a coercive aspect to them, elite litigants prudently stop short of threatening personal and direct retaliation against the city if their complaints against sykophancy are not taken seriously: they offer these reminders lest the demos wrongly calculates that supporting sykophantic prosecutions of the rich is ultimately beneficial to the city.

The Identity of Sykophants

Consistent with the efforts by elite litigants to mediate rather than amplify class differences over sykophancy is the way such litigants portray sykophants and their victims. Whereas class-hostile representations of litigation suggest that poor citizens sykophantically prosecute the wealthy, elite litigants avoid casting the problem in these explicit class terms. An elite litigant who depicted his unscrupulous opponent, whatever his actual social status, as a typical "poor man," risked alienating a jury composed of "poor men." To be sure, elite litigants sometimes attack their peers on the grounds that they have raised themselves from poverty to wealth through their sykophancy (Lys. 25.26, 30; Dem. 58.63; cf. Ar. Pl. 567–70, with 30–31).[73] The main thrust of this slur is not against average "poor men," however, but against impoverished men who are so unscrupulous as to gain wealth by sykophancy. Similarly, when elite litigants characterize their sykophantic opponents as *ponēroi*,[74] they—unlike conservative writers—appear to be employing the label primarily as a term of moral, rather than of social, denigration: they do not suggest that sykophants as *ponēroi* behave in a way typical of average Athenians.

Although it was clearly not advisable for a litigant to identify sykophancy too closely with "poor men," some litigants flirt with this identification. For example, a client of Isocrates asserts, "I think you all know that sykophancy is especially attempted by those who are clever speakers but possess nothing, against men who are weak at speaking but wealthy enough to pay money" (21.5). He is careful, however, to suggest that, if sykophancy involves the victimization of rich men by poor ones, it entails simultaneously the harassment of weak speakers by clever ones: most "poor men" in the jury would not identify themselves with these supposedly impoverished slick rhetoricians.[75] Likewise, Aeschines is careful not to go too far in casting Demosthenes as a lower-class sykophant: while he asserts that Demosthenes has forsaken the traditional aristocratic pursuits of hunting and exercise in the gymnasium for the hunting of the rich through sykophantic litigation (3.255–56), Aeschines does not suggest that Demosthenes' behavior, though antiaristocratic, is typical of "poor men."

Most elite litigants, in fact, go out of their way to distinguish between sykophants and "poor men" by placing sykophants in a moral category that sets them apart from decent men of all social classes. This is conspicuous, for example, when litigants represent sykophancy as a perverse career distinct from the respectable work of average men (see Chapter 2). In general, elite litigants are comfortable denigrating each other as lowly laborers before popular audiences: the public appears to have shared to some degree their view that certain careers were humiliating and degrading.[76] The topic must have been a sensitive one, however, since most Athenians worked in one way or another to make a living, and those engaged in most forms of "honest work" were probably not ashamed of their situations. When elite litigants represent sykophancy as a devious career, therefore, they are careful to make it clear that this work stands in utter contrast to the various honest livings that most average Athenians pursue. For example, Demosthenes distinguishes the sykophantic Aristogeiton from legitimate merchants—he is "a seller, a retailer, a trafficker *in villainy*" (25.46)[77]—and from other real workers as well: Aristogeiton is not engaged "in a craft, in farming, or in any other business" (25.51); instead "he likes to see everyone involved in trials, lawsuits and vile charges. That is the crop he sows, that is the trade he plies" (25.82).

Elite litigants further differentiate between sykophants and working Athenians by characterizing sykophantic labor as particularly degrading, since sykophants will do *anything* for a wage (*misthos*) (Dem. 59.43; Aesch. 1.20).[78] As one litigant puts it, sykophants "count as friends those who offer them money, and the quiet [*apragmonas*] and wealthy people[79] as their foes" (Dem.

58.65). The idea that sykophants "sell everything" (Dem. 58.34) leads readily to their association with prostitution and pimping. Aeschines, for example, accuses Timarchus of squandering his patrimony and then turning to prostitution and sykophancy to support himself (1.105).[80] Elsewhere, he claims that Demosthenes started life as a kept boy (kinaidos) and then matured into a sykophant (2.99; cf. 3.255–56; Apollod. Car. or Gel. fr. 13).[81] Andocides deploys this conception of the sykophant deftly to distract attention from the charge that he was involved in subversive activities as a member of an aristocratic political club. He labels one of his opponents a "sykophant and execrable fox [kinados]" (1.99), and asks him:

> Do you actually see fit to make mention of my *party* activity [hetaireias] and to speak ill of other men? You, however, did not have the decency to be the *party* boy [hētairēsas] of just a single man, but took a trifling sum of money from any willing man, as the court knows, and supported yourself by shameful acts even though you are ugly in appearance. (1.100)

Andocides puns on the root *hetair-* to contrast his own supposedly innocuous involvement in a political club (hetaireia) with his sykophantic opponent's outrageous prostitution (hetaireō).[82] If the sykophant could be cast as a prostitute, it was only natural to cast him as a venal pimp as well. Thus Apollodorus attributes two sources of income to Stephanus, pimping for Neaira and acting as sykophant (Dem. 59.39; cf. 59.68), and alleges that Stephanus pursued both enterprises at once when he sykophantically blackmailed the clients of Neaera (59.41) and her daughter (59.65).

The Victims of Sykophants

Elite litigants suggest not only that the sykophant is distinct from decent poor men, but also that he threatens poor and rich alike. Some litigants, in fact, submerge class differences altogether and pretend that all Athenians face the same risk of sykophantic harassment. For example, a wealthy defendant asserts before the Areopagus[83] that the threat of sykophancy is so universal that "even those who are yet unborn ought now to fear what is in store for them" (Lys. 7.1). Similarly, Andocides suppresses class differences, when he suggests that the verdict in his case will decide for the public—and thus not simply for men of his class—how to respond to sykophants (1.105).

Other elite litigants represent themselves as average men—no different from jurors—who are harassed by sykophants, and thus pretend that sykophants pose a serious threat to average Athenians as well as members of the leisure class. Euxitheus, for example, contrasts his own attempt to make an honest living (Dem. 57.32; cf. 57.36) with his opponent's career as a sykophant harassing working men like himself (57.32–34).[84] Just how far a litigant could manipulate this claim is evident when the wealthy banker Phormio's advocate protests that jurors should not allow sykophants to take "the property of those who work for a living" (Dem. 36.58): to characterize Phormio as "a working man" is to obscure the economic gap between himself and average Athenians and, at the same time, to exaggerate the vulnerability of real working men to legal harassment.[85]

Few litigants, however, document specific instances where their sykophantic opponents victimized average Athenians—other than themselves cast in this guise. For example, while Epichares asserts that Theocrines acts as sykophant against "many citizens" (Dem. 58.2), his alleged victims, with the possible exception of the shipowner Micon (58.5–13), appear to be persons prominent in public life (58.23, 35–36). Furthermore, although Demosthenes claims that Aristogeiton prosecuted the miserable (*talaiporos*) Phokides, as well as an unnamed coppersmith and a tanner (25.38), the supposed victims may well be persons active in public life, like Aristogeiton's other legal opponents, and not mere tradesmen.[86] By contrast, Demosthenes is more specific when he asserts that Meidias falsely prosecuted an average Athenian, Strato, and thereby brought about his disfranchisement. He describes this victim of the sykophantic Meidias as "a poor man [*penēs*], who was inexperienced in legal affairs [*apragmōn*], but otherwise not of poor character [*ponēros*], but rather a very good [*chrēstos*] citizen" (21.83).[87] Demosthenes makes the most of this alleged sykophancy against an average citizen: he asserts that because "the poorest and weakest of you run the greatest risk of being wantonly wronged," jurors should protect the interests of average Athenians by making an example of the sykophantic Meidias in the current case (21.123–24; cf. 21.141).

Notwithstanding Demosthenes' use of the Strato episode as an illustration of the threat sykophancy poses to the average Athenian, it was probably difficult to convince jurors that sykophants threatened them personally. Elite litigants therefore more commonly sound the alarm that sykophants harm Athenians collectively because they interfere with basic democratic institutions. For example, sykophants intimidate speakers in the Assembly with their threats and thus interfere with free and democratic debate (Dem. 18.138; Aesch. 3.226). Furthermore, sykophants interfere with the scrutiny (*euthunai*) of magistrates (Aesch. 1.107), harass the city's generals (Dem. 25.49–50), and twist the city's laws (Dem. 58.65). Moreover, when sykophants drop suits in exchange for payoffs, they subvert the legal authority of the popular courts and make themselves more powerful than jurors (Ant. 5.80; cf. And. 1.105; Dem. 25.50; Aesch. 2.145). Elite litigants suggest by such arguments that, even if men of their class are the immediate victims of legal harassment, all Athenians ultimately suffer as a result of it.

Pressing the Limits of Free Speech

Although most elite Athenians are careful in railing at sykophancy not to alienate their popular audiences, some take markedly antagonistic stances. These exceptional cases clarify by contrast the norms of interclass communications concerning sykophancy.

Lysias 25. The litigant whose speech is preserved as Lysias 25: *Defense against a Charge of Subverting the Democracy* (ca. 400 B.C.), finds himself in an awkward position when challenged at the review (*dokimasia*) required before he may enter office: he must explain before a popular jury why he remained in the city under the oligarchic Thirty (404/3 B.C.), when ardent democrats fled to join the opposition in the Piraeus.[88] He does little to dispel suspicions that he was a collaborator when he asserts, "I behaved just as the best of those in the Piraeus would have done, if he had remained in the city" (25.2), or when he explains that he sought merely to preserve his property (25.18). While the speaker's claims that he did not hold any office or sit on the Council under the Thirty (25.14) may be true, his complaints of democratic sykophancy reveal him as a sympathizer.

Consider, for example, how the speaker defends the Thirty's purge of democratic leaders:

> You are all aware that, under the previous democracy, many in charge stole public funds, while others accepted bribes at your expense, or by their sykophancy made your allies revolt. Now if the Thirty had kept their punishments for these persons alone, you yourselves would have considered them to be good men. But when in fact they thought it right to harm the majority [plēthos] because of the offenses of those persons, you were indignant, since you thought it awful that the crimes of the few should be spread over the whole city. (25.19)

The assertion that the Athenian people approved of the Thirty's purge of sykophantic demagogues, which also appears in Xenophon's slanted account of the episode (*HG* 2.3.12), should not be taken seriously: the demos surely took no pleasure in the condemnation of the leaders whose prosecutions they had supported (cf. Lys. 25.26).

The speaker reveals his political biases further when he asserts:

> At the end of it all, you would have been more pleased to punish those who engaged in sykophancy under the democracy than those who held office under the oligarchy. And with good reason, jurors: for it is manifest now to all that democracy comes into being due to the unjust acts of rulers in an oligarchy, whereas oligarchy has been established twice due to sykophants under the democracy. (25.27)

The suggestion that the demos would sooner punish their own sykophantic leaders than the participants in the oligarchies of 411 and 404/3 B.C. is absurd: it depends on the specious notion that at least some good comes out of an oligarchy—namely, the impetus to establish democracy—whereas democratic sykophants are responsible for something unqualifiably bad, the establishment of oligarchy.

The speaker's advice for the future is as striking in its antidemocratic implications as his reconstruction of the past is. He hints that men of his ilk may once more favor the establishment of an oligarchy, if jurors side with sykophants in cases like his own: "You should reflect that no human being is naturally either an oligarch or a democrat, but rather each man is eager to see established whatever constitution he finds advantageous to himself. It largely depends on you, therefore, whether a great many men shall desire the current state of affairs" (25.8). This analysis of human nature not only betrays a collaborator's outlook—personal advantage rather than political principle determines loyalty to a polity (cf. Isoc. 8.133)—but also constitutes a veiled threat that sykophancy under the democracy may prompt the speaker and others to join the enemies of the demos. The speaker makes this threat more explicitly, when he warns that the city's oligarchic enemies, now in exile, would rejoice to have their ranks increased by those "wronged by you" (25.24; cf. 25.6). Although other litigants hint that members of the city's elite, if victimized by sykophancy, can harm the majority, this direct threat is remarkable.

While some scholars have doubted that this speech was actually presented to the public because of its critical stance toward the democracy, there is reason to believe it was given publicly.[89] After all, the speaker does make some accommodations to popular sensibilities. He does not accuse the entire demos of sykophancy, as some conservative writers do, and he distinguishes the sykophants—his generic label for democratic politicians (25.24–25, 27, 29–30)[90]—against whom he rails from those in highest repute among the Piraeus faction (25.28). Whether these concessions to a popular jury's feelings were sufficient to win them over is open to speculation, however, since the result of the trial is unknown.

Isocrates. Although Isocrates did not ordinarily address the Athenian people face-to-face as orator, the pamphlets he circulated to advertise his rhetorical school and promulgate his political ideas take the form of orations that reproduce many of the features of Athenian public oratory.[91] This form was the natural choice for the presentation of political ideas, which were normally expressed in Athens through oratory, and allowed Isocrates to show prospective students the versatility of his rhetorical skills. Isocrates' oratorical pamphlets, however, diverge dramatically from democratic oratory in serving as vehicles for the advancement of a distinctly conservative, aristocratic point of view. As Ober observes, Isocrates "transubstantiate[s] democratic political slogans into an essentially aristocratic system of political values."[92]

Isocrates' treatment of sykophancy is emblematic of the tension between democratic form and aristocratic substance in his works. Isocrates vacillates between treating the subject of sykophancy with a caution consistent with that taken by orators directly addressing the demos, and offering a scathing critique of democratic sykophancy more in keeping with the acerbic comments of elite writers addressing their peers. Consider, for example, Isocrates' abrasive remarks on sykophancy in *On the Peace* (355 B.C.):

> I marvel if you [the Athenian people] cannot see at once that no class is more hostile to the people than base [*ponērōn*] orators and demagogues. For they very much want you, in addition to your other misfortunes, to lack your daily necessities, since they observe that those who are able to manage their affairs from their private means are on the side of the city and of our best counsellors, whereas those who live off income derived from the courts and assemblies are compelled by their need to be subservient to base orators and demagogues, and have deep gratitude [*charin*] for impeachments, indictments, and other acts of sykophancy they carry out. (8.129–30)

Although Isocrates follows the diplomatic practice of actual public speakers in not accusing the demos of sykophancy directly, he goes well beyond public speakers in laying bare the supposed financial dependency of poor jurors on sykophants, and in asserting that wealthier men therefore make better citizens than poor ones.

Likewise in his *Antidosis* (354/3 B.C.), Isocrates pays heed to some of the unwritten rules of interclass communication concerning sykophancy but violates others. Isocrates composed this work in response to criticisms leveled against him and his school in an *antidosis* suit he had recently lost (15.4–5). The *Antidosis* takes the form of a forensic speech in which Isocrates defends himself from a sykophant, Lysimachus, who has brought him before a popular court on a capital charge for corrupting Athens's youth.[93] This peculiar literary device allows Isocrates simultaneously to defend his school (he poses as a second Socrates) and to rail at the free rein given sykophants under the democracy. Although educational and political polemic are thus intertwined in the work, it is the latter that is relevant here.

At a number of points in the *Antidosis,* Isocrates respects the fictional court setting by adapting his view of sykophancy to a popular audience. For example, he rebukes his imagined jury on the grounds that "with you the accused have not even an equal chance with sykophants" (15.21), but stops short of a class-hostile reading of the situation:

> What is most awful is the fact that, when a man is himself on trial, he denounces slanderers, but when he sits in judgment upon another, he is no longer of the same mind regarding them. Yet surely intelligent men ought to judge others in the way they would wish others to judge them, reckoning that because of the audacity of sykophants it is impossible to foresee what man may be placed in peril and be compelled to plead, just as I am now doing, before men who are to decide his fate by their votes. (15.23)

Like elite litigants, Isocrates glosses over the social differences between litigants and jurors, and suggests that because all face an equal risk from sykophancy, all should unite against it (cf. Lys. 7.1). Isocrates also follows the normal practice of elite litigants when he distinguishes between sykophants and the demos: "Even if some of the citizens happen to be sykophants and evildoers like my prosecutor, it is not right to think all the rest are also of this type" (15.224; cf. 15.299–301).[94]

Elsewhere in the *Antidosis,* however, Isocrates is less charitable in assessing sykophancy under the democracy. He complains bitterly, for example, that "the city now takes such pleasure in putting the squeeze [*piezousa*] on moderate men [*epieikeis*] and making them low, while giving license to the base [*ponērois*] to say and do whatever they wish," that a sykophant like Lysimachus prospers (15.164). The assertion that the city, which is dominated by the majority, delights in the discomfiture of "moderate men"—that is, men of Isocrates' class—and favors the base is an unmistakably class-hostile analysis of the situation (cf. Dem. 12.19). In this case, the whole city is to blame, not simply aberrant demagogues, and the people support sykophancy not out of economic necessity (cf. Isoc. 8.129–30) but out of sadistic pleasure in "putting the squeeze" on the rich.[95] Evidence of Isocrates' class-hostile view of sykophancy also surfaces several times in the closing sections of the *Antidosis*. Isocrates fantasizes about a past in which men of his class dominated the city (15.308) and sykophants were punished as they should be, rather than employed as prosecutors and lawmakers as in contemporary Athens (15.313–15). Furthermore, Isocrates, like other conservative critics of the democracy, asserts that democratic sykophants, by their false charges, force gentlemen to turn against the city and become oligarchs (15.318).[96]

Presumably Isocrates was free to criticize democratic sykophancy in the relatively harsh way he does in his oratorical pamphlets because he was not addressing the public face-to-face as orators did. But apparently he hoped that his pamphlets would somehow reach a wider audience than the reading elite, and therefore, unlike other elite writers, he follows the conventions of democratic discourse to some extent. One may doubt, however, whether Isocrates' aristocratic views found a sympathetic audience outside of the narrow reading elite.[97] Even if on the whole his view of sykophancy is less manifestly class-hostile than, for example, that of Xenophon, it diverges enough from the norms of public discourse that average citizens would likely take offense at it.

The exceptional approaches to legal excess and abuse in Lysias 25 and Isocrates throw into relief those that members of the elite normally adopt when addressing the public. In general, while public speakers are critical of the Athenian people's toleration of sykophantic excess, they seek common ground with their audiences by representing sykophancy as a problem that transcends narrow class interests. In arguing that sykophancy is fundamentally antidemocratic and un-Athenian, they acknowledge that, if their complaints are to be taken seriously, they must prove that sykophancy is inconsistent with democratic rule and with the values of the majority of Athenians. Ober views this kind of accommodation by public speakers to democratic ideology as evidence of the power of the demos over the elite minority: "The demos ruled, not so much because of its constitutional 'sovereignty,' as because of its control over significant aspects of the symbolic universe of the Athenian political community."[98] There is much to be said for this point of view: elite speakers discuss sykophancy within the bounds and in the appropriate terms of democratic discourse and thereby acknowledge their audiences' power and authority over them. At the same time, it is significant that this power dynamic did not lead to the complete suppression of elite perspectives: while elite concerns about sykophancy were broached in conciliatory terms, they were nonetheless clearly and unmistakably expressed. It was, moreover, in the interest of the demos to take these concerns seriously, since, as elite litigants reminded their audiences, the city was dependent on the goodwill of its wealthy citizens for performance of liturgies and payment of the war tax. In this case, the public power of the demos over forensic verdicts and popular discourse was at least partially matched by the private power of the elite to use its wealth and resources for the good or detriment of the city.

SYKOPHANCY ON THE COMIC STAGE

Writers of Old Comedy (late fifth to early fourth century B.C.) in Athens regularly address political concerns and issues within their works. Several difficulties arise in assessing their treatment of political material. First, only Aristophanes' comedies have survived intact and the discussion therefore necessarily centers on him. Second, it is no easy matter to assess the political perspective of the surviving material. Quips made by individual characters do not necessarily reflect the poet's own political views, and even statements of a political nature presented by choruses as if authorial views cannot be taken entirely at face value.[99] Despite these difficulties, scholars have argued persuasively that comic writers embrace elite perspectives, but tailor their views to appeal to mass audiences.[100] Because Aristophanes and other comic writers were either members of the city's wealthy elite or at least closely connected with it,[101] they were well versed in, and probably sympathetic with, elite concerns about the demos's administration of the city. When comic poets addressed popular audiences, however, they were under considerable pressure to adapt their views so as to make them palatable to the city's majority: they competed with one another at the city's festivals and sought to win votes cast by judges chosen from, and presumably influenced by, the populace.[102] Attic comedy thus involved a social dynamic similar to that of public oratory: in each case elite Athenians competed to win the approval of popular audiences. Although comic writers enjoyed greater license to criticize the demos than elite orators did,[103] they too had a vested interest in adapting their criticism to a popular audience's sensibilities. Henderson thus observes that, although comic poets "typically championed minority positions, they did so from a stance of ideological solidarity with the official culture, with those who had sole power to act on such positions: the sovereign *dēmos*."[104]

Aristophanes' relatively moderate treatment of sykophancy is consistent with the general hypothesis that he is under pressure to adapt his elite perspectives before a popular audience. On the one hand, Aristophanes is highly attuned to elite complaints about sykophancy, presents them prominently, and often employs vocabulary and imagery that elite critics of the democracy do.[105] For example, Aristophanes quips that Athenians are always judging lawsuits (*Pax* 505; cf. *Eq.* 1317; *Nu.* 206–8); the Old Oligarch makes the same point ([X.] *Ath.* 3.2). Aristophanes' protagonists in *Birds* flee Athens because nonstop litigation makes it unlivable (*Av.* 33–41, 109–11); this is precisely the complaint of conservative critics of the democracy. Aristophanes and other comic poets jibe that Athens is full of sykophants (*Ach.* 829, 903–5; cf. Antiph. fr. 177); those hostile to the democracy heartily embrace this view (Theopomp. Hist. *FGrH* 115 F 281). Nonetheless, on balance Aristophanes does not advance a class-hostile reading of the situation. Although he enjoys more license than elite litigants to criticize democratic sykophancy and exercises that license freely, like elite litigants he discourages his audience from interpreting sykophancy along strict class lines. The basic resemblance of Aristophanes' approach to that of elite litigants is evident from his similar treatment of the dynamics of sykophancy: (1) the demos and sykophancy;

(2) the identity of sykophants; and (3) the identity of the victims of sykophants.

The Demos and Sykophancy

Aristophanes is clearly aware of class tensions surrounding the courts and litigation. He regularly plays on the elite complaint that lower-class jurors and sykophants have a symbiotic relationship. He characterizes jurors as poor men—some might even say "trash" (V. 673–74)—who depend on their three-obol wage for subsistence and therefore support a sykophant like Cleon, since he ensures that the courts are kept busy (Eq. 1359–61). In *Knights*, therefore, Cleon addresses jurors as "Brethren of the Order of the Three Obols, whom I feed by my loud denunciations, true or false" (255–56; cf. 973–85; V. 197).[106] The collusion between jurors and sykophants is encapsulated in an Aristophanic supercompound adjective that describes jurors' habits: they "wake up early, go to court, and toil to judge some sykophantic suits" (V. 505). Furthermore, Aristophanes' jurors are jealous of, and hostile to, rich litigants. The jury-addict Philocleon (his name derives from his fondness for the sykophantic Cleon) is aware of the softness of the hand of the rich defendant who reaches out to him in supplication on his way to court (V. 553–54). He is cynical of the posturing of rich defendants in court: "Some of them bewail their poverty, and exaggerate the misery they are in, until as he goes on he makes it out to be as great as mine" (V. 564–65). Philocleon delights in knowing that "the rich and the very grand shit in their clothes for fear of me" (V. 626–28). Aristophanes' jurors, moreover, are suspicious to the point of paranoia that members of the upper class are plotting against the demos, and this makes them believe demagogues when they falsely charge wealthy Athenians with treason, or rich men in allied states with fomenting rebellion.[107]

Although these features of Aristophanes' depiction of litigation and the courts make it clear that he is aware of class tensions concerning them, his comedy works to overcome rather than augment these. The very caricaturing of these tensions can be viewed as a step toward defusing them, but Aristophanes goes further than this in mediating class differences. In his ostensibly didactic role as comic poet and self-avowed enemy of sykophants (*V.* 1037–42), he exhorts the demos to stop supporting sykophancy. While Aristophanes is less charitable than elite litigants in explaining why the demos supports sykophants—stupidity, malice, and greed all play a role according to him—his criticisms, like theirs, ultimately take the form of friendly advice: he places the bulk of the blame for sykophancy on unscrupulous individuals, especially demagogues, and seeks to convince a popular audience that its interests are not served by cooperating with these sykophants. For example, in *Wasps,* Bdelycleon (whose name means "hater of Cleon," and who is closely identified with the poet: 650–51) points out that demagogues hog all the fruits of sykophancy to themselves, while poor jurors are left starving (673–79; cf. *Eq.* 797–804; *Pax* 632–48).

In keeping with Aristophanes' direct efforts to bridge class differences over litigation and the courts is the way he subtly undercuts the notion that class division is at the root of the problem. For example, in *Knights* (424 B.C.) Aristophanes plays upon the polarization of rich and poor when he presents the wealthy chorus of knights as arch-opponents of the sykophantic demagogue Paphlagon/Cleon and his three-obol dependents.[108] But Aristophanes undercuts this opposition through the course of the comedy: the gentlemen knights make an alliance with a lowly Sausage-seller, who challenges and eventually defeats Paphlagon/Cleon at his own game of sykophancy and demagoguery.[109] As this cross-class alliance is forged, the Sausage-seller, despite his lowly status, is ready to praise the ways of gentlemen (733–35). The knights for their part step off their high horses (metaphorically) and praise the Sausage-seller's sykophantic tactics. When the Sausage-seller threatens to reveal that Paphlagon/Cleon accepted bribes (830–35), the chorus of knights hails him: "You who have arisen as the greatest aid to all mankind, I envy you your ready tongue. If you go on attacking like this, you will be the greatest of the Greeks, and alone you will control the city's affairs and rule the allies, holding in your hand a trident with which you will make loads of money by shaking and disturbing them" (836–40). The knights are thus taken with the idea that the Sausage-seller will replace Paphlagon/Cleon as an extorter of money from the allies[110] and act as a Poseidon-sykophant in "shaking down" (i.e., blackmailing sykophantically) the members of Athens's sea-empire.[111] While the wealthy knights complain of sykophancy against the rich (259–65), apparently they are not troubled by the idea that non-Athenians may be victims of sykophancy.[112] Near the end of the comedy, moreover, the chorus leader asks but one favor of the victorious Sausage-seller, namely, that he may assist the Sausage-seller in his lawsuits (1254–56).[113] In these ways, Aristophanes suggests that interest in sykophantic profit knows no class bounds.

When Aristophanes' contemporary Eupolis wrote his *Maricas* (421 B.C.)—a comedy supposedly imitating *Knights* (Ar. *Nu.* 553–56; cf. Eup. fr. 89), but attacking the demagogue Hyperbolus (called "Maricas" within the play) rather than Cleon—he too may have sought to undercut the idea of class division over sykophancy. Eupolis apparently divided his chorus into opposing rich and poor sections, and in a surviving fragment, these sections are aligned on opposite sides, the poor favoring the sykophantic Maricas, the rich opposing him:

> *Maricas:* For how long now have you been with Nicias?
> *Character B:* I did not see him, except just now when he was standing in the agora.
> *Maricas:* The man admits that he has seen Nicias. Although why would he have seen him [there?], if he (Nicias) was not engaged in treason?
> *Hemi-chorus of Poor Men:* Did you hear, my agemates, that Nicias has been caught red-handed?
> *Hemi-chorus of Rich Men:* Are you crazy—could you catch a noble man in any crime?
>
> (fr. 193)

The way the Poor Men readily believe Maricas's absurd, sykophantic charge and the Rich Men jump to the defense of one of their own effectively caricatures the divisive character of sykophancy. Tammaro may be right to suspect, however, that the comedy ultimately brought about a reconciliation of rich and poor.[114] Plutarch, who preserves the fragment (*Nic.* 4.5), introduces Character B as an "unmeddlesome [*apragmōn*] poor man," and if this is accurate, he may have provided a vehicle for overturning the stereotype that poor men necessarily support meddlesome sykophants.

In his *Wasps* (422 B.C.), Aristophanes undercuts a strict class reading of sykophancy by focusing on a juror, Philocleon, who unlike his fellow jurors is a man of some property.[115] To be sure, Philocleon takes pleasure in his juror's wage (605–12) and identifies with his fellow jurors as a "poor man" relative to the rich and powerful (esp. 564–65). Philocleon, however, is not compelled by financial need to serve in the courts, but is "addicted" to jury service. His son, Bdelycleon, seeks to cure him of his ailment and convince him to take up the life of a gentleman. While poor jurors presumably do not have this option of a comfortable retirement, the focus on this sociologically atypical juror who does have a choice shifts attention away from the problem as one rooted in class and socioeconomic status, and paves the way for an imaginary solution to it.

Consistent with this downplaying of the class dimensions of sykophancy in *Wasps* is Aristophanes' translation of conflict concerning the courts into an intergenerational struggle.[116] While *Wasps* acknowledges and plays upon conflict between rich and poor over the courts, it focuses attention on the conflict between the elderly Philocleon and his son Bdelycleon. Although this conflict of generations proves impossible to resolve in the course of the play, the translation of class conflict into these terms distracts attention from the more troubling spectacle of ongoing class tension over sykophancy.

In Aristophanes' *Acharnians* (425 B.C.), the idiom of intergenerational strife also can be viewed as supplanting analysis of sykophancy in class terms. Whereas the aged jurors in *Wasps*, who fought in the Persian Wars, have adapted to the times and now relish serving in the courts (1095–97, 1112–13), the chorus of aged veterans of the glorious battle of Marathon (*Marathōnomachai*) in *Acharnians* complains that young, glib prosecutors (685) of the current generation harass their elders through litigation.[117] All too often, a young prosecutor overcomes his elderly rival with "verbal traps" (687), violently "assaulting, confounding, and confusing him" (688). For example, a ruthless young prosecutor Euathlus "outwrestled" the elderly Thucydides, son of Melesias in court (703–12).[118] The chorus captures in a pun the ignoble reversal of fortune men of their generation have suffered: formerly, the *Marathōnomachai* "pursued" the Persians, whereas now they find themselves "sued" in the courts (698–701).[119] They protest that if they must lose sleep (cf. V. 1037–42) over lawsuits, there should at least be a rule that litigants be of the same age (713–18). This presentation of sykophancy as an intergenerational issue should not be taken literally as evidence of conflict between young and old in the Athenian courts.[120] The supposed vulnerability of the *Marathōnomachai* before young prosecutors calls attention rather to the decline of Athens's traditional ideals: whereas formerly valor on the battlefield was held in high esteem, now slick rhetoric and newfangled arguments in court are the rage, and legal rather than martial prowess carries the day. Immediately after this choral interlude and as if in answer to it, Dikaiopolis appears onstage and announces that in his private market sykophants are to be excluded (725–26).[121] This juxtaposition suggests that Dikaiopolis's fantasy market represents, among other things, a return to the sykophant-free days of old about which the *Marathōnomachai* reminisce.[122]

That Aristophanes has gone to some trouble to depict sykophancy as an intergenerational rather than an interclass issue in this scene from *Acharnians* is evident from his suppression of class division on the topic. On the one hand, the *Marathōnomachai* are clearly not members of Athens's elite: they make their living as charcoal bearers (212–13, 325–36), and if one of them loses a lawsuit and pays a fine, he has no money left even to pay for a coffin when he dies (691; cf. *Pl.* 555–56). Curiously, however, these average Athenians identify closely with the legal plight of Thucydides (703–12), a well-known, conservative aristocrat. Because they too are elderly and suffer at the hands of malicious prosecutors, they identify with him. In addition, Thucydides is represented as a fellow Athenian who is harassed by the sykophantic outsider, Euathlus, whom they denigrate as a Scythian bowman (702–7).[123]

Aristophanes' rival Eupolis likewise portrays sykophancy as a gross deviation from the traditional values and ideals of the past. In his *Demes* (412 B.C.?), Eupolis conjures up from the dead four famous statesmen, Solon, Miltiades, Aristides, and Pericles, to offer advice to their countrymen during the difficult, late years of the Peloponnesian War. In a scene surviving in fragments (fr. 99.79–120), Aristides, who won the epithet "the Just" from his countrymen because of his reputation for fair dealing, sits in judgment of his polar opposite, a distinctly unjust modern-day sykophant. After the sykophant brazenly boasts of blackmailing a rich man from Epidaurus for profaning the Mysteries (fr. 99.86–89), Aristides orders him to be bound up (cf. fr. 99.104–5). The sykophant, however, threatens to sue for this "injustice" (fr. 99.103–11)—a doubly comic threat since Aristides is a paragon of justice and, moreover, dead. This sykophant, like sykophants in Aristophanes, is humiliated and ultimately banished (fr. 99.112). His banishment constitutes a victory not for a single class, although the victim happens to be a rich man, but for all just persons, as Athens's ideal past confronts and triumphs over the decadent present.

Conservative writers like Isocrates invoke the past not only because traditional values were respected in the good old days but also because the "best men" ruled the city at this time. Appeals to the past in comedy, by contrast, invoke the time of the Persian Wars as one of ideal values and circumstances, without openly advocating a return to an earlier, less democratic constitution. They suggest simply that men in the decadent present would do well to return to the ways of their ancestors and to shun sykophancy.

The Identity of Sykophants

Aristophanes is conscious of the class-hostile stereotype that sykophants are poor, lower-class men and plays upon it in a variety of ways. The sykophant in *Birds* appears in ragged costume (1416–21) and can thus be taken as a poor man;[124] Socrates' friend Chairephon is said to be a sykophant and a poor man (*penēs*) (Ar. fr. 552);[125] Aristophanes' knights naturally turn to a humble Sausage-seller for a counter-sykophant against the supposedly lower-class and sykophantic Cleon/Paphlagon. Aristophanes also exploits the notion that demagogues are men of lowly origins who have enriched themselves through sykophancy (*Pl.* 30–31, with 567–70; cf. Lys. 25.30).

The Litigious Athenian

If Aristophanes nods to the stereotype of the impoverished sykophant, however, like elite litigants he distinguishes sykophants from the vast majority of poor men (cf. [X.] *Ath.* 2.18). Sykophants are base (*ponēroi*) (*Ach.* 698–701; *Pl.* 920; cf. 900–901; fr. 424), but this designation is moral rather than social. The comic poet makes this particularly clear in his manipulation of the metaphor of sykophantic work: sykophants engage in a perverse trade that distinguishes them from honest workers like farmers and traders (*Av.* 1432; *Pl.* 903–5).[126]

Consistent with Aristophanes' care in distinguishing between sykophants and decent poor men are the words of a character in Menander (ca. 344–291 B.C.), who protests that "it is easy to scorn a poor man [*penēs*], even if he speaks the absolute truth; for he is believed to speak solely so as to make money. And straightaway, a man wearing a poor man's cloak [*tribōnion*] is labeled a sykophant, even if it happens that he is the one who has suffered a wrong" (*Georg.* fr. 1 Sandbach). This late fragment is interesting, because it attests both to the longevity of the stereotype that sykophants are poor men and to the effort even of a writer of new comedy to appeal to a popular audience by denying the validity of the association.[127]

The Identity of Victims

Aristophanes discourages not only the identification of sykophants with ordinary members of the demos but also the idea that the rich alone suffer from malicious prosecution. One of the sykophants in *Acharnians*, for example, attacks a desperately poor Megarian who comes to Dikaiopolis's market to sell his daughters (818–29). In the same play, the *Marathōnomachai*, poor charcoal bearers, fear sykophantic attacks (691, 698–718). In *Wasps*, Bdelycleon suggests that a member of the demos seeking his meager grain dole may find himself falsely accused of being an alien and thus not eligible for the distribution (718). In *Knights*, rich and poor alike "fart in fear" of Cleon (223–24), in no small part because of the way he wields sykophantic threats against his enemies (cf. 235–39). Indeed, Aristophanes suggests that all decent men are vulnerable to sykophants: public figures (*Eq.* 259–65, 288), private citizens (*Eq.* 773–76; cf. *Ach.* 693–702), Athenians and foreigners (passim), and even the comic poet himself (*Ach.* 377–82; cf. Ar. *Vita* 1.19–31 K-A). One need not be a wealthy man therefore to yearn for the quiet life, free of litigation, that Peisetairos seeks in *Birds* (33–41, 109–11).

If the sykophant is omnivorous, however, he has an epicure's taste, as Aristophanes characterizes it, for "the plump and rich" (*Pax* 639–40; cf. *Eq.* 1139–40), "the most fruitful of the foreigners" (*Eq.* 326), and "the choicest bits of the scrutinies of outgoing officials" (*Eq.* 824–26). This translation of motivation into terms of basic human appetite—"la politique du ventre," as Taillardat describes it[128]—is commonplace in comedy. Part of its appeal in this context lies in the fact that it explains behavior in terms of human nature rather than of class: hungry sykophants naturally seek out the delectable wealthy.

Even so, wealth is but one of many attributes that whet the sykophant's appetite, to judge from the way the sykophantic Paphlagon/Cleon is said to select his victims:

> You pick off as if they were figs [*aposukazeis*][129] officeholders subject to audit, pressing them to see which is green, or ripe, or not quite ripe. And if you discover someone who is a retiring type [*apragmon'*] and has a vacant look, after dragging him back from the Chersonese, you take hold of him with your slanders, you hook him, you twist his arm, and then devour him. Yes, and you keep an eye out for any citizen who is sheepish, rich, not base [*poneros*], and in fear of legal trouble [*pragmata*]. (*Eq.* 259–65)[130]

The ripeness of a victim is thus a function of intelligence (a vacant look invites attack) and demeanor (the sheepish make good victims). In Aristophanes and other comic poets, Nicias is a prime example of a man whose timidity, as well as his wealth, makes him a favorite victim of sykophants.[131] So too the wealthy Callias appears to be vulnerable by nature: his "feathers" are plucked not only by sykophants, but also by the mistresses he keeps (Ar. *Av.* 285–86).

Lest the rich and powerful receive more sympathy than they deserve, moreover, Aristophanes and his comic rivals make sure to point out that they are sometimes guilty of the charges that sykophants wield against them. Aristophanes suggests that the prominent general Laches, though victimized by a sykophantic prosecutor, is guilty as charged (*V.* 836–38; 240–44; cf. 554). Aristophanes' rival Cratinus jibes that when Callias is caught in adultery with Phocus's wife, he pays three talents to buy off the prosecution (fr. 81). In Eupolis's *Demes,* a rich man from Epidaurus may be ready to pay off a sykophant because he is guilty as charged of mocking the Mysteries (fr. 99.86–89).

When Aristophanes and other comic poets represent sykophancy in the terms sketched out here, they suggest that sykophancy is not a class issue but an Athenian one, and the entire city would benefit from a unified condemnation of it. The comic scenes in which sykophants are chased from the stage (discussed in Chapter 2) dramatize the point and invite collective repudiation of sykophancy.

But how hopeful is Aristophanes that men of different classes can accept his vision of sykophancy as a threat to all Athenians and unite to banish it from the city? Aristophanes' presentation of the problem suggests that he is not entirely optimistic that it can be resolved off the comic stage.[132] After all, Aristophanes depicts sykophancy as firmly rooted in the city's institutions—the popular courts (esp. *Wasps*), volunteer prosecution (esp. *Wealth* 900–925), and competitive politics (esp. *Knights*)—and although he works to extirpate it and represents himself as engaged in heroic labors against it (*V.* 1030, 1043), the challenge is indeed Heraclean.

One detects pessimism, for example, in Aristophanes' portrayal in *Wasps* of Bdelycleon's efforts to cure Philocleon's addiction to the courts. Although Bdelycleon is successful in keeping his father from serving as juror, toward the end of the comedy it appears that Philocleon may find himself in court once again—as a defendant. He drunkenly assaults passersby and leaves a trail of angry victims and lawsuits in his path (1332–34, 1392–93, 1443–45). When Philocleon disavows interest in the summonses and suits that are to be brought against him (1335–41), he does so not as a reformed devotee of the courts but as a defendant who does not wish to face the legitimate charges against him. The chorus reasonably expresses doubt, therefore, as to whether Philocleon wants to change his old ways: "For it is hard to depart from the nature that one has always had" (1457–58).[133]

A similar pessimism may be discerned in Aristophanes' depiction in *Knights* of the transformation of Demos, a personification and caricature of the Athenian people. Throughout most of the comedy (but cf. 1121–30), he is portrayed as a gawking and gullible abettor of the sykophantic Cleon. Toward the end, however, Demos is miraculously transformed: he is "boiled down" and thus rejuvenated and reformed into a responsible and enlightened citizen who will reject the panderings of sykophants (1357–63). But this sudden and remarkable transformation, late in the play, cannot entirely erase the depiction of Demos through the rest of the drama, and it can be taken as consistent with the cynical portrayal of Demos up to this point—that is, nothing short of boiling down Demos will change his nature. Even if this miracle cure is to be taken at face value within the comedy, it does not lend itself readily to imitation off the stage: the transformation depicted offers an image of the demos as it should be rather than as it is.[134]

If these two examples indicate that Aristophanes is cynical about the prospects of changing the demos, he nonetheless continues to attempt to do so through his comedy. In the case of sykophancy, he persists throughout his career in warning the demos of the threat it poses to the city. Like orators addressing the public, he translates this sensitive class issue into an unambiguous moral issue upon which men of all classes should agree, and thus at least helps mediate conflicting class perspectives.

Henderson has suggested that in general on the comic stage, "the community emphasizes its norms and discourages their violation, and by doing so as a festive entertainment allows for the release of pent-up tensions before they can become dangerous."[135] Aristophanes' treatment of the issue of sykophancy may be taken as a particular instance of this—an attempt to address and defuse a potentially divisive and dangerous class issue. Not all tensions, however, can be defused, and concerns over sykophancy—despite

Aristophanes' efforts in his comedies of the fifth century—did in fact figure prominently in the violent class conflict in the time of the Thirty (404/3 B.C.). Nonetheless, even after this unhappy episode, Aristophanes in his *Wealth* (388 B.C.) once more advanced the perspective that sykophancy was, rightly viewed at least, not a class issue, but a moral one.

Throughout much of the life of the democracy, elite Athenians complained about legal excess and abuse. For some alienated members of the elite, sykophancy was a flaw inherent in democracy and a direct threat to an aristocratic life-style and values. But concern over sykophancy was not confined to an extreme fringe, and complaints about it were not aired only in written works circulating among the literate elite. The issue resonated with meaning for the many, and presumably politically diverse, elite litigants represented in the corpus of Attic oratory, as well as for the smaller group of elite comic writers represented in surviving comic works. When these elite Athenians brought their complaints about sykophancy before mass audiences, they expressed their concerns about the democratic legal order and, in particular, how far the city would go to protect their persons and properties from what they viewed as legal excess and abuse.

The fact that elite Athenians kept addressing the subject of sykophancy in public contexts suggests that the issues it subsumed were never resolved, and this is not surprising since tensions over these were to a large extent inherent in the city's class structures and legal institutions. The airing of these tensions in public discourse was preferable, however, to the class violence under the Thirty that was fed by elite concerns about litigation under the democracy. It is significant, moreover, that elite Athenians addressing popular audiences not only complained of sykophancy but sought to win over their audiences to their point of view through image and argument. Whereas extreme critics of the democracy painted a generally bleak picture of the situation for their elite reading audiences, elite Athenians addressing the demos directly in the courts or through comedy attempted to bridge the gap between elite and masses on the subject of sykophancy. Although these elite Athenians engaged in a certain legerdemain to transform their pet peeve, sykophancy, into a matter of public concern, when they offered images of the sykophant as an enemy of rich and poor alike, they appealed to an ideal of social unity in which all Athenians, regardless of their actual differences, may have wished to believe.

Four

Public Suits and Volunteer Prosecutors

In classical Athens "anyone who wished" (*ho boulomenos*) could bring a public action. While Athens was by no means the only Greek polis to encourage private citizens to bring prosecutions on behalf of the state,[1] volunteer prosecution came to occupy a position of importance in democratic Athens that was without parallel in the rest of the Hellenic world. Although some forms of volunteer prosecution antedated the foundation of the Cleisthenic democracy (508/7 B.C.), democratic reform in the first half of the fifth century extended the scope of volunteer prosecution considerably (see Chapter 1). Throughout the life of the democracy, volunteer prosecution remained a vital institution and a hallmark of democratic rule (cf. [Arist.] *AP* 9.1–2). To moderns accustomed to public prosecution being conducted by state-appointed officials this arrangement may seem primitive. Athenians sometimes made use of state prosecutors (*sunēgoroi*) and could easily have entrusted public prosecution exclusively to them, had they deemed this desirable.[2] They preferred, however, to rely on private initiative for public prosecutions and maintained the system of volunteer prosecution from the time of the democratic reforms of the mid-fifth century to 322 B.C.

If Athenians embraced the principle of volunteer prosecution, however, they were uncomfortable with aspects of it. While elite citizens had their own reasons for complaint (see Chapter 3), the public at large was also concerned about basic facets of volunteer prosecution. The first part of this chapter argues that the public's concerns helped limit the scope of the use of volunteer prosecution, the second part that these concerns profoundly shaped how prosecutors who had recourse to it presented their roles to the public.

Volunteer Prosecution: Possibilities and Realities

Athenians distinguished between private suits, in which generally only an aggrieved party could act as prosecutor, and public suits, in which any adult male, normally a citizen, was allowed to prosecute (see Chapter 1). Volunteer prosecution could take any one of three forms:

1. In some circumstances a third party could intervene and lodge a public suit on behalf of another individual. For convenience, this will be referred to as "third-party litigation."[3]
2. An individual could bring a public suit on his own behalf.
3. An individual could pursue a public suit on behalf of the city.

While volunteer prosecution was available in all these circumstances, Athenians appear to have availed themselves of it primarily in the third form. This gap between what was possible and what was normal is curious. This section considers what is known about the first two forms of public prosecution, and explores the values and attitudes that inhibited their use.

HELPING THE WEAK

Athens's encomiasts praised the Athenian people for their willingness to intervene militarily in order to assist other Greeks who had been wronged by powerful bullies (Lys. 2.12, 14; cf. 2.22), and to take vengeance on their behalf (Dem. 60.11). Athenians invoked the same basic ideal in connection with life within the city: their laws provided "for the assistance of persons who have suffered wrong" (*ep' ōpheliai tōn adikoumenōn*) (Th. 2.37.3), by allowing any willing party to undertake a prosecution for a victim in certain circumstances.⁴ But just as Athenians were far from altruistic in assisting other Greeks militarily, so too they do not appear to have used volunteer prosecution to help their fellow citizens to any great extent. Let us consider first the ancient attribution of volunteer prosecution in this form to Solon, and then turn to the question of its use under the classical democracy.

Ancient writers associate volunteer prosecution closely with the Athenian statesman Solon (fl. ca. 590 B.C). For example, the Aristotelian *Athēnaiōn Politeia* (ca. 330 B.C.) includes among the three most democratic features of Solon's constitution "the permission granted to anybody who wished to take vengeance [*timōrein*] on behalf of wronged persons" (9.1; cf. Dem. 24.212–14; 22.25–30). Plutarch (ca. A.D. 100) expands on this tradition:

> Solon, thinking it necessary to make still further provision for the weakness of the multitude, gave every citizen the privilege of taking legal action on behalf of one who had suffered wrong. If a man was assaulted and suffered violence or injury, it was permitted to anyone who was able and willing [*tōi dunamenōi kai boulomenōi*] to indict the wrongdoer and prosecute him. The lawgiver in this way rightly accustomed the citizens, as members of one body, to feel and sympathize with one another's wrongs. We are told of a saying of his that is consonant with this law. When he was asked, apparently, what city was best to dwell in, he replied, "That city in which those who are not wronged, no less than those who are wronged, step forward to punish the wrongdoers." (*Sol.* 18.5 = fr. 40b Ruschenbusch)

These two passages raise many questions.

First, do these late sources preserve historical information about the origins of volunteer prosecution? Skepticism is in order whenever claims are made concerning Solon, since Athenians regularly credited Solon with demonstrably late democratic reforms and laws.⁵ In this case, however, the tradition does not appear to be a complete fabrication. Volunteer prosecution is certainly an old institution in Athens, and may even antedate Solon in some form; it is quite possible therefore that Solon extended the scope of volunteer prosecution as one of his many reforms.⁶ Further grounds for accepting the tradition is that in the case of [Arist.] *AP* 9.1 it does not appear to be merely a projection of contemporary practice onto the past, since third-party litigation was uncommon in the fourth century B.C.

Second, if the reform is historical, why would Solon have introduced it? The explanations provided in the sources betray the interests and assumptions of their authors. The *Athēnaiōn Politeia* labels the reform "democratic" and thereby posits that in Solon's time volunteer prosecution was, as in the fourth century B.C., a democratic institution. Plutarch casts the reform in his own ethical terms when he suggests it was intended to encourage citizens "as members of one body, to feel and sympathize with one another's wrongs." Nonetheless, it is plausible that Solon made it possible for anybody who wished to take vengeance on behalf of wronged persons (*AP* 9.1), and that the measure was designed, as Plutarch puts it, to enable an individual who was "able," that is, wealthy and powerful, to intervene on behalf of a weaker party. Such a reform would be consistent with Solon's concern, which is well attested in his surviving poems (e.g., fr. 36 West), to reduce civic tensions by enhancing the security of poorer citizens.

Third, did Solon conceive of volunteer prosecution as an act undertaken in the public interest? Although the *Athēnaiōn Politeia* frames the principle in personal terms—the volunteer prosecutor steps in to exact vengeance on behalf of the injured party—this does not rule out the possibility that volunteer prosecution of this sort had a public aspect as well in Solon's time. Indeed, the words that Plutarch attributes to Solon (*Sol.* 18.5; cf. Plu. *Mor.* 154d11–e2; D.L. 1.59.7–8), which may well be authentic, suggest that Solon envisioned volunteer prosecution as an act benefiting not only the individual victim but the city.[7]

Fourth, did the reform actually provide protection to the weak? This could only have happened if volunteer prosecutors actually stepped forward, or at least appeared ready to do so. But one must ask why a powerful man would assist a weaker one in this way, especially since he would thereby risk incurring the enmity of the victim's persecutor. This question is especially relevant in an ancient context, since Athenians, like other Greeks, were acutely attuned to considerations of self-interest and, while not entirely selfish, did not feel compelled to run considerable risks to assist others. Dover thus observes in his study of Greek popular morality: "Positive assertion that a good man should give help where it is needed, even if no claim can be based on kinship—and, presumably, even where there is no calculation of future advantage—is uncommon."[8] In a Solonian setting, those able and willing to act as third-party prosecutors were most likely propertied gentlemen who stood to gain something from this. By acting as volunteer prosecutor, an aristocrat might foster the dependence of a poor man on himself through legal patronage.[9] The role of volunteer prosecutor might be all the more enticing to him if the prospective defendant was a rival or enemy. In such a context, however, assistance of the weak was contingent on elite interests, and Solonian legislation concerning *ho boulomenos* should be viewed therefore not as democratic but as consistent with the preservation of aristocratic power and current social structures.[10]

Under the classical democracy, third-party prosecution could be carried out through a number of public actions, some of which may date back to Solon or earlier. For example, anyone could prosecute a criminal through *endeixis* or *apagōgē*, or bring a *graphē* for hubris, for wrongful restraint, for falsely listing someone as a state debtor, or for attesting to a false summons. Furthermore, any citizen could bring an *eisangelia* alleging abuse of parents, orphans, heiresses, or an orphan's estate ([Arist.] *AP* 56.6).[11]

Third-party prosecution appears, however, to have been uncommon in the classical period.[12] There are several explanations for this. First, although in Solon's time some rich men may have engaged in this as a form of patronage, the social and political ethos of the classical democracy discouraged such open displays of status inequity among citizens.[13] In general, where one-on-one patronage existed, it was probably a local phenomenon (e.g., Dem. 53.4), and it did not find a conspicuous outlet in civic institutions. In some areas, in fact, the city assumed the role of patron to less well-off citizens by providing state pay for service to the city, and thereby saved them from an unbecoming dependence on the wealthy. To the extent that legal patronage was practiced openly, it took the form of politicians bringing volunteer prosecutions on behalf of the people as a whole, not pro bono suits for weak individuals.

One-on-one legal patronage not only clashed with democratic principles, but also with Athenian ideals of manhood.[14] In general, Athenians appear to have believed that a man should either fight his own battles or steer clear of them in the first place. In a legal context, this meant that he should, if at all possible, prosecute his own suits. In this way, he could reestablish his manly reputation by taking vengeance personally for his opponent's slight to his honor (cf. Dem. 53.1–3). If a victim was unable to do this himself, it regularly fell upon his son to take vengeance on his behalf (Lys. 13.41–42).[15] Because this constituted an acknowledgment of weakness on the father's part, however, this alternative was probably exercised only in extreme cases—when the father was suffering from a restriction on his civic rights that prevented him from bringing suit (Dem. 58.1–3), or was aged or dead.

For an adult male citizen to accept legal patronage from another man through a third-party suit, moreover, was to place himself on a level with persons of lower status. Metics, for example, may have required the support of citizen patrons (*prostatai*) to pursue their legal interests.[16] Women, children, and the elderly too depended on the efforts of others, usually relatives, for representation in legal matters. A self-respecting male citizen would not seek to invite equation of his status with members of any of these groups.

Financial considerations may also have deterred individuals from accepting prosecutorial patronage. If a victim brought and won his own private suit, he could hope to receive a monetary award, but if a third party brought a public suit on his behalf, any fine imposed normally went to the state. Victims might think twice therefore about the benefit to be had from third-party suits.

Potential prosecutors also had good reason to avoid third-party suits. An angry defendant might interpret a prosecutor's intervention as a gratuitous insult and an act of enmity to be avenged through his own lawsuit. Furthermore, public suits normally involved considerable financial risks for the prosecutor who won less than one-fifth of a jury's votes. The likelihood of his receiving less than this minimum was heightened, moreover, by the public's suspicion that he was meddling in others' affairs. Even when volunteer prosecutors brought suits alleging a direct harm to the city, their opponents could accuse them of meddling in business that was not their own; a third-party prosecutor, who placed himself in the middle of an interpersonal dispute, could all the more be accused of meddling.

Given these unattractive features of third-party prosecution from the perspective both of victim and prosecutor, Athenians probably did not think of this form of volunteer prosecution as a very real option. Consider, for example, how one litigant surveys the legal options available to a harmed party (Dem. 22.25–27). He asserts that Solon provided a multiplicity of actions to those lodging suits, so that men of varying resources could choose actions consistent with their means: a weak man can either bring a lesser action (i.e., one bearing less risk for the prosecutor) or submit to arbitration. He passes over completely, however, the possibility that a weak individual might seek out a third-party prosecutor, presumably on the assumption that this is not ordinarily a viable option.

These considerations were so compelling as to discourage third-party litigation not only when the victim was a stranger, but even when he was a friend or relative.

Legal Assistance to Strangers

Volunteer prosecutors were especially unlikely to step forward to assist a stranger. In a society that embraced the notion that one should help one's friends and hurt one's enemies, obligations to strangers were minimal.[17] For example, when passersby witnessed frays in Athens, if they involved themselves at all, they tended to give verbal rather than physical support.[18] If strangers were unlikely to risk serious personal involvement in a fray that they happened upon in the streets, they were all the more unlikely to intervene as prosecutors in an extended and potentially costly legal fray on behalf of a stranger.

It is not surprising, therefore, that the ancient sources record so little of third-party prosecutions on behalf of strangers.[19] While such prosecutions may have taken place with greater frequency than the sources suggest and just have not survived as the subjects of extant orations, in this case one would expect litigants in other suits at least to allude to these, for example, to take credit for conducting them. But, while litigants regularly boast of their generosity to less fortunate citizens,[20] they do not include volunteer prosecutions in their lists of benefactions. To be sure, prosecutors sometimes claim that their opponents have treated the weak ruthlessly, but they do so while pursuing public suits on other grounds—alleging a wrong to the city (Lys. 31.18–19; Dem. 25.38; cf. 58.2) or themselves (Dem. 21.83–101).

That Athenians felt no obligation to pursue third-party prosecutions on behalf of strangers is especially clear from Demosthenes' speech in his public prosecution of Meidias for striking him in the face while he was serving as benefactor of a public chorus (*chorēgos*). In the course of his prosecution, Demosthenes describes at length how Meidias through a false suit brought about the disfranchisement of Strato, "a poor man" (21.83) who had decided in favor of Demosthenes rather than Meidias when arbitrating a dispute between them (21.83–101). To a modern observer it may seem curious that Demosthenes did nothing to help Strato in his dire circumstances, especially given his willingness to pursue on his own behalf a public suit for a mere slap in the face. Demosthenes, however, feels no need to explain to his Athenian audience why he did not intervene on behalf of Strato through a third-party suit or for that matter why he did not support him in any way at all.

To be sure, Strato may not have been as innocent as Demosthenes claims,[21] and this may have deterred Demosthenes from intervening on his behalf. But, at least as Demosthenes paints the scene, one might suppose the circumstances were ripe for Demosthenes' third-party prosecution of Meidias on Strato's behalf: this was a clear-cut case of abuse of a poor man by a rich man, and Demosthenes could have justified his volunteer prosecution in the way that so many prosecutors on behalf of the city do, namely, as an attempt to punish a personal enemy and simultaneously to serve the public interest. Yet Demosthenes is unapologetic about his failure to render assistance, presumably because he was under no obligation to help this average citizen who was caught in the crossfire between feuding rich men: Strato's personal misfortune was simply not Demosthenes' business. Consistent with this is Demosthenes' argument later that average Athenians have a vested interest in supporting men like Demosthenes who have the means to prosecute on their own behalf dangerous, powerful men like Meidias, since this is the only way such villains will be brought to justice (21.123–24; cf. 21.141).

Friendly Legal Assistance

The obligation to help relatives or friends could conceivably have encouraged third-party prosecutions. Indeed, relatives and friends were expected to regard one another's foes as their own and to lend assistance against them in litigation.[22] Actions based on friendly relations (*philia*), however, were susceptible to calculations of self-interest, as someone seeking a loan from his intimates might well discover.[23] So too in litigation, the assistance of relatives and friends was probably limited by practical considerations. It apparently went beyond the normal expectations of *philia* that a friendly supporter should risk the fine falling on an unsuccessful prosecutor in most public suits. In practice, therefore, relatives and friends did not normally assist one another in this way.

Relatives and friends could and did discharge their obligation to assist one another at law in a number of ways short of undertaking third-party prosecutions.[24] For example, they could lend each other money to help subsidize the costs of a suit through the association known as the *eranos:* members apparently pooled funds that could be drawn on by those with special needs, including litigants (Lys. 8.18; cf. Dem. 25.58). Or relatives and friends could provide litigants with witness testimony and act as supporting speakers (*sunēgoroi*) at trial.

The institution of *sunēgoria*, in fact, provided both a victim and his supporter with an attractive alternative to third-party prosecution.[25] It allowed the victim, as prosecutor, to present himself as the avenging party and thus fulfill social expectations that he behave in a manly fashion. At the same time, his *sunēgoros* could fulfill the obligations of *philia* by providing substantial support, without incurring the financial risks of volunteer prosecution. Indeed, while witnesses were at risk of being charged with false witnessing, *sunēgoroi* were not subject to prosecution for lying (Aesch. 2.170). Like all supporters of a litigant, however, *sunēgoroi* could be accused of lending assistance in return for money (this was illegal: Dem. 46.26), and *sunēgoroi* therefore often assert that they are motivated simply by *philia*.[26]

If relatives and friends preferred to act as *sunēgoroi* rather than third-party prosecutors, nothing prevented them from appealing to the ideal of mutual assistance among citizens associated with third-party prosecution. Hyperides, in fact, goes so far as to appeal to this ideal when serving as *sunēgoros* for a defendant, Euxenippus, facing an impeachment (*eisangelia*):

> Of the many good practices in our city, what is better or more democratic than this—that, whenever a private person [*idiōtēs*] is facing the danger of a trial and cannot conduct his own defense, any citizen who wishes [*ton boulomenon*] is allowed to come forward to help [*boēthēsai*] him and give the jury a fair statement of the case? (4.11; cf. 1.10)

When Hyperides casts the *sunēgoros* as a volunteer from the citizen body who renders assistance to the weak, he draws on the ideology of volunteer prosecution. That a *sunēgoros* should equate himself with a volunteer prosecutor attests to the appeal of the ideal that the strong should actively assist the weak in litigation. This equation, however, is forced, and not simply because Hyperides, as the supporter of a defendant, is manifestly not a volunteer prosecutor. First, *sunēgoria*—for prosecution or defense—did not require the same level of involvement as volunteer prosecution or entail the same risks. Second, the *sunēgoros* was not just "any willing citizen" volunteering on the basis of democratic principle, but normally a friend or relative of the litigant (cf. 4.13); those without such supporters did not benefit from *sunēgoria*.

The foregoing analysis suggests a variety of reasons why third-party prosecution was probably uncommon in classical Athens. A possible exception is prosecutions brought on behalf of orphans (in an Athenian context, orphans are children who have lost their fathers, but not necessarily their mothers as well),[27] since a number of factors encouraged these. Even here, however, there is reason to believe that third-party prosecution was uncommon.

Athenian law allowed volunteer prosecutions on behalf of orphans while they were still minors under a number of rubrics, including an "impeachment for maltreatment of orphans" (*eisangelia orphanōn kakōseōs*).[28] This *eisangelia* had several special features. It was without risk (*akindunos*) ([Arist.] *AP* 56.6; cf. Is. 3.46–47; Dem. 37.46), that is, a prosecutor who failed to receive one-fifth of the votes was not subject to any penalty, and it remained risk-free even when other *eisangeliai* became subject to risk around 330 B.C.;[29] the prosecutor paid no court fees (cf. Is. 3.47); and his speech was not subject to the usual time limits (Harp. 167.12–13 Dindorf). These special provisions suggest that Athenians sought to encourage prosecution on behalf of orphans, presumably on the grounds that they were exceptionally vulnerable and therefore merited extra protection. Additional impetus to extend them special protection came from the fact that many orphans were children of the state's war dead, and it was a basic tenet of civic ideology that the city would provide for the children of those who sacrificed their lives for it.[30]

One might suppose that the special terms governing this *eisangelia* made it an appealing action for third-party prosecutors to undertake. Underage male orphans, moreover, need not have felt public embarrassment that others were bringing suit on their behalf, since as minors they could not bring suits. But only two cases of *eisangelia* for orphans are attested. One case (Is. 11) was brought unsuccessfully by one guardian against another (both were relatives of the orphan in question); the details of the other case are obscure—Epichares alleges that the *rhētōr* Theocrines initiated an *eisangelia* against Polyeuktes, but dropped the charge in exchange for two hundred drachmas (Dem. 58.30–34).[31] Although Osborne is too quick to conclude that both *eisangeliai* were "moved very much in the interests of the prosecutor and not the ward," he is probably right that this *eisangelia* "hardly succeeds in protecting the interests of those unable to act for themselves."[32]

While *eisangeliai* for orphans may have been more common than the fragmented record indicates, their infrequency is also suggested by the numerous attested suits against guardians (*dikai epitropēs*) brought by male orphans who had reached the age of majority.[33] In some cases the defalcations of his guardians may not have been discovered until an orphan reached his majority, at which point the orphan—no longer a minor and now able to litigate in his own person—rather than a third-party was the preferred prosecutor. It is hard to believe, however, that relatives and friends were always oblivious to abuses against minor orphans: many may have been aware of abuses, but were reluctant to champion the wards' cause especially against guardians who may have been closer in relation to the wards than they. If one guardian was ready to accuse another, as in Isaeus 11, an *eisangelia* might be lodged, but otherwise wards might lack a willing advocate. If relatives and friends waited until a male orphan came of age and brought his own private suit, moreover, they could support him in the more limited capacity of *sunēgoroi* (Is. 7.6–7; Lys. 32.9–10) and discharge their obligations in this less risky manner.

The orphan upon reaching his majority was, however, in an awkward position as prosecutor.[34] Claims of peculation were difficult to prove, especially since written records, if kept at all, were easily manipulated by guardians. Furthermore, the public may have regarded the orphan as ungrateful to his guardians, and have been sympathetic with the common complaint of guardians that they were the subject of sykophantic attacks (Lys. fr. 43 Thalheim; Dem. 38.3, 20; cf. Aesch. 3.255). Moreover, if the orphan was unsuccessful in prosecuting his suit, he was subject to a financial penalty (*epōbelia*),[35] and even if successful, he might have difficulty, as Demosthenes did (Dem. 30; 31), in enforcing the court's verdict. The situation could only have been more difficult for female orphans and heiresses (*epiklēroi*), who were reliant on the legal agency of others even when they were no longer children. Humphreys is probably right in her pessimistic assessment of the general situation: "the laws offering protection from exploitation within the *oikos* were often completely ineffectual."[36]

The city could have assumed the role of legal patron of weak citizens, including orphans and heiresses, by entrusting state prosecutors with the protection of their interests, but Athenians viewed direct intervention by the state as inappropriate even in these circumstances.37 In their view no harm to a private individual constituted a threat to the collective interest that was so great as to *require* intervention by the city through its agents. To be sure, the city did make it possible for third-party prosecutors to intervene to protect the weak, but apparently few were ready to undertake this office, even under the favorable rules governing prosecutions on behalf of orphans. In general, Athens had no legal safety net for the weak, and Athenians were left to help themselves as they could through litigation.

HELPING ONESELF

If Athenians were reluctant to intercede on behalf of others through public actions, they were perhaps somewhat more comfortable with bringing public actions alleging harms to themselves.38 In all situations where a third party was allowed to bring a public suit on behalf of a victim, the victim was also permitted to bring public suit in his own person. After all, public suits were available to *anyone* who wished to bring them and this broad category included victims as well as third parties. Instances are recorded, for example, of victims bringing public actions for hubris (esp. Dem. 21), wrongful restraint (Dem. 59.64–70), and attesting to a false summons (Dem. 53.17).

Such suits, however, seem to have been relatively uncommon. Many victims probably preferred to bring private actions rather than public ones, so that any fine imposed would come to them (in public actions fines went to the state), and furthermore so as not to risk the statutory penalties applicable to unsuccessful prosecutors in most public actions. If a victim brought his own public action, moreover, he put himself in a peculiar position before the public. First, by prosecuting a public suit in a case where he was himself a victim,39 he invited comparison of his role with that of the third-party prosecutor acting for a helpless victim. To the extent the public viewed volunteer prosecution on behalf of private persons as a means of protecting the weak, they might look askance at an able prosecutor "volunteering" to help himself through a public action. Second, the prosecutor bringing a public suit on his own behalf also invited comparison of his role with that of the volunteer prosecutor of the most common public suits, namely, those claiming a direct wrong to the city. To the extent the public thought of public actions as vehicles for protecting the city's interests, they might wonder why a private wrong was being pursued through a public action. Although the public could be said to have an interest in all harms done to private persons, on the grounds that "men who punish those who wrong them prevent others from being wronged" (Is. fr. 32 Thalheim), Athenians tended to view injuries to individuals as matters for private suits rather than public ones.

These considerations in all likelihood discouraged individuals from pursuing, for example, the public indictment alleging hubris (*graphē hubreōs*).[40] If an Athenian was physically attacked and beaten, he could prosecute the aggressor through a private action for assault (*dikē aikeias*) or a public action for hubris. Although it is not clear precisely what Athenians expected the prosecutor of a hubris charge to demonstrate, it was probably incumbent on him to show that his opponent had acted not only violently but also so insolently as to degrade and humiliate him. For a prosecutor to choose the *graphē hubreōs* over the *dikē aikeias* was a significant decision. Demosthenes' client Ariston opted for a *dikē aikeias* at the prodding of friends and relatives: "they advised and urged me not to take upon myself matters which I should not be able to bear, or to appear to be bringing suit for the injuries I had suffered in a manner beyond my youth. I took this course, therefore, and, in deference to them, initiated a private suit" (54.1). Ariston insists, however, that his private action is a more modest one than the offense merits (54.13) and that his complaint is not merely a private one despite the form of the action (54.42). Ariston appears not to have been alone in choosing the less ambitious and lower risk *dikē aikeias* over the *graphē hubreōs*. Few indictments for hubris appear to have been lodged and no doubt fewer still were carried through.[41] Most prosecutors probably preferred, like Ariston, to bring the *dikē aikeias* and to complain of their opponents' hubris within the framework of this suit without actually bringing a public action for hubris (cf. Isoc. 20.2–5).[42]

Just how awkward it might be to bring a public action for hubris is illustrated by Demosthenes' prosecution of Meidias for striking him in the face while he was serving as *chorēgos*. After Demosthenes had won a public censure of Meidias through a *probolē* before the Assembly, he pursued his case before a popular court through a public action—either a *probolē* alleging hubris or a *graphē hubreōs*.[43] While some scholars believe, on the basis of Aeschines' claim that Demosthenes sold off the case to Meidias for thirty minae (3.52), that the surviving speech (Dem. 21) was not actually delivered, Aeschines may be lying or hostilely characterizing a fine that the court required Meidias to pay to Demosthenes.[44] In any event, Demosthenes' published speech against Meidias presents itself as one actually given and provides good evidence of the tensions involved in bringing a public action on one's own behalf.[45]

Demosthenes is conscious that jurors may be uncomfortable with two aspects of his suit: first, the fact that he is playing the role of public prosecutor in a case in which he is the harmed party and thus in the peculiar situation of "coming to his own rescue" (*boēthein hautōi*: cf. 21.106, 141); second, that he is presenting the injury to himself as one against the entire city. In his speech, therefore, he attempts to answer jurors' concerns in both these areas.

Demosthenes does not apologize for the oddity that he is bringing a public prosecution in a case where he is the victim, but rather seeks to turn this to his advantage. For example, he notes that although the prosecutor of a public suit would not ordinarily make a personal appeal to his audience for goodwill (*eunoia*) (cf. Lyc. fr. VI.1 Conomis), in this case, since he himself suffered hubris, it is appropriate to do so (21.5–7). Demosthenes goes so far as to seek credit for choosing to bring a public rather than a private suit, since he has thus waived the financial gain a private suit might have brought him (21.28). Later, too, he emphasizes his financial sacrifice as he explains the rules governing actions for hubris:

> Consequently, for hubris too [the lawmaker] permitted anyone who wished to prosecute, and he made the penalty entirely payable to the state; for, he considered, the man who turns to hubris wrongs not only the victim but the city, and revenge is sufficient compensation for the victim, who ought not to make money for himself from such offenses. (21.45)

Demosthenes notes in passing that such suits are open to prosecution by *anyone* (cf. 21.47), but does not elaborate since in this case the "volunteer" is the victim himself.

Demosthenes must also overcome his audience's suspicion that this was merely another episode in his ongoing feud with Meidias and thus not of public concern. Although Demosthenes acknowledges the private enmity that exists between himself and Meidias (21.74; cf. 21.29), he asserts that the harm done to him personally was also an affront to the public, since he was assaulted while serving the city as *chorēgos* (21.31–34; cf. 21.7–8, 21). He insists that Meidias's hubristic actions and way of life make him the enemy of all men, especially the helpless poor (21.142). Throughout his speech Demosthenes is at pains to demonstrate that the harm to him has a significant public dimension—testimony to the challenge he faces in persuading a jury that he is justified in bringing a public action for the slap he received.

One way Athenians could avoid the difficulties inherent in bringing public actions for harms to themselves was by framing their complaints as private actions. Another option, however, was also available: a harmed party could wait for an opportunity to take vengeance on his foe by bringing a suit against him alleging a direct harm to the city. In such cases—and they appear to have been common—the volunteer prosecutor could maintain that he was simultaneously serving the city and justly avenging himself on a personal enemy.

The Use and Abuse of Public Actions on Behalf of the City

Most public suits in Athens arose not in connection with injuries done to individuals as in both sets of circumstances just considered, but rather from direct offenses against the city. Athenians would have agreed that "everyone suffers wrong, whenever someone wrongs the city" (Pl. *Lg.* 768a1–2), and viewed public actions primarily as instruments for protecting the Athenian people from offenses against their collective interests. While Athenians recognized the importance of public actions on behalf of the city, they were well aware that these were vulnerable to abuse, primarily because the prosecutors pursuing them were volunteers.

CONCERNS OVER PUBLIC ACTIONS

Public actions were available against a variety of civic offenses including treason and desertion; theft or wrongful possession of public property, or failure to pay debts to the city; venality or other abuse of position by men in public life and civic administration; and illegal exercise of citizenship privileges by non-Athenians or Athenians subject to *atimia*.[46] Complaints of abuse are recorded concerning all types of public actions: contrary to much scholarly opinion no single type of action or group of related actions was inherently suspect—or, to put it more cynically, all public actions were more or less equally suspect. Two groups of actions illustrate this general point: actions used primarily against persons involved in public life, and actions bearing financial rewards for successful prosecutors.[47]

Policing Public Officials and Politicians

Fundamental to the protection of the interests of the Athenian people was the policing of officeholders and public speakers. Suits against these persons, in fact, probably constituted the majority of public suits coming before the courts. Hansen has observed that magistrates, generals, and *rhētores* were prosecuted most commonly through *euthunai, eisangelia,* and *graphē paranomōn,* respectively.[48] Since these actions were common, it is not surprising that the sources speak with some frequency of abuse in connection with each of them.

Officeholders were automatically subject to review and potentially to prosecution both upon entering office and leaving it. Apparently, however, challenges at the qualifying review of the *dokimasia* were infrequent and few candidates were rejected,[49] even though there was no restriction on the nature of the charges that could be leveled[50] and the prosecutor who stepped forward was not subject to risk (i.e., he was *akindunos*).[51] Candidates who were not qualified to serve on technical grounds or who were likely to be rejected on political grounds may normally have withdrawn their names from consideration in advance, so as to avoid the public humiliation of rejection.

If the *dokimasia* was only a formality for most officeholders, the mandatory review of the *euthunai* to which they were subject on leaving office was more to be feared.[52] A magistrate could be prosecuted not only for corrupt behavior, but also for honest mistakes (Hyp. 5.25–26). The first phase of the *euthunai* was supervised by state accountants (*logistai*) and culminated in a court review of magistrates' accounts. While anyone could bring a charge to the court's attention, publicly appointed *sunēgoroi* conducted the actual prosecution. A convicted magistrate was subject to a fine. In the second phase of the *euthunai*, nonfinancial complaints were invited, and charging parties were responsible for pursuing these in their own persons through separate actions, private or public.[53] A magistrate convicted in this second phase could be fined or punished, for example with *atimia*.

It is commonly claimed in the ancient sources that sykophants extort blackmail from officeholders by threatening to bring charges against them at their *euthunai*.[54] The officials who managed the review process were perhaps in an especially good position to extort money in this way: thus Aeschines claims that Timarchus, while serving as *logistēs*, demanded and received payoffs from guilty and innocent alike (1.107). But anyone possessing or claiming to have information concerning the illegal behavior of an officeholder could attempt blackmail. Because officeholders were vulnerable to accusations at their *euthunai*, even innocent men may have chosen to come to terms with their blackmailers rather than risk prosecution. Many officeholders who paid money to blackmailers, however, were probably guilty of the charges threatened.[55] Officeholders had many opportunities to reap personal profit from their positions, for example through bribe taking. Athenians in general were ambivalent toward bribery (see Chapter 3), and officeholders faced with the possibility of personal gain could easily rationalize the acceptance of a "gift" that in their view did the city no harm.

Although Athenians were aware of abuses in connection with the *euthunai*, prosecutions of officeholders were such an important democratic check on their abuse of power that it is unlikely any stigma attached to prosecutors. To be sure, Aeschines (1.1; cf. 2.182) seeks credit on the grounds that he has never prosecuted at *euthunai,* but in the same passage he also takes credit for not bringing *graphai* against any Athenian, and thus does not appear to be singling out prosecution at the *euthunai* as especially suspect.[56]

While the annual *euthunai* provided the best opportunity for making claims against most officeholders, special considerations made impeachment (*eisangelia*) the preferred action for the prosecution of generals at least in the fourth century B.C.[57] An *eisangelia,* which carried no statutory penalty for unsuccessful prosecution before ca. 330 B.C., could be brought immediately against an incompetent or unsuccessful general and remove him from office before he did more harm to the city and its soldiers. Prosecutors impeached generals frequently,[58] and the Athenian public, which held generals to an exceptionally high standard of accountability, seems to have been quick to punish those who fell short of expectations.[59] If, from a modern perspective, the frequent and sometimes capricious use of *eisangelia* against generals casts "a shadow over the Athenian democracy,"[60] on the whole Athenians appear to have been relatively comfortable with its use.

Athenians were aware, however, that *eisangelia* could, like other actions, be abused. A defendant could complain, for example, that a prosecutor was bringing false charges without any risk to himself and, in some cases, that he had chosen *eisangelia* over a more appropriate action because it was risk-free (Is. 11.31; Hyp. 1.12).[61] Such complaints may have led Athenians to modify the rules governing *eisangelia* in the late fourth century B.C. According to Pollux (8.53), Theophrastus (late fourth century B.C.) said that, whereas in other public suits a prosecutor who won less than one-fifth of the votes was subject to both a thousand-drachma fine and *atimia,* in *eisangelia* the unsuccessful prosecutor paid only the fine and was not subject to *atimia;* Pollux observes that this represents a shift from earlier times when the prosecutor of an *eisangelia* was completely *akindunos.* Modern scholars have tentatively dated this change of rules to the late 330s B.C. on the basis of evidence from the extant forensic speeches.[62]

Although this change of rules may well have come about, as Pollux speculates, due to concern that it was too easy to bring an *eisangelia,* one must not make too much of the reform. Some scholars have seen it as a response to a general trend of increasing abuse of *eisangelia* in the fourth century,[63] but this seems unlikely: contemporaries probably had little sense of long-term trends and were simply responding to conspicuous recent cases that called attention to the potential for abuse.[64] Whatever the source of contemporary concerns, they were not so great as to prompt a complete change of rules: prosecutors using *eisangelia* were made liable to the statutory financial penalties to which prosecutors of other public suits were subject, but remained exempt from the penalty of *atimia.*

Because *rhētores* held no elected or allotted office, they were not subject to *dokimasia* or *euthunai.* While they could be charged through a variety of public actions, including *eisangelia,* they were most commonly held accountable through the *graphē paranomōn,* an indictment alleging that a decree proposed in the Assembly contravened existing laws.[65] Any willing party could bring this action, but if he won less than one-fifth of the votes at trial, he was subject to the usual statutory penalties.[66] While a *rhētōr* convicted three times incurred *atimia,*[67] he could avoid becoming subject to this penalty by hiring or otherwise inducing another man to be the nominal sponsor of his decrees (Dem. 24.3, 14, 66; 59.43).

Any public action could be used as an instrument of political rivalry—Demosthenes thus claims that his rivals have employed *euthunai, eisangeliai,* and *graphai paranomōn* against him (18.249–50). Competing *rhētores,* however, appear to have used the *graphē paranomōn* with especially great frequency against one another. Most active *rhētores* probably found themselves defendants in a *graphē paranomōn* at some point in their political careers.[68] Scholars often note the opposite extremes of Aristophon of Azenia, who was said to have been acquitted seventy-five times on this charge (Aesch. 3.194),[69] and Cephalus who was supposedly never even indicted (Dem. 18.251). Although at trial the nominal issue was the legality of the proposed decree, jurors' verdicts could also be taken as indications of their confidence in, or displeasure with, the *rhētores* involved.[70] While indicted *rhētores* naturally accused their opponents of abusing this action, they were no doubt equally ready to indict opponents in pursuit of political advantage.

Actions Bearing Financial Rewards

Much modern discussion of the abuse of public actions in Athens centers on actions in which the successful prosecutor could lay claim to a financial reward:

1. The successful prosecutor of an *apographē*, an action for recovering state property illegally held by an individual, could claim a portion of the proceeds from the sale of the property. Lewis may be right that the text of Dem. 53.2, according to which the prosecutor's reward is three-quarters (*tria*) of the proceeds, should be emended to read one-third (*trita*).[71]
2. The successful prosecutor of a *phasis,* an action against an "object or property with which an offence had been committed,"[72] received half of the proceeds from the sale of the object or property in question; such actions were particularly common in connection with trade.
3. Throughout most of the classical period noncitizens attempting to pass themselves off as citizens could be indicted through a *graphē xenias*. Special rules introduced sometime in the fourth century went so far as to prohibit marriages between a citizen and noncitizen and to provide a financial incentive to prosecutors exposing foreigners in such unions (Dem. 59.16). A successful prosecutor received one-third of the sum obtained from selling off the convicted party and his or her property, and probably also one-third of the thousand-drachma fine imposed on the husband of a convicted alien woman. In the same period, a public action (*graphē xenēs enguēs*) was created for prosecuting a man who gave a foreign woman in marriage to an Athenian, passing her off as a citizen: if the accused was convicted, he lost his civic rights, his property was sold, and his prosecutor received one-third of the proceeds from this (Dem. 59.52).[73]

To judge by the heterogeneous nature of these actions, incentives were attached to them not on the grounds of any unifying legal principle, but rather on an ad hoc basis to encourage certain types of prosecutions. In fact, not even all types of *phasis* or all actions against foreigners masquerading as citizens had financial rewards attached to them.[74]

Most scholars have assumed that suits carrying financial rewards were especially attractive to unscrupulous prosecutors. Lofberg, for example, asserts that the "sycophant would naturally prefer" public suits that "yielded him money if he was successful," and Bonner and Smith follow his lead.[75] More recently, Sinclair has stated somewhat more cautiously, "These [financial] inducements were not the only cause but they were the major cause in the emergence of *sykophantai*."[76] Osborne, however, has argued that in the extant cases involving these actions prosecutors appear to be pursuing other ends than financial gain, and concludes: "Overall the evidence available to us does not justify the supposition that malicious litigation was either occasioned by, or a particular problem in, actions in which the prosecutor was rewarded."[77] Scholars have been reluctant, however, to accept Osborne's arguments. Harvey, for example, acknowledges that the sources rarely allege that a prosecutor is bringing a suit so as to win the financial reward attached to it, but maintains nonetheless that when a litigant alludes vaguely to monetary motives, "no doubt he often has this in mind."[78] In my view, Osborne may well be right that financial gain was not the primary motivation for many prosecutors of such actions. Whatever the truth may be about prosecutors' actual motivations, public concern over these actions does not appear to have been great, to judge from comments about each of them in the extant record.

Defendants in *apographai* have remarkably little to say about the venality of their opponents in pressing these actions.[79] One of Lysias's clients only speaks vaguely of the benefit (*ōphelēsein*) his prosecutors seek (9.16) and this need not be taken as a reference to the percentage they will receive if successful; in fact, he emphasizes throughout his speech that they are motivated by enmity for him (9.7, 10, 17, 22).[80] Another client of Lysias protests: "What calls for the highest indignation is that the disposition of men in public life today is such that *rhētores* do not speak about what will be best for the city, but rather about what will bring profit [*kerdainein*] to them—and you give them your votes" (18.16). This complaint concerning the venality of *rhētores* is vague and generic, however, and the speaker does not link it to the financial reward available in the current suit. Yet another client of Lysias accuses his opponents of being sykophants (19.9) but does not claim that they are motivated by the hope of getting a financial reward from this type of action. Instead, he expresses concern, as litigants in actions not bearing financial incentives also do, that jurors may seek to enrich the city's treasury by ruling against him (19.11).[81]

Lofberg asserts in connection with *apographai*, "The jurors were likely to be suspicious of a prosecutor in a suit of this type unless he made special efforts to put himself in the right light before them."[82] The primary evidence to support this is Apollodorus's statement at the beginning of an *apographē* that he relinquishes in advance the reward that will fall to him if he is successful (Dem. 53.1–2). Apollodorus assumes that it will strengthen his credibility if he makes it clear that he has no financial interest whatsoever in the case and is pursuing it, as he explains, strictly out of a desire to take vengeance on his enemies. For Apollodorus this strategy makes good sense: he is very wealthy and the reward he forsakes is relatively small (a portion of the 250 drachmas in question), and his interest in any event is most likely, as he states, to take vengeance on his enemies. Apollodorus's strategic choice does not constitute proof, however, that it was *necessary* for a prosecutor to address his audience's concerns about the financial reward available in an *apographē*.[83] A volunteer prosecutor in another *apographē* makes no apology for his prosecution of such a case but rather takes credit for not being venal: he asserts there is a dearth of prosecutors in the present case because the defendant has bought them off with his ill-gotten gains (Lys. 29.1).

Scholars have frequently associated sykophancy with the legal procedure of *phasis*, because not only of a possible etymological link between *phasis* and sykophancy, but also of the assumed corrupting effect of the availability of a financial reward.[84] Too much has been made, however, of Aristophanes' comic presentation of *phasis* in *Acharnians* (425 B.C.). Dikaiopolis speaks of *phasis* as an instrument of sykophants against Megarian goods before the outbreak of the Peloponnesian War (517–22; cf. 541–43).[85] Later in the comedy, two sykophantic accusers attempt to use *phasis* against foreign traders in Dikaiopolis's private marketplace (818–29, 908–58). The objects of this satire are marketplace informers who receive some reward—although Aristophanes does not mention this—if successful in their suits;[86] they probably bring their complaints before a magistrate, who rules on the spot in cases involving small sums (presumably most cases would be of this sort),[87] and if he rules against the accused, sells off his goods (cf. 517–22) and gives a portion of the proceeds to the person initiating the *phasis*. Although some might conclude from these episodes that Aristophanes regards *phasis* as a legal action that is abused more than others, he focuses on this procedure because *phasis* is the legal charge most closely associated with the marketplace, which figures so prominently in this comedy. That sykophancy also extends beyond the marketplace and is not limited to abuse of *phasis* is clear in Dikaiopolis's description of the sykophant-vessel as a lampholder for "bringing to light charges against magistrates undergoing their scrutinies" (*phainein hupeuthunous*) (938).[88] Moreover, just a year later in *Knights*, Aristophanes mentions *phasis* (300–302) as but one of many legal actions susceptible to abuse, and in his sykophant scenes in *Birds* and *Wealth, phasis* does not figure at all as a tool of sykophants.

Similarly, in forensic oratory *phasis* appears as an action that is subject to abuse, but not necessarily more than other actions are. For example, Epichares accuses Theocrines of having brought a *phasis* against a ship owned by a certain Micon, only to have dropped the suit (Dem. 58.5–13; cf. Isoc. 17.42). He asserts that Theocrines has thus violated the law requiring a prosecutor to pursue a *graphē* or *phasis* once it is filed, and since he probably dropped the suit because it was false, he has also violated another law providing for punishment of those bringing sykophantic charges against merchants and shipowners (58.10–13). Epichares makes it clear, however, that he does not regard the procedure of *phasis* as itself suspect:

> For what man would have desisted from an honest course of action by which he would have received the share of the money allowed by law, and have chosen instead to make a trifling gain by a compromise and thus render himself subject to these laws, when, as I said just now, he might have received half the sum involved in the *phasis*? No one would have done so, men of the jury, unless he knew that he was bringing a sykophantic suit. (58.13)

Epichares thus objects not to the honest pursuit of a financial reward through *phasis* but rather to the leveling of a false suit, which is dropped as soon as blackmail is paid.

There is little evidence concerning the use, let alone abuse, of the *graphai* that rewarded prosecutors for enforcing the laws concerning "mixed" marriages. As Osborne notes, Demosthenes 59: *Against Neaira* provides the sole example of a prosecution against a foreigner married to an Athenian, and enmity rather than pursuit of a financial reward appears to drive the prosecutors; and the same speech provides the only reference to a prosecution of a man for betrothing a noncitizen to an Athenian (59.53).[89] That so little appears concerning these suits in the ancient record may mean that they were uncommon and the measures largely symbolic expressions of the importance of keeping the Athenian stock "pure." In any event, one may doubt that the financial incentive was a decisive consideration for potential prosecutors: apparently Athenians brought *graphai xenias* that did not bear financial rewards with some frequency[90] and were ready, without a financial bonus, to volunteer the names of alleged noncitizens when the demes revised their citizen rolls in 346/5 B.C.[91]

Further evidence that Athenians did not view actions with financial rewards as especially susceptible to abuse can be found in the way that litigants list these and other public actions together indiscriminately as sykophantic tools.[92] That *apographai* and *phaseis* appear on such lists is unremarkable, since they were commonly used and thus like other actions also subject to abuse. In only one passage concerning legal abuse, in fact, are *apographai* and *phaseis* mentioned together, and here as part of a more general argument protesting abuse of *eisangelia* in the current case (Hyp. 4.32–35).

There is no reason to believe that a certain class of persons abused suits bearing financial rewards. Aristophanes' presentation of marketplace informers, viewed in isolation, might be taken as evidence that certain men "specialized" in pursuing *phasis*. Evidence from the orators, however, suggests that *phasis* was not a legal procedure monopolized by any particular group of persons, but rather one of many legal instruments available to a variety of persons, including *rhētores* (Aristogeiton: Dem. 25.78; Theocrines: Dem. 58.45; Stephanus: Dem. 59.43).

If Athenians were not especially suspicious of prosecutors bringing actions bearing financial rewards, how can this be explained? First, Athenians were accustomed to the use of financial incentives to elicit prosecutions and therefore were no doubt more comfortable than moderns with this.[93] Athenians also used financial incentives to encourage individuals with knowledge of crimes to step forward as informers (*mēnutai*), although these persons (sometimes slaves) were not required to carry through with a prosecution.[94] Second, because prosecutors of actions bearing financial rewards also risked a thousand-drachma fine and *atimia* if they failed to receive one-fifth of the votes, the possible reward may have been viewed in such cases as a reasonable counterbalance to the risks involved.[95] Third, Athenians were aware that an individual could profit from *any* kind of action if he used the threat of it to blackmail someone. At least the profit to be had from actions bearing financial rewards was allowed by law and prosecutors' motivations were subject to public scrutiny in the course of adjudication. These considerations made Athenians relatively comfortable with such actions, and they did little therefore to limit them.[96]

CONCERNS ABOUT VOLUNTEER PROSECUTORS

The foregoing survey suggests that Athenian concerns about the abuse of public actions were not suit-specific. The public's concerns, in fact, centered more on the person of the volunteer prosecutor than the particular type of action brought. Volunteer prosecutors of all types of actions, therefore, were under considerable pressure to justify their pursuit of a public suit.

Numerous tensions surrounded the volunteer prosecutor's role. First, although volunteer prosecution was open to "anyone who wished," in practice few had the resources and abilities to undertake a public action.[97] If volunteer prosecution was a foundation of the democracy, volunteer prosecutors were living proof of the limits of democratic egalitarianism.[98] The volunteer prosecutor was therefore in a delicate position as he addressed popular juries dominated by persons who were unable to play this prominent public role.[99] Second, volunteer prosecutors stepped into exceptionally active and aggressive public roles when they brought public actions, since these required extended and extensive effort. The public naturally wondered what kind of person, driven by what motivations, would choose to undertake this role.

Two intriguing passages, one from forensic oratory, one from the comic stage, address directly the public's misgivings concerning volunteer prosecutors. Near the opening of his *eisangelia* against Leocrates for treason (330 B.C.), Lycurgus complains of the public's prejudice against volunteer prosecutors like himself:

> Gentlemen, I would wish that, since it is beneficial to the city that there are men who bring lawbreakers to judgment here, the people would view this as a benevolent [*philanthrōpon*] activity. In fact, the opposite is true: anyone who takes on himself personal risk [*ton idiai kinduneuonta*] and incurs enmity [of defendants] on behalf of the public [*koinōn*], appears [to his fellow citizens] to be fond not of the city [*philopolin*], but of lawsuits [*philopragmona*]. This is neither just nor advantageous to the city. For three things in particular guard and preserve the democracy and the city's prosperity: first, the system [*taxis*] of laws; second, the vote of jurors; and third, the method of prosecution [*krisis*] that hands over crimes to them. The law exists to lay down in advance what must not be done, the accuser to report [*mēnuein*] those who are subject to penalty under the laws, and the juror to punish all who have been exposed by these two. Thus neither the law nor the vote of the jurors has any strength without someone to hand over offenders to them. (1.3–5)

This defense of volunteer prosecutors is interesting both for the concerns it acknowledges and for those it suppresses.

Lycurgus openly acknowledges that his audience may look on the volunteer prosecutor as overly active. He challenges this perception first by emphasizing the importance of the volunteer prosecutor's activities to the democracy and then, more subtly, by downplaying the aggressiveness of his role. Lycurgus speaks in abstract terms of "the method of prosecution" that brings forward offenders, as if the volunteer prosecutor is simply part of a larger process. He further minimizes the active role of the volunteer prosecutor when he depicts him as merely a reporter (*mēnuein*; cf. 1.146; Dem. 26.22) of offenses: this conflates the role of an informer (*mēnutēs*), who simply provides information against a wrongdoer, with the more active role of a volunteer prosecutor, who not only reports a crime, but prosecutes it in his own person. Finally, Lycurgus downplays the active and independent role of the prosecutor by merging his role with that of the laws: jurors judge offenders who have been exposed by both the laws and the prosecutor.

One might assume from Lycurgus's justification of his role that the public's suspicions of volunteer prosecutors arise primarily in connection with their apparent meddlesomeness and aggression; however, the public also suspected volunteer prosecutors of seeking to gain financially or politically from their suits. Lycurgus avoids these concerns entirely: he emphasizes that volunteer prosecution is solely a matter of private risk, without acknowledging that it can simultaneously be a source of private benefit.

Aristophanes likewise addresses the problematic status of the volunteer prosecutor in his sykophant scene in *Wealth* (388 B.C.). Dikaios cross-examines a blustering sykophant, who claims to be patriotic (*philopolis*) (900):

> *Dikaios:* Are you a good and patriotic citizen?
> *Sykophant:* As no other man.
> *Dikaios:* All right, answer a few questions for me.
> *Sykophant:* Go ahead.
> *Dikaios:* Are you a farmer?
> *Sykophant:* Do you think I'm so crazy?
> *Dikaios:* A trader?
> *Sykophant:* Yes, at least I pretend to be, whenever it suits me.[100]
> *Dikaios:* What do you do then? Did you learn some trade?

Sykophant: By Zeus, no.

Dikaios: How then have you been making a living, if, as you say, you do nothing?[101]

Sykophant: I am the superintendant [*epimelētēs*] of all affairs, public and private.

Dikaios: You? How's that?

Sykophant: I volunteer.[102]

Dikaios: But how could you be a good citizen, you thief, when you're hated for getting involved in what is no concern of yours?

Sykophant: You simpleton. Isn't it my concern to be the benefactor [*euergetein*] of my own city as best I can?

Dikaios: Is meddling in others' affairs [*to polupragmonein*] the same as being a benefactor?

Sykophant: Coming to the rescue of the established laws certainly is, and not permitting anyone to transgress them.

Dikaios: Is it not for that reason that the city puts jurors in office?

Sykophant: But who does the prosecuting?

Dikaios: Any volunteer.

Sykophant: Precisely, and, as I said, I am that person, and so the affairs of the city have fallen upon me.

Dikaios: By Zeus, if that is so, then the city has a base protector [*prostatēn*]. But couldn't you volunteer for something else, namely, to keep quiet and live an idle life?

Sykophant: You speak of a sheep's life, if there is no way to pass time.

Dikaios: Would you not change your ways?

Sykophant: Not even if you should give me Wealth himself and all the silphium in Libya as well.

(901–25)

Although MacDowell suggests that Aristophanes' attitude toward sykophants has mellowed by the time of *Wealth* since he allows the sykophant here, unlike those in his earlier plays, to defend himself at length,[103] the broader context makes it clear that Aristophanes' antipathy for sykophants has not changed. This sykophant is a member of a class hated by all Hellenes (878), a creature whose bite is to be shunned by charms (885), a leveler of false charges (864–65, 945–50), and obsessed with money (870–95) despite his assertion to the contrary in the passage above. Like other Aristophanic sykophants, he is therefore driven from the stage by gleeful assailants (see Chapter 2).

This scene illustrates how easily a glib sykophant can pose as a legitimate volunteer prosecutor. Like Lycurgus, this sykophant insists that he is a friend of the city (*philopolis*), not meddlesome (*polupragmōn*), and that without volunteer prosecutors like himself the laws would not be enforced and jurors would not hear cases. While Aristophanes stops short of a direct attack on the institution of volunteer prosecution,[104] his treatment suggests that there is something peculiar about this "job" for which anyone can volunteer.[105] The volunteer prosecutor's "profession" does not fall within recognized social categories—farming, trading, or crafting—and his public role defies easy categorization. When the sykophant pompously asserts he is "the superintendant [*epimelētēs*] of all affairs, public and private," he appropriates a title frequently applied to Athenian magistrates,[106] although as a volunteer he holds no formal office. Later, the sykophant suggests that he is the city's benefactor (*euergetēs*): while this designation, unlike *epimelētēs*, conveys the voluntary quality of his activity, it is an honorific better applied perhaps to public benefactors who spend money lavishly on the city than to volunteer prosecutors, who stand to profit from their activities.[107] Finally, Dikaios offers his own designation for the sykophant: he perverts the legitimate role of the city's protector (*prostatēs*) (cf. *Pax* 684), a title sometimes applied to prominent politicians.[108] Although the search for a proper designation for volunteer prosecutors takes a comic form here, the difficulty in finding an appropriate label reflects the inherently problematic and complex nature of the volunteer prosecutor's role.

While direct discussion of the problematic role of the volunteer prosecutor is uncommon in the ancient sources, excellent testimony to the public's concerns can be found in the way volunteer prosecutors seek to justify their roles before jurors. In general, prosecutors go out of their way to anticipate their opponents' objections to their motives. A speaker supporting an indictment of the younger Alcibiades for desertion appears initially to violate this norm when he opens his speech, "I do not believe, gentlemen of the jury, that you desire to hear any justification from those who have volunteered to prosecute Alcibiades" (Lys. 14.1). This turns out to be, however, a rhetorical introduction to the speaker's explanation of the public and private grounds for his participation in the prosecution (14.1–2).

Volunteer prosecutors tend to justify their roles by making some combination of the following claims:

1. I am a self-sacrificing public servant.
2. I am not meddlesome.
3. I am not interested in financial profit.
4. My opponent is a personal enemy; or alternatively
5. My opponent is *not* a personal enemy.

Let us consider each of these.

Patriotism

Volunteer prosecutors regularly assert that they are patriotic citizens (Lyc. 1.3; Dem. 23.190) who have come to rescue/assist (*boēthein*) the city and its laws (Lys. 22.3; Dem. 24.8; Aesch. 1.2).[109] In equating the city and its laws with helpless victims in need of legal assistance from volunteers, they adapt the ideal of third-party prosecution on behalf of weak individuals to their defense of the entire city. Volunteer prosecutors stress that in assisting the city in this way, they face considerable dangers (*kindunoi*): they risk not only the statutory penalties falling on unsuccessful prosecutors (Dem. 24.3; 53.1; Lyc. 1.3),[110] but also the enmity of their opponents, who may seek vengeance on them through lawsuits or other means (Dem. 23.1; 58.59–60; Lyc. 1.3; cf. Ant. 6.35).[111]

When volunteer prosecutors assert that they are risking great dangers for the benefit of the city, they link themselves to citizens risking their lives for the city on the battlefield.[112] Some prosecutors develop this connection explicitly. Epichares, for example, attributes to the frequent prosecutor, Theocrines, the boast that he has been "placed in the ranks" (*tetachthai*) against proposers of illegal decrees and "is on guard" (*phulattei*) against them (Dem. 58.45–46; cf. 58.34). A publicly appointed *sunēgoros* concludes his speech with the boast, "I have not deserted the city" (Din. 1.114). Aeschines asserts that his opponents have engaged in preparation (*paraskeuē*)[113] and are marshaled up in battle-array (*parataxis*) against the current suit (3.1), and invites jurors to take the proper side in this legal war: "Just as each of you would be ashamed to desert the rank [*taxin*] assigned him in war, so now you should be ashamed to desert the rank assigned you by the laws, sentinels [*phulakes*] of the democracy this day" (3.7). Similarly, Lycurgus groups together jurors, prosecutors, and the laws, as the three things that together "guard [*diaphulattei*] and preserve [*diasōizei*] the democracy" (1.3).[114] The claim of prosecutors, noted earlier, that they are coming to rescue (*boēthein*) the city also has a military ring to it.[115] These analogies between military service and volunteer prosecution not only glorify the prosecutor, but also provide him with a ready explanation for his voluntarism: he is "compelled" to serve the city, just as a soldier is in time of war.

The idea that a volunteer prosecutor is a guard of the democracy sometimes takes the form of the more humble image that he is a watchdog of the people (*kuōn tou dēmou*). This commonplace is well attested thanks to satirical comment on it. Aristophanes frequently mocks Cleon for pretending to be the people's watchdog while using volunteer prosecution for his own ends.[116] Nearly a century later, one of Aristogeiton's enemies attacks him on the grounds that while his friends claim he is a watchdog of the people he devours those whom he pretends to guard (*phulattein*) (Dem. 25.40). Another enemy of Aristogeiton says of him: "No one would use a sorry mongrel to guard a flock; yet some people say that, to keep watch on those who administer the state, one ought to employ any stray volunteers—who pretend to detect offenders, though they themselves need the most careful watching" (Dem. 26.22). Although the claim to be the people's watchdog was subject to mockery, its appearance even in the late fourth century in these passages (cf. Thphr. *Char.* 29.4a; Plu. *Dem.* 23.5) suggests that prosecutors continued to cast themselves in this role.

The image of the volunteer prosecutor as the city's watchdog was appealing in part because this depicted him in a protective, yet subservient, role as a loyal servant of the people. This might be more palatable to a popular audience than, for example, the image of the volunteer prosecutor as a superior patron (*prostatēs*).[117] Between these images of inferiority and superiority respectively, however, lay a middle ground: prosecutors could cast themselves as friends of the people, fulfilling the obligation of *philia* by assisting in litigation. Fifth-century politicians, no doubt largely on the basis of their activities as volunteer prosecutors, regularly claimed to be friends of the city (*philopoleis*) or of the people (*philodēmoi*).[118] In the fourth century too volunteer prosecutors draw on such images: Lycurgus casts himself as *philopolis* (1.3; cf. Ar. *Pl.* 900–901), and Epichares ridicules Theocrines' claim that "he loves you [the demos] next after his own relatives [*oikeious*]" (Dem. 58.30).[119]

Although some of these claims of patriotism were so banal as to draw satirical comment, in general prosecutors could not dispense with them entirely. As so often in public political discourse, banality is no obstacle to invoking a tried and proven phrase or image. It was not enough, however, for a volunteer prosecutor to justify himself on patriotic grounds; rather, he had to defend himself, explicitly or implicitly, from negative perceptions of his motivations.

Overactivity and Meddling

While volunteer prosecutors seek praise for their active service to the city, their opponents characterize this voluntarism hostilely as meddlesome overactivity. As Lysias's oligarchic client sourly puts it, the prosecutors at his *dokimasia* "neglect their own private affairs [*oikeiōn*] and attend [*epimelontai*] to those of others" (25.1).[120] Lycurgus addresses such concerns directly and on an abstract level when he argues that volunteer prosecution is a public service, not meddling (1.3; cf. Ar. *Pl.* 913–15). Most prosecutors, however, approach these concerns more obliquely and seek to show how they conform more or less to the social ideal of not being overly or unnecessarily active in the courts.

One tack a volunteer prosecutor could take is to anticipate charges of excessive zeal by asserting that he was an *apragmōn*. While some prosecutors go so far as to assert that they have never appeared in a lawsuit (Lys. 12.3; cf. Dem. 24.6), others make more limited claims concerning their inexperience. Aeschines, for example, asserts that he has never brought a *graphē* or prosecuted at the *euthunai* of an officeholder (1.1; cf. 2.182), but stops short of claiming that he has no experience at all in public litigation as a prosecutor of other types of public actions,[121] or as a supporting advocate (*sunēgoros*) in public suits brought in the names of others.

What could make an otherwise peaceful man bring a public prosecution? Litigants assert that they have been "forced" to act as volunteer prosecutors, for example, because they are outraged at the spectacle of public enemies harming the city. Euthycles thus explains how his sense of shame at a wrong done to the city induced him to indict Aristocrates for proposing an illegal decree:

> At present many of us—who are not clever at speaking, perhaps, and yet are better men than the clever speakers—are fearful of addressing you and therefore do not think even of examining any public question. You may be sure that I for one—I swear by all the gods—would have been reluctant to bring this indictment, if I had not thought it entirely shameful that at this time, when I see people engaged in a project disadvantageous to our city, I should hold my peace and remain silent—I who, on a former occasion, when I sailed for the Hellespont as trierarch, spoke out and prosecuted certain men who, in my opinion, were doing you wrong. (Dem. 23.5)

The final lines make one wonder just how inexperienced Euthycles is, since on at least one previous occasion indignation at a public wrong prompted him to act as volunteer prosecutor.[122] Other prosecutors claim that when the person harming the city is also their personal enemy, it would be doubly shameful not to seek vengeance. Some go so far as to chastise others who lack the conviction and courage to step forward: "While the rest kept quiet, I rose and accused these men" (Lys. 22.3); "Everybody urges us on . . . yet no one . . . declares that he is ready to incur the open enmity of Theocrines. Thus with certain people a sense of what is right is not strong enough to lead them to speak out freely" (Dem. 58.59).

A prosecutor could also attempt to dispel the impression that he was meddlesome by arguing that he was carrying out the obligations of a state office. This defense was available, for example, to individuals who had been selected by the Athenian people to serve as public prosecutors (*sunēgoroi*) in connection with the regular *euthunai* or in special situations.[123] A *sunēgoros* selected for prosecution in connection with the Harpalus affair exploits the fact that the people had chosen him precisely for this task by proclaiming to jurors that he is "ashamed you need us to encourage and goad you on" (Din. 3.15). Even *sunēgoroi*, however, could be suspected of excessive zeal in litigating (Ar. *Ach.* 685; *Eq.* 1359–63; cf. fr. 205; Dem. 20.152): individuals could put themselves forward for this office, and some no doubt did so to take advantage of the fact that *sunēgoroi*, as publicly appointed prosecutors, were not liable to the normal statutory penalties for unsuccessful prosecution (cf. Philem. Jun. fr. 3). When Demosthenes serves as a public *sunēgoros* against Aristogeiton, he therefore goes out of his way to dispel concerns over his motives:

> When I saw you in the Assembly selecting and appointing me as a prosecutor of this man, I was troubled and, by Zeus and all the gods, I did not wish it. For I was aware that he who plays such a part in your courts suffers for it in the end, not perhaps so as to feel it at once, but if he undertakes many such tasks and persists in so doing, he will soon become known for this. Nonetheless, I thought it necessary to obey your wishes. (25.13)

Although Demosthenes asserts that he became a *sunēgoros* reluctantly, this is doubtful: this office gave him an excellent opportunity to prosecute a political enemy, who had indicted him seven times and twice accused him at his *euthunai* (25.37).[124]

While a public *sunēgoros* could justify his prosecution as a formal obligation of office, other officeholders, including councilmembers, could argue that they were obliged morally, if not legally, by their positions to serve as volunteer prosecutors. The prosecutor of Philo at his *dokimasia* before the Council,[125] for example, asserts that his oath as councilmember requires him to expose unsuitable candidates (Lys. 31.2). Another councilmember justifies his prosecution of certain grain dealers before a popular court by arguing that it would be shameful to abandon the charge he initiated in the Council (Lys. 22.4).[126] Despite such claims of diligence in carrying out the duties of a councilmember, many prosecutors in such cases were probably also active as prosecutors when not members of the Council: a client of Antiphon, for example, clearly brought prosecutions before he joined the Council (6.12, 35), as well as after (6.49–50).[127]

Likewise, when Demosthenes prosecutes his fellow ambassador, Aeschines, at his *euthunai* for accepting bribes from Philip, he justifies his prosecution as a necessary extension of his own service as ambassador. Demosthenes defends himself against Aeschines' objection that he is denouncing one of his own colleagues by asserting that he must prosecute, since otherwise he may be mistaken for Aeschines' accomplice (19.188; cf. 19.223). Demosthenes argues, moreover, that he is in a better position than others to prosecute Aeschines, since as a fellow ambassador he has "the most accurate knowledge" of his offenses (19.257).

If a *rhētōr* happened to hold a state office, as Demosthenes did when he prosecuted Aeschines and Aristogeiton, he could justify his public suit as an obligation of his official position. Because *rhētores* were active as prosecutors even when they were not officeholders, however, they often had to rely on the public's recognition that, while it was good and proper that private persons (*idiōtai*) live quiet lives (cf. Dem. 18.308), the city relied on *rhētores* to be active in and out of the courts.[128] Indeed, while average citizens were under no obligation to volunteer to prosecute, persons in public life could be chastised for not acting in this capacity (Dem. 24.173). And as long as *rhētores* were active in prosecuting others prominent in public life and not private citizens,[129] they could reasonably expect their fellow citizens to judge their exceptional activity by its own standard.

Avarice and Venality

A generic charge against volunteer prosecutors is that they seek to enrich themselves through litigation or the threat of it and "live off sykophancy."[130] Some volunteer prosecutors confront such concerns directly. For example, they assert that they are "above money" (Dem. 58.29; cf. Th. 2.60.5), or point out that they did not succumb to their opponents' efforts to buy off the prosecution (Lys. 27.14–15; 30.34–35; 31.32; cf. 29.1). They emphasize that, far from expecting any financial gain, they are risking their own financial resources for the city since, if unsuccessful, they may be liable to the statutory fine of a thousand drachmas (Dem. 24.3; 53.1–2). Moreover, since charges of venality were nearly impossible to prove, prosecutors could argue on the basis of likelihood that they were not seeking financial gain. Thus, for example, Demosthenes preempts Aeschines' charge that he brought suit against his fellow ambassadors in order to blackmail them, by asserting that he had far more to gain by accepting Philip's bribes when he was ambassador than by blackmailing his fellow ambassadors for a mere portion of the bribes they had received (19.222).

A prosecutor's ability to convince jurors that he was not venal, however, was very much linked to his ability to persuade them that he was driven by other, honorable motivations. If he could persuade jurors that he was a self-sacrificing patriot or a genuine friend of the city, he might convince them that he was not acting in pursuit of base gain.[131] Many prosecutors seek to show that they are personal enemies of their opponents and are thus pursuing vengeance rather than financial profit. The thinking behind this curious (from a modern perspective) form of self-presentation requires some explanation.

Enmity: Pursuing Personal and Collective Vengeance

Athenian jurors appear to have been cynical enough about human motivations to assume that personal interests of some kind were present when an individual stepped forward in the exceptional role of volunteer prosecutor. When volunteer prosecutors draw attention to their enmity with their opponents, they provide jurors with a plausible explanation for their voluntarism and one that the public could be expected to view in a largely positive way.[132] The pursuit of vengeance (*timōria*) against an enemy was a matter of honor for Athenian men, and the public was sympathetic to this as long as it was carried out within certain parameters: while a violent physical assault on a personal enemy was likely to be perceived as a transgression of community norms and laws, vengeance through a lawsuit was well within the bounds of socially acceptable retaliation.[133]

At the same time, the volunteer prosecutor who declared that he was seeking personal vengeance could hope to persuade jurors that he was not acting from less honorable motivations. If a prosecutor could convince jurors that the defendant was his personal enemy, he had an immediate defense not only against the charge of venality—he was seeking vengeance, not money—but also against the charge of meddling, since it was certainly a man's business to punish his enemies (cf. Lys. 1.15–16). This popular justification of voluntarism assumes that there is something so straightforward and all-consuming in a man's pursuit of vengeance against a personal enemy as to leave no room for corrupting influences.

Consider how Theomnestus explains why he is prosecuting Neaira for masquerading as a citizen (Dem. 59). Although he stands to win a financial reward if successful in his prosecution, which Apollodorus supports as *sunēgoros*, he does not directly address the jurors' possible concerns about this, but rather focuses attention on the role of personal enmity in the prosecution. Theomnestus explains that he has every reason to regard Neaira's husband Stephanus as a personal enemy (59.1–14), and that he seeks a fitting retribution from Stephanus through this lawsuit (59.13): just as Stephanus attempted to drive Apollodorus from the city through litigation (cf. 59.9) and thus deprive Theomnestus of his relative, so now Theomnestus seeks to prove Neaira is an alien and thus deprive Stephanus of her company. One may infer that because he seeks this vengeance in the same coin (cf. 59.8), any financial reward he may win is incidental.

As a practical matter, however, the pursuit of private vengeance and the defense of public interests could hardly be in perfect accord with one another. Jurors may well have noticed, for example, how in some cases prosecutors lost sight of the public good as they spoke at length of their personal enmities (e.g., Dem. 53.4–18). It was therefore advantageous to prosecutors to reassure their audiences of the compatibility of the private and public dimensions of their suits. For example, when Aeschines pursues his personal enemy Timarchus through a public action, he offers this optimistic view of such prosecutions: "What is so frequently said of public suits is no mistake, namely, that very often private enmities correct public abuses" (1.2; cf. Dem. 22.1–3; 24.8). Another prosecutor however, finds it prudent to subordinate his private interests to public ones: he brought his suit because he had been deeply wronged by the defendant and, furthermore, because he saw that the people "had been wronged still more deeply" (Ant. fr. V.1 Gernet).

Perhaps the most brilliant portrayal of the compatibility of the pursuit of private vengeance and the protection of public interests is found in Lysias's prosecution at a special *euthunai* of Eratosthenes,[134] who had been one of the notorious Thirty in 404/3 B.C:

> It seems to me that our positions will be the reverse of what they were in former times: for previously the prosecutors had to explain their enmity toward the defendants, but in the present case one must inquire of the defendants as to the source of their enmity toward the city in committing such audacious offenses against it. It is not, indeed, from any lack of private enmity and suffering that I make these remarks, but because of the abundant reasons that all of us have for anger on personal or public grounds. (12.2)

Lysias deftly turns on its head the convention that a volunteer prosecutor should explain the source of his personal enmity with the defendant, when he asserts that his opponent in fact should explain *his* enmity toward the whole community. Despite this initial shift of the burden of justification to his opponent, however, Lysias goes on to invoke, and build upon, the normal convention. Lysias asserts that he has private grounds for hating the defendant (Eratosthenes was responsible for his brother's death during the Thirty's reign of terror: 12.16–34), and that *everyone* has private or public grounds for enmity against Eratosthenes. Thus, according to Lysias, private and public interests in punishing Eratosthenes are inseparable (cf. Lys. 13.1–3; 14.1–2).[135]

The frequency with which prosecutors justify their voluntarism on the grounds of personal enmity leaves no doubt that jurors found this compelling as an explanation of why an individual would take on a public action. Jurors probably also found this conceptualization of prosecution on behalf of the city appealing: just as private individuals pursued vengeance against their personal enemies through litigation, so too the personified city, aided by persons pursuing private vengeance, could be envisioned as taking vengeance on its enemies through public prosecutions. In any event, the justification of volunteer prosecution in these terms was so popular that in some cases prosecutors who were not actually enemies of a defendant may have attempted to cast their prosecutions in these terms (cf. Lys. 24.2), and in other cases those seeking to prosecute an individual may have sought out his private enemies and induced them to bring suit in their names so as to exploit the public's sympathetic attitude toward such prosecutions.[136]

Enmity: Envy and Rivalry

Although prosecutors routinely justify their voluntarism on the grounds of personal enmity, defendants could argue that they were on trial solely because their enemies were seeking to harm them out of envy, anger, or spite.[137] It is on this basis, for example, that Demosthenes attacks Aeschines for prosecuting Ctesiphon, who had proposed that the people honor Demosthenes with a crown and vote of thanks. He casts Aeschines as a sykophant (18.112, 118, 121) who uses the courts to air his personal abuse (*loidoria*) (18.123) and prosecutes out of "private enmity, envy, and pettiness" (18.279; cf. 18.13, 121). Demosthenes insists, however, that "an honorable citizen should never expect a jury empaneled in the public service to bolster up his own anger or enmity or other passions, and he will not go to court to gratify these" (18.278; cf. 18.123). He at least would never bring a false charge against Aeschines out of enmity or contentiousness (18.141; cf. 18.143), notwithstanding Aeschines' claims to the contrary (18.283).

Some volunteer prosecutors attempt to preempt such attacks on their motivations by denying that enmity has any role in their prosecutions. For example, Lycurgus asserts in his prosecution of Leocrates:

> It was not out of any enmity or contentiousness (*philonikian*) that I undertook this suit . . . A just citizen will not let private enmity induce him to bring a public prosecution against one who does the state no harm. On the contrary, it is those who break his country's laws whom he will look on as his personal enemies; offenses that affect the public will, in his eyes, offer public grounds for enmity toward offenders. (1.5–6)

Lycurgus stops short, however, of condemning private enmity categorically as a motivation for volunteer prosecution. He states only that one should not bring a *false* public prosecution out of private enmity, not that public prosecution arising in connection with enmity is necessarily corrupt.

When Euthycles prosecutes Aristocrates (Dem. 23), he likewise emphasizes that he is not driven by enmity. He opens his speech: "Men of Athens, let no one among you believe that I have come here to prosecute Aristocrates out of private enmity, or that I am thrusting myself so eagerly into a quarrel with him because I have detected some small and trivial error" (23.1). Later, he elaborates on the potentially corrupting effect of enmity on a volunteer prosecutor, noting that "it is the act of one who has suffered some private wrong or of a sykophant to speak against grants with which the recipient . . . could do the city no serious harm, whereas it is the act of a good and patriotic citizen to oppose proposals devised very much to the city's detriment" (23.190). Euthycles goes somewhat further than Lycurgus in his criticism of enmity as a motivation: whereas Lycurgus asserts that it is wrong to bring a false public prosecution out of personal enmity, Euthycles suggests that it is improper to bring an insignificant public charge against a personal enemy, even if it is true. Like Lycurgus, however, Euthycles stops short of a categorical condemnation of public prosecutions prompted by personal enmity: as long as the charge is true *and* not trifling, one may infer, it is acceptable for a private enemy to lodge it.[138]

The limited nature of the criticisms that Lycurgus and Euthycles level against public prosecutions driven by enmity is significant. Both recognize the prevalence of the practice and the public's general acceptance of it, and they seek therefore not so much to condemn it as to reap advantage from their exceptional roles as disinterested parties. This stance was probably especially popular among *rhētores* acting as volunteer prosecutors: while they could sometimes justify their prosecutions on the grounds that their opponents were enemies, they often prosecuted persons who were not personal enemies, and in such cases they could vaunt themselves as objective protectors of the city's best interests.

One may reasonably suspect that a prosecutor's assessment of whether enmity is a proper or improper motivation depends on his personal relationship with the defendant. On the one hand, prosecutors bringing public suits against personal enemies were well advised to make a virtue of this, and by acknowledging this openly, to preempt the possibly damaging disclosure of it later by an opponent, who might assert that this concealed motivation corrupted the prosecution.[139] On the other hand, prosecutors bringing public suits against strangers or mere acquaintances could maintain that this was evidence of their objectivity and interest solely in serving the state. As far as we know, these two positions were available to prosecutors throughout the history of the democracy: litigants did not, for example, gradually abandon the former for the latter in the face of growing public suspicion of enmity as a motivation for public prosecution. It was therefore up to a prosecutor to adopt and exploit whichever stance best fit his circumstances.

This chapter has argued, first, that although volunteer prosecutors were permitted to bring public actions on behalf of wronged individuals, including themselves, in practice Athenian assumptions and prejudices concerning the proper use of public actions discouraged such prosecutions. Second, even public actions that were commonly pursued, namely, those on behalf of the city, gave rise to a variety of concerns among Athenians. These concerns, however, appear to have centered not so much on the type of action used, since any action was susceptible to abuse, as on the motivations of the individuals volunteering as prosecutors. Good evidence of the level and scope of the public's concerns is found in the extensive self-justification in which volunteer prosecutors engaged to assure their audiences of their legitimate intentions. Indeed, when prosecutors offered defenses of their voluntarism, jurors could judge them along with the defendants actually on trial and, by issuing verdicts against prosecutors who seemed overzealous or corrupt, police the city's watchdogs.

Five

Private Quarrels and Public Disputes: Quarrelsomeness and Community Ideals

According to the scholia to Aristophanes,

> Once at Athens a man hired a donkey after some bargaining with its driver, just to carry a load to Megara. When they had agreed on these terms, they placed the freight upon him and set out. At midday when the summer heat beat down upon them and they could find no shelter, the owner of the freight lifted it off the donkey and used the donkey to shade himself. At this the driver launched into battle, declaring that he had hired out his donkey to carry freight, *not* to provide shade; to which the other replied that he had hired it to use as he wished. They took this quarrel about nothing into court.[1]

While Athenians agreed that one should not pursue a quarrel over "the shadow of an ass" to court,[2] there was no clear consensus as to precisely when an individual was justified in turning a private dispute into a public lawsuit. This was true, in no small part, because Athenians were ambivalent toward legal conflict: while litigation was a regular feature of civic life and its pursuit could be construed as consistent with manly ideals, it also represented a breach of social peace and a challenge to the cooperative ideals upon which communal life was based.[3]

Excellent testimony to the public's ambivalence toward the pursuit of litigation is found in the way Athenian litigants, especially those involved in private actions,[4] maneuver in their speeches between conflicting societal expectations of manly behavior and of cooperation. While litigants are not apologetic about defending their manly honor through lawsuits, they are at pains to reassure jurors that they are not in the least quarrelsome or contentious. In particular, litigants seek to reconcile the breach of social relations that their suits so often involve with social ideals about how those relations should function. Although litigants no doubt invoke cooperative ideals so as to win their suits, their appeals to these before large audiences constitute an ongoing public discourse concerning the nature of the Athenian community. Indeed, while the popular courts made it possible for Athenians to engage in litigation at a level unparalleled in the Greek world, they also gave Athenians a public forum for articulating and addressing societal concerns over dispute and conflict to an extent unmatched by other city-states.

Aggression, Cooperation, and Litigation

Athenian litigants found themselves in an awkward situation. On the one hand, Athenians expected a man not to shrink back from the aggression of others but to avenge, in or out of court, slights to himself and his dependents. On the other hand, Athenians viewed the unprovoked initiation of aggression or the unnecessary escalation of a conflict into a lawsuit as ugly manifestions of quarrelsomeness and contentiousness. Let us consider this tension and its impact on the posturing of litigants.

Athenians shared with other Greeks the basic assumption that when a man suffered at the hands of another, he should pursue vengeance (*timōria*) in his own person not only to right the wrong, but also to defend his reputation.[5] Two passages illustrate the social pressures on men to measure up to this basic standard of manly behavior by pursuing litigation.

Plato's Socrates, in his portrayal of the timocratic youth, explains to Adeimantus how social expectations might induce a youth to reject the example of his father, who shuns lawsuits and meddling (R. 549c2–6):

> "[The boy's mother] tells him that his father is unmanly [*anandros*] and too slack, and includes all the other complaints with which women nag in such cases."
>
> "Many indeed," said Adeimantus, "and others just like these."
>
> "You are aware, then," said I, "that even the houseslaves of such men say similar things in secret to the sons—ostensibly out of kindness, and if they observe a debtor or any other offender whom the father does not prosecute, they urge the boy to take vengeance on all such persons when he becomes a man and thus to prove himself more of a man than his father; and when the lad goes out he hears and sees the same sort of thing." (549d6–550a2)

This youth, spurred on by a pushy mother, houseslaves, and others in the community, attempts to distinguish himself from his unmanly father, and therefore becomes contentious (*philonikos*) and overly eager for honor (*philotimos*) (550b6–7). Although Plato identifies timocracy with Sparta (545a2–3), his portrayal of the sociology of legal behavior is almost certainly inspired by his native Athens, where litigation was a real option—as it was not for the most part in Sparta—for those pursuing honor.

That the pressures Plato condemns were real ones for Athenian men is confirmed in forensic contexts. Consider, for example, how Theomnestus characterizes the social pressures on him to prosecute Neaira:

> People came to me in private from all sides exhorting me to take vengeance for the wrongs he [Stephanus] had done us. They reproached me on the grounds that I was the most unmanly [*anandrotaton*] of humankind, if, being so closely related to them, I did not exact punishment for my sister, my father-in-law, my nieces, and my own wife. (Dem. 59.12)

Theomnestus clearly assumes that an Athenian audience will understand his concern over his manly reputation and therefore respect his decision to litigate (cf. Dem. 39.6; 34.2).

D. Cohen has argued on the basis of the prominent acknowledgment of vengeance in forensic oratory that both litigants and jurors view court as merely "another resource for enmity to draw upon, another arena where conflict may be pursued, where violence and revenge may be legally sanctioned."[6] Elements of this interpretation of Athenian litigation as an extension of feuding behavior are appealing. Litigants in Athens, and arguably in most societies, take an instrumental view of litigation,[7] and are therefore ready to use it for the pursuit, as well as the resolution, of conflict. Indeed, in some cases, Athenian litigants appear to be engaged in a cycle of vengeance and retaliation that might well be labeled feuding behavior (esp. Dem. 21), and for them the courts are no doubt arenas for the pursuit of personal vendettas. The critical question, however, is to what extent the community, as represented by large jury panels, tolerates or encourages this kind of behavior. To judge by the way litigants represent their behavior in the course of disputes and litigation, they do not expect the community to endorse unprovoked aggression, disproportionate retaliation, or contentious pursuit of a dispute. In fact, litigants know that to win their suits, they must reconcile their participation in litigation with social ideals of cooperative behavior.[8]

To understand the pressures on litigants to appeal to cooperative ideals before the popular courts, one must appreciate that for society at large legal competition represented a special and, in some respects, problematic contest (*agōn*). On the one hand, litigation, like many *agōnes*—for example, athletic contests or the rivalry among the rich to perform liturgies—involved a competition among individuals in a public setting in pursuit of honor and self-interest. On the other hand, a legal contest was distinct from these relatively peaceful *agōnes* in that it was inherently strifeful and regularly ugly, and sometimes arose when rivalry in these other agonistic settings went awry (cf. Dem. 21.13–18, 180). Because a legal contest often represented the culmination of a breach of social peace, litigants sometimes describe it as the domestic equivalent of the destructive *agōn* of war between states (Lys. 32.22; cf. Dem. 21.29).

The public viewed this strifeful *agōn* among fellow citizens with considerable ambivalence. While jurors enjoyed the spectacle of competition among powerful men and were sympathetic with the legitimate pursuit of manly vengeance, they brought to court communal concerns about the social ramifications of conflict and disputing behavior. For example, the aggressiveness of an individual currently involved in a trial might be directed toward another member of the community in the future and perhaps one less able to defend himself through legal or other channels (cf. Dem. 21.123–24). Furthermore, conflicts between individuals could get out of control and cause breaches of public peace, for example, in the form of scuffles and frays in the agora (Dem. 54.7–9), at public festivals (Dem. 21.1, 180), or in military camps (Dem. 54.3–6; cf. Lys. 3.45).[9] Therefore, while jurors were ready to endorse within limits manly behavior in the course of a dispute, they had good reason to be concerned about the social consequences of aggressive and quarrelsome behavior.

Because Athenians, like members of most societies, viewed quarrelsomeness as ugly,[10] it was in the interest of a prosecutor to persuade jurors that his suit was not trivial, especially when the pursuit of it might appear excessive. For example, a man prosecuting his stepbrother for using his name is at pains to assure jurors in his opening words that he is not bringing a frivolous suit, since this action has caused him significant harm (Dem. 39.1). Another litigant, bringing a suit for slander, is quick to point out that, while he would normally consider the prosecutor of such a suit to be too fond of litigation (*philodikos*), his opponent's gross slander warrants the current prosecution (Lys. 10.1–3).

Litigants in private suits, from which both of these examples derive, were under special pressure to justify their pursuit of a wrong to court. Whereas a public prosecutor could explain his pursuit of a relatively small, if not trivial (cf. Dem. 23.190), matter on the grounds that vigilance was essential where the community's interests were at stake (Dem. 24.192–93; 26.4), private citizens could not justify their pursuit of personal squabbles in this way. Moreover, whereas jurors might expect rival *rhētores,* who shared no social bond, to lash out at one another in public prosecutions, as they often did, jurors were more critical of private disputants, who frequently did share some social bond, when they pursued their differences to court.

Athenian institutions reflected and reinforced the view that a private difference should not be recklessly pursued through litigation. As noted in Chapter 1, deme judges had the authority to rule on private disputes involving sums under ten drachmas, presumably to keep petty matters from occupying court time. Furthermore, while it was illegal for prosecutors in public suits to settle with defendants, settlement was encouraged in private disputes: disputants were expected to make some effort to resolve their differences through informal or formal private arbitration, and were required in most cases to submit their differences to nonbinding public arbitration before bringing them to court.[11]

Litigants pursuing private disputes to court are conscious that jurors will wonder why, given the opportunities for settlement, they have come before a court. Typically, therefore, as they narrate the course of their disputes, they assert that, despite their heroic efforts to settle in private, their opponents have stubbornly refused to compromise.[12] Litigants express regret not only at the unnecessary escalation of their personal conflicts into lawsuits, but also at the deracination of these private matters from the private sphere. They point out, for example, that this entails a violation of privacy that is embarrassing for one or both disputants. Furthermore, they insist that friends and neighbors in the private realm are better able to evaluate disputants' competing claims, and protest that their opponents have intentionally forced the dispute from its original venue so as to dupe jurors who are unfamiliar with the local scene.[13] If the ideal of local solutions to private conflicts clashed with the reality of frequent litigation in the courts among private persons, this ideal played on an image of local community that jurors must have found appealing.[14]

Elite litigants, whose disputes dominate the ancient record, were probably under additional pressure to justify their presence in court, since the public might assume that they were in court not because this was the only way for them to resolve their conflicts, but because their resources allowed them to pursue disputes this far. By adopting a rhetoric of reluctance, elite litigants could hope to dispel the impression that they were hubristic rich men who were contentiously pursuing squabbles.[15]

The dichotomy between the opposing types of the *apragmōn* and the sykophant provided elite (and presumably other) litigants with an effective means of contrasting their own conciliatory behavior in the course of a dispute with the aggressive and uncooperative behavior of their opponents. On the one hand, litigants cast their opponents as sykophants who bitterly and vindictively seek out and pursue disputes (esp. Dem. 55.1). In behaving in this aggressive fashion, their sykophantic opponents apply boldness and daring, which might in other contexts be laudable manly qualities, to the antisocial pursuit of conflict.[16] On the other hand, litigants cast themselves as *apragmones* who act in a moderate and conciliatory manner at all stages of a dispute. The *apragmōn*'s peaceful character makes him avoid conflict in the first place, and if conflict arises, he seeks settlement before trial even if this is disadvantageous to him (Dem. 41.1). Only the magnitude of the wrong done him by the defendant (a prosecutor might claim) or the aggressive behavior of the prosecutor (a defendant might claim) has forced him to appear in court. His very presence in court is thus an anomaly, as a litigant in an early model speech explains: "It is clear to me now that sheer misfortune and necessity can force peaceful men [*apragmonas*] to appear in court, and quiet men to be bold and to speak and act contrary to their nature" (Ant. 3.2.1). When litigants claim to be *apragmones*, however, they are not rejecting societal expectations of manly behavior. The *apragmōn* makes it clear that he has the power and courage to respond aggressively in the course of a dispute, but *chooses* not to do so in deference to social ideals of cooperative behavior.[17] His reluctance is thus not evidence of weakness or cowardice, but rather of an uncontentious nature. Indeed, when he is provoked beyond reason by an antagonist, he is prepared to resist in a manly and honorable way through litigation. Herein lies much of the appeal of the stance of the *apragmōn:* his measured resistance to aggression is in keeping with both social ideals of manly behavior and cooperation.

When litigants cast themselves as peaceful *apragmones* and their opponents as aggressive sykophants, they offer jurors a choice between antithetical models not only of disputing behavior, but also more generally of social relations.[18] The next section looks more closely at some of the ways in which litigants appeal to and manipulate ideals of social relations as they seek to justify their participation in legal disputes.

Litigation and the Preservation of Social Relations

Just as litigants in Athens translate their disputes, which arise from complex circumstances, into the formal legal categories required for the lodging of lawsuits, so too they translate these disputes into social terms jurors will find compelling.[19] Litigation in Athens regularly brought before the public the troubling spectacle of disintegrating social relations. Private suits in particular were a source of communal concern, because they illustrated how easily friendly relations could become hostile ones, and thus exposed the fragility of social bonds.[20] Litigants acknowledge and exploit these concerns, when they translate their disputes before the popular courts into test cases of the ideal of friendly relations or *philia*.

Athenians applied the term *philia* both to relationships among kin and to those, more or less close, among persons outside of the family.[21] Within a nuclear family the bond of *philia* normally manifested itself in warm feelings and freely offered mutual support.[22] While outside of the family *philia* tended to operate more conspicuously on the principle of reciprocity (*charis*), that is, the exchange of favors, this is not to say it was primarily utilitarian and affection absent from it.[23]

In keeping with the exigencies of forensic oratory, litigants do not speak in abstract terms about the merits of *philia*, but rather seek to show in the context of particular disputes how their opponents have outrageously betrayed the familiar attributes of *philia*, especially intimacy (*oikeiotēs*),[24] trust, and the obligations of *charis*. When litigants cast their disputes in these terms,[25] they draw on powerful social ideals of cooperative and mutually beneficial relations within the city.[26] Litigants are so attracted to this manner of representing legal disputes, in fact, that they sometimes forcibly translate their disputes into this code. For example, although their disputes frequently have a significant financial dimension,[27] litigants tend to downplay this and stress instead that their opponents have violated norms governing social relations. Litigants also sometimes strain to transform their current enemies into erstwhile intimates so as to exploit social concern over the breach of *philia*. The following analysis considers how this understanding of the social meaning of litigation shapes the presentation of disputes involving members of three groups: kin; friends, neighbors, and demesmen; and bankers and their clients, and business associates.

FAMILY MATTERS

At times, legal disputes among kin brought before the public conflicts as sensational as those portrayed on the tragic stage. For example, a litigant prosecuting his stepmother for poisoning his father exploits the tragic resonances of his suit, when he compares the alleged poisoness to Clytemnestra (Ant. 1.17). More often, however, legal disputes among kin arose over more mundane matters connected with the transmission of family property from generation to generation: inheritance, guardianship, heiresses (*epiklēroi*), and dowries.[28] High mortality rates, frequent remarriage, and adoption made the Athenian family a dynamic unit in which strife over such matters could easily arise.[29]

Most litigation among kin, however, involved persons who were not members of the same nuclear family.[30] While the male head (*kurios*) of a nuclear family was alive, formal challenge to his authority by household members was unlikely, and when he died, litigation within the immediate family over inheritance and related matters was uncommon: if he left surviving blood descendants, the principle of division of property among them was straightforward, with sons receiving equal portions and daughters dowries.[31] But if there were no surviving offspring or an adopted son was to receive part or all of the estate, relatives from outside the nuclear family might well step forward to assert their rights before a court.[32] In the absence of public records of birth, marriage, and death, however, there was considerable confusion concerning family relationships, and jurors often had to evaluate the conflicting testimony of partisan witnesses concerning these.[33] While inheritance disputes involved a special procedure (*diadikasia*) that allowed for multiple claimants and in which, unlike in regular private suits, there was technically no wronged party,[34] in practice this did not make them any less rancorous than other disputes. Especially where large estates were involved, conflict was intense and disputes could be protracted over many years.[35]

While litigation among kin took place with some frequency, it did not accord well with social expectations of proper disputing behavior. As Humphreys observes, "One of the norms frequently emphasised [in forensic oratory] is that quarrels between kin should be settled without recourse to the courts—while quarrels within the nuclear family should not happen at all."[36] Although wealthier Athenians were more likely than average jurors to pursue their disputes with kin to court, family strife and concerns over it knew no class boundaries. Disputes among kin brought before jurors the failure of a fundamental form of *philia*,[37] and thus raised concerns about the foundations of society.

To judge by the self-justification in which litigating kinsmen engage, they were under strong social pressure to explain why they were opposing relatives at law. Kinsmen commonly express embarrassment that they are engaged in litigation with "the last persons with whom one should quarrel."[38] As one litigant explains: "I consider it the worst feature of my present troubles not that I am unjustly placed in peril, but that I am contesting with kinsmen, against whom even to defend oneself is not a pretty thing; for I would not regard it as a lesser misfortune to harm my relatives in my own defense than to have been originally injured by them" (Is. 1.6).[39] Litigants assert, however, that if relatives are the last persons with whom one should quarrel, they are also "the last persons who should wrong one" (Dem. 48.1; Lys. 32.1, 10) and act as enemies (Is. 1.5–8; 5.9–10; Dem. 27.65). This misfortune, they insist, compels them to appear in court.[40]

One concern of disputing kin is that they may appear to value money and property, which are commonly at the root of their disputes, over kinship. They therefore often represent themselves as interested only in their due, even willing to accept a financial loss in the interest of preserving good relations (cf. Is. 5.29). They point out that their opponents, by contrast, subordinate even the bonds of kinship to the pursuit of gain (Is. 9.25; cf. 1.8; fr. 22 Thalheim; Lys. 32.17; Dem. 45.54; 48.46).

Furthermore, while litigants in most private actions attempt to convince jurors that they have done their best to reach private settlements, litigating kin appear to be under especially strong pressure to demonstrate this. They commonly appeal to the ideal that family matters deserve family solutions, and reproach their opponents for rejecting formal or informal private arbitration.[41] In so doing, they exploit their audience's general assumptions about the autonomy of the *oikos*: while the city's laws regulated aspects of the *oikos* and this made it possible for kin to bring suit, Athenians viewed the *oikos* ideally as a self-regulating unit, able to resolve problems arising in connection with it. In particular, litigants maintain that a family resolution of a dispute is preferable, because family members and close friends, who know the disputants and the circumstances of the dispute, are the best arbitrators of it,[42] and because this best preserves the privacy of the family. Indeed, when kinsmen dispute before Athenian courts, they commonly expose one another's dirty laundry, making allegations concerning sexual misbehavior and bad citizenship.[43] Although such charges were also common in suits involving unrelated disputants, they gained credibility when made by kin, who might be thought to possess intimate knowledge of one another's peccadilloes, and therefore could be more damaging.

Two forensic speeches illustrate how litigating kin maneuver around the tensions surrounding their legal contests. In the first case, Lysias 32: *Against Diogeiton*, a *sunēgoros* accuses his wife's grandfather Diogeiton (who also happens to be her uncle: 32.4–5) of defrauding her and her two brothers of the estate over which he was guardian.[44] The speaker begins by acknowledging that his situation is awkward: "I regard it as most shameful to dispute with one's relatives, and I know that you disapprove not only of those who are guilty of wrong but also of anyone who is unable to tolerate some disadvantage at the hands of kinsmen" (32.1). Immediately, however, the speaker blames his opponent for the removal of the dispute from its private setting, since he refused to abide by the judgment of friends who assembled to arbitrate the matter (32.2).[45] The centerpiece of the speech is the speaker's recreation of this assembly (32.11–18). According to the speaker, Diogeiton's daughter, the mother of the defrauded children, asked him to assemble her father and their friends so she might present an account of her difficulties, "although she had not previously been accustomed to speak in the presence of men" (32.11). While Diogeiton was reluctant to attend, he eventually gave in to the pressure of his friends and came to the gathering (32.12). The speaker proceeds to report the impassioned speech Diogeiton's daughter gave, berating her father for treating his own family members in such a despicable manner (32.12–17). Her words reduced the group to tears (32.18) but had no effect on Diogeiton (cf. 32.2).

While this vignette most obviously explains why the prosecution has been forced to pursue its complaint before a public court, at the same time it presents jurors with the illusion that they are at a private assembly and privy to the case that a woman, who was not permitted to address an Athenian court, might present to friends. In inviting members of the jury into this imagined private realm, the speaker puts them in the position of the personal friends who witnessed the speech at first hand. Whereas that original audience was unable to make Diogeiton treat his kin as he should, the current audience has the power to do precisely this. In so doing, it will protect not only Diogeiton's oppressed relatives but also the community: "For Diogeiton is reducing all people to such a state of suspicion toward one another that neither living nor dying can they place any more trust in their nearest relations than in their worst enemies" (32.19). Thus conceived, this family dispute provides jurors with an opportunity to confirm the fundamental social importance of the bonds of familial *philia* that Diogeiton has devalued.

Demosthenes 48: *Against Olympiodorus* also involves a dispute over the transmission of family property, though under very different circumstances. The prosecutor is suing Olympiodorus, his brother-in-law and also a blood relation (48.1; cf. 48.6), for damages on the grounds that he violated his oath to share the proceeds from the estate of a common relation, Comon. This litigant acknowledges that it is awkward to sue a relative, but insists, "I have been forced to do so because of the magnitude of the wrongs that he has done me" (48.1). In keeping with his claim that this lawsuit was his last resort, the speaker explains how on two separate occasions he went out of his way to avoid litigation with Olympiodorus by seeking private solutions to their differences.

The first series of negotiations between the speaker and Olympiodorus took place after Comon's death, when much to the speaker's surprise his brother-in-law asserted that he too was a blood relation of Comon and therefore had a claim on the estate (48.6). The two summoned all their relatives to a meeting where they discussed at leisure Olympiodorus's claim (48.7). The outcome was that he and Olympiodorus agreed in writing and by oath to share the estate and collaborate in fending off any rival claimants (48.8–11). The speaker explains that he accepted this arrangement so as to avoid a court encounter in which he might be forced to say unpleasant things about his kinsman and hear something unfriendly (*anepitēdeion*) from him in turn (48.8).

This collaborative arrangement, however, broke down.[46] When others put in claims to the estate (48.20), litigation ensued, and although Olympiodorus won possession of the entire estate, he refused to share it as promised with the speaker (48.29–32). Olympiodorus, moreover, "refused to refer our differences to our relatives and friends, who had precise knowledge of all the circumstances of the case," since he knew that these persons—unlike a popular court—would be able to see through his lies (48.40). The current prosecution, therefore, is a direct consequence of Olympiodorus's intransigeance.

The speaker expresses regret that Olympiodorus has forced this private matter to become a public one, because this puts him in the awkward position of speaking openly of matters best kept out of the public view. He points out, however, that "this fellow is himself to blame for my mentioning the things which I am about to tell you, since he shamelessly refused to settle our differences through our relatives" (48.53). The speaker proceeds to relate with gusto how Olympiodorus's despicable behavior is due to the fact that he is under the sway of his mistress (48.53–55).

The speaker suggests that, if this lawsuit brings a private dispute into the public sphere and thus forces the public revelation of private peccadilloes, it also provides an opportunity for jurors to enter into and set right a disruption of the private sphere. He encourages the jurors to play the role of reconcilers (*diallaxantes*) of the disputants (48.3; cf. 48.58)—a role normally played by friends of the litigants in the private realm.[47] This litigant is well aware that

Athenian juries could not actually intervene and reconcile litigants in the course of a trial,[48] and he therefore goes on to say that, if they cannot do this, they should vote for the just cause—presumably his own. His appeal is nonetheless significant: it suggests that ideally at least jurors should seek to restore good relations among disputing kin, just as their friends in the private sphere might.

Other litigants, when their kin turn out to be less than kind, make no pretense of seeking evenhanded arbitration from jurors, but rather invite jurors to act as kinsmen and friends in supporting them against their false relatives. For example, after Apollodorus casts doubt on his brother Pasicles' paternity because Pasicles failed to support him in his claim against Phormio,[49] he appeals to the jurors on the grounds that his father's generosity to the city makes them his natural "helpers and friends" (Dem. 45.84–85). A client of Antiphon is even more direct: "avenge the dead man, and in so doing give me, a lonely orphan, your aid. For you are my kin; those who should have avenged the dead and supported me are his murderers and my opponents" (1.3–4; cf. Dem. 28.20). In such cases, litigants suggest that where private relations have failed, not only should the community, as represented by large juries, affirm the importance of the bonds in question by a favorable verdict, but also step in directly to fill the gap created by their failure.

FRIENDS, NEIGHBORS, AND DEMESMEN

While disputes among kin represented the most dramatic disruptions of social relations coming before Athenian courts, litigation involving nonkin also frequently brought the disintegration of social bonds to the public's attention. To be sure, some litigants do not appear to have enjoyed lengthy relations before becoming involved in litigation with one another. For example, the requirements of civic life sometimes created circumstances in which conflict arose among virtual strangers: service in the army (Dem. 54), assignment to carry out a liturgy (Dem. 42), or the execution of a liturgy (Dem. 47) could all lead to litigation between mere acquaintances. In many attested suits, however, opposing litigants appear to have enjoyed friendly relations (*philia*) or even to have been close friends (*philoi*) for some time before coming into conflict.[50] Litigants in these circumstances are conscious of the social tensions concerning the breach of such relationships, and therefore invoke many of the same ideals concerning dispute resolution that litigating kin do: persons bound by *philia* should not quarrel in the first place, but when they do, they should seek reconciliation outside of court. At the same time, they—like litigating kin—justify their participation in lawsuits on the grounds that their opponents have failed to respect these ideals.

While an Athenian audience might perceive any form of litigation among persons bound by *philia* as socially disruptive, the breach of social relations raised special concerns about the nature of communal life when litigants came from the same locality. Although the city at large could be conceived of as a single community held together by the glue of *philia* (cf. Isoc. 4.45; Dem. 25.87–88), as a practical matter most Athenians experienced community and *philia* through their daily social interaction with one another on the local level. Next we consider how litigants who are neighbors and/or fellow demesmen acknowledge and manipulate juror's concerns about disputes among persons associating closely within the local community.

Neighbors

In most societies neighbors have exceptional opportunities for the forging of close social bonds, on the one hand, and for quarreling, on the other hand, and ancient Athens was no exception (cf. Hes. *Op.* 346). Ideally, neighbors enjoyed peaceful relations, cooperated with one another in matters of mutual interest, and even assisted one another in hard times.[51] Where neighbors were relatives, as may often have been the case,[52] ideals of proper kin behavior also encouraged good relations. Actual relations among neighbors, however, frequently fell short of these ideals, and sometimes neighbors not only failed to get along but also came into open conflict that culminated in litigation.[53] Two cases from the Demosthenic corpus illustrate how litigating neighbors justify their involvement in unneighborly litigation.

Neighborly relations could easily become strained over issues of land ownership, water rights, and drainage. In Demosthenes 55:

Against Callicles, a defendant in a suit for damages responds to the claim of his neighbor, Callicles, that a wall the defendant's father had built next to the roadway separating their two adjacent properties caused water to run off onto Callicles' property and damage it. The defendant maintains that the whole case is a sykophantic ruse and part of a long-term effort by Callicles to drive him out of the deme ("village") through lawsuits and thereby take over his land (55.1–2, 31–35). In particular, he argues that his father had built the wall in question many years earlier to prevent the flooding of his property and no complaint had been leveled against him (55.3–12); that Callicles had increased his own vulnerability to flooding by encroaching on the road with a wall he constructed (55.22); and that, in any event, Callicles' losses were minimal (55.24–25). The defendant, however, not only makes specific claims about drainage and property lines, but also presents this suit as one in which neighborly relations are conspicuously at stake. He makes this clear from the start, when he generalizes, "There is nothing worse than having a neighbor who is base [*ponērou*] and covetous [*pleonektou*]" (55.1). He maintains that if Callicles has his way, an absurd situation would arise: anyone in the neighborhood suffering flood damage could bring suit against the speaker (55.20). When floods cause damage elsewhere in Attica, however, customarily neighbors do not claim the right to recover damages from one another and this is only reasonable (55.28). The difference between Callicles' and the speaker's attitudes toward matters involving neighbors could hardly be greater: whereas the speaker kept his peace about Callicles' infringement on the road despite the risks this posed to his property, Callicles goes so far as to sue a neighbor whose property he has himself damaged (55.29).

The speaker portrays Callicles as not only a bad neighbor but also a betrayer of the long-standing friendly relations between their two families: "Before they [Callicles and his relatives] undertook to engage in sykophancy against me, my mother was on friendly terms with theirs and the women used to visit one another regularly, as was natural, since both lived in the country and were neighbors, and since, furthermore, their husbands had been friends while they lived" (55.23). Whether this picture of uninterrupted friendship between the two families is true or not, the speaker suggests by including these details that social ideals transcending the particular dispute are at stake.[54] He suggests, moreover, that consistent with Callicles' violation of ideals of neighborly behavior and *philia* is his behavior as a disputant: Callicles has not allowed the conflict to be resolved privately by persons familiar with the local situation, because he hopes to be able to deceive the jurors, who are unacquainted with the circumstances of the dispute, into ruling in his favor (55.9; cf. 55.35).

A further instance of litigation among neighbors is found in Demosthenes 53: *Against Nicostratus*.[55] Although the case is a public suit, as so often a volunteer prosecutor has stepped forward to avenge wrongs he claims to have suffered at the hands of a personal enemy. The prosecutor, Apollodorus, devotes much of his speech to narrating how enmity initially arose between himself and his neighbor, Nicostratus, and the course it took in and out of the courts. While Apollodorus provides this account to explain his readiness to volunteer as public prosecutor, he seeks at the same time to rouse the jurors to outrage at Nicostratus for his betrayal of social ideals of *philia*.

Apollodorus paints a rosy picture of the friendship he and Nicostratus once enjoyed:

> Nicostratus, whom you see here in court, men of the jury, was my neighbor in the country and a man of my own age. Although we had known each other for a long time, after my father died and I went to live in the country, where I still live, we associated even more with one another since we were neighbors and of similar age. As time went on we became very close [*oikeios*]; indeed I came to feel on such close terms with him that he never failed to win any favor he asked of me. He, on his part, was useful to me in looking after my affairs and managing them, and whenever I was abroad on public service as trierarch, or on private business of my own, I used to leave him in charge of everything on the farm. (53.4)

Apollodorus persists throughout his speech in idealizing his relationship with Nicostratus as one of intimate *philia*. He asserts that he proved himself a true friend (*alēthinos philos*: 53.7, 8, 12) by assisting Nicostratus when he was taken captive by pirates and held for ransom. Whereas Nicostratus's own relations failed to assist him, Apollodorus helped bring about his release and then, through gifts and loans of money, rescued him from the grips of those who had lent him a portion of his ransom (53.7–13).

Apollodorus asserts that Nicostratus, by contrast, acted not as a *philos* but an enemy. Rather than repay this enormous debt of gratitude (*charis*), he did his best to harm Apollodorus so as to prevent him from collecting on his loans (53.13). Nicostratus helped Apollodorus's opponents at law by disclosing his legal arguments to them in advance of trial (53.14); he induced another man to indict Apollodorus as a state debtor and thereby forced him to pay a large fine (53.14–15); he was responsible for acts of predation on Apollodorus's property (53.15–16), one of which was designed to provoke him to an illegal act of violence that would have made him subject to a *graphē hubreōs*; and, finally, Nicostratus assaulted and attempted to kill Apollodorus to prevent him from carrying through a lawsuit against Nicostratus's brother, Arethusius, for his role in the earlier indictment of Apollodorus as state debtor (53.17).[56]

When Apollodorus casts Nicostratus's treatment of him as an egregious violation of their intimate *philia,* however, he is almost certainly exaggerating the true nature of their previous relationship. At the end of the passage cited earlier (53.4), Apollodorus discloses that Nicostratus actually worked for him; thus their relationship had a distinct economic aspect to it, and if they were on friendly terms, they were hardly *philoi* on an equal footing as Apollodorus implies elsewhere.[57] Furthermore, when Apollodorus speaks of the friendly gifts and loans he made to his neighbor, one must keep in mind that Apollodorus—when not busy being a good neighbor—was a banker who sought profit through his financial transactions, and this may well be at the roots of his dealings with Nicostratus. That Apollodorus nonetheless translates his suit against Nicostratus into a test case of *philia* is testimony to his belief that the jurors will be anxious to preserve the social ideals at stake and therefore rule in his favor.

The Litigious Athenian

Demesmen

Even when neighbors did not develop the close bonds of *philia* claimed in the two cases just discussed, they were often bound to one another as members of the same deme. To be sure, because deme membership was hereditary after the Cleisthenic reforms (508/7 B.C.) and followed a man even if he moved from one locale to another, neighbors were not necessarily members of the same deme; especially within the urban center of Athens neighbors may often have belonged to different demes, since the city attracted part- and full-time residents from the surrounding countryside. But throughout most of Attica geographic mobility was limited and neighbors were usually fellow demesmen, and Athenians thus often treat these two categories as if synonymous.[58]

Most Athenians experienced communal life largely through their participation in the life of the deme. Although the polis could be idealized as a "face-to-face society" in which citizens all knew one another, it was only on the level of deme that this could be a reality.[59] Fellow demesmen shared with one another a common identity that they reaffirmed by their participation in social, political, and religious activities at the deme level. Along with this shared identity came certain expectations of behavior, including the ideal that demesmen, like relatives and friends, should support each other at law rather than litigate against one another (Lys. 27.12; cf. Dem. 52.28; Ar. *Nu.* 1218–19).[60] Although this ideal must have been violated often, since the frequent interaction among demesmen provided sources of friction as well as opportunities for good social relations, its violation was especially prominent when individual demesmen found themselves at law with the corporate deme before a popular court. The legal confrontation between a demesman and the deme, normally represented by the local magistrate known as the demarch,[61] conspicuously called into question the ideal of deme solidarity.

Consider, for example, how one litigant, confronting his fellow demesmen in a lawsuit over a piece of property he had mortgaged to the deme, portrays the awkwardness of his situation:

> My wish, men of the jury, would have been never to suffer wrong at the hands of any of my fellow citizens; or, if that were impossible, to oppose at law men with whom it would not trouble me to quarrel. As it is, the most grievous thing possible has happened to me: I have been wronged by my fellow demesmen, whose robbery I cannot easily overlook, but whose enmity is unpleasant, since I am obliged <to share their sacrifices> and attend their common gatherings . . . I beg you therefore to excuse me, if at my early age I have ventured to address a court; I am compelled by those wronging me to act contrary to my natural character. (Is. fr. 4 Thalheim)

Although in this fragment the speaker stops short of describing his relation with his fellow demesmen as one of *philia*, he makes it clear that enmity with them is unnatural. His characterization of his awkward situation, in fact, recalls the statements of litigating kin who express regret at being compelled to litigate against persons with whom they have such close relations.[62] If this litigant suggests that this breach of happy relations among demesmen is akin to a breach of familial relations, however, he also highlights a distinctly unpleasant dimension of it: this legal dispute arises because of the abuse of an individual by the group to which he belongs.

Another instance of a demesman confronting his deme at law is found in Demosthenes 57: *Against Eubulides,* in which Euxitheus appeals to a popular court to reinstate him as citizen after his fellow demesmen struck him from the list of citizens during the revision of the deme rolls in 346/5 B.C.[63] Euxitheus presents himself as a victim of a conspiracy among fellow demesmen: a faction (57.2, 7, 17) of his enemies (57.6, 8, 48),[64] who resented his honest administration of the office of demarch (57.63), manipulated the deme's review of the citizenship list so as to disfranchise him (57.9–13). Just as angry kin expose one another's dirty laundry to the courts, Euxitheus reveals to a jury composed of Athenians from other demes (cf. 57.57) the scandalous behavior of his fellow demesmen. He asserts that "in no deme will you find more outrageous transactions than in ours," and proceeds to describe how his opponents make it possible for citizenship to be bought and sold within the deme (57.58–60). The failure of his fellow demesmen to treat one of their legitimate members as they should thus prompts this litigant to seek support from outside his local community in the higher authority of a popular court representing the Athenian community at large (57.56).

FINANCIAL RELATIONSHIPS: BANKERS AND TRADERS

Because bankers and traders involved in legal disputes over large-scale transactions could afford logographers' speeches, their legal contests are well attested in extant forensic oratory. The surviving speeches provide good evidence of how litigants involved in suits arising in connection with financial arrangements package their relationships and disputes for public presentation.

Bankers and traders were under special pressures when they addressed popular courts, first, because jurors apparently viewed them and their activities as marginal and somewhat suspect. Athenian citizens tended not to engage directly in capital-focused and aggressively profit-oriented activities like banking and trade, because these clashed with traditional economic activities based on agriculture. Non-Athenians—namely, metics and foreigners—who were not allowed to own land, and other persons of low social status (e.g., former slaves who had gained citizenship) stepped into this vacuum and seized the opportunity to enrich themselves.[65] When bankers and traders appeared before popular courts, they had to confront not only the ambivalence of jurors toward their activities, but also envy of their often conspicuous wealth. If jurors could not help but feel some envy toward the wealthy Athenian litigants who regularly came before them, they were all the more likely to be jealous of wealthy litigants who were noncitizens or, as in the case of the banker Pasio, only recently enfranchised.

Litigating bankers and traders are aware that jurors may regard them as avaricious outsiders and hold their financial success against them, and therefore are at pains to bridge the gap between themselves and jurors.[66] Frequently, they convert their financial relationships with their opponents into the common coin of familiar social bonds, and their disputes over money into conflicts involving basic social principles, in particular, the norms of *philia*. This could, but did not necessarily, involve a gross distortion of reality.

On the one hand, financial relationships involving bankers or traders in some cases probably did partake of *philia,* as the Athenian public understood it. After all, these relationships regularly involved direct personal contact between individuals and mutual trust (*pistis*), and over time the individuals involved might become friends and intimates.[67] On the other hand, financial relationships often bore but a superficial resemblance to other social relationships subsumed under the rubric of *philia.* The presence of trust and personal interaction in these relationships probably did not normally make them very intimate ones, notwithstanding claims of litigants to the contrary. Many financial relationships appear to have been opportunistic ones forged between persons having little in common with one another except their financial transactions. Although *philia* was a flexible concept and calculations of self-interest could be compatible with it,[68] these relationships based overtly on profit did not jibe very well with conventional understandings of it. Because Athenians idealized *philia* as a relationship based on the exchange of favors not of money, they were unlikely to speak of *philia* and gain (*kerdos*) in the same breath.

Despite these obstacles to presenting their financial relationships and disputes in terms of *philia,* litigants often do just this, even when they must strain to do so. The subsequent discussion looks first at how litigants in banking disputes draw on and manipulate the ideal of *philia,* and then considers how litigants in disputes concerning maritime loans tend to emphasize a breach of contract rather than of *philia.*

Bankers

Athenian bankers were active in holding deposits securely for clients and in extending loans, both personal and maritime, from these deposits and their own private funds.[69] While some individuals relied on friends and family to assist them in these ways, others turned to bankers out of necessity or choice.[70] Foreign traders, who lacked trusted connections in Athens with whom they could deposit funds or from whom they might borrow, regularly had recourse to bankers. Wealthy Athenians turned to bankers for a variety of reasons: they were convenient and generally trustworthy holders of deposits, and they could provide loans to the wealthy, who were often cash poor, to meet private or public obligations. Attitudes toward bankers were probably mixed: bankers, like their modern counterparts, could variously be described as "enjoying a reputation for honesty because of their profession" (Isoc. 17.2) or as an execrable tribe (Antiph. fr. 157.11–12).[71]

Aspects of the banker-client relationship invited equation of it with other social relationships subsumed under *philia*. Banking regularly involved a personal relationship between banker and client based on trust (*pistis*),[72] and a client could be said to "use" (*chraomai*) a banker—the same idiom is applied to close social relationships.[73] But evidence of real social intimacy between bankers and their clients is thin, and to the extent a client "used" a banker, this was very much an extension of his "use" of the bank (Isoc. 17.4), and not an independent relationship. This did not, however, stop litigants from idealizing this relationship as one of intimate *philia*. Both bankers and their clients appealed to this ideal so as to legitimize their relationships before jurors who were not altogether comfortable with them and to amplify the magnitude of the betrayal of trust leading to litigation.

Consider, for example, how the son of Sopaeus, a foreigner from the Bosporus, presents his charge that the Athenian banker Pasio stole money deposited with him (Isoc. 17).[74] From the outset, Sopaeus's son downplays the financial character of the dispute:

> This trial, men of the jury, is an important one for me. For I have at stake not only a large sum of money, but also my reputation, since I risk being thought to desire unjustly what belongs to another; that is what gives me the greatest concern. Sufficient property will be left to me even if I am robbed of this sum, but if I should be thought to have brought suit for so large a sum of money without just cause, I would have an evil reputation as long as I live. (17.1)

In keeping with this idealization of what is at stake in this suit is the way Sopaeus's son idealizes his relationship with his banker, which is based on a contract (17.2), as one involving intimate *philia*.

While the relationship clearly originated in a financial arrangement between strangers—Sopaeus's son deposited money with

Pasio only after Pythodorus, a Phoenician, introduced the two (17.4), Sopaeus's son suggests that it became more personal. When enemies from his homeland sought to seize the funds deposited with Pasio, he turned to Pasio for friendly help in concealing the deposit: "When I found myself in such great difficulties, men of the jury, I related my troubles to Pasio; for I was on such familiar terms [*oikeiōs*] with him that I placed the greatest trust [*pisteuein*] in him, not only in matters of money, but in other affairs as well" (17.6).[75] While trust (*pistis*) is a normal feature of intimate *philia*, it may be present in less close social relations as well, and Sopaeus's son provides no evidence of frequent contact or friendly association to support his claim of intimacy with Pasio. Pasio's willingness to cooperate with Sopaeus's son in concealing his money is hardly evidence that *philia* budded between banker and client: the concealment of wealth in banks was a normal practice,[76] and Pasio had good reason, whether Sopaeus's son was his friend or not, to keep quiet about the deposit since he could profit from its use while he held it. Later too Sopaeus's son appeals to *philia*, when he asserts that it is unlikely that he would lodge a sykophantic charge against Pasio and thereby "become an enemy of the man with whom, of all the inhabitants of Athens, I happened to be on terms of greatest familiarity [*malist'* . . . *chrōmenos*]" (17.47). The current enmity between the two is not proof, however, of their prior intimacy: even if Sopaeus's son's statement that he was on closer terms with his banker than he was with other Athenians is true, this does not mean that the *philia* between them was anything but superficial. That Sopaeus's son seeks, despite these difficulties, to depict his relationship with Pasio as a close bond of *philia* is significant: he thus suggests that his relationship with his banker, which is difficult to categorize in traditional social terms, partakes of the same *philia* that Athenians cherish, and that his Athenian jury therefore has a vested interest in protecting this social principle against those who, like Pasio, are ready to betray it.

A similar idealization of the banker-client relationship, in this case by a banker, is found in Demosthenes 49: *Against Timotheus*.[77] This speech was presented by Pasio's son, Apollodorus, when he sued to collect money that Pasio had allegedly lent on several occasions to Timotheus, a prominent Athenian general. The relationship between Pasio and Timotheus was to all appearances an opportunistic one for both men. Timotheus had an urgent and unmet need for loans, personal and maritime. Pasio had access to vast financial resources and, as a former slave, was willing to extend credit to Timotheus, in hopes that "he would not only recover his money, but would be in a position to obtain whatever else he might wish" (49.3). Consistent with the formal financial nature of their relationship, Pasio kept careful records of his loans to Timotheus (49.5; cf. 49.43, 59).

This does not stop Apollodorus, however, from suggesting that the dispute has arisen because of Timotheus's violation of *philia*. While Apollodorus does not directly assert that Timotheus enjoyed *philia* with Pasio, he implies this when he responds to Timotheus's claim that Pasio actually lent money on one occasion to a Boeotian admiral, not to Timotheus, with the query, "From what motive of *philia* would my father have lent the thousand drachmas to the Boeotian admiral whom he did not even know?" (49.50). Furthermore, Apollodorus describes the dynamics of the relationship in terms typically associated with *philia*, when he emphasizes that Pasio took pity on Timotheus in his distress (49.17; cf. 49.2–3) and therefore lent him assistance,[78] and protests that Timotheus refuses to acknowledge either the actual debt or the debt of gratitude (*charis*) he owes Pasio (49.1, 2, 4, 27, 54).[79] Thus, when Apollodorus laments that Timotheus will pay back what he has borrowed only when confronted with a hostile legal action (*di' echthras kai dikēs:* 49.4), he is expressing concern not only over the current state of hostilities but also over the inversion of prior *philia* that this represents. That his opponent has betrayed personal trust (49.64) out of base greed (49.65–68) makes this violation of social ideals all the more shocking.

While bankers were an important source of credit in Athens, professional moneylenders were also active in extending loans. They appear to have enjoyed a less favorable reputation than bankers, however, and to have been associated with usury.[80] When moneylenders appeared as litigants before popular courts, therefore, they were probably under strong pressure to represent their financial relationships and disputes in traditional social terms.

Consider, for example, the dispute described in Demosthenes 37: *Against Pantainetus* over a mining loan.[81] The speaker Nicobulus, to all appearances a professional moneylender, complains that Pantainetus, to whom he had lent money for operating a mining franchise leased from the city, betrayed the *philia* between them. Nicobulus asserts that Euergus, a friend of the two (37.15, 26) who also happened to be Nicobulus's business partner (37.4), introduced them and that they then arranged a loan by contract (37.5, 10). When Pantainetus fell out with Euergus and won a lawsuit against him (37.6–8), however, Pantainetus also became hostile to Nicobulus, who had been absent during the earlier litigation: "When I returned from my voyage, at first he pretended that he was glad to see me, but when the time came for him to do what was right, he became surly with me. I saw that he was friendly [*philon*] to all men until he got some advantage and obtained what he wanted, and thereafter he became their enemy and quarreled with them" (37.15). Although Nicobulus expresses hurt at this unfriendly treatment, his characterization of his relationship with Pantainetus in terms of *philia* appears to be based exclusively on their financial relationship and the fact that they share a friend in common. Consistent with this packaging of the relationship is the indignation that Nicobulus expresses at the fact that Pantainetus has brought suit alleging that Nicobulus wrongfully ejected him from the mine (the same claim that Pantainetus had successfully pursued against Euergus): whereas Pantainetus should feel gratitude (*charis*) for the friendly financial assistance Nicobulus gave him, he has instead brought a sykophantic suit (37.35; cf. 37.49–50).[82] That the actual relationship between Nicobulus and his opponent was an impersonal, financial one, however, is suggested by Nicobulus's protest late in his speech that he is not, as Pantainetus claims, a professional moneylender: "If a man has worked as I have, going to sea on perilous journeys, and from his small profits has made these loans, because he wishes to confer favors [*charisasthai*] and prevent his money from slipping away unnoticed, why should one set him down in that class?" (37.54). Surely, however, Nicobulus protests too much.[83] In all likelihood, he was in the business of making money rather than friends, and he presents this dispute as one involving the decline of *philia* into enmity so as to translate the financial relationship involved and the ensuing dispute into social terms his audience will find compelling.

Traders

Because Athens was a major trading center, men from different locales often met one another and entered into agreements involving maritime loans there.[84] Typically in these transactions, a professional moneylender, speculator, or banker contracted with a maritime trader to provide a high-interest loan, the principal and interest of which came due when the trader's vessel safely completed its voyage; but if the ship sank or was seriously damaged and therefore unable to complete its voyage, the trader was no longer responsible for the loan. Athenians had a vested interest in the smooth operation of these arrangements, especially those concerning the transport of grain, since the city relied on imported grain to feed its populace. They therefore not only allowed traders of any nationality involved in disputes over maritime loans access to the courts, but they also made special provisions to expedite adjudication of such suits under the rubric of "monthly suits" (see Chapter 1). As scholars often note, suits involving maritime loans were apparently common enough that litigants could take for granted that jurors were acquainted with how maritime loans worked. Several speeches in the Demosthenic corpus involving claims of fraud in connection with maritime loans (Dem. 32; 34; 35; 56) provide good evidence of how litigants in these circumstances presented themselves and their disputes to Athenian audiences.[85]

Litigants in suits concerning maritime loans do not ordinarily pretend that their opponents have betrayed *philia,* but rather emphasize that they have violated a contractual relationship.[86] To be sure, litigants had good reason to speak of their contracts in these suits: the existence of a written contract was a requirement for bringing a *dikē emporikē*—the favored action in disputes involving maritime loans, since it was available to non-Athenians and relatively speedy—and if there was no written contract, the defendant could lodge a procedural objection (*paragraphē*). Litigants could have protested, however, that their opponents had breached not only a contract but also *philia*, and could thus have capitalized on jurors' concerns over the latter as litigants in other financial disputes do. That they do not appeal to *philia* probably reflects their assumption that jurors would simply not regard such claims as credible because the relationship between trader and lender was so manifestly a commercial one founded on the pursuit of profit.

When litigants in these circumstances complain that their opponents have broken a contract, however, in keeping with the normal discourse of the Athenian courts they do their best to place this violation in a broader social and civic context. Typically they characterize the breach of contract as a threat to cooperative social life, which is based on trust (*pistis*) and fairness (*ta dikaia*), and moreover as an attack on the city's trade interests, which depend on the proper observance of contracts. In so doing, they—like litigants appealing to the ideal of *philia*—seek to establish that they are "insiders" defending community values and interests, and their opponents "outsiders" threatening both of these. This competition among litigants to prove themselves the true insiders, however, takes on a special dimension in maritime suits, since one or both litigants were often non-Athenians and hence, in civic terms, very much outsiders. Two examples illustrate how this dynamic of creating insiders and outsiders operates in disputes over maritime loans: the first (Dem. 35) involves an Athenian and a non-Athenian, the second non-Athenians on both sides (Dem. 56).

When an Athenian confronted a non-Athenian in court, he must have enjoyed a distinct advantage over his opponent, since his audience of fellow Athenians would identify with him and be predisposed to believe that his non-Athenian opponent was an unscrupulous outsider.[87] An Athenian litigant, Androcles, brazenly exploits this situation in Demosthenes 35: *Against Lacritus*. Androcles asserts that he and Nausicrates of Carystus had provided a maritime loan to two men from Phaselis, Artemo and Apollodorus, which they refused to repay on the grounds that their vessel had been lost. Since Artemo died before he could sue him, however, Androcles brought a *dikē emporikē* against Artemo's brother Lacritus, since he had inherited his brother's estate (35.3–4) and had played a part in the arrangement of the contract (35.15–16). Lacritus, however, lodged a procedural protest (*paragraphē*) against Androcles' suit on the grounds that there was no contract between him and Androcles and that Androcles' suit was accordingly inadmissible. In such circumstances, the issue raised by the *paragraphē* had to be resolved by a separate trial, in which the original prosecutor appeared as defendant, before the initial suit could proceed. In the surviving speech, Androcles, the original prosecutor, defends himself against Lacritus's *paragraphē*.

From the outset Androcles exploits Athenian prejudice toward outsiders:

> The Phaselites, men of the jury, are up to no new tricks, but are just doing what they usually do. For they are the cleverest people at borrowing money in your emporium, but, as soon as they get it and draw up a maritime contract, they immediately forget the contract and the laws, as well as the fact that they are under obligation to pay back what they have taken. They consider that, if they pay their debts, it is as if they have lost some of their own private property, and, instead of paying, they invent sophisms, *paragraphai*, and pretexts. Indeed, they are the most villainous and dishonest of men, and here is proof: although many Greeks and barbarians frequent your emporium, the Phaselites alone have more suits, when the courts sit, than all the others combined. That is the sort of people they are. (35.1–2)

Throughout his speech, Androcles builds on this image of Phaselites as sykophantic outsiders against whom Athenians must unite. He expresses outrage, for example, that "in our own city we have been robbed [*sesulēmetha*] of our own possessions by Phaselites, just as if rights of reprisal [*sulōn*] had been given to Phaselites against Athenians" (35.26). The image is a telling one: for Athenians to tolerate this legal abuse of one of their own by an outsider is tantamount to the absurdity of giving foreigners special license to collect plunder in Athens.[88] While Androcles' appeal to Athenian solidarity against outsiders is remarkable for its directness, the prejudices upon which he plays were no doubt present whenever non-Athenians appeared before Athenian courts.

Despite Androcles' "single-minded jingoism and xenophobia,"[89] he stops short of asserting that his Athenian audience should side with him regardless of the legitimacy of his case. These Phaselites have flagrantly violated their contract (esp. 35.17–25) and have attempted to manipulate legal procedures to avoid honoring it: this is wrong and contrary to the city's laws concerning contracts (35.45; cf. 35.1–2). In violating their contract, moreover, these Phaselites have circumvented the city's law restricting Athenians and metics to loaning money for transport of "grain or other specified articles" to Athens (35.50–54).[90] Their actions not only put Androcles—who, as an Athenian, is subject to this law—in the embarrassing position of appearing to have made an illegal loan (35.11, 50), but also represent a direct harm to the city, since it has not received the benefit expected from a loan extended by one of its citizens (35.54; cf. 35.5).[91] Androcles thus maintains that it would be both just and in the interest of the city to find in his favor (35.56) against this unscrupulous outsider.

Whereas Androcles could exploit the civic tie between himself and jurors, when non-Athenians confronted one another in Athenian courts, neither party could do so. Such litigants could argue, however, that, if not Athenians in name, they—unlike their opponents—were bound to their audiences by common social values and regard for Athenian interests, and that this was, in fact, the basis for their participation in litigation. Demosthenes 56: *Against Dionysodorus* provides a vivid example of how a non-Athenian litigant goes about establishing such a bond between himself and jurors.

The speaker, Dareius, presents the circumstances of his case as follows. For the transport of grain from Egypt to Athens, he and Pamphilus—both probably metics—lent three thousand drachmas to two traders, Dionysodorus and Parmeniscus, who were probably neither Athenians nor metics.[92] When the price of grain dropped in Athens, however, the traders took their cargo to Rhodes and sold it there instead, and subsequently refused to pay back the full amount of the loan. Thus, they not only broke their contract, but also circumvented the Athenian law that citizens and metics could only make loans to traders bringing cargoes back to the Piraeus. Dareius asserts that, while Dionysodorus and Parmeniscus claimed that their ship was damaged and could not make it back to Athens, they continued to use this very ship for trade between Egypt and Rhodes. In the face of this patent fraud and his opponents' unwillingness to submit to arbitration (56.16, 18, 43), Dareius brings a *dikē emporikē* for damages against them.

Like Androcles in the suit just considered, Dareius places his contractual dispute within a broader social context. He asserts that maritime contracts involve not only the parties to them but also the city, which lenders trust (56.2) to enforce contracts; thus it is only right that the city come to their aid when they have been wronged (56.1–2, 4). At the same time, Dareius makes it clear that the city's own interests are at stake. For example, because of unscrupulous profiteers like his opponents, the price of grain rose in the city (56.8). Furthermore, it is very much to the advantage of his Athenian audience to enforce contracts, since thus "lenders will be more ready to risk their money, and the business of your port will be increased" (56.48). Thus Dareius suggests that principles of fair dealing and considerations of Athenian interests bind him and his Athenian audience to one another and set them apart from, and against, his shameless opponents.

The foregoing survey suggests that Athenians conceive of litigation as a challenge to the cooperative relationships on which society is founded, and therefore expect litigants to reconcile their participation in litigation with the social ideals threatened by it. Whether litigants insist that they are acting to preserve the ideal of *philia* or, as in disputes over maritime contracts, principles of trust and fair dealing, they seek to prove that they, rather than their opponents, are true members of the community who adhere to its cooperative values.[93] While litigants appeal to these social ideals because they know this will help them win their suits, their appeals have a social significance for Athenians at large. Although Athenians had opportunities to reflect on community ideals in a variety of civic contexts, when they served on large panels of jurors or were present in court as spectators they had an especially good opportunity to do so, since these ideals were conspicuously onstage. Athenians serving on juries were not merely passive observers of the construction of social ideals in the courts but active participants in the process. Every verdict issued was, among other things, a verdict on the competing visions of community that litigants offered. In this way Athens's courts provided a venue not only for the adjudication of individual disputes but also for the articulation and confirmation of collective ideals.[94]

Ideals and Realities

It is reasonable to ask whether the pressure on litigants to appeal to ideals of cooperative behavior in the popular courts had any impact on the actual behavior of Athenians outside of court. Were Athenians aggressive, disputatious, and keen to litigate, and yet ready to appeal in court to ideals of cooperation?[95] On this question, I would take a middle ground between the pessimistic position of D. Cohen that the courts had little effect on aggression in Athenian society and essentially reinforced patterns of feuding behavior, and the optimistic view of Herman that the "civilized" standard of the courts actually prevailed in Athenian society.[96] While there is surely a gap between the collective ideals of cooperation articulated in the courts and individual behavior outside of them, the courts and the peaceful values institutionalized within them in all likelihood had real and salutary effects on disputing behavior.

Athenian disputants, especially those who were members of the elite, had good reason to adjust their disputing behavior because their disputes, if unresolved, were likely to end up before a popular court that would evaluate their behavior, at least in part, by community standards of tolerance and cooperation.[97] Although disputants in Athens and elsewhere do not always behave rationally, especially when making decisions in the heat of the moment, in most cases Athenian disputants had ample time to reflect on what disputing behavior over the course of time would help them achieve their goal of victory over a rival. While litigants once in court could cast their behavior at earlier stages of the dispute, no matter how aggressive, as cooperative and tolerant, peaceful gestures—for example, willingness to submit to private arbitration—that were publicly witnessed would make these claims more credible. Effective self-fashioning as an *apragmōn* began at the outbreak of conflict and culminated in self-presentation in court.

In particular, Athenian disputants were under considerable pressure to moderate their use of force, since jurors would not look favorably on unprovoked physical aggression or disproportionate retaliation (Dem. 54.17–19; cf. Ant. 4.2.2; 4.4.6). To be sure, this did not always stop disputants from striking one another, but it encouraged a degree of restraint that might otherwise have been absent. For example, disputants in Athens tend to avoid committing acts of violence in broad daylight or where witnesses are present: in forensic oratory allegations of reckless violence often place the acts in question at nighttime and/or in an isolated place.[98] If disputants acted cautiously out of fear that open violence would lead to their condemnation by a popular court rather than because they embraced cooperative and peaceful values, the result was nonetheless a positive one for civic peace. Further evidence that disputants were conscious that violent acts might lead to condemnation by a court is found in the way disputants seek to provoke their opponents to actionable outbursts of violence. For example, Apollodorus maintains that his enemies sent a citizen boy to pluck flowers from his rose bed in hope of provoking Apollodorus to engage in an act of hubris against him (Dem. 53.16).

Demosthenes' behavior when Meidias slapped him in the face in public illustrates well how the availability of the courts could alter the behavior of disputants. Demosthenes did not respond in kind, but rather initiated a public lawsuit against Meidias. While some members of the audience judging the suit may have wondered why Demosthenes did not respond physically to this flagrant insult,[99] his decision to bring suit was not only defensible, but also, as Demosthenes intelligently presents it, compatible with the role of the popular courts in controlling the violent outbursts of aggressive citizens (21.123–24). If Demosthenes intended his lawsuit to be an even greater blow to his opponent than the slap he had suffered, the fact that he did not respond physically is significant: the courts gave Demosthenes and other Athenians an alternative to violence.[100]

Six

Beyond the Letter of the Law

An important dimension of the Athenian discussion of legal excess and abuse yet to be considered is the high level of concern among Athenians that knowledgeable experts, well versed in the laws and adept at legal argument, may win unjust verdicts. Athenian attitudes are pithily summed up in a quip of Menander: "The laws are a splendid thing; but a man who looks too closely to the laws is clearly a sykophant" (fr. 545 K-T).[1] Though hardly unique among the world's peoples in their concerns over legal expertise, Athenians were perhaps especially sensitive to this. The mass of Athenians were conscious that an elite minority, because of education and training, had distinct advantages over average Athenians in formulating and presenting legal arguments. This expertise was highly problematic: it not only clashed with egalitarian ideals concerning the conduct of civic life under the democracy, but also gave elite individuals real power to do wrong to other citizens and to the city itself. In this chapter we consider first some of the roots of Athenian concerns over legal expertise and then the impact of these concerns on how litigants presented themselves and their arguments based on laws, procedural rules, and written contracts.

Popular Perceptions of Law and Legal Expertise

Athenian jurors were reluctant to concede too much authority to legal argument in court for two basic reasons. First, they brought to court a perspective on the nature of justice and the purpose of adjudication that privileged the community's sense of "what is right," broadly defined, over a rigid legal standard. Second, jurors were concerned and arguably even insecure about the ability of glib experts to employ legal argument deviously.

THE NATURE OF JUSTICE

Some scholars argue on the basis of the Heliastic oath sworn by Athenian jurors that they must have felt bound to apply and enforce the city's laws closely and conscientiously.[2] Indeed, jurors swore to vote in accordance with the laws and the decrees of the Assembly and Council; where no law was in existence, in keeping with their most just judgment; and without favor or enmity.[3] Oaths were generally taken seriously in Athens,[4] and even unscrupulous persons might hesitate to violate them (cf. Dem. 57.63). Litigants, when it serves them (cf. Arist. *Rh.* 1375b16–18), therefore remind jurors of their oath.[5] Lycurgus goes so far as to warn jurors that, while they cast their votes in secret, the gods will know how they vote (1.146; cf. Dem. 19.240).

One must wonder, however, what impact this oath had on the way jurors actually applied laws. They apparently swore the oath, which was lengthy (cf. Dem. 24.149–51), only once a year when they were selected to serve (cf. Isoc. 15.21), and they swore it collectively, rather than individually.[6] Furthermore, even if jurors were mindful of their oath when voting, few were likely to feel that they were in violation of it however they voted. First, the oath only required them to vote in accordance with the laws, and most laws were sufficiently vague that jurors could vote as they wished with little fear that they were violating their oath. Second, while the oath privileged the laws and directed jurors to rely on their "most just judgment" only where no law applied, jurors may have felt they were carrying the oath out by remaining faithful to the "most just judgment" clause: indeed, litigants sometimes treat this clause as if it were the essence of the oath (Dem. 58.61, cf. 23.96–97).

This is not to say that jurors took the laws lightly. Most probably agreed with the vague notion, to which litigants often appeal, that the city's laws are authoritative (*kurioi*),[7] and were flattered to be addressed as guardians of the law.[8] While a rhetorical handbook could group the laws together with other forms of proof (Arist. *Rh.* 1375a22–25), litigants treat the laws as if they have special authority and jurors probably accepted this.[9] Because the laws were held in high regard, litigants are careful not to criticize them directly. To be sure, a rhetorical handbook could advise litigants that, if a law happens to oppose them, they should argue that "law is laid down for the public benefit, but this law harms the city," and that "it is a public service to annul bad laws" ([Arist.] *Rh. Al.* 1443a23–28). As E. Harris observes, however, in the extant orations Athenian litigants do not have recourse to these direct challenges to laws.[10]

All of this, however, is testimony to the fact that jurors valued legality and held the laws in high esteem, not that they felt bound to apply individual laws to the letter.[11] While law was in a certain uncontroversial sense a standard (*kanōn*: Lyc. 1.8–9; cf. Aesch. 3.199–200) of the courts, jurors determined how and whether to enforce laws on the basis of a more fundamental standard—namely, their sense of "what is just" (*ta dikaia*). The primacy of this standard is evident when litigants speak of a particular law as just (Dem. 24.34; Hyp. 3.22) or argue that a claim is not only consistent with law but also just (Isoc. 19.16).[12] So too litigants sometimes appeal to a standard of justice that transcends particular laws when they speak of the "common law of all men" (Dem. 23.61; cf. Isoc. 18.34; Lys. 1.2),[13] or cite laws from other city-states in support of their cases (Lyc. 1.129).[14] If justice is a criterion by which the laws themselves can be evaluated, however, litigants stop short of asserting bluntly that a law is unjust. One litigant magnanimously concedes that, even if the law does not support his opponents, they should prevail if their cause is just (Dem. 44.8); still, it was best for litigants to present their own claims as justified both by law and principles of justice (Ant. 5.86; Is. 11.35; Dem. 19.179).

Several basic limitations of the city's laws, in fact, made it necessary for jurors to issue verdicts on the basis of their understanding of what was just in light of community norms. First, the body of laws as a whole was manifestly an incomplete expression of community norms. Prosecutors draw attention to this fact when they urge jurors to view as a crime something that has not been written down (Lys. 31.27; Lyc. 1.8–9), or to enforce written and "unwritten laws" simultaneously (Lys. 6.10).[15] Indeed, whereas magistrates were expressly forbidden to enforce "unwritten laws" (And. 1.85–87), jurors were apparently free to do so.[16]

Second, individual laws were highly abbreviated and approximate expressions of norms.[17] A prosecutor attempting to show that his opponent has violated a law thus points out: "It was too much of a task for the lawgiver to write all the words that have the same effect, but by mentioning one he showed his meaning in regard to them all" (Lys. 10.7). Litigants in fact regularly appeal, like this prosecutor, to the "intent of the lawgiver."[18] When they do so, they are not engaging in a search into legislative history but attempting to show how their interpretations of laws are consistent with community norms.[19]

Third, because laws gave no indication of how strict enforcement was to be, it was incumbent on jurors to determine this case by case. Jurors were free to take into account a host of factors, including the character of litigants and the city's best interests (see Chapter 1). Furthermore, Athenians contrasted the humanity of laws under democracy with the harshness of those under oligarchic regimes (Dem. 24.24) and took pride in the fact that they applied laws humanely.[20] The public did not expect all laws to be enforced with the same vigilance (Dem. 25.85–87) and held public persons to a higher standard of behavior than private ones (Dem. 24.193). Indeed, where private persons were involved, jurors were especially receptive to appeals to gentleness (*praotēs*), compassion (*sungnōmē*), and humanity (*philanthrōpia*).[21] How much lenience should prevail in a particular case was a matter for contention among litigants, who depending on their interests characterized this as consistent (Lys. 18.1; 19.53) or at odds with justice (Lyc. 1.33; cf. Din. 1.55).[22]

THE ABILITY OF LEGAL EXPERTS

Jurors hesitated to place too much weight on the letter of the law in adjudication because they were conscious not only of the limitations of laws as expressions of "what is right" but also of the susceptibility of laws to manipulation. Their concerns focused not so much on the law-making process or the safekeeping of written versions of the city's laws as on the ability of litigants to manipulate laws in court.

Litigants take for granted that their audiences will accept laws cited in court as legitimate expressions of shared values and interests. While indictments of proposed decrees and laws must have given rise to some doubts concerning law making—"*rhētores* rarely let a month go by without legislating to suit their private ends" (Dem. 24.142)—in general Athenians appear to have been confident that the city's laws were untainted.[23] Apparently, Athenians also believed that their laws were recorded accurately and secure from physical tampering. For most of the fifth century, laws and decrees were inscribed on stone and displayed publicly. Writing on stone could be and sometimes was erased by interested parties: the Thirty erased democratic laws when they came to power ([Arist.] *AP* 35.2), and a client of Lysias alleges that Nicomachus inserted some laws and erased others for payment when he was involved in revision of the city's laws between 410 and 399 B.C. (30.2, 5).[24] On the whole, however, the possibility of physical tampering with inscribed laws does not seem to have caused much anxiety.[25] After all, stone was less destructible than other materials used for public posting, such as the painted boards (*sanides*) employed for some public notices,[26] and would likely show evidence of any physical tampering. Starting toward the end of the fifth century, all new laws were copied onto papyrus and placed in the city's new archive in the Metroön, and only some laws were inscribed on stone (see Chapter 1). Athenians do not appear to have worried about the substitution of forged laws for those copied on papyrus: the laws were under guard (Aesch. 3.75; cf. 2.89) and the life of the public slave who supervised the archive (Dem. 19.129) probably depended on his preventing abuses.[27] Lycurgus's hypothetical possibility, "Suppose someone should enter the Metroön and erase one law" (1.66), is proposed as something outrageous and unlikely. Athenaeus (407c) relates an anecdote alleging that Alcibiades erased the name of a comic writer Hegemon of Thasos from a legal charge recorded in the Metroön, but this is dubious testimony: other sources indicate that legal charges were displayed by the statues of the eponymous heroes in the agora, and the mention of a comic writer suggests that the episode is derived from a comic source.[28]

While Athenians trusted that the city's laws reflected collective values and interests and were secure from physical tampering, they were well aware that laws as presented in court were the instruments of partisan advocates. Litigants were responsible for selecting and transcribing the laws they planned to cite and brought these to court themselves or, where public arbitration preceded trial, gave them to tribal officials who conveyed them to court in sealed jars (*echinoi*) along with other documents produced at arbitration. The involvement of state officials in the latter context may have ensured that litigants did not surreptitiously deposit additional laws in the *echinoi* so as to surprise opponents in court,[29] but this did not guarantee that the laws originally deposited were relevant to the case. The laws produced in court, moreover, were conspicuously subject to partisan interpretation: claims of twisting the laws (Lys. 10.6–20; Isoc. 18.11; Is. 11.4, 36; Dem. 44.49; Aesch. 3.28, 35, 37, 199–200; Din. fr. IX.3 Conomis) or quoting in a misleading fashion from them (Dem. 18.121; 24.191; Aesch. 3.35) fly back and forth in forensic oratory.[30]

Jurors' uneasiness both toward writing and the spoken word made them reluctant to rely too much on litigants' appeals to the precise wording of laws. Let us consider how their attitudes toward each of these contributed to their skepticism toward legal arguments.

Writing

Despite the increased use of writing during the classical period in public life and administration in general and in litigation in particular, it is likely that few Athenian citizens could read and write with much facility.[31] Aristophanes jokes that all Athenians can forage among the laws and browse through decrees in the agora (*Av.*

1286–89), but for the average Athenian the real situation was probably closer to that depicted by Aristophanes' rival, Cratinus: a character in his *Laws* asserts that while he does not know his letters (*grammata*), he can speak (sc. the laws?) aloud from memory well (fr. 128). Another comic writer quips, "Our laws are like those fine [*leptois*] webs that a spider weaves upon the walls" (Pl. Com. fr. 21). This was perhaps doubly true for the average Athenian: he might perceive not only the substance of the laws but also their written form as a web of subtlety.[32]

Because the average Athenians who dominated juries were less than fully literate, they were ambivalent toward written laws in the courts. While jurors could appreciate the advantages of fixed, publicly inscribed laws, they were not ready to trust absolutely in words they could not themselves easily read.[33]

Special considerations made jurors distrustful of the written word where private documents, like wills and contracts, were involved: because they were suspicious, perhaps rightly so, that these documents were easily forged, they expected litigants to provide witnesses to confirm their authenticity.[34] Concerns over forgery, however, do not appear to have extended to the laws transcribed by litigants. The best explanation for this is that litigants were unlikely to forge laws, because the penalty for citing a nonexistent law was death (Dem. 26.24) and the likelihood of discovery great since consultation of the archives would readily reveal a fabrication.[35]

Jurors' concerns about the laws as written objects arose primarily from the fact that literate litigants, unlike their audiences, enjoyed direct access to the laws and thus, as Hedrick observes, were in a position to know them intimately and misconstrue them in legal argument.[36] Ideally, the laws could be consulted by "anyone who wished" (*ho boulomenos*) (And. 1.84; cf. Dem. 20.93) and were available to rich and poor alike (E. *Supp.* 433–37). These egalitarian ideals existed in tension with the reality that the majority of Athenians had only limited ability to read the written laws.[37] This reality was perhaps nowhere more evident than when elite litigants, who were probably in most cases literate, interpreted written laws before juries composed of considerably less literate citizens.

Because elite litigants realize that the gap in literacy between themselves and their audiences puts them in an awkward position, they tend to avoid drawing attention to this divide.[38] They often present their knowledge of the laws as the result of casual inquiry and usually suppress the fact that they have consulted archived laws in the Metroön.[39] When litigants expose their opponents as men who know the laws too well (Dem. 57.5; 58.24) or who are too clever in using them (Lys. 10.13), they are probably exploiting jurors' insecurities about laws as written objects since literacy was a prerequisite for expert knowledge of the laws.[40] Litigants making such attacks, however, tend not to speak specifically of their opponents' literacy, most likely since this same criticism could easily be turned back against them.[41]

In presenting arguments based on the laws, moreover, litigants tend to avoid pressing "the letter of the law." On the one hand, litigants hail the written laws as a source of precise (*akribēs*) information (Dem. 35.51; 46.10).[42] On the other hand, a man looking to the laws too precisely (*akribōs*) could be labeled a sykophant (Men. fr. 545 K-T; cf. Ant. 3.3.3; Dem. 58.15, with 24).[43] Most Athenians would probably have embraced the ideal of a flexible, unwritten standard of justice articulated by Gorgias in his model funeral oration. Gorgias praises the Athenian war dead, who regularly serve as exemplars of civic values, on the grounds that they "much preferred gentle fairness to a rigid sense of right, and directness of speech to precise points [*akribeias*] of the law" (82 B 6.12–14 D-K).[44] In this view, the way to determine what is right and fair is through honest speech rather than subtle application of written law (cf. Dem. 18.111).

The Spoken Word

If Athenians agreed that it was better to rely upon honest speech than precise points of written law, they were also aware that speech was not always honest and that the oral presentation and interpretation of laws in the courts were further reasons not to trust absolutely in appeals to them. While litigants consulted the laws in their written form and jurors were well aware of their origin in writing (cf. Dem. 21.224), in court jurors met them primarily in oral form. Litigants in the course of their speeches could call upon court secretaries to read aloud laws or excerpts from them. Having an agent of the city read these laws out may have given them an aura of authority and reliability and encouraged audiences to believe that "the voice of the laws is your [i.e., the people's] voice" (Dem. 42.15).[45] But litigants selected the laws to be read out, and the partisan nature of the process was manifest whenever a litigant directed the secretary, "Read *for me* the law itself" (Dem. 46.10; cf. Lys. 1.30, 31). Some litigants, in fact, dispensed with readings by a court secretary and provided their own paraphrases of laws (Hyp. 3.13–17, 21–22). This practice prompts one litigant to warn, "Do not let my opponent talk about a few select phrases that have a benevolent sound to the ear" (Dem. 24.191).[46]

The oral quality of laws in the courts, however, was most conspicuous not in the presentation of the texts of laws but in litigants' legal arguments. This oral argument was manifestly a part of a speaker's overall rhetorical strategy and was subject to the same suspicions that rhetoric in general was.[47] Litigants remind jurors how easily written decrees and laws lose their fixity and stability in the oral medium. For example, Aeschines protests against Demosthenes that "the decrees stand as they were originally written, whereas the words of sykophants are spoken to fit the day and occasion" (2.66). Aeschines likewise plays on his audience's awareness of the gap between rhetoric and law when he criticizes Demosthenes on the grounds that "the orator and the law should speak the same language" (3.16).[48]

In the face of their opponents' supposed rhetorical manipulation of laws, litigants often urge jurors to consider the "law itself" (Dem. 21.46; 46.8, 10; Aesch. 3.15, 22, 30). What they mean, of course, is that jurors should heed *their* rhetorical interpretations of laws rather than their opponents'. Epichares in his prosecution of Theocrines proposes another solution to the problem: "The honorable course for you, men of the jury, is not to put the laws or your own selves in the power of those who speak, but to keep the speakers in your power, and distinguish between those who speak well and lucidly, and those who speak what is just; for it is concerning justice that you have sworn to cast your votes" (Dem. 58.61). Although Epichares' paraphrase of the juror's oath is a loose one, jurors were probably sympathetic to the idea that where legal arguments couched in rhetoric seemed confusing, as must often have been the case, they were to have recourse to their basic sense of "what is just."[49]

Because jurors were suspicious of legal expertise based on knowledge of the written or spoken word, litigants had good reason to suppress information concerning their association with professionals closely identified with knowledge of either sort. No litigant would want to vaunt his training in speaking under a rhetorician or sophist (cf. Dem. 35.15) or advertise the fact that he had consulted with, or purchased a written speech from, a logographer.[50] Such disclosures might lead to the accusation of professionalism, and damage a litigant's credibility with jurors.

When elite litigants disguised their legal expertise, they sought to avoid calling attention to the considerable gap in education and experience between themselves and jurors. To be sure, jurors were familiar with some, and perhaps many, of the laws brought before them, and were also acquainted with rules governing litigation.[51] But this hardly gave them the expertise possessed by many elite litigants, who were able to read and interpret the city's laws with facility. One litigant explicitly acknowledges this gap between jurors and experienced litigants as he expounds upon the Heliastic oath:

> Every man keeps his oath who does not, through enmity or favor or other dishonest motive, vote against his better judgment. Suppose that a juror does not apprehend some point that is explained [*didaskomenos*] to him, he does not deserve to be punished for his failure to understand it. The man who is subject to the curse is the knowledgeable litigant who betrays or deceives the jury. (Dem. 23.97)

If this indulgent attitude toward jurors' errors appears patronizing, the divide assumed between experienced litigant and juror was a real one, and jurors were conscious of it. Confirmation of this is found in the way litigants present their legal knowledge and frame their legal arguments before popular audiences.

Amateurism and Legal Argument

We consider, first, how litigants of all sorts tend to present themselves as legal amateurs; second, how they take into account jurors' concerns about legalities when they discuss legal procedures; and, third, how some of the same public attitudes that induce litigants to tread carefully when making legal arguments affect the way they present arguments based on written contracts.

LEGAL AMATEURS

While most litigants seek to avoid appearing too knowledgeable about legal matters or too adept at legal argument,[52] private persons (*idiōtai*) were under more pressure than public speakers (*rhētores*) to do so. If a litigant sought to give the impression that he was, like the average juror, an *idiōtēs*, and therefore deserved indulgence when presenting his case and dealing with legal questions, he had to be especially careful not to appear too well versed in the law. After all, as an *idiōtēs* he had no reason to be intimately familiar with the city's laws (Dem. 20.93). It was therefore incumbent on logographers, who wrote the speeches for the *idiōtai* represented in the extant forensic orations, to provide their clients with effective legal arguments where called for, but without calling into question their status as amateurs.

Idiōtai avoid giving the impression that they are legal experts by citing laws sparingly: in general, they support their cases more by the reading out of witness testimony than by the citation of laws.[53] When *idiōtai* cite several laws or display subtle knowledge of legal procedures, they feel that they must explain how they became so familiar with legal matters. A common strategy is to blame the opposing litigant for "forcing" one to become acquainted with laws or legal rules. For example, one of Hyperides' clients prefaces his paraphrase of several laws with an address to his opponent: "You have made me so very fearful that I may be ruined by you and your cleverness, that I have been searching [*exetazein*] the laws night and day and studying [*meletan*] them to the neglect of everything else" (3.13; cf. Dem. 54.17). This image of the frantic amateur forced to engage in a legal cram session is consistent with the speaker's general stance as a helpless lover, duped into signing a disadvantageous contract.

Although Hyperides' client represents his inquiry into the laws as that of an amateur, his disclosure that he has consulted the laws directly and without assistance could undercut this claim in the eyes of jurors. Ariston, a young man prosecuting a private suit for assault, is more coy, as he explains how he obtained information about legal actions. Rather than acknowledge that he is literate and has consulted the laws directly or that a logographer has done so on his behalf, he asserts that family and friends communicated the relevant information to him orally (Dem. 54.1). So too, when he engages later in exegesis of the purposes of different actions (54.17–19), he makes sure to represent his knowledge as secondhand (54.18).

A different approach to the problem of portraying legal research is taken by another young *idiōtēs,* Epichares, who is pursuing a public action (*endeixis*) against the *rhētōr* Theocrines to avenge his father's disfranchisement at Theocrines' hands. Epichares emphasizes that while Theocrines, as a *rhētōr,* knows the laws all too well (Dem. 58.24) and has the ability to distort them through tricks of speech (58.61), he is himself an inexperienced speaker who cannot embellish the laws through rhetoric (58.41, 61). Although Epichares cites a number of laws and discusses them in some detail, he shrewdly presents his knowledge as if it were not of the laws but of Theocrines' crimes: after citing a fourth law against Theocrines, he states, "I admit that I have searched [*exētakenai*] into most of the things that the defendant has done" (58.19).

It was important for *idiōtai* not only to downplay their involvement in legal research, but also to avoid giving the impression that their legal arguments were overly subtle. Antiphon in one of his model speeches suggests that, if an opponent protests the subtlety (*akribeia*) of one's legal arguments (cf. 3.3.3), the appropriate response is that he has forced them to be "close and subtle" (*lepta de kai akribē*) by his outrageous conduct, and that they are in fact truthful (3.4.2; cf. 3.2.1–2). Most litigants, however, prefer not to acknowledge that there is anything subtle about their interpretations of law. For example, a client of Lysias reproaches his opponent for thinking he is so clever that he can manipulate the city's laws by quibbling over them (10.13; cf. Dem. 57.5), and contrasts his own straightforward approach:

> Well, gentlemen of the jury, I think you all know that I am speaking correctly [about the law], whereas this man is so obtuse that he cannot understand a word that is said. I would therefore like to instruct him [didaxai] about these matters from other laws as well, in the hope that even now on the speaker's platform he may be educated and in the future desist from making legal trouble for us. (10.15)

While this *idiōtēs* assumes a didactic role in educating his opponent about what the laws mean, he makes it clear that this is due not to his expertise but his opponent's ignorance.[54] Other *idiōtai* also characterize the legal instruction they provide to their opponents not as expert exegesis but as a lesson in the obvious that a reading aloud of the "law itself" imparts (Is. 8.30; Dem. 35.51–52).

Idiōtai avoid displays of legal virtuosity not only in the popular courts but also in the city's other courts, although evidence for practices in the latter is limited. For example, although litigants before the Areopagus in cases involving intentional wounding naturally address the issue of intent (Lys. 3; 4), they treat this in a straightforward manner that is consistent with their emphatic stances as *idiōtai*.[55] Litigants in the city's other homicide courts, which may have been manned by the Areopagites,[56] probably operated under similar constraints. In Lysias 1: *On the Murder of Eratosthenes*, a speech apparently given before the homicide court of the Delphinion, a defendant claims to have committed justified homicide in slaying his wife's lover. Although this speaker cites a number of laws,[57] he poses as a simple and trusting man, who has acted consistently with the values of all Greeks (1.2) and who should not be entrapped by Athens's laws (1.49). These examples suggest that the persons manning the Areopagus and special homicide courts were, like the jurors sitting on popular courts, suspicious of legal expertise.[58]

While experienced public speakers were assumed to be more knowledgeable than average citizens about the city's laws (Dem. 24.66; cf. 19.102), even they do not flaunt their legal knowledge and expertise.[59] Consider, for example, how the *rhētōr* and frequent litigant Apollodorus has Theomnestus explain why he is turning the rest of the prosecution of Neaira over to Apollodorus: "He is older than I and more experienced [*empeiroterōs*] with the laws" (Dem. 59.15). This downplays Apollodorus's considerable legal experience in two ways. First, Theomnestus says only that Apollodorus is *more* experienced with the laws than he, not that Apollodorus is in an absolute sense knowledgeable concerning them. Second, Theomnestus suggests that Apollodorus's experience is not the result of frequent litigation, but a natural consequence of his greater age. As further justification for handing the prosecution over to him, Theomnestus observes that Apollodorus has taken particular (*akribōs*) care "concerning all of these things" (59.15): while Apollodorus has obviously looked specifically into the relevant laws (cf. 59.16, 52, 87),[60] Theomnestus's vague statement acknowledges merely that he has looked into the details of the case (cf. Dem. 58.19).

Although a *rhētōr* played a didactic public role as adviser of the demos in and out of court,[61] it was best for him not to draw attention too directly to his superior role in providing "instruction" concerning laws and decrees. For example, while Lycurgus in his prosecution of Leocrates knowledgeably cites numerous decrees (1.114–25) and even Spartan law (1.129), he justifies this to his audience on the general principle that "instruction by numerous examples makes your decision an easy one" (1.124), but stops short of casting himself personally as their "instructor."

When a *rhētōr* was involved in a suit arising from an indictment for proposing an illegal decree (*graphē paranomōn*) or one for proposing an unsuitable law (*graphē nomon mē epitēdeion theinai*), he could hardly avoid discussing the city's laws and the rules of law making, since these were very much at issue. In such cases a copy of the existing law and the proposed decree or law were placed on display in court for comparison. Yet even in these cases, *rhētores* present their legal arguments as straightforward and simple. For example, a prosecutor of a *graphē paranomōn* who cites numerous laws concerning homicide (Dem. 23.22–62) suggests that his audience is fully aware of the meaning of these (cf. 23.31).[62] He anticipates the objection that he is arguing too closely about the wording of a law ("By Zeus, we are being sykophantic about the matter") by asserting that his arguments are not mere quibbles but fundamental to the written law and to "the common law of all men" (23.61). Similarly, when Diodorus cites numerous laws (Dem. 24.19–72) in his prosecution of Timocrates for proposing and carrying an unsuitable law, he insists that this is necessary since his opponent has violated so many rules of law making, and in fact he is citing only some of the laws broken (24.61; cf. 24.18). He asserts that his arguments are not overly precise but rather that the rules themselves are precise: "Every condition that must be observed when new laws are to be enacted . . . is laid down with precision and clarity [*akribōs kai saphōs*]" (24.17; cf. 24.32). He argues that Timocrates should be held to a high level of accountability, since he is not an *idiōtēs*, who could claim inexperience in proposing laws, but rather is experienced in composing and introducing laws for a wage (24.66). To convict Timocrates would not be to apply the laws rigidly, but merely to enforce fairly laws that are themselves firm and severe in the case of *rhētores*, since their crimes harm the city (24.193; cf. 26.4).

The danger of a *rhētōr*'s placing too much emphasis on the laws is well illustrated by Aeschines' unsuccessful prosecution of Ctesiphon through a *graphē paranomōn* alleging he had illegally proposed that Demosthenes be rewarded with a crown for his public service. Throughout his speech (Aesch. 3), Aeschines appeals to the laws and insists that they be enforced as written. Because Ctesiphon and Demosthenes are sophistic manipulators of the laws, Aeschines must step forward to defend them: "Against their tricks I will introduce your laws as my supporting speakers [*sunēgorous*], as indeed I earnestly try to do throughout this whole prosecution" (3.37). In particular, Aeschines encourages his audience to follow the stern example of an earlier generation of jurors, who "convicted a man of proposing an illegal decree, not just when he had overleaped all the laws together, but if he had violated a single syllable" (3.192). In keeping with his appeal to this rigid standard, Aeschines offers his audience an analogy:

Just as in carpentry when we wish to know what is straight and what is not, we apply the carpenter's rule [*kanona*], which serves as our standard, so too in indictments for illegal decrees there lies ready as a rule of what is just this tablet, containing the decree proposed and the laws transgressed. Show that these agree with one another Ctesiphon, and then take your seat. (3.199–200)

Aeschines thus asserts that, at least in evaluating the legality of public decrees, one should look to the existing laws as a precise standard.[63]

Demosthenes, however, succinctly dismisses Aeschines' legal claims in his speech defending Ctesiphon: "As for Aeschines' confusing jumble of arguments about the laws transcribed for comparison, by the gods, I do not believe that you understand the greater part of them, and I myself was unable to comprehend many of them; I can only offer a plain, straightforward argument, based on what is right [*tōn dikaiōn*]" (18.111). Whether Demosthenes or Aeschines had the stronger legal claims,[64] Demosthenes presents his position in a way that is clearly more compatible than Aeschines' with a popular audience's sensibilities: what is simple and right should naturally be preferred over sykophantic legalities.[65] This may well have contributed to Demosthenes' stunning defeat of Aeschines, who won less than one-fifth of the jurors' votes and was therefore subject to the usual statutory penalties.[66]

These examples suggest that even under the special circumstances in which the city's laws were explicitly at issue and on display in court and knowledgeable *rhētores* engaged in debate concerning them, the public did not welcome subtle legal argument. The appearance of legal sophistication was therefore all the more to be shunned by *idiōtai* arguing cases where the laws were not themselves the focus of debate.

PROCEDURAL ARGUMENTS: LEGALITIES AND TECHNICALITIES

Although any legal claim could be construed as legalistic, arguments concerning procedural matters were especially susceptible to criticism. While appeals to procedural rules, which were often an important component of laws, were routine in forensic argument, a

Beyond the Letter of the Law

litigant dwelling on these was vulnerable to attack on the grounds that he was quibbling over fine points to distract attention from substantive issues. Litigants therefore address procedural questions cautiously and along with, rather than in place of, substantive arguments. Let us consider first how litigants treat regular procedures and then barring actions.

Regular Procedures

While prosecutors could often select from two or more actions in lodging a suit,[67] defendants were free at trial to criticize the action chosen. For example, defendants in public actions regularly protest that the prosecutor should have brought a private action instead. This type of objection was vulnerable to the sort of criticism with which Demosthenes responds to Meidias's complaint that he should have brought a private suit (*dikē*) against him rather than seek a public censure (*probolē*) in the Assembly: "It is typical of a guilty defendant, I think, to try to evade the method being used to bring him to punishment, by saying that a different method should have been employed" (21.27; cf. 22.28). In general, therefore, when defendants object that they are being charged through a public rather than a private action, they emphasize that this involves a gross misapplication of the action in question.

Hyperides, for example, speaking as *sunēgoros* on behalf of Euxenippus, objects that Polyeuctus has flagrantly misused the public action of *eisangelia* in bringing it against a private citizen:

> In public trials, gentlemen of the jury, jurors should refuse to listen to the details of the prosecution until they have first considered the point at issue and the written response of the defendant, to see if the suit is legally valid. By Zeus, it is wrong to maintain, as Polyeuctus did in his speech for the prosecution, that defendants should not insist [*ischurizesthai*] on the *eisangelia* law, which ordains that *eisangeliai* apply not to every Athenian, but only to *rhētores* who speak against the interests of the people. (4.4)

While Hyperides characterizes his procedural objection as peremptory and devotes a good part of his speech to advancing it (4.1–10, 27, 30), he is careful to address at length the substantive claims of

Euxenippus's accusers as well. Like most litigants offering a procedural protest, Hyperides is not about to risk the outcome of a case entirely on it.

Similarly, Isaeus's client Theopompus complains that his opponent has brought an *eisangelia* for the maltreatment of an orphan against him where a *dikē* is clearly the appropriate action (11.34–35). Theopompus argues that *eisangeliai* on behalf of orphans are reserved for cases arising from the administration of an estate, and are not meant to be used in cases like the present one in which property outside the estate is in question. His opponent's devious and sykophantic (11.31; cf. 11.36) intent is to bring a suit in which he bears no financial risk (11.31),[68] while exposing Theopompus to the great personal risk that *eisangeliai* entail. Theopompus protests that this is neither consistent with what is fair (*ta dikaia*: 11.32, 35) nor legal (11.35).[69]

Because an *eisangelia* was so distinct from a *dikē*, defendants may have had some reason to believe that jurors would sympathize with their protests that the former was being used in place of the latter. Some defendants, however, are comfortable in objecting even where the procedures are less distinct from one another. Hyperides' client Lycophron, for example, protests that the wrong kind of public action has been brought against him for adultery:

> You accuse me in your *eisangelia* of undermining the democracy by breaking the laws; but you transgress every law yourself, by presenting an *eisangelia* where the laws require indictments [*graphai*] before the *thesmothetai*. Your object was to bring the action without risk [*akindunos*] and to have the opportunity of writing tragic phrases in the *eisangelia*. (1.12)

Lycophron suggests that his opponent has brought an *eisangelia* rather than a *graphē*, first, to avoid paying a fine if unsuccessful (cf. 1.8) and, second, to make the charge seem more serious than the situation warrants (cf. 1. fr. 3a). Although Lycophron may be right about his opponent's strategy, his objection may have seemed weak: after all, jurors might reason that both public charges were serious ones and view his opponent's avoidance of a *graphē*, in which unsuccessful prosecution might result in a fine, as a reasonable exercise of prosecutorial choice.

Epichares attempts to exploit just such assumptions on the part of jurors, when as prosecutor he anticipates Theocrines' protest that the wrong kind of public action has been brought against him, an information (*endeixis*) in place of an indictment (*graphē*) (Dem. 58.48). Epichares poses a rhetorical question: "Why do you, Theocrines, try to teach [*didaskeis*] me all the ways a man may avenge himself upon his enemies, instead of making a defense in the action in which you have come into court?" (58.52). Epichares' suggestion that Theocrines is attempting to instruct him on legal procedures is a pointed one, since he casts Theocrines as a sykophant who is all too familiar with a variety of legal procedures (58.24). Jurors may have agreed with Epichares that the two procedures were similar enough that any complaint on the part of Theocrines would be a mere quibble. To be sure, from the perspective of a defendant the difference between the two actions could be substantial, since if charged through *endeixis* he might be arrested and imprisoned before trial.[70] But to jurors it may have seemed that both *endeixis* and *graphē* involved serious charges against a defendant, and that the differences between them during the pretrial phase were therefore of little consequence.

While in the preceding case Theocrines' procedural objection against the use of *endeixis* is presented from the slanted perspective of his prosecutor, a defendant's actual protest against *endeixis* appears in Antiphon 5: *On the Murder of Herodes*, one of the earliest extant forensic orations (ca. 420–411 B.C.).[71] In this speech a Mytilenean, Euxitheus, defends himself against the charge that he murdered an Athenian. Much of Euxitheus's speech is concerned not with the charge of murder, however, but with the objection that, while his opponents should have brought a private suit for murder (*dikē phonou*) against him before the Areopagus, they have instead used the procedure of *endeixis*, followed up by summary arrest (*apagōgē*), to bring him before a popular court as a malefactor (5.8–19; cf. 5.85–96).[72] Euxitheus argues that his opponents deviously selected *endeixis* so as to confine him before trial and thus prevent him from preparing his case (5.18). Euxitheus is careful, however, to avoid giving the impression that he seeks acquittal on a technicality. As he embarks upon his excursus on the proper use of procedures, he observes:

> I shall prove to you that the methods used to involve me in today's trial were entirely illegal and violent. Not that I wish to evade trial before a popular court; I would place my life in your hands even if you were not under an oath and I were being tried under no particular law, since indeed I am confident of my innocence of the present charge and in the justice of your verdicts. No, my object is to let the violent and illegal behavior of the prosecution furnish you with evidence as to the character of the rest of their case against me. (5.8)

Thus Euxitheus shrewdly suggests that what follows is not a quibble about procedural distinctions but has a direct bearing on the credibility of the prosecution's case (cf. Dem. 33.27). This self-conscious presentation of a procedural argument in an early oration suggests that from an early date litigants (or the logographers advising them) recognized that jurors might be hostile to such arguments.

Barring Actions

Whereas procedural objections raised at trial enjoyed no privileged status but rather had to compete with other arguments for jurors' attention, in special circumstances a litigant could lodge an action in advance of trial that barred the pursuit of other actions. "Barring actions," as modern scholars have labeled these, were available exclusively in connection with private suits and were of two sorts, *diamarturia* and *paragraphē*.[73]

A *diamarturia* was available to an individual who wished to assert a claim to an estate on the grounds that he had a prima facie right to inherit, for example, because he was the only son of the deceased. The procedure took this name, because it required the testimony (*marturia*) of a witness to the claimant's relation to the deceased. A *diamarturia* constituted a peremptory claim to the estate that could only be set aside if the witness was accused and convicted of giving false testimony.[74] It could be lodged in anticipation of rival claims not yet made, or after claims had already been filed with a magistrate. Its appeal lay in the fact that it gave an heir immediate control of an estate without having to prevail over rival claimants at the *diadikasia*.

In certain private suits, a defendant could lodge a *paragraphē* at the magistrate's preliminary inquiry (*anakrisis*) on the grounds that the action against him was inadmissible. Once a *paragraphē* was initiated, it took priority over the original suit and came before a jury as an independent suit in which the original defendant was now the prosecutor. The circumstances in which a *paragraphē* could be lodged were, however, quite limited.[75] For example, a defendant in a *dikē emporikē* could lodge a *paragraphē* on the grounds that there was no written contract between him and his accuser. A defendant whose opponent had granted him a formal release from legal obligations on an earlier occasion could also bring a *paragraphē*. It is noteworthy that *paragraphē* was not available to persons complaining, as in some of the cases surveyed previously, that their opponents should have brought private rather than public actions. Although Athenians were ready to provide a legal mechanism for pursuing some kinds of procedural protests, they were not ready to endow procedural complaints in general with this status.

As barring actions, *diamarturia* and *paragraphē* resemble one another formally, and, in fact, *paragraphē* appears to have developed from *diamarturia* and to have assumed some of its functions from ca. 400 B.C.[76] Each procedure was the subject of considerable discussion when used. While litigants initiating these procedures could maintain they were legitimate instruments that kept others from making false claims, their opponents could protest that the resulting deviation from "straight adjudication" (*euthudikia*) was unfair to them.[77] Litigants on both sides were under pressure to persuade jurors that they were not placing undue weight on procedural subtleties.

Diamarturia. A prosecutor in a suit charging that his opponent provided false witness at his own *diamarturia* protests at length against this barring action:[78]

> That *diamarturiai* are of all forms of trials [*agōnōn*] the most unjust, and that those having recourse to them are most deserving of your resent-

ment, one can see very clearly from the following facts. In the first place, they are brought not by necessity, as the other forms of procedure are, but by the deliberate choice of the one swearing to them. If in the matter of disputed claims there is no other way of getting a judgment than by a *diamarturia*, it is perhaps necessary to make one. But if it is possible without a *diamarturia* to obtain a hearing before all tribunals, is not the use of one a mark of recklessness and utter desperation? For the lawgiver did not make it obligatory on contending parties to put in a *diamarturia*, but allowed them to do so, if they chose, as if he were testing the character of each of us, to see how we stand in regard to doing something reckless. Furthermore, if it rested with those who file *diamarturiai*, there would be neither popular courts nor trials; for the nature of *diamarturiai* is to block all these things and to prevent all cases from being brought into court, at least if the filer gets his way. (Dem. 44.57–59)

This tirade is remarkable, as it constitutes a critique not only of the way an opponent has used a legal procedure but also of the procedure itself.

Of particular interest is the way this litigant asserts that *diamarturia*, unlike other procedures, is unnecessary. By this he apparently means that, because rival claims to an inheritance are ordinarily resolved in due course by a *diadikasia* before a popular court (cf. 44.11), *diamarturia* is an unnecessary procedure that only an aggressive person would initiate. While the speaker concedes that *diamarturia* may actually be necessary in other circumstances where it might facilitate rather than block adjudication,[79] he maintains that in inheritance disputes this is not the case and, in fact, the law allows *diamarturia* simply to test men's moral character, since only the reckless will have recourse to it. If this is a dubious explanation for the establishment of a legal procedure, it effectively exploits the public's suspicions that only an unscrupulous individual would force a deviation from the normal course of litigation. In keeping with this hostile characterization of *diamarturia*, moreover, the speaker classifies it as a form of trial (cf. Is. 6.4), although in fact it is a procedure that seeks to prevent a trial from occurring (as he himself observes at the end of the passage quoted) and in the current suit he is in the role of aggressor as the prosecutor of a *dikē pseudomarturiōn*.[80]

Similarly, a client of Isaeus characterizes *diamarturia* as a devious alternative to "straight adjudication" (*euthudikia*: 6.3) that is unfair to rival claimants and an attack on the jurisdiction of popular courts over inheritance disputes (6.4). Moreover, he objects: "The purpose of their *diamarturia* is to throw the risk [*kindunos*] in these matters[81] upon their opponents, whereas even if they lose their case on this occasion and the estate is held to be subject to adjudication, they may, by bringing forward a rival claim, twice compete at law over the same property" (6.52). The speaker's assertion that *diamarturia* places legal risks solely upon the challenger is misleading, as there were apparently financial risks on both sides.[82] More accurate probably is the speaker's observation that *diamarturia* in effect gave a claimant two independent chances to win an inheritance: if unchallenged, he automatically received the inheritance in question; if challenged and defeated, he could still make a claim on the estate at the *diadikasia*. His loss of a false-witness suit might reduce his chances of winning a claim at the *diadikasia*, but this loss was not necessarily so prejudicial as to deter him from pursuing at least a part of the estate at a *diadikasia*;[83] he could claim that the jury in the earlier trial had been bamboozled and make his arguments anew before a fresh panel.

Because these criticisms of *diamarturia* appear in the speeches of parties bringing false-witness suits against persons attesting to *diamarturiai*, they no doubt exaggerate the procedure's potential for abuse. Consistent with these attacks on *diamarturia* as a devious procedure, however, is the way another litigant makes a merit out of his decision *not* to use it:

> If I observed that you [the jurors] prefer *diamarturiai* to direct actions [*euthudikias*], I would have brought forward witnesses to show that the estate is not subject to adjudication since Apollodorus adopted me in accordance with the laws. But since I am aware that by this method the rights [*ta dikaia*] of the case cannot be fully made known to you, I have myself come forward to explain the facts, so that they may bring no charge against us of being unwilling to submit to such a trial. (Is. 7.3)

Although this speaker probably did not lodge a *diamarturia* because he was in a poor position to do so,[84] he makes a virtue out of necessity. Like litigants criticizing their opponents for using *diamarturiai*, he characterizes the procedure as a deviation from direct adjudication that may be legal, but is inconsistent with "what is right" and with the principle that popular courts should decide such matters.[85]

It is difficult to know how seriously jurors would have taken these various objections to *diamarturia*. Harrison suggests, "There seems to have been a certain feeling—probably it was not much more—that there was something slightly evasive in employing the *diamarturia*."[86] But criticisms leveled against the use of *diamarturia* may well have had an air of plausibility. After all, even if *diamarturia* was a common procedure in the context of settling estates, it involved a deviation from the "straight adjudication" before a popular court that was the norm for most types of claims, and for this reason may have appeared questionable. Furthermore, jurors may well have suspected that the procedure was as likely to be used by a false claimant seeking to evade the *diadikasia* as by a legitimate heir. When litigants protested the use of *diamarturia*, therefore, jurors may have been ready to believe that the objections raised were not legal nit-picking.

Paragraphē. The survival of eight speeches delivered in trials involving *paragraphai* gives us relatively more information about the role of procedural arguments in these suits. Six of the eight, however, are those of the prosecutor of the *paragraphē* (the defendant in the original suit), whereas only two are those of the defendant in the *paragraphē* (the original prosecutor).[87] This distribution means that more praise than criticism of this procedure is found in the extant speeches. In general, prosecutors of a *paragraphē* praise it as a measure designed to keep sykophantic suits from reaching court (Dem. 33.2; 36.2–3; Isoc. 18.2–3). Defendants argue, by contrast, that this deviation from direct adjudication (*euthudikia*) (Dem. 34.4; cf. 45.6) is an instrument for sykophantic evasion; one litigant therefore groups it together with other dishonest devices, "sophisms, *paragraphai*, and pretexts" (Dem. 35.2).

Consider, for example, the contrasting views of *paragraphē* presented in connection with its use in a dispute over funds that Apollodorus alleged Phormio had stolen from the estate of his father, Pasio. When Apollodorus brought suit against Phormio many years after Pasio's death despite having settled with him earlier and given him discharge from future obligations, Phormio lodged a *paragraphē* asserting that the formal discharge granted him by Apollodorus made his suit inadmissible (Dem. 36.25) and sykophantic (36.3, 24). Phormio's advocate asserts preemptively at the opening of his speech: "We have filed a *paragraphē* against the suit, not so that we may evade the issue and waste time, but so that, if Phormio shows he has committed no wrong whatsoever, he may win in your court an acquittal that will be authoritative [*kuria*]" (36.2). When Apollodorus lost this *paragraphē*, he prosecuted one of Phormio's witnesses, Stephanus, for giving false testimony (Dem. 45; 46), and in his prosecution he presents a very different picture of *paragraphē*. Apollodorus alleges that Phormio "contrived and concocted a plot," whereby he entered a *paragraphē* and provided false witnesses to support his action (Dem. 45.5–6). That Apollodorus considers the use of a *paragraphē,* and not simply the suborning of witnesses in support of it, devious is evident from his complaint that Phormio took advantage of the fact that by the rules governing *paragraphai* his side spoke first: in this way Phormio (actually Phormio's advocate) was able to win over the jury through his lies, and "he made such an impression on the jurors that they refused to hear a single word from me" (45.6).[88]

While discussion of the procedure of *paragraphē* itself was an important part of *paragraphē* trials, so too naturally was argument based on the particular procedural violation alleged. In fact, prosecutors of *paragraphai* seize the opportunity provided by the assertion of a formal procedural complaint to make allegations concerning abuses of procedure that are not themselves grounds for *paragraphai*. For example, although violation of a statute of limitation was not grounds for lodging a *paragraphē*, several prosecutors of *paragraphai* protest that their opponents are guilty of this (Dem. 33.27; 36.26–27; 38.17).[89] While they do not go so far as to present this objection as the basis of their *paragraphai*, they do not distinguish clearly between this and the actual basis. They may rightly have calculated that jurors would not be inclined to worry over the distinction but would consider together all allegations concerning procedural violations in reaching a verdict.

Although procedural arguments were very much a part of *paragraphē* trials and jurors probably allowed litigants considerable freedom here, if anywhere, to argue on the basis of procedural rules, litigants on both sides recognize that it would be a mistake to limit themselves to debate over proper procedures and thus address substantive issues as well.[90] Often litigants explicitly remark that they will not rely solely on arguments concerning procedural issues but will prove that they are in the right in the original dispute (Dem. 32.1–2; 34.3–4). One litigant makes his rationale for doing so explicit: "So that no one, men of Athens, may suppose it is because I am at a disadvantage regarding the rights [*tois . . . dikaiois*] of the matters at issue that I have recourse to this *paragraphē*, I wish to show that in every one of his charges against me he is lying" (Dem. 37.21; cf. 37.1). It is testimony to Athenian concerns about arguments based on legal fine points that even in *paragraphai*, where procedural issues are unavoidable, litigants tend to downplay their dependence on such claims.

In many *paragraphē* trials, litigants must not only maneuver around jurors' concerns over their use of procedural arguments but also determine how best to frame and press their claims based on contracts. The next section focuses on how litigants in *paragraphai* and other suits involving contracts meet this challenge.

ENFORCING THE LETTER OF A CONTRACT

Some of the same popular attitudes and concerns that shape how litigants treat laws and procedural rules also affect how they frame their appeals to written contracts. Litigants recognize that just as jurors may be hostile to them if they appeal too rigidly to the letter of the law, so too jurors may disapprove of them if they press the terms of a contract too far.

There were a number of reasons for jurors to associate laws and contracts with one another. Both were fixed, written sources of authority that a litigant could have read out in support of his case.[91] Furthermore, each involved rules that had been agreed upon: thus Aristotle suggests that a litigant could argue, "A contract is a law applying to individuals and particulars," and "In a general sense, a law is a kind of contract" (*Rh.* 1376b7–10; cf. [Arist.] *Rh. Al.* 1422a3–4). Although litigants do not express the relationship between laws and contracts so analytically, they equate the two: for example, one litigant points out that his opponent "insists [*ischurizetai*] on his private contract with me, although he has transgressed our common contracts with the state [i.e., the laws]" (Hyp. 3.31; cf. Dem. 25.16).[92]

Because of the affinity between laws and contracts, Aristotle advises litigants that similar arguments may be applied to the two (*Rh.* 1376b15–17), and indeed in the extant forensic speeches litigants treat arguments based on each in similar ways. For example, litigants appeal to contracts, as to laws, as sources of precise (*akribēs:* Dem. 33.36; 35.25) information that expressly (*diarrhēdēn:* Dem. 56.11; 35.51–52) address the matters in dispute and assert that they should be regarded as authoritative (*kurios:* Dem. 35.43; cf. Hyp. 3.13) and binding (*ischuros:* Dem. 56.48). Furthermore, litigants depict written contracts, like texts of laws, as fixed sources of authority that should be trusted more than the shifting, unstable oral arguments of their opponents (Dem. 33.36; 35.1–2, 22). But appeals to contracts, as to laws, are ultimately constrained by the public's discomfort with rigid appeal to written authority: litigants can characterize inflexible appeals to contracts, as to laws, as insisting on (*ischurizomai*) fine points and inconsistent with what is right (*ta dikaia*) in a particular case (Hyp. 3.31; 3.13).[93]

Despite these basic similarities in the ways litigants treat laws and contracts, contracts differed from laws in important respects, and this could work either in favor of or against arguments that jurors should enforce contracts. On the one hand, a litigant could demand strict enforcement of a contract on the grounds that individuals entered contracts willingly and for a specific purpose (Dem. 56.2). While Plato argues that citizens should obey the city's laws on similar grounds, namely, because they contract to follow them (esp. *Cri.* 50a5–54d1), the point of entry into this contract is not so clearly demarcated and its terms far more complex. A litigant could argue, moreover, that there was something universal about the sanctity of agreements between persons that made it especially important to enforce contracts (Isoc. 18.27–28; cf. Arist. *Rh.* 1376b11–14).

On the other hand, contracts were less reliable than the city's laws as sources of authority for a number of reasons. Whereas the lawmaking process was public and subject to close scrutiny, contracts were made in private—though often in the presence of witnesses—and were not subject to state supervision. Furthermore, whereas copies of laws were guarded in the city archive, contracts were less well protected even when deposited in the hands of third parties for safekeeping (cf. Dem. 33.16–18). Because of these differences, litigants could cast doubt on contracts in ways that they could not on laws. At trial, therefore, litigants seeking the enforcement of a contract did well to bring in as witnesses persons who had been present at its signing and those to whom the contract had been entrusted (cf. Arist. *Rh.* 1376b2–5).

Jurors seem to have allowed litigants in maritime suits considerable latitude in pressing contractual claims.[94] This is consistent with the special nature of the actions involved, *dikai emporikai*, which could be brought only if a contract existed between the disputants, or *paragraphai* protesting that no such contract existed and therefore a *dikē emporikē* lodged was not admissible. Furthermore, jurors were probably inclined to hold the parties to maritime agreements to the terms of their contracts, since they could be assumed to be men of experience who had entered contracts knowingly and with an eye to their profitability, and because it was in the city's interests that these contracts function properly. Accordingly, litigants in these circumstances unabashedly advance their contractual claims. One litigant, for example, who claims that his opponent, Lacritus, has made off with money lent to his brother (now deceased) for the shipping of wine, stresses that he had a contract with Lacritus's brother. He asserts that Lacritus has no respect for the law or contracts (Dem. 35.1); he asks twice that the contract in question be read to the court (35.10–13, 37); and he discusses it closely ("I will take up the clauses of the contract one by one, and show that in no single instance have these men done what is proper": 35.17) and at length (35.18–25). Furthermore, he emphasizes the precise (35.25) and express (35.52) terms of the contract and insists it is both fair and in the interest of the city that the contract be upheld as binding (35.54–56). Likewise, another client of Demosthenes involved in a maritime dispute vigorously advances his contractual claims (56.6–7, 11) and insists that contracts should be binding (56.48–50).[95] He reassures his audience, however, that he was ready to compromise to avoid litigation: "We were not unaware, men of the jury, of our just claim under the agreement, but we thought it necessary to suffer some loss and make a concession, so as not to appear overly fond of litigation [*philodikoi*]" (56.14).[96]

In disputes over contracts that were less conspicuously commercial in nature and involving less experienced parties, however, jurors may have been less receptive to contractual claims and less inclined to hold that a contract was binding. For example, a client of Hyperides prosecuting a certain Athenogenes (Hyp. 3) asserts that he was duped into signing an unfair contract with his opponent and therefore should not be held to its terms.[97] Hyperides' client describes the situation as follows. When he fell in love with a slave boy belonging to Athenogenes and sought to purchase him, Athenogenes, with the assistance of his mistress, tricked the speaker into buying not only the boy but also the boy's father and brother, along with the perfume business in which they all worked. Furthermore, Athenogenes manipulated the speaker into agreeing by contract to assume the perfume business' debts, which he represented as minimal. Once Hyperides' client took over the business, however, he discovered that the outstanding debts were huge—in fact, many times the price he had paid for the business and the slaves. He therefore brought suit against Athenogenes to recoup his losses.

In arguing that his contract should not be binding, Hyperides' client presents himself as an innocent lover, manipulated by a plotting sykophant (cf. 3.25).[98] Athenogenes, he asserts, laid a trap for him and thereby forced him to consent to the agreement (3.18; cf. 3.12). His description of the circumstances under which this agreement came into being draws attention to the manipulation involved: "When I accepted his proposals, he immediately took a document from his lap and began to read the contents, which were the text of an agreement with me. I listened to it being read, but I was in a hurry to complete the business for which I had come" (3.8).

Although this speaker is clearly literate (3.10, 13), he suggests that his opponent made devious use of his literacy by reading the contract aloud while the speaker listened in a state of distraction. Hyperides' client also points out that he had no friend, who presumably could have prevented him from entering into this duplicitous contract, present as witness (3.8). Only later, when creditors came forward seeking to collect some five talents in debt from the speaker (3.9), did he call together his friends and family members to read a copy of the agreement. What they found was that, although some minor debts were expressly noted in the contract, the large debts were not listed but rather were "mentioned as an unimportant item in an addendum, which ran 'and any debt which Midas [the slaveboy's father] may owe to any other person'" (3.10). When the speaker and his supporters confronted Athenogenes, he pretended not to know of any debts and responded simply that "he had in his possession a written document concerning these matters" (3.12).[99]

In light of this deception, Hyperides' client maintains, it is absurd for Athenogenes to insist (*ischurizesthai*: 3.18, 31) on the terms of the contract: "Athenogenes will presently tell you that the law states that whatever agreements one man makes with another are binding. Yes, my friend, at least agreements that are just. But if they are unjust, the opposite is true: the law forbids that they be binding" (3.13). The laws that Hyperides' client proceeds to cite, however, state no exception to the law of contracts (3.13–18, 21–22) and apply only loosely to the circumstances of his case.[100] His protest thus appears to be based very much on considerations of fairness: the general rule that contracts are binding should surely not be applied in the case of a duplicitous contract. Just as another litigant protests that jurors should not allow him to be "ambushed" by the laws (Lys. 1.49), so too Hyperides' client urges his audience not to tolerate a situation in which an honest man is "ambushed" by a fraudulent contract (3.12, 18).[101]

If jurors were ready to overrule the terms of a written contract in some cases, they appear to have been all the more prepared to overrule the specifications of a written will.[102] Two considerations made jurors reluctant to rely too heavily on wills. First, as litigants often point out, wills could be forged (Is. 7.2; 9.2; fr. 2 Thalheim; Dem. 45.29; cf. Arist. Pr. 950b5–8).[103] Second, even if a will was not forged, its terms might be unfair (Is. 9.27–31). Thus one litigant urges jurors that they should not hold valid a will that is "contrary to law, what is just, and the intention of the deceased" (Is. 1.35; cf. 1.26).[104] Jurors were probably sympathetic to such arguments and ready to privilege them over the authority of written wills (cf. Ar. V. 583–86).[105] This angered some wealthy Athenians, for whom adjudication of inheritance disputes was especially important, and therefore when the Thirty came into power they acted to eliminate grounds on which jurors could overturn wills, "so that there might be no leeway to sykophants" ([Arist.] AP 35.2).

To judge by the way litigants presented themselves and their arguments before popular courts, Athenian juries were inclined to view legal sophistication and subtle argumentation based on written authority with considerable suspicion. This did not stop litigants from advancing, and sometimes pressing vigorously, claims based on laws, procedural rules, and contracts. Yet, in general, it was critical for litigants in these circumstances to reassure jurors that their claims were founded ultimately on a communal standard of fairness that any member of their audiences could understand and embrace. This downplaying of legal expertise before lay juries is hardly surprising; in a modern context professional lawyers arguing before citizen juries often adopt a similar strategy. In an Athenian context, however, there was no professional judge, as there is in a modern U.S. setting, before whom more technical claims could be presented; this reduced considerably the likelihood that written sources of authority in Athens would be upheld to the letter.

While Athenian jurors' distrust of legal sophistication could be viewed as evidence of excessive insecurity on the part of the uneducated citizens dominating juries, jurors in fact had good reason to be uneasy about subtlety in legal argument and insistence on legal fine points. Athenian laws and procedural rules were not designed to sustain the weight of close analysis and argument, and could be manipulated easily by experienced litigants. Indeed, in Athens the development of legal rhetoric far outpaced the growth of jurisprudence, and jurors did well therefore to look beyond the laws, as interpreted by sophisticated litigants, in issuing verdicts. In relying ultimately on their own sense of "what is fair" rather than on any external standard of authority, jurors confirmed that in adjudication, as in all matters within the democracy, the authority of the people was supreme.

Conclusion

> The public seems . . . to have a love-hate
> relationship with law. It sees law as a bag of tricks, a
> bottomless pit of artifice and legalism; but it also
> sees law as a shining sword of justice, a powerful
> weapon of public purpose.
> —L. Friedman ([1989] 1599)

Friedman's observation concerning the American public's "love-hate relationship" with law could well be applied to the Athenian public. The discussion of legal excess and abuse in Athens attests unmistakably to Athenian ambivalence toward litigation under the democracy. While Athenians took pride in the unique status of law in their city and in the role of the popular courts under democratic rule, they were concerned about many aspects of litigation.

Athenian concerns reflected fundamental questions about litigation within the city. Under what rules and within what parameters should litigation be conducted? What role should experts and expertise play in the process? How much assistance should a litigant receive from supporters, and should this take the form of advocacy by third-party prosecutors? When the city is the "victim" of an offense, who should volunteer to prosecute on its behalf and what are legitimate motivations for doing so? When is it appropriate to turn a private quarrel into a lawsuit, and how can the pursuit of litigation be reconciled with communal ideals of cooperative behavior? How should courts respond to complaints about the use of the legal process, and in particular how far should juries composed of average citizens go in accommodating the special concerns of elite litigants?

To some extent Athenians responded to these diverse concerns by modifying legal rules and institutions. Athenians grappled creatively with the problem of balancing incentives and disincentives for prosecuting suits, and from the end of the fifth century they required disputants in most private actions to submit to public arbitration before pursuing their suits to court. In general, however, Athenians were reluctant to limit access to the courts and left it to jurors representing the community and its values to evaluate case by case the use of litigation. By appealing to shared values, litigants sought to persuade jurors of the appropriateness of their legal behavior and of the sykophantic and antisocial nature of their opponents' actions.

Although litigants no doubt characterized legal excess and abuse as challenges to shared values because this helped them win favorable verdicts, for the community this public discussion encouraged reflection on what the role of litigation should be within the democracy. While the issues involved were at their roots complex and the problems addressed in some sense insoluble, jurors through their verdicts could show pleasure or displeasure at how a litigant framed and answered basic questions about the place of litigation within the city. Jurors' verdicts, in turn, had to be taken into account by future litigants and the logographers assisting them not because verdicts set legally binding precedents, but because they were indications of, among other things, the attitudes of popular audiences concerning proper legal behavior.

Although the Athenian discussion of legal excess and abuse was ongoing and intense, it is best viewed as evidence not of a profound legal crisis or the sorry state of the democratic legal system but of the fundamental importance of the issues at stake. Concerns over legal excess and abuse pertained most directly to litigation and the courts, but they also reflected basic questions about the nature of private and public life within the democracy. Jurors may have been drawn to serve in the courts because lawsuits brought onstage intriguing and sometimes troubling questions about litigation in the city. Litigants discussed the specific circumstances of their cases and also addressed questions concerning the proper use of litigation. This explicit "metalegal" discussion was not only allowed by court rules but expected by jurors. Thus, in every trial in Athens litigation itself was potentially on trial.

It should be clear by this point that to speak of Athenians categorically as "litigious" or to decry Athenian "litigiousness" is to overlook a complex web of social meanings and tensions within the Athenian discussion of legal excess and abuse. For Athenians these matters were controversial ones touching ultimately on basic aspects of life under the democracy. If the past can provide a lesson for the present, the Athenian experience suggests that discussion of and concern about legal excess and abuse are inevitable in a democratic society that values access to courts and yet remains conscious that the pursuit of litigation is not necessarily synonymous with the pursuit of justice.

Notes

Introduction. Litigiousness, Ancient and Modern

1. Lieberman (1981); W. K. Olson (1991); Glendon (1994). On the promulgation of this view, see Galanter (1983) 5–11, (1986) 3–5, (1994) 643–62; Hoffer (1989) 295–97.
2. Galanter ([1983] 6) credits Manning ([1977] 767) with this coinage.
3. For an aggressive litigant as a "cancer," see Dem. 25.95. For an analogy between lawsuits and diseases, see Strabo 6.1.8.37–40 (claiming to cite Plato). For addiction to service on juries as a disease, see Ar. V. 85–135.
4. See Goldstein (1987); Freckelton (1988).
5. *New York Times*, April 26, 1996, D20.
6. Ibid., June 8, 1983, A23.
7. Friedman (1989) 1599.
8. I use *legal system* loosely to denote Athenian legal institutions, not to suggest that Athenians were orderly or systematic in designing these. S. Todd ([1993] 21) goes too far, I think, in positing that there was "a latent logic behind the system, even if not an explicit legal theory" (cf. Christ [1994] 258).
9. On the high level of citizen involvement in Athenian courts, see MacDowell (1978) 40; cf. Garner (1987) 3. Contrast the modern American situation, as described by Friedman (1989) 1593.
10. On the inclusion of these items (*pinakia*) in graves, see Kroll (1972) 9–10, 262–63; cf. Lang (1995) 59–64.
11. I follow S. Todd ([1993] 93) et al. in adopting the spellings *sykophants*

and *sykophancy* to distinguish these Athenian words, which were used primarily in connection with legal matters, from their modern English derivatives, which do not have this association.
12. Ober ([1989] 341–48) conveniently catalogs the extant speeches, some of which were not delivered in court.
13. See S. Todd (1993) 36–38; E. Harris (1995) 7–16; cf. Harvey (1990) 103–6.
14. Worthington (1991) does not persuade me that the complex ring composition found in some extant speeches was not present in the version presented in court.
15. See D. Cohen (1989) 95–99.
16. On the formation of the canon of the ten Attic orators, see Worthington (1994); Smith (1995).
17. On the uneven distribution of speeches, see Ober (1989) 49, 349.
18. For the synchronic approach to the study of Athenian attitudes, see Dover (1974) 30 (for the period 425–325 B.C.); Ober (1989) 36–38 (for 403–322 B.C.); Hunter (1994) 6–7 (for 420–320 B.C.).
19. For a survey of criticisms of Athenian democracy from ancient to modern times, see J. Roberts (1994); cf. Wood (1988) 5–41.
20. Lofberg (1917) 9–10; cf. 19.
21. For example, Lofberg ([1917] 23) takes the conservative Isocrates' complaints about sykophancy in his *Antidosis* as typical of "the attitude of the bulk of the Athenians toward it."
22. Followers of Lofberg include Bonner (1927) 65; Bonner and Smith (1938) 2.69; Ehrenberg (1951) 345–46, (1973) 215–16; J. Jones (1956) 123; Carter (1986) 49, 82. Hunter ([1994] 126) does not embrace Lofberg's sociopolitical assumptions concerning sykophancy, but accepts his view of the situation as a crisis.

When C. R. Kennedy (1891) characterizes the sykophant for his nineteenth-century audience as a "common barretor, informer, pettifogger," contemporary class bias also colors his picture. Hay ([1989] 359) notes the use of the class-charged "common informer" in connection with *qui tam* proceedings in eighteenth- and nineteenth-century Britain.
23. A. H. M. Jones ([1957] 58) was one of the earliest scholars to point out that elite sources present a distorted picture of "sykophancy."
24. Osborne (1990) 99; cf. S. Todd (1993) 93.
25. Osborne (1990) 99, building on Finley ([1962] 1974) 23.
26. Harvey (1990) criticizes Osborne's position primarily on philological grounds: he rightly points out that Athenians used the root *sukophant*-pejoratively and thus "sykophancy" could not in their view be a good thing. Harvey does not, however, come to terms with the class issues raised by Osborne's treatment. Hunter ([1994] 228 n. 20) well ob-

serves of their exchange that "their disparate conclusions are a cause for concern.... It may well be time for a major work on this subject, since Lofberg's classic study ... is much out of date."
27. Galanter (1983) 49–50, (1986) 20–26; cf. Nelson (1988) 686–91. On perceptions of law in "popular legal culture," see Macaulay (1989); Yngvesson (1989); Friedman (1989).
28. Galanter (1983) 36; cf. Kagan (1983) 152; Greenhouse (1982) 31.
29. Galanter (1986) 38. For case studies of "outsiders" as litigants, see H. Todd (1978); Engel (1984).
30. Galanter (1983) 64; cf. (1994) 662–69; Nelson (1988) 686–89.
31. For balanced criticism of Galanter's views, see Nelson (1988).
32. "Drunk Drivers' Protection Act" is President Clinton's characterization of the proposed bill (*Washington Post*, May 5, 1995, A1).
33. A number of essays on the subject cited here are collected in Greenhouse, Engel, and Yngvesson (1994).
34. Engel (1987) 636.
35. Engel (1984) 577–81.
36. Greenhouse (1989) 271.
37. Ibid., 252.
38. Galanter (1983) 11.
39. Galanter ([1983] 41) and Hoffer ([1989] 299–306) review the scholarly literature. Useful discussions of "litigiousness" in other societies include Frier (1985) 27–41 (ancient Rome); Sharpe (1983) (early modern England); Kagan (1983) (Castile, 1500–1700); Hay (1989) (England, 1750–1850).
40. Ann Landers (*Washington Post*, Oct. 30, 1994, F4), commenting on a reader's letter concerning the woman who sued McDonald's when burned by coffee purchased there; for the lawyer's response, see *Washington Post*, Jan. 16, 1995, B10.
41. *New Republic*, Oct. 31, 1994, 43.
42. Engel (1984) 581.
43. Galanter (1983) 59; cf. (1986) 12–14. On the hazards of comparing litigation rates from different societies, see Galanter (1983) 51–61; cf. (1994) 669–81; Nelson (1988) 683–84. Useful discussions of litigation rates in modern Western democracies include Atiyah (1987) (comparing the United States and Britain); Markesinis (1990) (on England, Germany, and the United States); Blankenburg (1994) (on the Netherlands and West Germany).
44. Engel (1984) 552.
45. Galanter (1983) 61.
46. Greenhouse (1989) 254.
47. Thus Greenhouse (1989) 253. It is often difficult to tell whether

persons speaking of "litigiousness" are decrying the quantity or quality of litigation, or both; on this ambiguity, cf. Kagan (1983) 155.

Chapter One. Litigation in Democratic Athens

1. On Athenian law before 508/7 B.C., see Ruschenbusch (1968); Stroud (1968); Gagarin (1981), (1986); Ostwald (1986) 5–15; Sealey (1994) 113–32.
2. On the diverse connotations of demos, see Lewis (1990) 260–63. On *isonomia*, see Ober (1989) 74–75 with n. 50; Raaflaub (1995) 49–51, (1996) 139–45.
3. On the Ephialtic reforms, see Ostwald (1986) 47–80; Wallace (1989) 77–87; Marr (1993); Raaflaub (1995) 36–42; Rihll (1995); DeBruyn (1995) 87–110. On the jurisdiction of the Areopagus, see Wallace (1989) 97–121; Hansen (1991) 288–95; DeBruyn (1995).
4. Garner ([1987] 42–43) notes some of these factors. On the fifth-century surge in litigation, see S. Todd (1993) 152–53.
5. See de Ste. Croix (1961); Meiggs (1972) 220–33; Fornara (1979); Rhodes (1985) 39; Koch (1991), (1993); S. Todd (1993) 329–32.
6. On the Periclean citizenship law, see Patterson (1981); Rhodes (1981) 331–35; Walters (1983); Manville (1990) 215–18; French (1994); Boegehold (1994).
7. On this shadowy episode, see Stadter (1989) 336–39.
8. On this proliferation of regulation, see Ostwald (1986) 410–11; cf. Garner (1987) 42–43. Sophocles' *Antigone* (441 B.C.), which explores the conflict between a tyrant's decrees and unwritten customs (453–55), may reflect contemporary concerns over the city's growing body of legal regulation.
9. On the new politicians, see Connor (1971).
10. On the sophists, see Guthrie (1971); Kerferd (1981); de Romilly (1992). On the development of rhetoric in the classical period, see G. Kennedy (1963); Cole (1991).
11. For discussion of the logographer's role, see Lavency (1964); Dover (1968) 148–74; Usher (1976); Worthington (1991), (1993); S. Todd (1993) 95–96; Hunter (1994) 233 n. 46.
12. See Galanter (1983) 36.
13. For a stimulating exploration of how the possibility of litigation affects disputing behavior in Athens, see Scafuro (1997), esp. 42–50, 69–84.
14. S. Todd ([1993] 156–57) suggests that growing urbanization in fifth-century Athens may have taken its toll on social relations and made Athenians more willing to litigate against one another, but, as he rightly observes, "Athens may have been more 'urbanized' than any other polis, but that is not saying very much" (156 n. 13).

15. See MacDowell (1986) 123–50.
16. Greenhouse (1982) 31.
17. See S. Todd (1993) 69–70; cf. Rhodes (1995). For general criticism of evolutionary models, see Humphreys (1985a) 248–50; D. Cohen (1995) 3–6, 13–19.
18. Recent surveys of Athenian democratic institutions include Sinclair (1988); Stockton (1990); Hansen (1991). On Athenian demography, see Hansen (1985), (1991) 90–94, (1994); cf. Rhodes (1988) 271–77.
19. See Rhodes (1972).
20. See Hansen (1991) 239–40.
21. Hansen ([1991] 240–42), however, argues that from the late fifth century most officeholders were unpaid.
22. Ibid., 205–24, for an overview of the legal actions discussed in this paragraph.
23. Ibid., 272.
24. Ibid., 269–70.
25. Ibid., 178–224, for an excellent overview.
26. On the number of court days, see Hansen (1979). On jury sizes, see Rhodes (1981) 728–29; Hansen (1991) 186–87; S. Todd (1993) 83 with nn. 9, 10. On methods of jury selection, which varied over time, see Boegehold (1995) 21–42.
27. See Markle (1985) on wages (265 with n. 1) and wage equivalents (293).
28. On the social composition of juries, I follow Markle (1985) 281–89; cf. Ober (1989) 142–44. While most jurors, rich or poor, were probably farmers, and litigants often appeal to them on this basis (Markle [1990] 164), this is not grounds (*pace* S. Todd [1990b] 169) for rejecting the common classification of jurors as "poor men": most jurors were involved with agriculture in some capacity and were, relative to elite Athenians, also "poor men."
29. On the Eleven and their public slaves, see Hunter (1994) 144–49; cf. E. Harris (1994b).
30. On the special homicide courts, see MacDowell (1963) 58–89; Boegehold (1995) 43–50. It is debated whether the *ephetai* who manned these courts were Areopagites (thus Carawan [1991]) or jurors from the popular courts (thus Wallace [1989] 102–5).

In the 340s B.C., the Areopagus was charged with investigating certain crimes against the people and with issuing a preliminary verdict on them, but this verdict could be overturned by a popular court: on the new procedure (*apophasis*) involved, see Carawan (1985); Wallace (1989) 113–19; Hansen (1991) 292–94; DeBruyn (1995) 117–46, 201–4.

31. Worthington ([1989] 205) argues, however, that in some cases political trials could last two or three days.
32. E. Harris ([1994a] 136) argues that *dikastēs* should be translated "judge." On the problem of translating *dikastēs*, see S. Todd (1993) 82–83.
33. On the relation of the popular courts to Assembly, I follow Ober ([1989] 144–47) over Hansen ([1978]; cf. [1989b]).
34. See Lofberg (1917) 10–11; Dover (1974) 92; Ober (1989) 145–47.
35. See S. Todd (1993) 299; cf. Ober (1989) 140.
36. On the judicial role of the Assembly, see Hansen (1991) 158–59; of the Council, Rhodes (1972) 144–207.
37. See Hansen (1991) 162–63.
38. See Ostwald (1986) 410–11, 479. Fragments of Plato Comicus, if they antedate the reforms described in the text, may be indications of contemporary concern about the situation: one compares the laws to a spider's web (fr. 21); another claims that they are constantly changing (fr. 239).
39. My description of the reforms of 410–399 B.C. in the text draws especially on Hansen (1991) 162–75. Details are controversial: see also Harrison (1955); MacDowell (1975); Rhodes (1984, 1991); Ostwald (1986) 509–24; Robertson (1990).
40. On the testimony of Lys. 10.15–20, see Hillgruber (1988) 64–81; S. Todd (1993) 260.
41. S. Todd ([1993] 57–58; cf. Robertson [1990]) challenges the view that a comprehensive code was actually produced.
42. On the Metroön as state archive, see Boegehold (1972); Thomas (1989) 68–82; West (1989); Sickinger (1994); Hunter (1994) 130–31.
43. See Hansen (1991) 212.
44. As noted earlier, however, this action dates back at least to 415 B.C. (And. 1.17).
45. See Hansen (1991) 176.
46. For the view that the reforms in law making were designed to prevent snap votes of the Assembly from overturning the democratic constitution, see Harrison (1955) 35; Sinclair (1988) 67.
47. Advocates of the "rule of law" theory include Wolff (1970) 22–28, 68–80; Sealey (1982) 302, (1987) 146–48; Ostwald (1986) 497–524; Hansen (1991) 174; E. Harris (1994a) 132. Skeptics include Sinclair (1988) 84; Ober (1989) 299–304; S. Todd (1993) 299–300; D. Cohen (1995) 34–57.
48. Ober (1989) 301.
49. Hansen ([1990] 240 n. 117) collects the numerous citations.
50. Thus the demos could reasonably be said to be most authoritative (*kuriōtatos*): see Dem. 59.88; cf. [Arist.] *AP* 9.1; Lys. 1.36.

51. Ober (1989) 300.
52. Because laws were to serve the demos, a proposed law or decree could be indicted on the grounds that it was unsuitable or damaging to the democracy: see Hansen (1991) 175.
53. On the accretive nature of Athenian law, see Humphreys (1988) 488 n. 36.
54. See D. Cohen (1995) 35–36; cf. Wallace (1993), (1994).
55. On the state's regulation of family property, see Humphreys (1993) 4–5. On the authority of the *kurios*, see Hunter (1994) 9–42.
56. See D. Cohen (1991) 221–28; cf. (1995) 143–62. On gossip in Athens, see Hunter (1994) 96–119.
57. See S. Todd (1993) 61–62.
58. Ober (1989) 303.
59. D. Cohen (1991) 209; cf. Ober (1994a) 89–90.
60. On reconstructing democratic principles in this way, see A. H. M. Jones (1957) 41; Raaflaub (1989) 33–34.
61. Plato is critical of the payment of a wage to jurors (*Grg.* 515e2–7) that makes this domination of the courts by the masses possible.
62. Isocrates takes a very different view of the desirability of precision in the laws: he holds that gentlemen do not need an abundance of precise laws to guide them and criticizes the democracy for its excessive legislation (7.39–42; 4.78; 12.144; cf. Ephor. *FGrH* 70 F 139).
63. For the lawmaker as craftsman, see Pl. *Lg.* 858b2–c1; Arist. *Pol.* 1274b7–9.
64. In the *Republic,* however, Plato appears less enamored of legal regulation: see Humphreys (1988) 477–78.
65. On *epieikeia* in Aristotle's legal philosophy, see Triantaphyllopoulos (1985) 17–23.
66. D. Cohen (1995) 35–36.
67. See S. Todd (1993) 167–200; cf. Gauthier (1972) 136–56.
68. On the legal status of women, see Sealey (1990); Just (1991); S. Todd (1993) 201–31; Hunter (1994) 9–42; Foxhall (1996).
69. See S. Todd (1993) 184–94.
70. On the torture of slaves, see Thür (1977); S. Todd (1990a) 33–35; duBois (1991); Hunter (1994) 89–94; Mirhady (1996); Thür (1996); Gagarin (1996).
71. For a survey of Athenian legal actions, see S. Todd (1993) 102–9.
72. See MacDowell (1978) 54; Hansen (1991) 193.
73. I follow Johnstone (forthcoming) in adopting this convention.
74. See Osborne (1985b) 40–44; Hansen (1991) 193–94; S. Todd (1993) 160–61. D. Cohen ([1995] 121–22) rightly points out that the Athenian situation is not as novel as some scholars make it out to be.

75. On the time allotted to various suits, see Rhodes (1981) 719–28; MacDowell (1985); Worthington (1989); Hansen (1991) 187–88. On varying jury sizes, see note 26.
76. MacDowell ([1978] 257) points out that Athenians do not appear to have distinguished between "damages" and "fines."
77. In some public actions, however, the successful prosecutor received a financial reward: see Chapter 4.
78. See Hunter (1994) 120–53. Hunter (124) prefers the designation "private initiative" to "self-help," on the grounds that the latter can have pejorative connotations.
79. On pretrial procedures and court rules, see MacDowell (1978) 235–59; S. Todd (1993) 123–46.
80. See Calhoun (1919) 191.
81. See [Arist.] *AP* 16.5, 26.3, 53.1, with Rhodes (1981) ad loc.; Humphreys (1983) 239, 247.
82. For this dating of the innovation, see MacDowell (1971a) 271; cf. Hunter (1994) 209 n. 32. On public arbitration, see Hunter (1994) 62–66, with 203 n. 1; Scafuro (1997) 383–92. The *anakrisis* before deme judges may well have been abbreviated in cases involving more than ten drachmas that were to be handed over to public arbitrators: see S. Todd (1993) 128 n. 8; Hunter (1994) 140.
83. On this innovation, see Bonner (1905) 46–48; Calhoun (1919) 191.
84. S. Todd ([1993] 129) challenges the argument of Boegehold (1982) that the *echinos* was used in similar fashion at the *anakrisis*.
85. For allegations of abuse in connection with the *echinos*, see Chapter 6, note 29.
86. On *sunēgoroi*, see Bonner (1905) 82–84; Calhoun (1913) 85–89; Lavency (1964) 79–95; G. Kennedy (1968) 419–26; Humphreys (1985b) 317–18; S. Todd (1993) 94–95; Hunter (1994) 140; Crook (1995) 30–37. On some occasions, a litigant's tribe might provide *sunēgoroi:* And. 1.150; Dem. 23.206; Hyp. 4.12.
87. See Rhodes (1981) 722.
88. On this interrogation (*erōtēsis*), see Carawan (1983).
89. On rules concerning hearsay, see MacDowell (1978) 243; S. Todd (1990a) 28–29; Scafuro (1994) 192 n. 77.
90. See Boegehold (1995) 21–22.
91. On the offering of alternate penalties, see S. Todd (1993) 133–34. On the length of supplementary speeches, see MacDowell (1985) 525–26.
92. See MacDowell (1978) 254–58; S. Todd (1993) 139–44.
93. See Hunter (1994) 176–81. On the few instances where imprisonment could occur, see MacDowell (1978) 256–57.
94. On the difficulty of collecting fines imposed in private suits, see

Harrison (1971) 2.187–90; S. Todd (1993) 144–45. Herman ([1994] 116) overestimates the extent to which court decisions were carried out.
95. On *parastasis*, see Harrison (1971) 2.94. Rhodes ([1981] 661) suggests this sum was returned to successful prosecutors. Com. Adesp. fr. 526 characterizes eager litigants (perhaps all Athenians) as "men who are the best of all Greeks in depositing the *parastasis*."
96. On *prutaneia*, see Harrison (1971) 2.92–94. Under the Athenian empire, *prutaneia* could be reduced or waived as a special privilege to Athenian *proxenoi*: see de Ste. Croix (1961) 272–74.
97. On these statutory penalties, see Gerst (1963) 47–83.
98. Hansen ([1976] 65; cf. [1991] 192), followed by MacDowell (1990b) 327–28, believes that the *atimia* entailed only loss of the right to prosecute the type of action in which the prosecutor had failed, E. Harris ([1992] 79–80) that it entailed loss of the right to bring a public prosecution of any type.
99. See Harrison (1971) 2.183–85, who notes (2.184) that in the special case of *paragraphai*, the *epōbelia* fell on whichever party lost.
100. Harrison (1971) 2.179.
101. See Calhoun (1913) 58–59 n. 6; Lofberg (1917) 86–87; Hansen (1976) 59–60 n. 23, cataloging fifteen cases in which the prosecutor may have withdrawn with impunity, and four in which a prosecutor who failed to pursue a suit was fined and punished with partial *atimia*.
102. See Lofberg (1917) 88.
103. On collection of fines in public suits, see Harrison (1971) 2.185–87; S. Todd (1993) 144. On lenience toward state debtors, see Hansen (1976) 59.
104. For *endeixis* as the normal procedure against *atimoi*, see Hansen (1976) 94–95.
105. Thus Harrison (1971) 2.188, citing Dem. 35.46; 56.4.
106. See Harrison (1971) 2.179–83.
107. On false-witness suits, see Berneker (1959); S. Todd (1990a) 36–38; Scafuro (1994). On retrial, see Behrend (1975); Scafuro (1994) 179–80; in general, a man could not be brought up twice on the same charge (Dem. 36.25).
108. On this mysterious action, see S. Todd (1990a) 36 n. 31, (1993) 104; Scafuro (1994) 170.
109. See S. Todd (1990a) 25. On dealing with reluctant witnesses, see also Carey (1995a).
110. S. Todd ([1993] 105 n. 4) observes that "it is possible but not certain" this action was available only to persons wrongly imprisoned for *moicheia* (i.e., adultery and related offenses).

111. Arbitrators, for example, were subject to *eisangelia:* see [Arist.] *AP* 53.6; cf. Dem. 21.86.
112. On jury tampering, which seems to have been uncommon, see Calhoun (1913) 64–77; Wankel (1982) 37–38; MacDowell (1983) 63–69; Harvey (1985) 88–89. On safeguards against this, see Boegehold (1995) 21–42.
113. See Scafuro (1994) 180.
114. On measures against sykophants, see Lofberg (1917) 89–95; Harvey (1990) 106–7; Christ (1992). S. Todd ([1993] 93–94) rightly challenges Harvey's ([1990] 106) view that there must have been some legal definition of sykophancy.
115. Harvey ([1990] 106 n. 12) rightly rejects Crawley's argument ([1970] 81), based on Poll. 8.46, that *graphai* against sykophants were actually *probolai.*
116. On the other hand, in his zeal to list as many actions against sykophancy as possible Isocrates may be labeling an *eisangelia* available for use against *rhētores* as one directed specifically against sykophants; for Isocrates' conflation of the two groups, see 8.129–30.
117. Epichares asserts that *endeixis* and *apagōgē* are available against sykophants (Dem. 58.10–11), but as Harrison ([1971] 2.228 n. 3) points out, sykophants may not have been mentioned in the law cited. When Pollux (8.47) mentions *phasis* against sykophants, he may also be speaking loosely, *pace* E. Cohen's defense ([1973] 89–92) of this late testimony.
118. On alleged instances of *probolai* against sykophants, see Christ (1992) 340 n. 20.
119. See Lofberg (1917) 95.
120. See Scafuro (1994) 180.
121. See Christ (1992).
122. Cf. the rule that a man on his third conviction for proposing illegal decrees became *atimos* (Antiph. fr. 194.13–14; D.S. 18.18.2).
123. For this estimate of the size of Athens's leisure class, see Ober (1989) 128–29. On the frequent participation of its members in litigation, see Ober (1989) 112–13; Humphreys ([1985b] 331) speaks of Athens's elite as a "litigating class"; Frier ([1985] 276; cf. 35–36) describes Rome's upper class in these same terms.
124. On the problematic nature of elite complaints concerning false suits, see Chapter 3.
125. On liturgies, see Christ (1990) 148–51; Gabrielsen (1994). Litigation could arise when wealthy men sought to transfer their liturgies to their peers through the *antidosis* procedure (Dem. 42); when a trierarch sought to collect naval equipment from a trierarch of the

previous year (Dem. 47); when a *chorēgos* was assaulted while performing his liturgy (Dem. 21).
126. On the legal advantages of the wealthy, see Isoc. 20.19–20; Dem. 21.112; 44.28; 45.67; 51.11; Arist. *Rh.* 1372a11–14; Plu. *Sol.* 5.2. Modern treatments of the topic include Dover (1974) 111; Ober (1989) 217–19; Osborne (1990) 100.
127. Although one might argue that this was only fair, inasmuch as suits involving large sums were more complicated than those involving smaller sums, any dispute, regardless of the sum involved, could be complicated, and privileging suits involving large sums in this way can therefore be viewed as unegalitarian.
128. I follow Hedrick ([1994] 167) in translating *dikē* as "legal case" here.
129. See Ober (1989) 192–205; Sagan (1991) 273–89; Raaflaub (1996); Cartledge (1996).
130. On honor and shame in Greek culture, see Cairns (1993); cf. Williams (1993).
131. On trial as *agōn*, see Garner (1987) 59–71; S. Todd (1993) 67–68; D. Cohen (1995) 61–86. On trial as a problematic *agōn* for Athenians, however, see Chapter 5.
132. On bystanders at trial, see Bers (1985) 8; Hunter (1994) 232 n. 41; Boegehold (1995) 27. On success at litigation and reputation, see Dover (1974) 238.
133. The Greekless reader should be aware that *timē, timōria, timēsis,* and *atimia* are all etymologically related.
134. On status competition through performance of liturgies, see Christ (1990) 150.
135. On envy as a factor in the courts, see Ober (1989) 205–14.
136. Thus S. Todd (1993) 160–61, building on Osborne (1985b) 43; D. Cohen (1995) 112, 188. For reservations concerning such a model, see Carey (1994b) 182–83; Christ (1994) 259, (1996) 382.
137. See Hoffer (1989).
138. On judicial binding curses, see Faraone (1991); Gager (1992) 116–50. On judicial prayers, see Versnel (1991) 79–81; Gager (1992) 175–99.
139. On litigation and gamesmanship, see Frier (1985) 30–31.
140. Lofberg (1917) 94.
141. On these and other dirty tricks, see Calhoun (1913) 40–96; Lofberg (1917). On claims of lying, see Harvey (1985) 77, 81; Hunter (1994) 222 n. 15.
142. See S. Todd (1993) 67–68.
143. On such networks, see Calhoun (1913) 40–96 (although he exaggerates the role of "clubs"); Sinclair (1988) 141–45.
144. See Ober (1989) 309.

145. Cf. the common allegation that logographers sell out clients to their opponents: Dem. 58.19; Aesch. 2.165; 3.173.
146. On the use of legal agents, see Lofberg (1917) 48–59.
147. Most of the discussion of litigation in Athenian forensic oratory would probably not be allowed before a U.S. jury.
148. Contra Leisi (1908) 114.
149. See Hay (1989) 391–92.
150. On the difficulty of pursuing charges of abuse, see Lofberg (1917) 93; cf. Hay (1989) 354.
151. On these practices, see Chapter 3.
152. See Christ (1990) 159–60.
153. See Ober (1989) 152–55; Ober and Strauss (1990); Hall (1995).
154. See Markle (1985) 293.
155. Thus Markle (1985) 285; cf. Hansen (1991) 188–89.
156. See Bers (1985) 14; Boegehold (1995) 39.
157. On dikastic *thorubos*, see Bers (1985) 13.
158. On the tension between these diverse considerations, see D. Cohen (1995) 115.
159. On the importance of character at trial, see Dover (1974) 294; Hunter (1994) 101; Scafuro (1997) 57–66.
160. See Humphreys (1985b); S. Todd (1990a) 27. While witnesses no doubt sometimes told the truth, I am not persuaded by E. Harris ([1995] 12) that "we have strong grounds for accepting any statement made by an orator that is supported by the evidence of witnesses."
161. See Dover (1974) 309–10.
162. See Dover (1974) 292–95; J. K. Davies (1981) 92–100; Vannier (1988) 103–68; Ober (1989) 226–33; Christ (1990) 150. Johnstone (forthcoming) argues that it is defendants in particular who appeal to *charis*.
163. See Christ (1990) 155 with n. 36.
164. Maine ([1861] 1917) 44–45.
165. Lofberg (1917) 12; cf. Dorjahn (1935) 290–92.
166. S. Todd (1993) 147; cf. Sinclair (1988) 210–11; Cartledge (1990a) 42–44.
167. Scholars in critical legal studies (see Hunt [1988]) emphasize that law in modern societies is hardly free of political and social influences.
168. S. Todd (1993) 29; cf. Maio (1983); D. Cohen (1995) 118.
169. On this question, see also S. Todd (1993) 90–91.
170. Cf. A. *Pr.* 326, where Zeus is said not to be subject to democratic scrutiny (*hupeuthunos*).
171. On the problem of what constitutes a "political trial," see Bauman (1990) 2–3; Hansen (1991) 204.
172. Even the conservative Isocrates acknowledges as much (7.67).

173. See Hansen (1979).
174. On Athenian court sites, see Boegehold (1995) 91–113.
175. Boegehold (1995) collects the testimonia for the use of the Odeion (185–86) and the Stoa Poikilē (183–84) as courts.
176. See Boegehold (1995) 36–37.
177. Thus de Ste. Croix (1961) 101 n. 2; Bers (1985) 11 n. 41.
178. Hunter ([1994] 67) suggests that public arbitration aimed to keep "some private disputes from the time and expense involved in a court case. It also made court procedures more efficient, by forcing disputants to assemble and submit their evidence in writing at the arbitration hearing."
179. Hansen ([1991] 189) estimates the annual cost to the state of jury pay as between twenty-two and thirty-seven talents.
180. E. Cohen ([1973] 27) argues that these suits were filed monthly and expeditiously decided, Hansen ([1983] 170) that they were filed monthly and heard within a month. On this issue, cf. S. Todd (1993) 334–35. MacDowell (1976), followed by S. Todd (1993) 336–37, is right to doubt the view of E. Cohen ([1973] 93–95) that there were special courts for *dikai emporikai*.
181. According to Dem. 21.47, a *graphē hubreōs* was also to be heard within thirty days: see MacDowell (1990b) 266–67.
182. On delaying tactics, see MacDowell (1990b) 305–8; cf. E. Cohen (1973) 11.
183. E. Cohen (1973) 39–40; cf. Isager and Hansen (1975) 85.
184. Extraordinary forces sometimes interfered with the courts. Under the Thirty (404/3 B.C.), the popular courts did not meet, and private suits at least were not heard again until 401 B.C. (Isoc. 21.7; Lys. 17.3; with MacDowell [1971a] 267). Financial constraints due to wartime expenditure led to the suspension of private actions for a period in the 360s B.C. (Dem. 45.3–4), and again in 348 B.C. (Dem. 39.17); on these episodes, see Hansen (1991) 189; on the dating of the reference in Dem. 39.17 to 348 B.C., see Carey and Reid (1985) 179–80; Humphreys (1989) 184.
185. See Rhodes (1981) 591.

Chapter Two. The Invention of Sykophancy

1. Earlier discussions of sykophancy include Lofberg (1917); Bonner (1927) 59–71; Bonner and Smith (1938) 2.39–74; Voegelin (1943) 84–110; MacDowell (1978) 62–66; Bockisch (1981); Osborne (1990); Harvey (1990); S. Todd (1993) 92–94.
2. Harvey (1990) 105.
3. On these puns, see the subsequent discussion in this chapter.

4. On ancient speculation, see Lofberg (1917) vii; Latte (1931a) 1128–29.
5. On diverse modern etymologies, see Lofberg (1917) vii–viii; Bockisch (1981) 4.11–12; Harvey (1990) 105 n. 6.
6. On the fig's cultural associations, see Olck (1909); on its sexual connotations, Buchheit (1960); Henderson (1991) 117–19.
7. Lewis ([1993] 210 n. 6) rightly observes that the earliest datable use of *sukophant-* is Ar. fr. 228 (427 B.C.); Cratin. fr. 70 (before 424 B.C.) could antedate this; and [X.] *Ath.* 1.14 (420s B.C.?) is the earliest prose evidence. Harvey ([1990] 105) misses the Aristophanic fragment, and thus takes the occurrences in Ar. *Ach.* (425 B.C.) as the earliest datable ones.
8. Marr ([1983] 53 n. 9) suggests it may have been a comic coinage.
9. Harvey ([1990] 119–21) collects most of the testimonia for classical usage of *sukophant-*.
10. See Osborne (1990) 85; Harvey (1990) 113.
11. Bockisch ([1981] 4.11) maintains that, whereas in the fifth and early fourth centuries B.C. sykophancy was intimately connected with the struggle between democrats and oligarchs, this was not so in the late fourth century. This overlooks the prominent place of sykophancy in conservative criticism of the democracy throughout the fourth century (see Chapter 3).
12. In the classical period, *parasitos* and *kolax* can both mean "parasite" or "flatterer": see Brown (1992) 98–102 contra Nesselrath (1985) 88–121. *kolax* sometimes appears in the company of *sukophant-*: Cratin. fr. 227; Theopomp. Hist. *FGrH* 115 F 281; Men. *Theoph.* fr. 1.16–17 Sandbach; cf. X. *Mem.* 2.9.8. On the postclassical usage of *sukophant-*, see Lofberg (1920); Schneider (1977); Osborne (1990) 84 n. 2.
13. Harvey (1990) 110–14 (the enumeration in the text is mine). For surveys of modern definitions, see Lofberg (1917) ix–x; Osborne (1990) 83–84; Harvey (1990) 110.
14. Thus Lofberg (1917) 32, 46; Bonner and Smith (1938) 2.72; Adkins (1976) 316–18; MacDowell (1978) 62–64; Rhodes (1981) 444; Ostwald (1986) 480 n. 81.
15. Osborne (1990) 91–93.
16. See Lofberg (1917) x. For the close association of sykophancy and false witnessing, see also Ar. *Ec.* 561–62; Pl. *R.* 575b7–8; Dem. 58.65; 33.37; Theopomp. Hist. *FGrH* 115 F 110, F 281; Diph. fr. 31.16–17.
17. The following individuals are linked with sykophancy:
    Gorgias: Ar. *Av.* 1694–1705.
    Socrates: Ar. *Nu.* 757–83 (but the root *sukophant-* is not used). Plato (*R.* 340d1–341a9) ironically characterizes Socrates as syk-

Notes to Pages 50–51

ophantic; Xenophon (*Mem.* 4.4.11) denies that Socrates is a sykophant.
Disciples of Socrates: Chaerephon: Ar. fr. 552; cf. V. 1408; Aeschines the Socratic: Lys. fr. 1 Thalheim; Plato: Ephipp. fr. 14 *ap.* Ath. 509b.
Isocrates: Dem. 35.15 and 38–42, with 2; cf. Isoc. 15.237–38.
18. Cf. Fisher (1976) 36.
19. Harvey (1990) 107–9. In the notes to follow, I draw on Harvey's catalog and make my own additions.
20. McGlew ([1997] 46) well observes of the sykophant in Aristophanes' *Wealth*, "He is the 'other' of democratic civic identity," but I see no reason to reject, as McGlew does, the idea that he represents simultaneously a social type.
21. While arguably most forms of insult are based on exclusion from the group, the allegation of sykophancy is distinct in that it identifies an individual as a representative of a complex negative social type, whose attributes stand in strict opposition to civic and social ideals.
22. For the sykophant as savage (*ōmos*), see Dem. 18.212, 275; 25.63, 83, 84; Isoc. 15.315; as a wolf, X. *Mem.* 2.9.1–2; Men. *Mon.* 603 Jaekel; cf. Dem. 25.40; Philippid. fr. 30; *Suda* θ368.1–3; Harvey ([1990] 109) collects further animal images. On *praotēs* as a democratic ideal, see Dover (1974) 202.
23. For the sykophant as a criminal, see Ar. *Pl.* 30–31; Diph. fr. 31.12–17; Theopomp. Hist. *FGrH* 115 F 281; with further passages in Harvey (1990) 109; as a barbarian, Ar. *Ach.* 517–19, 725–26; *Av.* 1699–1701; Aesch. 2.183; 3.172.
24. See Dem. 25.82; cf. Ar. *Pl.* 877–79; Arist. *Rh.* 1382a7. For isolation of the sykophant from the group, see Lys. 25.19; Isoc. 15.299–301; Aesch. 2.145.
25. Edmunds (1987) 17. On the place of this imagery in Greek thought, see Edmunds 5–16.
26. See Dem. 25.74; 57.33; Hyp. 1.2; cf. Dem. 58.29; Heracl. Crit. fr. 1.4 Pfister.
27. See Dem. 36.54; Hyp. 1.2.
28. *polupragmōn*: Ar. *Pl.* 913; Isoc. 15.230, 237; cf. Ar. *Pax* 191; X. *Mem.* 2.9.1; Lyc. 1.3. *periergos*: Aesch. 3.172; Heracl. Crit. fr. 1.4 Pfister; cf. Dem. 39.2.
29. *tarattō*: Ar. *Ach.* 688; *Eq.* 66, 251, 308, 358, 840, 867, etc.; V. 1285; *Pax* 654; Isoc. 18.43; Dem. 25.19, 42, 50. *kukaō*: Ar. *Ach.* 688, 707, 939; *Eq.* 251, 866; *Pax* 654; cf. Dem. 18.111. *seiō*: Ar. fr. 228; *Eq.* 840; *Pax* 639; Ant. 6.43; Telecl. fr. 2; Heracl. Crit. fr. 1.4 Pfister.
30. See Lys. 7.40–41, with 7.1; 18.9; 25.26; Dem. 55.35; Aesch. 2.124; with additional passages in Harvey (1990) 117–18.

31. See Ar. Av. 1468; Is. 11.4; Demad. fr. 79 de Falco; cf. Ar. Nu. 434, 776, 1455; Pl. R. 405c1–3; Dem. 21.91.
32. See also Dem. 25.36, 49, 50, 94; 58.45.
33. Burkert (1985) 76.
34. *miaros:* Dem. 18.289; 21.103; 25.41, 58; 36.58. *akathartos:* Dem. 25.63. Lacking in *hugieia:* Ar. Ach. 956; Dem 18.242; 58.12. *kataratos:* Dem. 18.212; 25.82; cf. Ar. Ach. 934. *asebēs:* Dem. 25.52, 53, 63. *anosios:* Aesch. 2.5.
35. *kathairō:* Ar. V. 1043; Lys. 12.5; Diph. fr. 31.12–17; cf. Dem. 25.63. For the common notion that the city should be "cleansed" of some undesirable element, see Parker (1983) 263 n. 38.
36. On purification and scapegoat rituals including the one at the Thargelia, see Parker (1983) 257–80; Bremmer (1983); Burkert (1985) 75–84. On the role of figs in the scapegoat ritual in Athens and Kolophon, see Bremmer (1983) 312–13. On the cultural importance of the idea of the *pharmakos,* see Bennett and Tyrrell (1990) 235–41; cf. Sagan (1991) 168–85.
37. Parker (1983) 263 n. 37.
38. Elsewhere Theopompus labels Athens a city that is full of sykophants (*FGrH* 115 F 281).
39. Harvey ([1990] 119 n. 51) observes that Charondas, who probably lived during the sixth century B.C., cannot be the lawgiver for Thurii, founded in 443 B.C.; according to D.L. 9.50, Protagoras wrote a code of laws for Thurii. Arist. *Pol.* 1274b5–7 also casts Charondas as an enemy of legal abuse, claiming that he was the first to institute the practice of denunciation for false witnessing. On Charondas, see Link (1994) 166–68; on legends concerning Greek lawgivers, see Szegedy-Maszak (1978).
40. On Thurian concern over sykophants, see also Ephor. *FGrH* 70 F 139.11–14; cf. Plu. *Mor.* 519b8–10.
41. Dover (1974) 30. Harvey ([1990] 115 n. 40) takes the similar imagery applied to sykophants in comedy and oratory as evidence of direct borrowing of the latter from the former, but this need not be the case.
42. For this interpretation of the basis of *phasis* in these scenes, see MacDowell (1991) 188.
43. Only one of the four is named, a certain Nicarchus (*Ach.* 908).
44. The use of *phasis* by the two sykophants in *Acharnians* is legitimate under the laws of Athens, but violates the rules of Dikaiopolis's private marketplace.
45. The last two passages cited, from *Acharnians,* lie outside the sykophant scenes, but are closely connected with them.
46. Since the sykophant is already wearing a *tribōnion* (897), he is pre-

sumably dressed in an even more ragged one. For the *tribōn* as a poor man's garment, see Stone (1981) 173–74.
47. Stripping and reclothing are regular features of scapegoat ritual in and out of Athens: see Bremmer (1983) 305.
48. On Aristophanes and Cleon, see Connor (1971) 168–75; Bauman (1990) 49–60; Carawan (1990) 138 with nn. 3, 4; Atkinson (1992) 56–61. Aristophanes also casts the following politicians as sykophants: Alcibiades (*Ach.* 713–16; cf. fr. 205), Euathlus (*Ach.* 703–12; fr. 424), Hyperbolus (*Ach.* 846–47; *Eq.* 1356–63; *Nu.* 874–76; cf. Eup. fr. 193); see further Sommerstein (1996) 347–48.
49. On the imagery of disturbance in *Knights*, see Edmunds (1987) 1–2, 5–20.
50. On the nightmare imagery, see Sommerstein (1983) ad loc.
51. Some believe the allusion is to *Olkades:* see K-A ad Ar. *Olkades* t. iv.
52. For the sykophant as a strangler, see Ar. *Eq.* 775; as parricide, *Ach.* 703–18.
53. On metics as sykophants, see Christ (1992).
54. On the heroic image, see Mastromarco (1989).
55. For this dating of the trial, see Hansen (1976) 142. On Aristogeiton (*PA* 1775), see Sealey (1960).
56. On the authenticity issue, I follow Hansen ([1976] 144–52) over Sealey ([1993] 237–39).
57. For the sykophant as an overturner of the city, see also Apollod. Car. or Gel. fr. 13; of its laws, Dem. 18.111; 21.91; cf. Crit. 88 B 22 D-K.
58. Sealey ([1993] 238) suggests, "The details cannot be dismissed as the fanciful distortion of a zealous litigant; the speaker claims to produce the mutilated man as a witness."
59. Aristogeiton tears (*sparattō*) his legal victims apart (Dem. 25.50); for this image applied to sykophantic prosecution, see also Ar. *Ach.* 688; cf. *Pax* 641. For litigation as a form of cannibalism, see Telecl. fr. 2; contrast Hes. *Op.* 276–80, asserting that justice (*dikē*) keeps men from devouring one another as animals do.
60. Din. 2.9–10 also describes Aristogeiton's jail episode, and draws a similar moral from it.
61. See Osborne (1990) 84; cf. Gagarin (1997) 24.
62. Cf. Connor (1994) 41.
63. On ridicule in comedy, see Henderson (1990) 293–307.
64. On the familiarity of such puns, see MacDowell (1971b) 14; Dunbar (1995) 742. For play on *suko-*, see also Ar. *Eq.* 259, 529 = Cratin. fr. 70; *V.* 145, 897; *Av.* 1699; *Pl.* 946; Dem 25.48; Arist. fr. 667 Rose; cf. Antiph. fr. 177; Alex. fr. 187. For play on *-phant-*, see Ar. *Ach.* 725–26; *Av.* 1694; Men. fr. 545 K-T; for evidence of this in the orators, see note 74.

65. In the first sykophant scene in *Acharnians*, there is a brief postponement of identification: the sykophant enters at 818, is identified at 825, and then departs at 829. For postponement on an even more compact scale, see Ar. fr. 228, where three verbs hinting at sykophancy are followed by a fourth verb of the root *sukophant-*.
66. Cf. S. D. Olson (1992).
67. For this association in comedy and elsewhere, see Chapter 3.
68. I take the participle *echontes* as concessive.
69. Cf. *Pl.* 881–82, where the sykophant falsely accuses his well-dressed interlocutors of theft, and Cratin. fr. 171.58–76, where unjustly acquired wealth is the basis of a sykophantic prosecution. For a different interpretation of *Av.* 1410–11, see Dunbar (1995) ad loc.
70. Sommerstein ([1987] ad *Av.* 1423; cf. Dunbar [1995] ad loc.) points out that a similar joke may be behind Ar. fr. 228.
71. See S. D. Olson (1992) 313.
72. The intruder's sociological status is complex: although he appears wearing a poor man's cloak (*tribōnion*) (897), he was recently rich; he is linked, however, to the class of *rhētores*, who are said to start out as poor men, but to get rich by corruption (567–69; cf. 30–31). In this case the intruder has come full circle and returned to his natural state of poverty.
73. Wealth has made no such promise *in propria voce*, but cf. 460–65 and 1178, with the modern discussion of the problem of the "two plots" of *Wealth* (see Konstan and Dillon [1981] 371–83; S. D. Olson [1990a] 223–24). The sykophant's charge that Wealth is destroying the democracy (945–50) is unambiguously false.
74. For the common wordplay that an opponent's sykophancy is manifest (*phaneros*), see Is. 11.4; Dem. 18.118; 21.116; 33.16; 36.3; 37.3; 55.2, 26, 28.
75. An exception is found in Dem. 52.33, where the litigant speaks of sykophancy only in the final section of his speech.
76. On the legal context of Isoc. 18.52–54, see Carawan (1991) 3–5. On contrived homicide charges, see Calhoun (1913) 48–54.
77. On dikastic *thorubos*, see Bers (1985).
78. See Osborne (1990) 84, 93–94.
79. Aeschines and Demosthenes, for example, bandy the allegation of sykophancy back and forth in their speeches against one another (Aesch. 2; 3; Dem. 18; 19).
80. For testimonia concerning the *sanides*, see Boegehold (1995) 236–37. On the public posting of names, see Hunter (1994) 229–30 n. 29.
81. Written evidence might be available if an individual failing to win one-fifth of the votes in a public suit did not pay the statutory penalty

Notes to Pages 64-66

of a thousand drachmas and therefore had his name publicly recorded as a state debtor: see Chapter 1.
82. See Humphreys (1985b) 349; cf. 326.
83. Thus Lofberg (1917) 23; Bonner and Smith (1938) 2.45; Ehrenberg (1951) 343; J. Jones (1956) 123; Ostwald (1986) 81; Carter (1986) 105; Stockton (1990) 99.
84. See Isoc. 15.288; Dem. 58.63; Arist. Rh. 1382a7; Diph. fr. 31.12-17; cf. Isoc. 8.129-30; Nicol. Com. fr. 1.1-2.
85. Osborne (1990) 93.
86. ergazomai: Ar. Av. 1430; Dem. 25.82; 57.33; cf. Ant. 2.2.12. ergasia: Dem. 58.65; cf. [Arist.] Rh. Al. 1424a31-32; Dem. 20.152. ergastēria: Dem. 39.2; 40.9; cf. 32.10; 37.39. ergon: Ar. Av. 1430, 1450; Lys. 25.3. technē: Ar. Av. 1423; Isoc. 15.314; cf. Dem. 33.38. For sykophancy as a pseudo-technē, see Ar. Pl. 905; Dem. 25.51. zēn ek tou sukophantein: Ar. Av. 1433-35; And. 1.99; X. HG 2.3.12; Isoc. 15.164; Dem. 58.63. bios: Ar. Av. 1451-52; Ec. 562-63.
87. Calhoun ([1913] 79-81), followed by Lofberg (1917) 59-68, takes the figure ergastēria as evidence of "clubs of sykophants," and argues (95-96 n. 3) that these were not temporary groupings; for criticism of this view, see Osborne (1990) 93 n. 33; Harvey (1990) 115 n. 39. Ehrenberg ([1951] 344) takes seriously the idea that sykophancy is a bios. Harvey ([1990] 115 n. 39) seems ready to entertain the idea that sykophancy is a technē.
88. For the opposition of litigation and labor (ponos), see Hes. Op. 27-34, with Michelini (1994) 227.
89. For the idea that sykophants are not farmers, see Ar. Pl. 903; Lys. 20.12; Dem. 25.82; cf. Ar. Av. 1697-99; and that farmers are not sykophants, Ar. Pax 190-91; Hyp. 3.25-26 (context mutilated).
90. For the figure dikorrhaphein, see also Ar. Nu. 1483; Apollod. Car. or Gel. fr. 13.12. The translation of this in the text borrows from Arrowsmith.
91. Alternatively, the sykophant can be said to "do nothing" (Ar. Pl. 906; cf. Diph. fr. 31.10-17) and thus to be in violation of the "law against idleness" (Dem. 57.32); on this law, see Wallace (1989) 62-64, 120-21; DeBruyn (1995) 79-81.
92. Contra Harvey (1990) 114.
93. On such figures, see Wyse (1904) 591; Dover (1974) 26.
94. On the dichotomy apragmōn and polupragmōn, see Nestle (1927); Ehrenberg (1947); Grossmann (1950) 126-37; Dienelt (1953); Kleve (1964); Connor (1971) 175-94; Dover (1974) 188-89; Adkins (1976); Allison (1979); Lateiner (1982); Carter (1986); Edmunds (1987) 31-33; Demont (1990) 89-106.
95. Carter (1986) 27.

247

96. Thus S. Todd (1990b) 164; Osborne (1990) 99 n. 47; Ober (1989) 175 n. 37.
97. Osborne ([1990] 94 n. 34) rightly criticizes Lofberg ([1917] 73–85) for his identification of several "typical Athenian sycophants."
98. See Osborne (1990) 99 n. 47.
99. Although outside of the courts *apragmōn* can be a pejorative label (Th. 2.40.2; cf. 2.63.2), in the courts it bears positive connotations; *apragmōn* at Dem. 21.83 need not be taken as pejorative.
100. Harvey (1990) 114–16. For the possibility of living off the proceeds of informing in eighteenth-century England, see Hay (1989) 356.
101. Harvey ([1990] 114–15) makes too much of the tendentious claims of one litigant (Hyp. 1.2) that his opponent is a perpetual (*athanatos*) sykophant who invests his illicit profits with a friend and uses the income to support his ongoing sykophancy.
102. Harvey (1990) 115–16.
103. On contemporary criticism of Athenian "sykophancy," see further in Chapter 3.
104. See [X.] *Ath.* 1.14; Ar. *Eq.* 837–40, 1408; *Pax* 639–40; *Av.* 145–47, 1410–69; Eup. fr. 245; Th. 1.77.1; Lys. 25.19; cf. Lofberg (1917) 68–72.
105. See Ar. *Ach.* 515–19, 818–29, 908–58; Eup. fr. 99.86–89; Dem. 12.19; Heracl. Crit. fr. 1.4 Pfister; Plu. *Cim.* 10.8–9; cf. Ar. *Pl.* 877–79.
106. Note especially the early (420s B.C.?) use of *sukophant-* in [X.] *Ath.* 1.14.
107. In Th. 1.77.1, this view is attributed to Athens's subjects; for the debate over the meaning of this passage, see Hornblower (1991) 122–23. Note the close association of *philodikein* and sykophancy: see esp. [Arist.] *Rh. Al.* 1444a30–32; cf. Turner (1946) 5.
108. De Ste. Croix ([1972] 383–86) argues that this passage refers to the enforcement not of the Megarian decree (mentioned at *Ach.* 530–38 as a later measure), but rather of customs regulations. For the sykophant as a bad coin, see Ar. *Pl.* 862, 957; cf. *Ra.* 718–37.
109. See Loraux (1986); cf. Ziolkowski (1981).
110. Hunter (1994) 110. On negative stereotypes in comedy, see Henderson (1990) 297, 311. On the negative type of the *kinaidos* in Athenian discourse, see Winkler (1990).
111. On these *topoi*, see Walters (1980); Ziolkowski (1981).
112. See Loraux (1986).
113. For ideologies as vehicles for suppressing cultural tensions, see Geertz (1973).

Chapter Three. Litigation and Class Conflict

1. Concern over litigation probably also played a role in the oligarchic interlude of 411 B.C.: see Ant. fr. III.1 Gernet. It is not clear, however, what measures the Four Hundred took in connection with the popular courts: see [Arist.] *AP* 29.4; 31.1; with Rhodes (1981) ad loc.; Lewis (1993) 210.
2. The Thirty probably blamed, as later conservatives did (Lys. 25.19; Isoc. 15.318), Athens's loss of empire on sykophantic demagogues who had legally harassed Athenian subjects.
3. For the figure of fifteen hundred, see Isoc. 7.67; 20.11; Aesch. 3.235; [Arist.] *AP* 35.4; with Rhodes (1981) ad loc. On the purge, see Krentz (1982) 131–47; Rhodes (1981) 415–22; Ostwald (1986) 481–84; Christ (1992) 343–46 (arguing that the Thirty continued to use the same pretext).
4. Although [Arist.] *AP* 35.2 does not say that the Thirty eliminated the popular courts (cf. Rhodes [1981] ad loc.), the Council, which was controlled by the Thirty, appears to have usurped their powers (X. *HG* 2.3.11–12).
5. For the Thirty's use of judicial murder, see also Lys. 13.8–12, 18–22; X. *HG* 2.4.8–10.
6. On Athenian demography, see Chapter 1.
7. See Ober (1989) 128–29; cf. Christ (1990) 148–50.
8. On elite attributes, see Ober (1989) 11–13. On wealth as the primary distinguishing attribute of the elite, see Rosivach (1991) 190; cf. Sagan (1991) 252–56.
9. See Markle (1985) 267–71; Ober (1989) 11, 194–96; Rosivach (1991) 190.
10. See Ober (1989) 27–30.
11. Ibid., 12.
12. On concealment of wealth, see Gabrielsen (1986); E. Cohen (1992) 194–201. On liturgy avoidance, see Christ (1990); cf. Stanley (1993).
13. See Gabrielsen (1987); Christ (1990) 160–68.
14. While the charge against him may have been false, his payment was part of an open, public settlement: see Harvey (1990) 110.
15. On the threat of litigation as a tool in disputes in Athens, see Scafuro (1997) 69–84, 396–98.
16. Harvey ([1990] 111 n. 27) collects thirty-four instances of allegations of sykophantic blackmail.
17. See Ar. *Eq.* 259–65; *Pax* 639–43; Ant. 5.80; And. 1.105; Lys. 7.1; 25.3; X. *Mem.* 2.9.1; Aesch. 1.107.
18. Many scholars too readily accept elite protests of innocence, for ex-

ample, Lofberg (1917) 32–48; Ehrenberg (1973) 215–16; Carter (1986) 105, 129; Garner (1987) 67. Osborne ([1990] 98) is rightly skeptical of such protests; cf. Humphreys (1977–78) 103.
19. On blackmail of guilty persons, see Lys. 20.7, 10; 27.2; of both guilty and innocent, Lys. 7.1; Aesch. 1.107.
20. See Dem. 25.49–50; 58.32, 34; Isoc. 18.10, 14; Pl. Cri. 45a6–9. Harvey ([1990] 115 n. 41) points out that the sums cited in such contexts are relatively large, at least by the standards of average Athenians.
21. For claims of guilty payoffs, see Lys. 27.6, 14; 29.1, 6; Aesch. 2.148; cf. Ar. Eq. 438–39.
22. Cf. Pl. Cri. 44e–45a, with Osborne (1990) 96–97.
23. On Athenian attitudes toward bribery, see Wankel (1982); J. Roberts (1982) 52–64; MacDowell (1983); Harvey (1985); Strauss (1985).
24. For *kindunoi* as legal threats here, see Ober (1989) 212.
25. On the bias of elite sources concerning sykophancy, see Adkins (1976) 307–11; Osborne (1990) 95–96; Harvey (1990) 103–4.
26. On the limited extent of literacy in Athens, see W. Harris (1989) 65–115.
27. On elite critics of the democracy, see A. H. M. Jones (1957) 41–72; Raaflaub (1989), (1992); Ober (1994b).
28. On the class overtones of *ponēros* in the discussion of sykophancy, see Adkins (1976) 310; Harvey (1990) 109 n. 20; Christ (1992) 338 n. 11. On the overlap of moral and social terminology in Greece, see Adkins (1960), (1972); Dover (1974) 34–45, 109–12; Donlan (1978) 109–10; Schulz (1981) 3.128–29; Brock (1991) 160 n. 2.
29. In elite-elite discourse, *dēmos* ("the people") can designate not the whole people (*populus*), but the common people (*plebs*): see Ober (1989) 4; Lewis (1990) 262.
30. On elite Athenians as the most likely prosecutors of their peers, see Osborne (1985b) 44–48; cf. Cartledge (1990a) 54–58. On the distorted depiction of prosperous new politicians, like Cleon, who were active in the courts, as poor men, see Connor (1971) 151–63; Adkins (1976) 310, 318; Carter (1986) 125; cf. Ober (1989) 235–36.
31. See S. Todd (1993) 151–52.
32. On the *Antidosis*, see the subsequent discussion in this chapter.
33. Examples of this complaint are collected in Chapter 2, note 104.
34. Cf. the claim of Theopomp. Hist. FGrH 115 F 281 that Athens is full of sykophants.
35. Harrison ([1971] 2.93 n. 3) rightly observes that this must be an exaggeration.
36. See Ostwald (1986) 481 with n. 87.
37. Cf. also Th. 6.53.2; Plu. Arist. 26.1.

38. See Adkins (1976) 308 n. 10; Christ (1992) 344 n. 41.
39. Some writers speak of sykophancy in connection with democratic Syracuse (D.S. 11.87; Plu. *Tim.* 37.1) and Thurii (Ephor. *FGrH* 70 F 139; D.S. 12.12.2; cf. Plu. *Mor.* 519b). For the view that a monarch would not tolerate sykophants, see Dem. 18.235; Dem. 12.19; Theopomp. Hist. *FGrH* 115 F 110. Ar. *Ach.* 903–4 takes for granted that oligarchic Boeotia has a dearth of sykophants, but [Arist.] *Rh. Al.* 1424b10–14 considers sykophancy a possibility under an oligarchy.
40. For the time of the Persian Wars as one free of sykophancy, see Ar. *Ach.* 698–701; V. 1095–97; Eup. fr. 99.79–120; cf. Ar. *Eq.* 1331–63.
41. Cf. the antidemocratic tradition that Theseus, after founding the democracy, was attacked by a sykophant, Lukos ("Wolf") (*Suda* θ368.1–3).
42. For the pun connecting *sukon* and *sukophant-*, see Chapter 2.
43. On Athens's fertile production of sykophants, see also Antiph. fr. 177; Eub. fr. 74; Plu. *Arist.* 26.1; cf. Dem. 25.48. These witticisms play upon Athenian boasts (e.g., Ar. fr. 581) of the city's agricultural bounty.
44. On the common characterization of litigation as wrestling, see Garner (1987) 61–62.
45. For the ideal that a man should not "need" lawsuits, see also Isoc. 15.238; cf. Antiph. fr. 281. On the closely associated ideal of "minding one's own business," as presented in Plato, see Adkins (1976) 301–3.
46. On aristocratic life-style under the democracy, see Kurke (1992). On aristocratic "style" in Xenophon, see Johnstone (1994).
47. See Murray (1990) 149–61.
48. For sykophancy as a topic at symposia, see also Ar. *Eq.* 529 = Cratin. fr. 70; as a topic for private griping among the elite, Thphr. *Char.* 26.5–7.
49. For a caricature of such complaints by rich men, see Antiph. fr. 202.
50. For the similar complaint that one must fawn on (*therapeuō*) the multitude in a democracy, see Ar. *Eq.* 59, 799, 1261; Isoc. 1.36.
51. J. K. Davies ([1971] 331) argues that Xenophon, in attributing poverty here to Charmides, son of Glaukon, has confused him with his homonym, Charmides, son of Aristoteles, whose property was confiscated by the city after his condemnation in 414 B.C. for profaning the Mysteries. Xenophon is vague, however, about the source of Charmides' financial hardship.
52. See O. J. Todd, *Xenophon IV* (Cambridge, Mass., 1923) 580.
53. For *lambanō*, which is used here of the transformed, grasping Charmides, applied to the venal sykophant, see Dem. 12.19, 58.62–63;

cf. X. *Mem.* 2.9.4. For *lambanō* in the Greek vocabulary of bribery, see Harvey (1985) 82–83.
54. For Charmides as a model of quietude in Plato's *Charmides*, see Carter (1986) 56–63.
55. For the idea that it takes a sykophant to beat one, see also Ar. *Eq.* 275–81, 435–44; cf. Apollod. Car. or Gel. fr. 1.
56. On the historical Ischomachus, see J. K. Davies (1971) 265–68; Pomeroy (1994) 259–64.
57. Konstan ([1985] 41) aptly describes Philocleon's home court in *Wasps* as a paradigm of aristocratic *autarkeia*.
58. I take *ekrithēn* here to refer to judgment rather than condemnation; cf. X. *Mem.* 2.9.5. If one follows the Loeb and Budé editors and Pomeroy (1994) in translating it as "condemned," the question several lines later about the outcome of the cases in question makes no sense.
59. Lit.: "he said it was very easy to take [sc. money] from sykophants."
60. On the historical Archedemus (*PA* 2326), see Connor (1971) 35–36; Millett (1989); Osborne (1990) 96–98.
61. He is depraved (Ar. *Ra.* 420–25); a non-Athenian (Ar. *Ra.* 422; Eup. fr. 80); an embezzler of the people's property (Lys. 14.25).
62. On the avoidance of private patronage in democratic Athens, see Chapter 4.
63. Compare how in Aristophanes' *Knights* (discussed later), the wealthy knights cheer on the lower-class Sausage-seller against the sykophantic Paphlagon/Cleon.
64. Although scholars often label Archedemus a sykophant because of his shrewd tactics (Lofberg [1917] 56 n. 54; Carter [1986] 112; Osborne [1990] 88), for Xenophon Archedemus is emphatically not a sykophant.
65. For *charis* as the common coin of aristocratic relations, see esp. Plu. *Cim.* 10.8–9 (relating how friends help one another against sykophants).
66. Note, however, that the original idea is Socrates': this entails a sort of inversion of Pl. *Cri.* 44e-45a, where Crito knowledgeably advises Socrates on how to deal with sykophants.
67. On public oratory in Athens as a vehicle for mediating differences between rich and poor, see Ober (1989) 205, 308.
68. On the freedom of public speakers to criticize popular audiences, see Dover (1974) 23–25; Ober (1989) 318–24.
69. On such concerns, see A. H. M. Jones (1957) 58–61; Ober (1989) 200–201; cf. Sinclair (1988) 208–9.
70. On such claims, see Ober (1989) 201, 225.
71. For *charis* invoked against sykophants, see Ant. 2.2.12; Lys. 21.17; Isoc. 18.64; cf. Lys. 19.9; Dem. 52.33. The sykophant can be cast as an antiliturgist: see Dem. 25.78.

Notes to Pages 93–102

72. On liturgy avoidance, see Christ (1990).
73. On this slander, see Ober (1989) 235.
74. On this common designation of sykophants, see Harvey (1990) 109 with n. 20.
75. On suspicion of clever speakers, see Dover (1974) 25–28; Ober (1989) 170–74.
76. See Dover (1974) 32–33, 40–41; Balme (1984); Markle (1985) 284; Ober (1989) 272–77; Rosivach (1991) 192–93; cf. Meikle (1996).
77. For the taker of a bribe as a "retailer," see Dem. 23.201, with Harvey (1985) 85.
78. Harvey ([1985] 84–85) points out that *misthos* can refer to a legitimate wage or a bribe.
79. Blass brackets *kai plousious*.
80. On the close association of prostitution and bribery, see Harvey (1985) 85–86.
81. On the social meaning of *kinaidia*, see Winkler (1990).
82. For the pun on *hetair-* and likely pun on *kinados* (fox) = *kinaidos*, see MacDowell (1962) 137.
83. Litigants before the Areopagus argue in very much the same way as litigants in the popular courts: see Chapter 6.
84. On Euxitheus's posturing here, see Ober (1989) 221–23.
85. Cf. Ant. 2.2.12: a liturgist asserts against his sykophantic opponents, "I made my money not from litigation but from hard work."
86. Ober ([1989] 274) takes the two unnamed tradesmen as politicians.
87. In general I am persuaded by MacDowell's ([1990b] ad loc.) interpretation of this passage over Markle's ([1985] 287–88 n. 40; cf. Ober [1989] 210–11), but I do not see *apragmōn* as a term of disparagement. In my view, Demosthenes is saying that Strato is a *penēs* and thus naturally without legal experience (*apragmōn*), but just because he is a *penēs*, one should not assume he is *ponēros*. For a *penēs* as an *apragmōn*, cf. Eup. fr. 193 *ap.* Plu. *Nic.* 4.3.
88. On Lysias 25, see Weissenberger (1987) 84–148; Murphy (1992).
89. Cf. Murphy (1992) 543–44 contra Dover (1968) 188.
90. See Lateiner (1981) 151. Isocrates also regularly condemns democratic politicians as sykophants: see 8.133; 12.12–13, 139–42; 15.315–19.
91. On the circulation of epideictic speeches, see Trevett (1996) 377.
92. Ober (1994b) 169 (assessing Isocrates' *Areopagus*); cf. Too (1995) 6. Wallace ([1989] 163) argues that Isocrates' political position is elitist rather than oligarchic.
93. On the legal setting of the *Antidosis*, see Bonner (1920).
94. Some manuscripts omit the part of Isoc. 15.224 quoted in the text.

253

95. For *piezō* applied to sykophantic blackmail, see Ar. *Eq.* 259. Lys. 28.3 applies the same image to the burden of the *eisphora*.
96. Cf. Pl. *R.* 565b5–c4; Arist. *Pol.* 1304b19–24; Lys. 25.27.
97. Ober ([1989] 48) classifies Isocrates' political pamphlets as "elite/elite literature."
98. Ibid., 338.
99. See Hubbard (1991).
100. For the view that Aristophanes is politically conservative, see de Ste. Croix (1972) 355–71; Henderson (1990) 284, 313; Cartledge (1990b) 43–53; cf. Sommerstein (1996) 335–36. This is disputed by Heath (1987) 29–43; cf. Carrière (1979) 168–71.
101. See Henderson (1990) 291–92.
102. On the selection of judges, see Pickard-Cambridge (1968) 95–98.
103. I am persuaded by Halliwell (1991) that the traditions concerning occasional restrictions on comic license are suspect.
104. Henderson (1990) 274.
105. On the basis of these similarities, de Ste. Croix ([1972] 362–63 n. 10) identifies Aristophanes' perspective fully with that of "the propertied class."
106. On Aristophanes' criticism of dikastic pay, see de Ste. Croix (1972) 362 n. 8 (collecting twenty-two citations).
107. For treason as a sykophantic charge, see Ar. *Eq.* 235–36, 257, 278–79, 452, 465–67, 476–79, 626–29, 862–67; V. 344–45, 464–65, 481–83, 488–89, 506–7, 953; Eup. fr. 193. For the sykophantic charge of fomenting rebellion, see esp. Ar. *Pax* 639–43. Thucydides too emphasizes the demos's fears of conspiracy within the city (6.53) and of rebellion among allies (8.1).
108. On the enmity between Cleon and the knights, see Bugh (1988) 107–14; Carawan (1990).
109. See Brock (1986) 20–22.
110. For Cleon as a sykophantic harasser of allies, see *Eq.* 313, 326–27, 361, 438, 801–2, 832–35, 974–76, 1034, 1070–71, 1196–98, 1407–8; V. 669–77; *Pax* 639–48.
111. On the imagery here, see Edmunds (1987) 7.
112. Cf. Aristophanes' cynical portrayal of the Theban trader in *Acharnians*: he is none too happy when a sykophant harasses him, but delights at the prospect of importing sykophants into his homeland and reaping profit from their tricks (906; cf. 957–58).
113. The assignment of these lines to the chorus leader is controversial: see Harder (1996) 42.
114. Tammaro (1973–74) 189–90.
115. My reading of *Wasps* draws on Konstan (1985) 35–38; but cf. S. D. Olson (1996).

116. See Konstan (1985) 39. On the intergenerational metaphor in Aristophanes, see Hubbard (1989); Crichton (1991); Strauss (1993) 153–66; Sutton (1993) 15–37.
117. For prosecutors cast as young men, see also Ar. V. 687–91; Av. 1431; cf. V. 1037–42; Nu. 1003–4.
118. For Euathlus and the courts, see also Ar. V. 592–93; fr. 424; Cratin. fr. 82; Pl. Com. fr. 109.
119. For the pun on *diōkō*, see also Ar. V. 1205–7.
120. Contra Carter (1986) 120–24.
121. Bowie ([1982] 32) notes the thematic link.
122. S. D. Olson ([1991] 203) observes that Dikaiopolis's market involves a return to the past in its preference for barter over cash.
123. Euathlus is denigrated in similar terms in Ar. fr. 424. On the possibility that he was in fact of Scythian ancestry, see MacDowell (1990a) 362–64.
124. On the difficulty of determining the social status of the sykophant in *Wealth*, see Chapter 2.
125. For an unnamed disciple of Plato cast as a poor sykophant, see Ephipp. fr. 14 *ap.* Ath. 509b.
126. On these metaphors in Aristophanes, see Chapter 2.
127. On forensic play in new comedy, see Scafuro (1997).
128. Taillardat (1965) 395–98.
129. Aristophanes puns here, as so often, on *sukophant-*. I am not persuaded by Henderson ([1991] 118, 176) that *aposukazeis* also involves a double entendre portraying Cleon as a homosexual rapist.
130. In my view Brunck's transposition of 264–65 to follow 260 is unnecessary.
131. See Plu. *Nic.* 4–5, citing Telecl. fr. 44; Eup. fr. 193; Ar. *Eq.* 358; Phryn. Com. fr. 62.
132. On the tension between utopian resolution and real life in Aristophanes, see Henderson (1990) 312.
133. Bowie ([1987] 125) well observes of Philocleon, "his youthful disregard for the courts is as disordered, from the city's point of view, as his earlier senile obsession with them."
134. On Demos's transformation, see Brock (1986); S. D. Olson (1990b) contra Edmunds (1987) 43–49. Bennett and Tyrell ([1990] 252) in my view take too optimistic a view of this transformation.
135. Henderson (1990) 295.

Chapter Four. Public Suits and Volunteer Prosecutors

1. See Ziebarth (1897); Humphreys (1988) 469, with 485 n. 13.
2. *Sunēgoroi* can designate state prosecutors of public suits, or advocates

speaking in support of litigants in private or public suits: see Mac-Dowell (1971b) 198–99; cf. (1978) 61–62.
3. I borrow the label from Osborne (1985b) 41.
4. Th. 2.37.3 is probably referring to volunteer prosecution: see Gomme (1945) ad loc. For other expressions of the ideal of assisting wronged parties, see Bolkestein (1939) 90–91, 128.
5. See Hansen (1989a); Rhodes (1993).
6. On the possibility that Draco's homicide law allowed volunteer prosecutors to enforce the exile of murderers, see Bonner and Smith (1930) 1.167–68; but cf. Hansen (1976) 115; Gagarin (1981) 61, 163. On the origins of volunteer prosecution, see also Calhoun (1927) 72–87; Gerst (1963) 24–46; Latte ([1931b] 1968) 263–82; Ruschenbusch (1968) 47–53; Winkel (1982) 283–88; Sealey (1994) 125–32.
7. On Plutarch's attribution of these words to Solon, see Fisher (1992) 77–78. Fisher (76–81; cf. Winkel [1982] 287–88) rightly challenges Ruschenbusch's position ([1968] 53; cf. Sealey [1994] 129) that third-party prosecution in Solon's time and in the classical period had no public dimension. S. Todd ([1993] 111–12) takes such actions as evidence of the community's "marginal interest" in protecting the weak.
8. Dover (1974) 278. On Greek attitudes toward charity, see Bolkestein (1939) 67–286; Hands (1968); Dover (1974) 177–78; Rosivach (1991) 193–95.
9. Humphreys ([1988] 470) suggests that volunteer prosecution was "a weapon for moderates, especially well-to-do commoners, to use against arrogant aristocrats, either in their own defense or on behalf of poorer clients."
10. Eder ([1986] 288) argues persuasively that the codification of law in both Athens and Rome confirmed "the political power of the leading social group." On the social significance of the codification of laws in Greece, see Thomas (1996).
11. Sealey ([1994] 125–32) surveys many of the actions that third-party prosecutors could employ. On *endeixis* and *apagōgē* against *kakourgoi*, see Hansen (1976) 36–53.
12. See Osborne (1985b) 52.
13. See Millett (1989); Arnaoutoglou (1994) contra Gallant (1991) 159–66; Dillon (1995).
14. Presumably in Solon's time too the acceptance of legal patronage clashed with ideals of manhood.
15. See Hunter (1994) 127.
16. S. Todd ([1993] 198) questions the dependence of metics on *prostatai* for legal support.

17. See Dover (1974) 180-84; Blundell (1989) 26-59.
18. Hunter ([1994] 138-39) in my view overestimates the willingness of passersby to intervene. Evidence of physical assistance is scarce: Lys. 3.7 is dubious, Dem. 53.17 vague. I would also agree with Humphreys ([1985b] 330-33) over Hunter (232 n. 41) that one should be skeptical when litigants represent witnesses at trial as bystanders.
19. For a possible exception, see Dem. 58.30-34, discussed later in this chapter.
20. See Dover (1974) 177-78.
21. See MacDowell (1990b) 314.
22. See Dover (1974) 304.
23. See Millett (1991) 119-120, 127-59. On *philia*, see further in Chapter 5.
24. See Calhoun (1913) 40-96.
25. Rubinstein, in a paper presented at the 1996 meetings of the APA, persuasively challenges the traditional view (e.g., S. Todd [1993] 94-95) that *sunēgoria* was relatively uncommon.
26. For the charge that a *sunēgoros* is bought, see Lyc. 1.138; Dem. 44.3; cf. 21.112; 48.36. For defenses against this charge, see [Arist.] *Rh. Al.* 1444a35-b3; Calhoun (1913) 85-89.
27. See MacDowell (1978) 93.
28. See Harrison (1968) 1.115-21; Rhodes (1981) 629-31.
29. See Rhodes (1981) 630.
30. See Lacey (1968) 140-41; Goldhill (1987) 63-64.
31. Osborne ([1985b] 48-49) observes that the second case appears to be part of ongoing political rivalry between Theocrines and his competitors.
32. Osborne (1985b) 49. Osborne (49 n. 45) also notes that only a single case of *phasis* on behalf of orphans is attested (Dem. 38.23).
33. Osborne ([1985b] 57) collects five known cases. On this action, see Harrison (1968) 1.119-21.
34. An orphan was supposed to bring his *dikē* within five years of the end of guardianship (Dem. 38.17).
35. See Harrison (1968) 1.120.
36. Humphreys (1993) 5.
37. The laws cited at Dem. 43.54 and 43.75 do not justify Ruschenbusch's claim ([1968] 54-55) that in the fourth century the volunteer prosecutor in *eisangeliai* for wrongs done to orphans and *epiklēroi* merely reported his charge to the archon, who then carried out the prosecution in court.
38. Osborne ([1985b] 52) in my view overstates the extent to which Athenians pursued *graphai* on their own behalf.
39. On the vexed question as to whether Athenians would designate a

graphē brought by a harmed party as private (*idia*), see Gerst (1963) 63–67; MacDowell (1990b) 247, 267–68; E. Harris (1992) 77–78. Special rules may have applied to such suits, for example, a prosecutor may not have been subject to penalty if he dropped his suit: see Dem. 59.64–71, with Hunter (1994) 207 n. 18.

40. On hubris and the *graphē hubreōs*, see MacDowell (1990b) 17–23, 263–68; Fisher (1992) 36–82; S. Todd (1993) 270–71; D. Cohen (1995) 143–62; Cairns (1996).
41. Osborne ([1985b] 50–51) observes that two cases are recorded, Is. 8.41 and Dem. 45.4, and that the latter did not come to court. Fisher ([1992] 43) suggests that these suits were probably "relatively infrequently brought to trial."
42. See S. Todd (1993) 270–71.
43. MacDowell ([1990b] 13–17) argues that the action was a *probolē*, E. Harris ([1992] 73–74), a *graphē hubreōs*. If the action was a *probolē*, it may have been *akindunos:* see Harrison (1971) 2.64; MacDowell (1990b) 268.
44. For criticism of Aeschines' testimony, see E. Harris (1989) 134.
45. On Dem. 21, see MacDowell (1990b); Wilson (1991); Ober (1994a); D. Cohen (1995) 93–100.
46. For a survey of public actions, see S. Todd (1993) 98–122.
47. Although actions bearing financial rewards could be used against persons involved in public life, they were by no means limited to this group.
48. Hansen (1991) 205.
49. See Hansen (1991) 220; but cf. Rihll (1995) 93–97. If a candidate was rejected at the *dokimasia*, he was prevented from entering office, but suffered no additional penalty.
50. In the extant cases prosecutors charge defendants with collaborating with the Thirty, even though this violates the terms of the Amnesty of 403 B.C.: see Adeleye (1983); Weissenberger (1987); S. Todd (1993) 285–89; Hunter (1994) 106–8.
51. See Hansen (1975) 29–30.
52. Hansen ([1991] 224) argues, however, that actual prosecutions at the *euthunai* were not that frequent. The description of *euthunai* in the text draws on Hansen 222–23.
53. Hansen ([1975] 29–30) observes that prosecutors at the *euthunai* were apparently not subject to the statutory penalties that applied in most public actions.
54. See Ar. *Ach.* 936–39; *Eq.* 259–60, 824–26; Ant. 6.43; Dem. 25.50; cf. 18.249–50; 25.37; Lofberg (1917) 45–46; Ostwald (1986) 211–12.
55. See Ar. *V.* 100–102, 553–54, 570–71; Lys. 27.14–15; 30.34–35.
56. On the ambiguity of *graphai* here, see note 121.

57. See Hansen (1975) 62–63; J. Roberts (1982) 167.
58. For varying estimates of frequency, see Hansen (1975) 60, 63–64; J. Roberts (1982) 175; Knox (1985) 143; Sinclair (1988) 150. S. Todd ([1993] 305) is right to point out the difficulties inherent in such calculations.
59. See J. Roberts (1982) 178; S. Todd (1993) 306.
60. Hansen (1975) 65; cf. Sagan (1991) 181–85.
61. On complaints about a prosecutor's choice of action, see Chapter 6.
62. Hansen ([1975] 30) argues on the basis of Dem. 18.250 that the rule must have changed before 330 B.C. Bonner and Smith ([1930] 1.296–98), however, rightly point out that this passage need not be taken as evidence of a rule change.
63. See Sinclair (1988) 158; Stockton (1990) 102.
64. Cf. Frier (1985) 39: "the litigious . . . often . . . provoke law into doing new things. In this they are indispensable agents of legal change."
65. See Hansen (1974).
66. See Hansen (1975) 29 n. 4.
67. See Hansen (1991) 207.
68. See ibid., 208–9.
69. On the tradition concerning Aristophon, see Sinclair (1988) 162.
70. On the legal and political dimensions of these *graphai*, see Yunis (1988).
71. Lewis (1966) 191 n. 67; but cf. Humphreys (1988) 486–87 n. 25. On *apographē*, see Osborne (1985b) 44–47, 54–55; S. Todd (1993) 118–19.
72. MacDowell (1991) 198; cf. Lipsius (1908) 2.309–16.
73. On these measures, see Berneker (1967) 1473–78; Harrison (1968) 1.26–28; Scafuro (1994) 156–57.
74. On unrewarded types of *phasis*, see MacDowell (1991) 197–98; of *graphai xenias*, see discussion in the text.
75. Lofberg (1917) 26; Bonner and Smith (1938) 2.42.
76. Sinclair (1988) 73.
77. Osborne (1985b) 48; cf. (1990) 84.
78. Harvey (1990) 112; cf. Hunter (1994) 126.
79. For a catalog of attested *apographai*, see Osborne (1985b) 54–55. Osborne (46) doubts that prosecutors normally sought financial gain through these suits.
80. Litigants regularly take for granted that if a prosecutor is motivated by enmity, he is not seeking financial profit: see discussion in the text. On Lysias 9, see MacDowell (1994).
81. For these concerns expressed in *eisangeliai*, see Hyp. 4.32; Lys. 30.22; cf. A. H. M. Jones (1957) 58–61.

82. Lofberg (1917) 30.
83. Note that Apollodorus, when joining in the prosecution of a *graphē xenias* bearing a reward (Dem. 59), does not feel compelled to decline in advance the reward.
84. See esp. Lofberg (1917) 26–28.
85. Compare the arrangement in eighteenth- and nineteenth-century Britain by which incentives were provided for private prosecution of infractions of customs and excise regulations: see Hay (1989) 355 n. 41.
86. MacDowell ([1991] 194–95) is probably right that, notwithstanding Aristophanes' silence, *phasis* was rewarded in such cases in the fifth century.
87. For evidence of this practice in the fourth century, see MacDowell (1991) 193.
88. This use of *phainein* to describe how the sykophant will make trouble for magistrates is consistent with the comedy's focus on *phasis*.
89. Osborne (1985b) 44.
90. For attested cases, see Scafuro (1994) 194 n. 96. For claims of abuse, see Ar. V. 718; *vit. Ar.* 1.19; Dem. 49.66–67; cf. Cratin. fr. 251; Ar. fr. 237.
91. On the *diapsēphisis* of 346/5 B.C., see Whitehead (1986) 104–9, 292–301; Scafuro (1994) 191 n. 64. For alleged abuses, see Dem. 57; Is. 12; Aesch. 1.114–15; cf. 2.182.
92. In lists of abused actions, *apographē* appears with *dikē* and *graphē* at Lys. 13.65 (Osborne [1985b] 46 n. 32 believes that *apographē* does not have its technical meaning here), and with *graphē* at Lys. fr. 26a Thalheim; *phasis* appears with *graphē* at Isoc. 15.99 and Dem. 59.43, with *apagōgē* and *endeixis* at Dem. 25.78, with *graphē, endeixis,* and *apagōgē* at Dem. 39.14, and with *graphē* and *endeixis* at Dem. 58.45.
93. Financial incentives were also provided for prosecution elsewhere in the Greek world: see Ziebarth (1897); Humphreys (1988) 471. Hdt. 4.68 asserts that Scythian prophets who conduct a successful prosecution divide the convicted party's goods.

    This kind of arrangement is not entirely without parallel in the United States. Under the 1986 amendments to the False Claims Act, anyone can bring a civil suit against a party submitting a false claim to the U.S. Treasury and, if successful, receive a part of the penalty imposed: on these *qui tam* actions, see Caminker (1989); Lee (1990); Park (1991); Reidinger (1996) 50–54. On *qui tam* actions in eighteenth- and nineteenth-century Britain, see Hay (1989) 354–68.
94. See Hunter (1994) 89, with 210–11 n. 2. The practice of offering a reward (*mēnutron*) to informers is attested as early as Hom. *h.Merc.* 264.

95. For explicit comparison of financial risks and benefits by a prosecutor in a public action not bearing a financial reward, see Dem. 24.3.
96. Contrast the situation in eighteenth- and nineteenth-century Britain as described by Hay (1989) 354–68: concerns over abuse of *qui tam* prosecutions, in which a successful prosecutor received a financial reward, led to increasing state monopolization of public prosecution.
97. Cf. Hansen (1991) 266–68.
98. Osborne ([1985b] 52) is more cautious, suggesting that volunteer prosecution "could be socially conservative." Hay and Snyder ([1989a] 29–30) characterize the American preference for public prosecutors by the time of the Revolution as a democratic reaction against the class inequalities of private prosecution.
99. *Rhētores*, who frequently served as volunteer prosecutors, also faced this difficulty when they addressed the Assembly: see esp. Ober (1989).
100. For the idea that a sykophant might pose as a trader, see also Dem. 33.2.
101. To accuse a sykophant of being someone who "does nothing" is to insinuate that he lives off criminal activities (cf. 869, 909, 939). This accusation also involves a comic paradox, since his profession entails above all "doing everything," that is, meddling.
102. Here and later Aristophanes plays on the designation of the volunteer prosecutor as "any willing person" (*ho boulomenos*).
103. MacDowell (1978) 63; challenged by Carter (1986) 87, and Sommerstein (1984) 324. On the scene, see also Fisher (1976) 69–70; Adkins (1976) 308–10; McGlew (1997) 46.
104. Adkins ([1976] 310) goes too far in maintaining that Aristophanes' objection is to any such prosecution, false or not.
105. On sykophancy as a "job," see Chapter 2.
106. See Rhodes (1981) 785, s.v. *epimelētai*; cf. Whitehead (1993) 68–69.
107. For *euergetēs* as an honorific, see Whitehead (1983) 61; (1993) 54–55.
108. See Connor (1971) 110–15; Rhodes (1981) 97, 344–61; Ober (1989) 316–17; cf. Millett (1989) 33–36.
109. On the figure *boēthein* in the courts, see Latte ([1931b] 1968) 282 n. 26.
110. Where these penalties did not apply, a defendant could protest that a prosecutor was acting without risk (*akindunos*): see Hyp. 1.12; cf. Is. 11.31.
111. For enmity as a risk of public life in general, see And. 4.1; Dem. 57.63; Din. fr. LXXXVII Conomis.
112. On *kindunos* in Athenian ideology, see Dover (1974) 161–63; Christ (1987); Crane (1992) 240–44.

113. The word applies equally well to martial and (devious) legal preparations: on its use in the latter sense, see Chapter 2.
114. Epichares ridicules corrupt prosecutors like Theocrines who claim to ensure the safety (*sōteria*) of the people (Dem. 58.63; cf. 13.16–17).
115. For *boēthein* applied to Athens's soldiers, see Ziolkowski (1981) 104–5.
116. For Cleon as watchdog, see Ar. *Eq.* 1017–34, V. 894f., with further testimonia in Brock (1991) 161 n. 3; cf. Taillardat (1965) 403–5. For similar imagery applied to other politicians, see Eup. fr. 220; X. *Mem.* 2.9.2, 7.
117. Although ancient sources speak of leaders of the demos as *prostatai* (see note 108), it is not clear that a *rhētōr* would be so bold as to characterize himself as such in popular discourse.
118. See Connor (1971) 101–3.
119. Cf. the assertion that a *rhētōr* should have the same friends and enemies as the city (Dem. 15.33).
120. For a less extreme statement of the priority of a man's private affairs over matters of public concern, see Dem. 36.53–54. On public prosecution conceived as meddling outside the *oikos*, see Adkins (1976) 318.
121. It is not clear, however, whether Aeschines is using *graphē* in a generic sense ("public action"), or in the more specific sense of a particular kind of public action. E. Harris ([1995] 36–37) argues that Aeschines was not a frequent public prosecutor.
122. For other prosecutors driven by a sense of shame and indignation, see Aesch. 1.1–2; Lyc. 1.5–6; fr. X–XI.2 Conomis.
123. On circumstances in which officeholders were required to carry out prosecutions, see Gerst (1963) 111–20; Harrison (1971) 2.6–7; MacDowell (1978) 235–37. On public *sunēgoroi*, see Bonner and Smith (1938) 2.26–38; Rhodes (1981) 597; S. Todd (1993) 92.
124. One of the grounds on which Sealey ([1993] 238) challenges the authenticity of Dem. 25 is that, apart from 25.13, "there is no evidence that prosecutors were elected for the procedure of *endeixis*." But, as Hansen ([1976] 146) observes, such a practice is plausible in the late fourth century.
125. Prospective councilmembers underwent *dokimasia* before members of the outgoing Council, but if rejected here, they could appeal to a popular court ([Arist.] *AP* 45.3).
126. On this *eisangelia*, see S. Todd (1993) 316–20.
127. See Rhodes (1972) 112, 148; Gagarin (1997) 246.
128. On the different expectations of *rhētores* and *idiōtai*, see Ober (1989) 104–12, 174–89, 306–11.
129. For the assertion that public prosecutions should not be used against *idiōtai*, see Dem. 25.38–41; Hyp. 4.9, 27–28.

130. On this trope, see Chapter 2.
131. Note, however, how Thucydides' Pericles treats the claims that he is *philopolis* and "above money" as separable (2.60.5).
132. On personal enmity in public prosecution, see Hunter (1994) 127, 228 n. 21; D. Cohen (1995) 101–6; Rhodes (in Mitchell and Rhodes [1996]) 25–26.
133. On the limits of retaliation, see Chapter 5.
134. For this identification of the action involved, see S. Todd (1993) 113.
135. For rhetorical analysis of Lys. 12.2, see Grau (1972) 50–53.
136. Calhoun ([1913] 53 n. 1) may be right that this is how Epichares became the prosecutor of Theocrines (Dem. 58). Cf. the practice of calling forth a man's enemies as witnesses: see Humphreys (1985b) 338–39.
137. See Dover (1974) 192. In addition to the passages discussed in the text, see And. 1.104; Lys. 9.22; Is. 12.8; Dem. 21.29; 57.49; cf. 5.6; Pl. *Ap.* 23e2–24a1, with 22e6–23a2. For envy (*phthonos*) as a corrupt motivation, see Lys. 24.1–3 (where it is distinguished from enmity); Dem. 57.6 (where it is linked to enmity).
138. For the disavowal of enmity in the prosecution of a *dokimasia*, see Lys. 31.2; cf. 26.15.
139. Note, however, how Demosthenes in his prosecution of Aristogeiton suppresses enmity as a motivation, though it is surely present (cf. 25.37), since he can justify his participation by the fact that the Assembly appointed him *sunēgoros* (25.13).

Chapter Five. Private Quarrels and Public Disputes

1. Schol. VAld Ar. V. 191.
2. On this proverb, see MacDowell (1971b) 157.
3. On the anthropology of dispute, see Nader and Todd (1978) 1–40; Comaroff and Roberts (1981); Geertz (1983); Humphreys (1985b), (1986); W. Davies and Fouracre (1986); Starr and Collier (1989); Gagos and Minnen (1995); D. Cohen (1995) 9–24.
4. While concerns over quarrelsomeness arise in public actions, especially when volunteer prosecutors are seeking vengeance against personal enemies, they are especially conspicuous in private actions and these therefore provide most of the source material for this chapter.
5. I am not persuaded by Herman ([1994] 108; cf. [1993], [1995]) that Athenian attitudes toward vengeance differed significantly from those of other Greeks.
6. D. Cohen (1995) 183. Cohen (87–118) argues that litigation in Athens is a manifestation of feuding behavior.
7. On this general tendency of litigants, see Hay (1989) 391–92.

8. In my view D. Cohen ([1995] 97) overestimates jurors' toleration of aggression, while Herman ([1994] 109) goes too far in the opposite direction in maintaining that "the 'primitive' code [of vengeance] had lost its hold over their minds."
9. For the idea that Athens's laws are designed to discourage the escalation of violence, see Dem. 54.17–19, with Herman (1994) 112.
10. On "quarrelsomeness" as a social idea, see Frier (1985) 39–40; for Athenian attitudes toward it, see Dover (1974) 234. On the general tension between competitive and cooperative virtues in Greek culture, see Adkins (1960), (1972); Dover (1974) 230–34.
11. On private arbitration, see Hunter (1994) 55–62, with 206 n. 16; Scafuro (1997) 117–41, 393–99; on public arbitration, see Hunter (1994) 62–66, with 203 n. 1; Scafuro (1997) 383–92. On these and other options of dispute settlement, see Scafuro (1997) 31–42. Another alternative to trial was the "oath challenge": see Mirhady (1991a).
12. See Hunter (1994) 57, 187.
13. On the ideal of local adjudication, see Humphreys (1985a) 245, (1985b) 316; Hunter (1994) 58.
14. On the representation of the local community in the city's courts, see Humphreys (1983) 248, (1985b) 316.
15. On the association of hubris with the rich, see Fisher (1992) 20–21.
16. For the sykophant as bold (*thrasus*), see Isoc. 15.316; Dem. 25.97; Aesch. 1.105; as reckless (*tolm-*), Ar. *Ec.* 560; Isoc. 15.317; 18.22; Is. 11.13; Dem. 25.9 (these instances are taken from the catalog of Harvey [1990] 108). For prosecuting as a false show of manliness, see Lys. fr. 26a Thalheim.
17. A self-assured man could also ignore the aggression of his opponent on the grounds that he was beneath contempt and an unworthy adversary: see D. Cohen (1995) 69, 73.
18. Note how the sykophantic Aristogeiton is said to reject *charis* and *philia* (Dem. 25.52). For the sykophant as an enemy of good social relations, see Chapter 2.
19. On the transformation of disputes into legal categories, see Galanter (1983) 19; into "appropriate conventions," S. Roberts (1983) 22; cf. Humphreys (1986) 58; into legal stories, Johnstone (forthcoming); cf. Brooks and Gewirtz (1996).
20. On the fragility of social relationships in Athens, see Humphreys (1985b) 340; Millett (1991) 119–20.
21. On *philia*, see Dover (1974) 180–84; Blundell (1989) 26–59; Millett (1991) 109–26; Konstan (1996), (1997). Although scholars commonly group relatives and friends together under the designation *philoi*, Konstan (1996) argues that in an Athenian context *philoi* nor-

mally is used only of friends, while the abstract *philia* subsumes a wide range of bonds, including those between friends or relatives.
22. See Millett (1991) 127–39.
23. See Konstan (1995) 331, (1996) 86 contra, e.g., Millett (1991) 116–26.
24. *oikeiotēs* connotes personal closeness but without the self-disclosure often associated with friendship in a modern context (cf. Konstan [1997] 69).
25. Scafuro ([1997] 131–36) discusses the role of "the ideology of friendship" in arbitrations and reconciliations.
26. On *philia* as a social ideal in Athens, see Konstan (1996) 76, (1997) 71–72, 75. Konstan ([1997] 72) observes, "A person who was a good friend was the model of a good citizen."
27. Ar. *Ec.* 655–61 thus asserts that if private property is eliminated, there will be no need for private suits.
28. See Humphreys (1986) 58; Hunter (1994) 49.
29. On the Athenian family, see Lacey (1968); Humphreys (1993).
30. Hunter ([1994] 48–55, 68–69) surveys the evidence.
31. See S. Todd (1993) 215–21.
32. On the frequent involvement of agnates due to the rules governing inheritance, see Humphreys (1986); cf. Hunter (1994) 50.
33. On the critical role of witnesses in such cases, see Scafuro (1994) 172–77.
34. See S. Todd (1993) 119–20.
35. See MacDowell (1978) 103–8; D. Cohen (1995) 163–80.
36. Humphreys (1993) 5; cf. Millett (1991) 129–30; Hunter (1994) 54–55.
37. Humphreys ([1986] 87–88) observes that as a practical matter bonds of *philia* among kin were considerably looser outside of the nuclear family than within it.
38. See Dover (1974) 275.
39. Cf. how a litigant prosecuting his stepbrother speaks vividly of his "struggling with his yoke mate" (*zugomachein*) (Dem. 39.6; cf. Hyp. fr. 245 Jensen).
40. Litigating kin regularly claim to be victims of circumstance or chance: Ant. 1.2; Is. fr. 22 Thalheim; Dem. 48.1; cf. Is. 1.6; Dem. 40.1–2; and to be acting under compulsion: Ant. 1.2; Dem. 40.1–2; 48.1–2.
41. See Hunter (1994) 57. Hunter (58, 205 n. 13) is probably right that most disputes among kin were in fact settled by private arbitration of some kind.
42. See ibid., 58.
43. Humphreys ([1986] 67) aptly observes that lawsuits among kin gave the juror a "voyeur's view of the dramas of private life"; cf. Hunter (1994) 51, 64.

44. On Lys. 32, see S. Todd (1993) 202–3; Foxhall (1996) 147–49; Scafuro (1997) 46–50.
45. The friends (*hoi philoi*) referred to here may have included relatives: see Lys. 32.12.
46. It is not clear that this arrangement was illegal (contra Humphreys ([1993] 6); the speaker shows no embarrassment about it. On contracts involving illegal activities, see S. Todd (1993) 264.
47. See Hunter (1994) 205–6 n. 14.
48. Litigants could apparently agree to settle with one another even as the jury's votes were counted: see Is. 5.17–18; Wyse (1904) 425–27; Scafuro (1997) 393–94. While Is. 5.29 suggests that in such cases the jury may have given final approval to the settlement, this hardly made the jury active "reconcilers" of the disputants.
49. For similar doubts raised about kinship on the basis of behavior in litigation, see Dem. 39.34; cf. 40.12, 47.
50. Contrast the modern American setting, where "litigation tends to be between parties who are strangers" (Galanter [1983] 24).
51. On mutual support among neighbors, see Gallant (1991) 155–58.
52. Humphreys ([1986] 59) observes that "patrikin were often neighbours, at least in rural areas."
53. For litigation among neighbors in early modern England, see Sharpe (1983).
54. On the idealization of *philia* here and elsewhere in the speech, see Millett (1991) 139 with n. 17.
55. On Dem. 53, see Millett (1991) 53–59; E. Cohen (1992) 210–13; D. Cohen (1995) 102–3.
56. Apollodorus proceeded with his *graphē pseudoklēteias* (53.17) against Arethusius, succeeded in having him fined by a court (53.18), and then brought the current suit against Nicostratus when Arethusius tried to avoid paying the fine by transferring his assets to Nicostratus (53.19–29).
57. On the presentation of this economic relationship in social terms, see Millett (1991) 53–58; cf. E. Cohen (1992) 210–11. On *philoi* conceived as equals in democratic Athens, see Arist. *EN* 1157b36; Konstan (1995) 332–33, (1996) 74.
58. See Whitehead (1986) 231; cf. Millett (1991) 140.
59. On the deme as a "face-to-face society," see Osborne (1985a) 89; Whitehead (1986) 226, 231. On the fiction invoked by public speakers that Athens was such a society, see Ober (1989) 150.
60. See Humphreys (1985b) 340–41, 343–45; Osborne (1985a) 42; Whitehead (1986) 227–31.
61. See Whitehead (1986) 128–30.
62. Ibid., 230.

63. On Dem. 57, see Osborne (1985a) 146–51; Whitehead (1986) 296–301; Humphreys (1986) 60–62; Scafuro (1994) 165–68; Carey (1994a) 104–6. On other possible cases, notably Is. 12, arising from this revision of the deme rolls, see Whitehead (1986) 107 with n. 108; Scafuro (1994) 183 nn. 11, 12.
64. Note the similar complaints of conspiring enemies in Is. 12.8, 10–12.
65. E. Cohen ([1992] 145) stresses that some bankers and traders were Athenians; on Athenians in the world of trade, see Mossé (1983); von Reden (1995) 34.
66. This is a good example of how public disputing, as Humphreys ([1985a] 244) observes, can illuminate "areas of ambiguity or uncertainty in social relationships."
67. See Humphreys (1985b) 348; E. Cohen (1992) 62–66, 100; Millett (1991) 212.
68. See Arist. EN 1156a10 and EE 1236a33–35, with Millett (1991) 115–16.
69. The nature and scope of Athenian banking are disputed: Millett ([1991] 197–217, 238–41) argues for a "primitivist" view, E. Cohen (1992) for a "modernist" one; Morris (1994) suggests the truth may lie somewhere between these two positions. I am persuaded by E. Cohen ([1992] 136–50) over Millett ([1991] 202) that bankers extended maritime loans.
70. Millett ([1991] 206–9) argues that bankers were lenders of last resort, used primarily by noncitizens, E. Cohen ([1992] 24–25) that bankers played a broader role than this.
71. Millett ([1991] 197) observes that the Antiphanes fragment is the only passage generalizing a negative attitude toward bankers; E. Cohen ([1992] 24) believes that "as a group bankers enjoyed high esteem and credibility," but makes no mention of Antiphanes' barb.
72. See E. Cohen (1992) 6.
73. On the social resonances of *chraomai*, see ibid., 66.
74. On Isoc. 17, see Millett (1991) 208–9; E. Cohen (1992) 38–40. On Pasio and his banking family, see E. Cohen (1992) 61–110; Trevett (1992) 1–49.
75. For the claim that a banker-client relationship is *oikeios*, see also Dem. 52.23.
76. See E. Cohen (1992) 191–201.
77. On Dem. 49, see Millett (1991) 125–26; E. Cohen (1992) 37–38; cf. Trevett (1991).
78. Cf. Dem. 53.8–12, where Apollodorus claims to have acted as a *philos* in assisting Nicostratrus in his distress.
79. On the emphasis on *charis* here, see Millett (1991) 125–26.
80. On professional moneylenders, see ibid., 179–96.

81. On Dem. 37, a speech by the prosecutor of a *paragraphē*, see Isager and Hansen (1975) 191–96; Carey and Reid (1985) 105–17; Millett (1991) 194–96.
82. On the exploitation of the idea of *charis* here, see Millett (1991) 194.
83. Ibid., 194. For similar posturing by a litigant, see Dem. 33.4.
84. On maritime loans, see de Ste. Croix (1974); Isager and Hansen (1975) 74–84; Millett (1991) 189–93; E. Cohen (1992) 136–60; S. Todd (1993) 337–39.
85. Three of the four maritime loan suits are *paragraphai* (Dem. 32; 34; 35); the fourth (Dem. 56) is a *dikē blabēs* brought as a *dikē emporikē* (see Isager and Hansen [1975] 84–86, 209–10).
86. Carey and Reid ([1985] 200 n. 50) remark on the striking emphasis on contracts in such suits.
87. For the idea that sykophancy is practiced by non-Athenians, see Chapter 2.
88. On the meaning of *sulai*, see Pritchett (1991) 116–32.
89. Dover (1974) 84.
90. On the rules governing the grain trade, see S. Todd (1993) 321; on the problem of the applicability of the law cited at Dem 35.51 to the circumstances of Dem. 35, see Todd 321 n. 8.
91. For similar appeals to Athenian interests, see Dem. 32.23; 34.50–52.
92. On the status of the parties, see Carey and Reid (1985) 197–98.
93. For *pistis* and *philia* as "building stones of society" in Hellenic thought, see von Reden (1995) 28.
94. On ideals of community arising in the context of legal disputes, see Greenhouse, Engel, and Yngvesson (1994); cf. Humphreys (1985b) 355.
95. Cf. Galanter (1983) 58 n. 247: "Populations which embrace ideals of harmony and conciliation may use courts at high rates while disparaging litigation."
96. D. Cohen ([1995] 101) argues that while the courts appear to have discouraged the escalation of conflict into homicide, they had little effect on lesser forms of violence. Herman ([1994] 102) credits the courts for the fact that Athens was "as judged against comparable European societies past and present, a remarkably peaceful society, exhibiting probably less violence than is generally assumed by modern scholars."
97. Cf. Galanter (1983) 12: "Litigation . . . profoundly affects what happens at earlier stages by providing cues, symbols, and bargaining counters which the actors use in constructing (and dismantling) disputes."
98. For nighttime violence, see Lys. 3.6–9; fr. 75 Thalheim; Dem. 53.17; 54.5, 7–9; Aesch. 1.59; cf. Lys. 1.23–28; drunkenness is often al-

leged to play a role in such episodes (cf. Fisher [1992] 101). For violence in isolated locations or indoors, see Lys. 3.12–13; fr. 75 Thalheim; Dem. 53.17; Aesch. 1.59.
99. See D. Cohen (1995) 94–95.
100. Cf. Christ (1996) 383.

Chapter Six. Beyond the Letter of the Law

1. Cf. A. Solzhenitsyn in Berman (1980) 8: "A society based on the letter of the law and never reaching any higher fails to take advantage of the full range of human possibilities. The letter of the law is too cold and formal to have a beneficial influence on society."
2. Thus Meyer-Laurin (1966) 28–31; E. Harris (1994a) 132–37; cf. Carey (1996) 34 n. 8. For challenges to this position, see Biscardi (1970); Humphreys (1988) 488 n. 37; S. Todd (1993) 54–55; D. Cohen (1995) 61; Scafuro (1997) 50–66.
3. For reconstructions of the Heliastic oath, see Fränkel (1878); Harrison (1971) 2.48.
4. See Dover (1974) 248–50.
5. E. Harris ([1994a] 133, with 149 nn. 6, 7) collects the numerous references to the Heliastic oath in forensic oratory.
6. For testimonia naming the Ardettos Hill as the site of the oath taking, see Boegehold (1995) 186–87.
7. Hansen ([1990] 240 n. 117) collects the ancient references.
8. For use of this figure, see Aesch. 3.7.
9. On laws as a form of proof, see Mirhady (1991b); S. Todd (1993) 58–60; Carey (1996), and cf. (1994a).
10. E. Harris (1994a) 140; cf. Carey (1996) 36.
11. Cf. D. Cohen (1995) 115: "Athenians articulated principles of legality, but at the same time conceived of the courts as operating within a matrix of political and social forces rather than isolated from them."
12. See Dover (1974) 186–87, 306–9; cf. Humphreys (1983) 248.
13. See de Romilly (1971) 38–49; Carey (1996) 43.
14. See S. Todd (1990a) 32.
15. The city could be said to be governed by both written and unwritten laws (Th. 2.37.3). Unwritten laws were often associated with traditional religious practices (Lys. 6.10; S. Ant. 454–55). On the concept of unwritten law, see Hirzel (1900–1903); de Romilly (1971) 25–38; Ostwald (1973); Thomas (1996) 16–19; Carey (1996) 37–38.
16. See Hansen (1991) 170.
17. For the discussion of this by philosophers, see Chapter 1.
18. On appeals to the lawgiver's intent, see Triantaphyllopoulos (1985) 19; Hansen (1989a) 80 n. 46; Thomas (1994b).

19. Humphreys ([1988] 488 n. 37; cf. Ober [1989] 300) wonders whether jurors were very conscious of the "distinction between laws and other normative statements." In my view, however, it is not so much that jurors failed to distinguish between the two—litigants addressing juries do not seem to confuse norms and laws, and their audiences probably did not either—as that jurors necessarily applied the city's laws in light of their understanding of norms.
20. See Dover (1974) 202.
21. On these values in the courts and elsewhere, see Dover (1974) 191–202; de Romilly (1979); cf. Humphreys (1983) 240.
22. See Dover (1974) 195–98.
23. For allegations of corruption in the law-making process, see also Din. 1.41–45; cf. Eub. fr. 74.6.
24. On this dark portrayal of Nicomachus's activities, see S. Todd (1996) 109; cf. suspicions concerning scribes in Athens (see Wankel [1982] 44–45) and elsewhere in Greece (see Thomas [1994a] 38–40). For allegations of tampering with inscriptions other than those recording laws, see Arist. *Rh.* 1400a32–36; Dem. 57.64. For the possibility of desecrating the city's inscribed laws, see Cratin. fr. 300; Ar. *Av.* 1054.
25. Contrast the high level of concern about erasure in other Greek states during both the archaic period (see Hölkeskamp [1992] 100; Camassa [1994]) and classical period (see Thomas [1994a] 38).
26. On manipulation of the *sanides,* see Boegehold (1972) 27 with n. 21. Even less durable than the *sanides* were the wax tablets on which magistrates recorded legal charges in the fifth century: see Ar. *Nu.* 759–74, with Boegehold (1972) 27.
27. On public slaves as scribes and record keepers, see Hunter (1994) 148; cf. Thomas (1989) 80–81.
28. See Boegehold (1972) 27 n. 20.
29. Litigants do, however, offer a variety of complaints in connection with the depositing of items in the *echinoi:* see Dem. 28.1; 45.57–58; 46.25; 49.19; 54.27, 31; Harrell (1936) 26; Hunter (1994) 65.
30. Carey ([1996] 41) rightly observes: "The potential for manipulation is not perceived, or at least not presented, by litigants as a flaw in the laws but simply a result of individual unscrupulousness."
31. On literacy and law in Athens, see Maffi (1988); W. Harris (1989) 65–115; Thomas (1989) 68–82; Robb (1994) 125–56; Hedrick (1994). On the ability to read and write, see W. Harris (1989) 102, 104; Hedrick (1994) 162–65.
32. For legal arguments as *leptoi,* see Ant. 3.4.2; cf. Ar. *Nu.* 320, 1496. On suspicions concerning literacy and the literate in comedy, see Slater (1996) 99–105.

33. Thomas ([1994a] 35) observes that there is little direct criticism of the public use of writing in Athenian sources.
34. On the limited acceptance of unwitnessed documents even in the fourth century, see Humphreys (1985b) 322; S. Todd (1990a) 29 n. 15, 33 n. 23; Scafuro (1994) 164 contra Pringsheim ([1955] 1961) 2.405. On Greek suspicions concerning forgery, see Thomas (1989) 41–42.
35. I am persuaded by West ([1989] 533) and Sickinger (1994) over Thomas ([1989] 78) that a filing system was in place to facilitate access to the documents in the archive.
36. Hedrick (1994) 168.
37. See Hedrick (1994) 160–67.
38. Theophrastus's "Shameless Man" makes the mistake of flaunting his literacy: he is a frequent litigant, who shows up for trial armed "with a document jar [*echinos*] in the fold of his cloak, and sheaves of written notes in his hands" (*Char.* 6.8). The "written notes" are presumably his speech; for a written speech as a source of suspicion, see also [Arist.] *Rh. Al.* 1444a18–28.
39. S. Todd ([1993] 58 with n. 11) gathers the evidence, and observes that fourth-century litigants, if they give any provenance at all for laws, cite *stēlai* more often than they do the Metroön. He suggests that this may mean, contrary to prevailing scholarly opinion, that Athenians in fact continued to inscribe laws regularly even after the late fifth-century founding of the archive. In my view, however, this manner of citation can be explained by the fact that litigants were reluctant to acknowledge their consultation of the archives in the Metroön; on possible negative perceptions of archiving of laws, see Hedrick (1994) 173.
40. Knowledge of writing and ability to manipulate the laws go hand in hand in Aristophanes' description of an adept litigant as a *kurbis,* "a walking statute-board" (*Nu.* 448).
41. For an exception of sorts to this general rule, see Hyp. 3.8, 12.
42. For *akribeia* applied to writing, see also Arist. *Rh.* 1413b8–9. On the concept of *akribeia,* see Kurz (1970); Trede (1983); Triantaphyllopoulos (1985) 145–47. Trede (407) suggests that *akribeia* designates "un idéal de précision quasi scientifique."
43. For similar sentiments, see Antiph. fr. 281 ("the man who does no wrong has no need of law"); Men. *Mon.* 382 Jaekel ("due measure [*kairos*] is a far greater thing than the laws"); Arist. *EN* 1137b34–1138a2 (a man who is fair [*epieikēs*] "is not absolute about his rights [*akribodikaios*], but is content to receive a smaller share although he has the law on his side"). On *akribeia* used pejoratively, see Dover (1974) 190.

44. For exegesis of Gorgias's vocabulary here, see Triantaphyllopoulos (1985) 145–47; cf. Th. 3.46.4 (Diodotus speaks pejoratively of "exacting [akribeis] jurors"); 5.90 (the Melians link justice and fairness with arguments that fall short of akribeia). Jurors might be flattered, however, to be told that they examine the laws closely (akribōs) when judging men of their own class (Dem. 26.15).
45. For the "voice" of written laws, see also Dem. 34.4; cf. Svenbro (1993) 28–30, 109–22, 172–74.
46. On direct quotation of laws and other written material in the courts, cf. Bers (1997) 152–54.
47. On distrust of rhetoric, see Dover (1974) 25–28; Ober (1989) 165–77.
48. For the rhētōr as a threat to the laws, see also Critias 88 B 22 D-K.
49. On this passage, cf. Ober (1989) 176.
50. On negative views of logographers, see Lavency (1964) 107.
51. See E. Harris (1994a) 135–36; Calhoun (1944) 36.
52. See Dover (1974) 192; Carter (1986) 108–9; Carey (1996) 41.
53. See S. Todd (1990a) 31–32.
54. Contra Humphreys ([1983] 248), the speaker does not privilege "expert knowledge of law."
55. Although some sources characterize the Areopagus as sober and revered (Lys. 6.14; Isoc. 7.38; Aesch. 3.20; cf. Wallace [1989] 126–27), Ober ([1989] 141) is probably right that the sociopolitical conditions here were not very different from those of the popular courts.
56. On the ephetai manning these courts, see Chapter 1, note 30.
57. On his legal arguments, see E. Harris (1990); Carey (1995b); cf. Herman (1993).
58. Legal argumentation is also minimal in Ant. 1 (presented before the Areopagus: see Gagarin [1997] 119) and Ant. 6 (presented before the homicide court of the Palladion). Cf. Ant. 3.4.2: a litigant in a model speech for use before the Palladion apologizes for the akribeia of his legal argumentation. The evidence does not, in my view, support Carawan's ([1991] 10) position that judges in the ephetic courts had "a better working knowledge of the legal principles and procedural rules than did the dicastic juries."
59. Even learned citation of poetry could be criticized by an opponent: see Dem. 19.250, with Ober (1989) 172–73.
60. Cf. Dem. 46, in which Apollodorus, prosecuting a private suit, cites no less than nine laws.
61. On the rhētōr as an instructor, see Ober (1989) 185–86; Yunis (1996).
62. See Humphreys (1988) 476.
63. For law as a kanōn, see also Lyc. 1.9; as a flexible kanōn, Arist. EN 1137b29–31.

64. E. Harris ([1994a] 141–48) challenges the majority view that Aeschines had the stronger legal case.
65. Compare Demosthenes' claim in his prosecution of Aeschines as fellow ambassador: because he is "so reluctant to play the sykophant in these matters or to ask you [the jurors] to do so," he will not press for punishment of Aeschines if he has violated the laws merely out of ignorance (19.102).
66. On the outcome and Aeschines' supposed departure from Athens, see Wankel (1976) 1.39–40.
67. On procedural choice in Athens, see Chapters 1 and 4.
68. On this special feature of *eisangeliai*, see Chapter 4.
69. Humphreys ([1983] 248 n. 30) goes too far in characterizing the argument of the speech as one "based almost entirely on legal technicality."
70. See Hansen (1976) 11–13.
71. On the speech's date, see Gagarin (1997) 4. On the action as *endeixis*, see Hansen (1976) 14.
72. On the speaker's procedural claims, see Gagarin (1989) 17–29; Manuwald (1995).
73. For an overview of these actions, see S. Todd (1993) 135–39. On *diamarturia*, see Gernet ([1927] 1955); Harrison (1971) 2.124–31; Isager and Hansen (1975) 132–37; MacDowell (1978) 213–14. On *paragraphē*, see Wolff (1966); Harrison (1971) 2.106–24; Isager and Hansen (1975) 123–32; MacDowell (1978) 212–19. One could also keep a suit from coming to trial by filing a countersuit: see Calhoun (1913) 48–54; Harrison (1971) 2.131–33.
74. On false-witness suits challenging *diamarturiai*, see Scafuro (1994) 172–78.
75. See Isager and Hansen (1975) 125–29, 227.
76. See S. Todd (1993) 136–38.
77. For *paragraphē* as a deviation from *euthudikia*, see Dem. 34.4; 45.6; for *diamarturia* as such, Is. 6.3–4, 43, 52, 59; 7.3. On these claims, see Wyse (1904) 492.
78. On the oddity of being one's own witness, see Harrison (1971) 2.127; S. Todd (1993) 136 n. 15.
79. Harrison ([1971] 2.130 n. 1) suggests that the speaker is thinking of the sort of situation described in Lys. 23.13; on *diamarturia* in Lys. 23, see S. Todd (1993) 136.
80. Wyse ([1904] 234) believes that in a *diamarturia* "there is strictly neither plaintiff nor defendant"; Harrison ([1971] 2.181–82), that the party lodging a *diamarturia*, if challenged, was "technically the plaintiff."
81. I follow Wyse (1904) in rejecting Naber's emendation of *toutōn* to *pantōn*.

82. See Harrison (1971) 2.131, 185; cf. 2.181–82.
83. I am not convinced by S. Todd ([1993] 138) that "[d]efeat in *paragraphē* or *diamarturia* was surely so prejudicial to your chances in the original case that you would have dropped your claim or accepted any terms which your opponent was prepared to offer."
84. See Wyse (1904) 551.
85. Litigants in extant false-witness suits arising in connection with *diamarturiai* do not always discuss *diamarturia* as a procedure: in Is. 2, a defense speech, there is no mention of the procedure; in Is. 3, a prosecution speech, the speaker castigates the lodger of the *diamarturia* for "daring" to use it, but does not complain about the procedure itself.
86. Harrison (1971) 2.130.
87. The extant speeches (cataloged in S. Todd [1993] 138 n. 19) by prosecutors of *paragraphai* are Isoc. 18; Dem. 32; 33; 36; 37; 38; by defendants Dem. 34; 35.
88. A client of Isocrates, prosecuting in what is apparently the first trial ever involving *paragraphē* (18.1), explicitly defends the reversal of speaking order (18.1–3).
89. Isager and Hansen ([1975] 126–27, 227) list the few situations where statutes of limitation applied in Athens, and argue that these were not grounds for *paragraphai*.
90. See Isager and Hansen (1975) 130–31; MacDowell (1978) 219; S. Todd (1993) 138.
91. On the general similarity of laws and contracts, see S. Todd (1993) 267.
92. Because contracts were regulated by law, an individual who violated a private arrangement could also be said to be transgressing the city's laws: see Dem. 35.1, 54; 56.1–3; cf. 18.210.
93. For *ischurizomai* used of "pressing the law," see Dem. 33.27; Hyp. 4.4; cf. Lys. 13.85; Dem. 40.40; of "pressing" the terms of a will, see Is. 1.3, 18.
94. See Carey and Reid (1985) 200–201 with n. 50.
95. Carey and Reid ([1985] 200 n. 50) remark on the exceptionally heavy reliance of this speaker on a contract.
96. On Dem. 35 and 56, see also Chapter 5.
97. The suit is a *dikē blabēs:* see S. Todd (1993) 266. On the speech, see Scafuro (1997) 61–64; cf. Meyer-Laurin (1965) 15–19.
98. For the contrast between lover and sykophant, see also Lys. 3.44.
99. Athenogenes apparently had a copy of the document; the original was deposited with Lysicles (3.9).
100. S. Todd ([1993] 257) points out that "[t]he speaker's problem is that he claims to have been cheated by the small print in a contract, and it is striking that he can find no law explicitly dealing with this."

101. The verb used in each case is *enedreuō*.
102. On will making and the special role of adoption in it, see S. Todd (1993) 221–25; Rubinstein (1993).
103. On suspicions that wills are forged, see Wyse (1904) 386–87; Thompson (1981) 14–15; Hunter (1994) 50.
104. Compare how litigants argue that their interpretations of laws hold to *ta dikaia* and are consistent with the intent of a long-dead lawmaker.
105. On "nonlegal" arguments in inheritance cases, see Hardcastle (1980).

Select Bibliography

Adeleye, G. 1983. "The Purpose of the *dokimasia*." *GRBS* 24:295–306.
Adkins, A. W. H. 1960. *Merit and Responsibility: A Study in Greek Values.* Oxford.
———. 1972. *Moral Values and Political Behaviour in Ancient Greece: From Homer to the End of the Fifth Century.* London.
———. 1976. "*Polypragmosune* and 'Minding One's Own Business': A Study in Greek Social and Political Values." *CP* 71:301–27.
Allison, J. W. 1979. "Thucydides and ΠΟΛΥΠΡΑΓΜΟΣΥΝΗ." *AJAH* 4:10–22.
Arnaoutoglou, I. 1994. "Associations and Patronage in Ancient Athens." *AS* 25:5–17.
Atiyah, P. S. 1987. "Tort Law and the Alternatives: Some Anglo-American Comparisons." *Duke Law Journal*, pp. 1002–44.
Atkinson, J. E. 1992. "Curbing the Comedians: Cleon versus Aristophanes and Syracosius' Decree." *CQ*, n.s., 42:56–64.
Badian, E., ed. 1966. *Ancient Society and Institutions: Studies Presented to Victor Ehrenberg.* Oxford.
Balme, M. 1984. "Attitudes to Work and Leisure in Ancient Greece." *G&R* 31:140–52.
Bauman, R. A. 1990. *Political Trials in Ancient Greece.* London.
Behrend, D. 1975. "Die ἀνάδικος δίκη und das Scholion zu Plato *Nomoi* 937d." In Wolff (1975) 131–56.
Bennett, L. J., and W. B. Tyrrell. 1990. "Making Sense of Aristophanes' *Knights*." *Arethusa* 23:235–54.

Berman, R., ed. 1980. *Solzhenitsyn at Harvard: The Address, Twelve Early Responses, and Six Later Reflections.* Washington, D.C.

Berneker, E. 1959. "ψευδομαρτυρίων δίκη." *RE* 23.2. 1364–85.

———. 1967. "ξενίας γραφή." *RE*, 2d ser., 9.A.2. 1441–79.

———, ed. 1968. *Zur griechischen Rechtsgeschichte.* Darmstadt.

Bers, V. 1985. "Dikastic *thorubos.*" In Cartledge and Harvey (1985) 1–15.

———. 1997. *Speech in Speech: Studies in Incorporated Oratio Recta in Attic Drama and Oratory.* Lanham, Md.

Biscardi, A. 1970. "La *gnome dikaiotate* et l'interprétation des lois dans la Grèce ancienne." *RIDA* 17:219–32.

Blankenburg, E. 1994. "The Infrastructure for Avoiding Civil Litigation: Comparing Cultures of Legal Behavior in the Netherlands and West Germany." *Law and Society Review* 28:789–808.

Blundell, M. W. 1989. *Helping Friends and Harming Enemies: A Study in Sophocles and Greek Ethics.* Cambridge.

Bockisch, G. 1981. "Sykophanten." In Welskopf (1981) 4.11–25.

Boegehold, A. L. 1972. "The Establishment of a Central Archive at Athens." *AJA* 76:23–30.

———. 1982. "A Lid with Dipinto." In *Studies in Attic Epigraphy, History and Topography Presented to Eugene Vanderpool.* Hesperia Suppl. 19:1–6. Princeton, N.J.

———. 1994. "Pericles' Citizenship Law of 451/0 B.C." In Boegehold and Scafuro (1994) 57–66.

———, ed. 1995. *The Lawcourts at Athens: Sites, Buildings, Equipment, Procedure and Testimonia. The Athenian Agora* 28. Princeton, N.J.

Boegehold, A. L., and A. C. Scafuro, eds. 1994. *Athenian Identity and Civic Ideology.* Baltimore.

Bolkestein, H. 1939. *Wohltätigkeit und Armenpflege im vorchristlichen Altertum.* Utrecht.

Bonner, R. J. 1905. *Evidence in Athenian Courts.* Chicago.

———. 1920. "The Legal Setting of Isocrates' *Antidosis.*" *CP* 15:193–97.

———. 1927. *Lawyers and Litigants in Ancient Athens.* Chicago.

Bonner, R. J., and G. Smith. 1930–38. *The Administration of Justice from Homer to Aristotle.* 2 vols. Chicago.

Bossy, J., ed. 1983. *Disputes and Settlements: Law and Human Relations in the West.* Cambridge.

Bowie, A. M. 1982. "The Parabasis in Aristophanes: Prolegomena, *Acharnians.*" *CQ*, n.s., 32:27–40.

———. 1987. "Ritual Stereotype and Comic Reversal: Aristophanes' *Wasps.*" *BICS* 34:112–25.

Bowman, A. K., and G. Woolf, eds. 1994. *Literacy and Power in the Ancient World.* Cambridge.

Bremmer, J. 1983. "Scapegoat Rituals in Ancient Greece." *HSCP* 87: 299–320.
Brock, R. W. 1986. "The Double Plot in Aristophanes' *Knights.*" *GRBS* 27:15–27.
———. 1991. "The Emergence of Democratic Ideology." *Historia* 40: 160–69.
Brooks, P., and P. Gewirtz. 1996. *Law's Stories: Narrative and Rhetoric in the Law.* New Haven, Conn.
Brown, P. G. McC. 1992. "Menander, Fragments 745 and 746 K-T, Menander's *Kolax,* and Parasites and Flatterers in Greek Comedy." *ZPE* 92:91–107.
Buchheit, V. 1960. "Feigensymbolik im antiken Epigramm." *RhM* 103: 200–229.
Bugh, G. R. 1988. *The Horsemen of Athens.* Princeton, N.J.
Burkert, W. 1985. *Greek Religion.* Translated by J. Raffan. Cambridge, Mass.
Cairns, D. L. 1993. *Aidos: The Psychology and Ethics of Honour and Shame in Ancient Greek Literature.* Oxford.
———. 1996. "Hybris, Dishonour, and Thinking big." *JHS* 116:1–32.
Calhoun, G. M. 1913. *Athenian Clubs in Politics and Litigation.* Austin, Tex.
———. 1919. "Oral and Written Pleading in Athenian Courts." *TAPA* 1:177–93.
———. 1927. *The Growth of Criminal Law in Ancient Greece.* Berkeley.
———. 1944. *Greek Legal Science.* London.
Camassa, G. 1994. "Verschriftung und Veränderung der Gesetze." In Gehrke (1994) 97–111.
Caminker, E. 1989. "The Constitutionality of *Qui Tam* Actions." *Yale Law Journal* 99:341–88.
Carawan, E. M. 1983. "*Erotesis:* Interrogation in the Courts of Fourth-Century Athens." *GRBS* 24:209–26.
———. 1985. "*Apophasis* and *eisangelia:* The Role of the Areopagus in Athenian Political Trials." *GRBS* 26:115–40.
———. 1990. "The Five Talents Cleon Coughed Up (Schol. Ar. *Ach.* 6)." *CQ,* n.s., 40:137–47.
———. 1991. "ΕΦΕΤΑΙ and Athenian Courts for Homicide in the Age of the Orators." *CP* 86:1–16.
Carey, C. ed. 1989. *Lysias: Selected Speeches.* Cambridge.
———. 1994a. "'Artless' Proofs in Aristotle and the Orators." *BICS* 39: 95–106.
———. 1994b. "Legal Space in Classical Athens." *G&R* 41:172–86.
———. 1995a. "The Witness's *Exomosia* in the Athenian Courts." *CQ,* n.s., 45:114–19.
———. 1995b. "Rape and Adultery in Athenian Law." *CQ,* n.s., 45: 407–17.

———. 1996. "*Nomos* in Attic Rhetoric and Oratory." *JHS* 116:33–46.
Carey, C. and R. A. Reid, eds. 1985. *Demosthenes: Selected Private Speeches*. Cambridge.
Carrière, J.-C. 1979. *La carnaval et la politique: Une introduction à la comédie grecque, suivie d'un choix de fragments*. Annales littéraires de l'Université de Besançon 212. Paris.
Carter, L. B. 1986. *The Quiet Athenian*. Oxford.
Cartledge, P. 1990a. "Fowl Play: A Curious Lawsuit in Classical Athens (Antiphon frr. 57–9 Thalheim)." In Cartledge, Millett, and Todd (1990) 41–61.
———. 1990b. *Aristophanes and His Theatre of the Absurd*. Bristol.
———. 1996. "Comparatively Equal." In Ober and Hedrick (1996) 175–85.
Cartledge, P., and F. D. Harvey, eds. 1985. *Crux: Essays Presented to G. E. M. de Ste. Croix on His 75th birthday*. London.
Cartledge, P., P. Millett, and S. Todd, eds. 1990. *Nomos: Essays in Athenian Law, Politics and Society*. Cambridge.
Christ, M. R. 1987. "Danger and Its Rewards: A Study in Athenian Self-Presentation." Ph.D. dissertation, Princeton University.
———. 1990. "Liturgy Avoidance and *Antidosis* in Classical Athens." *TAPA* 120:147–69.
———. 1992. "Ostracism, Sycophancy, and Deception of the Demos: [Arist.] *Ath. Pol.* 43.5." *CQ*, n.s., 42:336–46.
———. 1994. Review of S. Todd (1993). *BMCR* 5.3:256–60.
———. 1996. Review of D. Cohen (1995). *BMCR* 7.5:379–84.
Cohen, D. 1989. "Greek Law: Problems and Methods." *ZSS* 119:81–105.
———. 1991. *Law, Sexuality, and Society: The Enforcement of Morals in Classical Athens*. Cambridge.
———. 1995. *Law, Violence and Community in Classical Athens*. Cambridge.
Cohen, E. E. 1973. *Ancient Athenian Maritime Courts*. Princeton, N.J.
———. 1992. *Athenian Economy and Society: A Banking Perspective*. Princeton, N.J.
Cole, T. 1991. *The Origins of Rhetoric in Ancient Greece*. Baltimore.
Comaroff, J., and S. Roberts. 1981. *Rules and Processes: The Cultural Logic of Dispute in an African Context*. Chicago.
Connor, W. R. 1971. *The New Politicians of Fifth-Century Athens*. Princeton, N.J.
———. 1994. "The Problem of Athenian Civic Identity." In Boegehold and Scafuro (1994) 34–44.
Crane, G. 1992. "The Fear and Pursuit of Risk: Corinth on Athens, Sparta and the Peloponnesians (Thucydides 1.68–71, 120–21)." *TAPA* 122:227–56.
Crawley, L. W. A. 1970. "**ΓΡΑΦΗ ΣΥΚΟΦΑΝΤΙΑΣ**." In B. F. Harris (1970) 77–94.

Crichton, A. 1991. "The Old Are in a Second Childhood: Age Reversal and Jury Service in Aristophanes' *Wasps*." *BICS* 38:59–79.

Crook, J. A. 1995. *Legal Advocacy in the Roman World*. Ithaca, N.Y.

Davies, J. K. 1971. *Athenian Propertied Families*. Oxford.

———. 1981. *Wealth and the Power of Wealth in Classical Athens*. New York.

Davies, W., and P. Fouracre, eds. 1986. *The Settlement of Disputes in Early Medieval Europe*. Cambridge.

DeBruyn, O. 1995. *La compétence de l'Aréopage en matière de procès publics*. Historia Einzelschriften 90. Stuttgart.

Demont, P. 1990. *La cité grecque archaïque et classique et l'idéal de tranquillité*. Paris.

Détienne, M., ed. 1988. *Les savoirs de l'écriture en Grèce ancienne*. Lille.

Dienelt, K. 1953. "Ἀπραγμοσύνη." *WS* 66:94–104.

Dillon, M. P. J. 1995. "Payments to the Disabled at Athens: Social Justice or Fear of Aristocratic Patronage?" *AS* 26:27–57.

Dimakis, P., ed. 1983. *Symposion 1979: Vorträge zur griechischen und hellenistischen Rechtsgeschichte*. Cologne and Vienna.

Donlan, W. 1978. "Social Vocabulary and Its Relationship to Political Propaganda in Fifth-Century Athens." *QUCC* 27:95–111.

Dorjahn, A. P. 1935. "Anticipation of Arguments in Athenian Courts." *TAPA* 66:274–95.

Dover, K. J. 1968. *Lysias and the Corpus Lysiacum*. Berkeley.

———. 1974. *Greek Popular Morality in the Time of Plato and Aristotle*. Berkeley.

duBois, P. 1991. *Torture and Truth*. New York.

Dunbar, N., ed. 1995. *Aristophanes: Birds*. Oxford.

Eder, W. 1986. "The Political Significance of the Codification of Law in Archaic Societies: An Unconventional Hypothesis." In Raaflaub (1986) 262–300.

———, ed. 1995. *Die athenische Demokratie im 4. Jahrhundert v. Chr.* Stuttgart.

Edey, H., and B. S. Yamey, eds. 1974. *Debits, Credits, Finance and Profits: Studies in Honour of W. S. Baxter*. London.

Edmunds, L. 1987. *Cleon, Knights, and Aristophanes' Politics*. Lanham, Md.

Ehrenberg, V. 1947. "*Polypragmosune*: A Study in Greek Politics." *JHS* 67:46–67.

———. 1951. *The People of Aristophanes*. Oxford.

———. 1973. *From Solon to Socrates*. London.

Engel, D. M. 1984. "The Oven Bird's Song: Insiders, Outsiders, and Personal Injuries in an American Community." *Law and Society Review* 18: 551–82.

———. 1987. "Law, Time, and Community." *Law and Society Review* 21:605–37.

Euben, J. P., J. R. Wallach, and J. Ober, eds. 1994. *Athenian Political Thought and the Reconstruction of American Democracy.* Ithaca, N.Y.
Falkner, T. M., and J. de Luce, eds. 1989. *Old Age in Greek and Latin Literature.* Albany, N.Y.
Faraone, C. A. 1991. "The Agonistic Context of Early Greek Binding Spells." In Faraone and Obbink (1991) 3–32.
Faraone, C. A., and D. Obbink, eds. 1991. *Magika Hiera: Ancient Greek Magic and Religion.* Oxford.
Finley, M. I. 1962. "Athenian Demagogues." *Past & Present* 21:3–24. Revised in *Studies in Ancient Society,* 1–25. London, 1974.
Fisher, N. R. E., ed. 1976. *Social Values in Classical Athens.* London.
———. 1992. *Hybris: A Study in the Values of Honour and Shame in Ancient Greece.* Warminster.
Forer. L. 1975. *The Death of the Law.* New York.
Fornara, C. W. 1979. "The Phaselis Decree." *CQ,* n.s., 29:49–52.
Foxhall, L. 1996. "The Law and the Lady: Women and Legal Proceedings in Classical Athens." In Foxhall and Lewis (1996) 133–52.
Foxhall, L., and A. D. E. Lewis, eds. 1996. *Greek Law in Its Political Setting.* Oxford.
Fränkel, M. 1878. "Der attische Heliasteneid." *Hermes* 13:452–66.
Freckelton, I. R. 1988. "Querulent Paranoia and the Vexatious Complainant." *International Journal of Law and Psychiatry* 11:127–43.
French, A. 1994. "Pericles' Citizenship Law." *AHB* 8:71–75.
Friedman, L. M. 1989. "Law, Lawyers, and Popular Culture." *Yale Law Journal* 98:1579–1606.
Frier, B. 1985. *The Rise of the Roman Jurists.* Princeton, N.J.
Gabba, E., ed. 1983. *Tria Corda: Scritti in onore di A. Momigliano.* Como.
Gabrielsen, V. 1986. "ΦΑΝΕΡΑ and ΑΦΑΝΗΣ ΟΥΣΙΑ in Classical Athens." *C&M* 37:99–114.
———. 1987. "The *Antidosis* Procedure in Classical Athens." *C&M* 38:7–38.
———. 1994. *Financing the Athenian Fleet: Public Taxation and Social Relations.* Baltimore.
Gagarin, M. 1981. *Drakon and Early Athenian Homicide Law.* New Haven, Conn.
———. 1986. *Early Greek Law.* Berkeley.
———. 1989. *The Murder of Herodes: A Study of Antiphon 5.* Studien zur classischen Philologie 45. Frankfurt a.M.
———, ed. 1991. *Symposion 1990: Vorträge zur griechischen und hellenistischen Rechtsgeschichte.* Cologne, Weimar, and Vienna.
———. 1996. "The Torture of Slaves in Athenian Law." *CP* 91:1–18.
———, ed. 1997. *Antiphon: The Speeches.* Cambridge.
Gager, J. G. 1992. *Curse Tablets and Binding Spells from the Ancient World.* Oxford.

Bibliography

Gagos, T., and P. van Minnen. 1995. *Settling a Dispute: Toward a Legal Anthropology of Late Antique Egypt.* Ann Arbor, Mich.

Galanter, M. 1983. "Reading the Landscape of Disputes: What We Know and Don't Know (and Think We Know) about Our Allegedly Contentious and Litigious Society." *UCLA Law Review* 31:4–71.

———. 1986. "The Day after the Litigation Explosion." *Maryland Law Review* 46:3–39.

———. 1994. "Predators and Parasites: Lawyer-Bashing and Civil Justice." *Georgia Law Review* 28:633–81.

Gallant, T. W. 1991. *Risk and Survival in Ancient Greece: Reconstructing the Rural Domestic Economy.* Stanford, Calif.

Garner, R. 1987. *Law and Society in Classical Athens.* London.

Garnsey, P. D. A., M. K. Hopkins, and C. R. Whittaker, eds. 1983. *Trade in the Ancient Economy.* London.

Gauthier, P. 1972. *Symbola: Les étrangers et la justice dans les cités grecques.* Nancy.

Geertz, C. 1973. "Ideology as a Cultural System." In *The Interpretation of Culture: Selected Essays,* 193–233. New York.

———. 1983. "Local Knowledge: Fact and Law in Comparative Perspective." In *Local Knowledge: Further Essays in Interpretive Anthropology,* 167–234. New York.

Gehrke, H.-J., ed. 1994. *Rechtskodifizierung und soziale Normen im interkulturellen Vergleich.* Tübingen.

Gernet, L. 1927. "La diamartyrie, procédure archaïque du droit athénien." *TvR* 6:5–37. Reprinted in *Droit et société dans la Grèce ancienne,* 83–102. Paris, 1955.

Gerst, K. 1963. "Die allgemeine Anklagebefugnis in der attischen Demokratie." Ph.D. dissertation, Munich.

Glendon, M. A. 1994. *A Nation under Lawyers: How the Crisis in the Legal Profession Is Transforming American Society.* New York.

Golden, M. and P. Toohey, eds. 1997. *Inventing Ancient Culture: Historicism, Periodization, and the Ancient World.* London.

Goldhill, S. D. 1987. "The Great Dionysia and Civic Ideology." *JHS* 107:58–76. Reprinted in Winkler and Zeitlin (1990) 97–129.

Goldstein, R. L. 1987. "Litigious Paranoids and the Legal System: The Role of the Forensic Psychiatrist." *Journal of Forensic Sciences* 32:1009–15.

Gomme, A. W. 1945. *A Historical Commentary on Thucydides.* Vol. 1. Oxford.

Grau, P. 1972. *Prooemiengestaltung bei Lysias.* Bonn.

Greenhouse, C. J. 1982. "Nature Is to Culture as Praying Is to Suing." *Journal of Legal Pluralism and Unofficial Law* 20:17–35.

———. 1989. "Interpreting American Litigiousness." In Starr and Collier (1989) 252–73.

Greenhouse, C. J., D. Engel, and B. Yngvesson. 1994. *Law and Community in Three American Towns*. Ithaca, N.Y.
Grossman, G. 1950. *Politische Schlagwörter aus der Zeit des Peloponnesischen Krieges*. Zurich.
Guthrie, W. K. 1971. *The Sophists*. Cambridge.
Hall, E. 1995. "Lawcourt Dramas: The Power of Performance in Greek Forensic Oratory." *BICS* 40:39–58.
Halliwell, S. 1991. "Comic Satire and Freedom of Speech in Classical Athens." *JHS* 111:48–70.
Halperin, D. M., J. J. Winkler, and F. I. Zeitlin, eds. 1990. *Before Sexuality: The Construction of Erotic Experience in the Ancient Greek World*. Princeton, N.J.
Hands, A. R. 1968. *Charities and Social Aid in Greece and Rome*. Ithaca, N.Y.
Hansen, M. H. 1974. *The Sovereignty of the People's Court in Athens in the Fourth Century B.C. and the Public Action against Unconstitutional Proposals*. Odense.

———. 1975. *Eisangelia: The Sovereignty of the People's Court in Athens in the Fourth Century B.C. and the Impeachment of Generals and Politicians*. Odense.

———. 1976. *Apagoge, Endeixis and Ephegesis against Kakourgoi, Atimoi and Pheugontes: A Study in the Athenian Administration of Justice in the Fourth Century B.C.* Odense.

———. 1978. "*Demos, Ecclesia*, and *Dicasterion* in Classical Athens." *GRBS* 19:127–46.

———. 1979. "How Often Did the Athenian *Dikasteria* Meet?" *GRBS* 20:243–46.

———. 1983. "Two Notes on the Athenian *Dikai Emporikai*." In Dimakis (1983) 167–75.

———. 1985. *Demography and Democracy: The Number of Athenian Citizens in the Fourth Century B.C.* Herning.

———. 1989a. "Solonian Democracy in Fourth-Century Athens." *C&M* 40:71–99.

———. 1989b. "*Demos, Ekklesia*, and *Dikasterion*. A Reply to Martin Ostwald and Josiah Ober." *C&M* 40:101–6.

———. 1990. "The Political Powers of the People's Court in Fourth-Century Athens." In Murray and Price (1990) 215–43.

———. 1991. *The Athenian Democracy in the Age of Demosthenes*. Oxford.

———. 1994. "The Number of Athenian Citizens *secundum* Sekunda." *EMC/CV* 13:299–310.

Hardcastle, M. 1980. "Some Non-legal Arguments in Athenian Inheritance Cases." *Prudentia* 12:11–22.
Harder, R. E. 1996. "Zur Personenverteilung in Aristophanes' 'Rittern.'" *Hermes* 124:29–44.

Bibliography

Harrell, H. C. 1936. *Public Arbitration in Athenian Law.* Columbia, Mo.
Harris, B. F., ed. 1970. *Auckland Classical Essays Presented to E. M. Blaiklock.* Auckland.
Harris, E. M. 1989. "Demosthenes' Speech against Meidias." *HSCP* 92: 117–36.
———. 1990. "Did the Athenians Regard Seduction as a Worse Crime Than Rape?" *CQ*, n.s., 40:370–77.
———. 1992. Review of MacDowell (1990b). *CP* 87:71–80.
———. 1994a. "Law and Oratory." In Worthington (1994) 130–50.
———. 1994b. "'In the Act' or 'Red-Handed'? *Apagoge* to the Eleven and *Furtum Manifestum.*" In Thür (1994) 169–84.
———. 1995. *Aeschines and Athenian Politics.* Oxford.
Harris, W. V. 1989. *Ancient Literacy.* Cambridge, Mass.
Harrison, A. R. W. 1955. "Law-making at Athens at the End of the Fifth Century B.C." *JHS* 75:26–35.
———. 1968–71. *The Law of Athens.* 2 vols. Oxford.
Harvey, F. D. 1985. "*Dona Ferentes:* Some Aspects of Bribery in Greek Politics." In Cartledge and Harvey (1985) 76–117.
———. 1990. "The Sykophant and Sykophancy: Vexatious Redefinition?" In Cartledge, Millett, and Todd (1990) 103–21.
Hay, D. 1989. "Prosecution and Power: Malicious Prosecution in the English Courts, 1750–1850." In Hay and Snyder (1989b) 343–95.
Hay, D., and F. Snyder. 1989a. "Using the Criminal Law, 1750–1850: Policing, Private Prosecution, and the State." In Hay and Snyder (1989b) 3–52.
———, eds. 1989b. *Policing and Prosecution in Britain, 1750–1850.* Oxford.
Heath, M. 1987. *Political Comedy in Aristophanes.* Hypomnemata 87. Göttingen.
Hedrick, C. W., Jr. 1994. "Writing, Reading, and Democracy." In Osborne and Hornblower (1994) 157–74.
Henderson, J. 1990. "The *Demos* and the Comic Competition." In Winkler and Zeitlin (1990) 271–313.
———. 1991. *The Maculate Muse: Obscene Language in Attic Comedy.* 2d ed. Oxford.
Herman, G. 1993. "Tribal and Civic Codes of Behaviour in Lysias I." *CQ*, n.s., 43:406–19.
———. 1994. "How Violent Was Athenian Society?" In Osborne and Hornblower (1994) 99–117.
———. 1995. "Honour, Revenge and the State in Fourth-Century Athens." In Eder (1995) 43–60.
Hillgruber, M. 1988. *Die zehnte Rede des Lysias.* Berlin.
Hirzel, R. 1900–1903. Ἄγραφος Νόμος. Abhandlungen der königlich

sächsischen Gesellschaft der Wissenschaften, philologisch-historische Classe 20, no. 1. Leipzig.

Hoffer, P. C. 1989. "Honor and the Roots of American Litigiousness." *American Journal of Legal History* 33:295–319.

Hölkeskamp, K.-J. 1992. "Written Law in Archaic Greece." *PCPS*, n.s., 38:87–117.

Hornblower, S. 1991. *A Commentary on Thucydides*. Vol. 1. Oxford.

Hubbard, T. K. 1989. "Old Men in the Youthful Plays of Aristophanes." In Falkner and de Luce (1989) 90–113.

―――. 1991. *The Mask of Comedy: Aristophanes and the Intertextual Parabasis*. Ithaca, N.Y.

Humphreys, S. 1977–78. "Public and Private Interests in Classical Athens." *CJ* 73:97–104.

―――. 1983. "The Evolution of Legal Process in Ancient Attica." In Gabba (1983) 229–56.

―――. 1985a. "Law as Discourse." *History and Anthropology* 1:241–64.

―――. 1985b. "Social Relations on Stage: Witnesses in Classical Athens." *History and Anthropology* 1:313–69.

―――. 1986. "Kinship Patterns in the Athenian Courts." *GRBS* 27:57–91.

―――. 1988. "The Discourse of Law in Archaic and Classical Greece." *Law and History Review* 6:465–93.

―――. 1989. "Family Quarrels." *JHS* 109:182–85.

―――. 1993. *The Family, Women and Death: Comparative Studies*. 2d ed. Ann Arbor, Mich.

Hunt, A. 1988. "The Theory of Critical Legal Studies." *Oxford Journal of Law* 6:1–45.

Hunter, V. 1994. *Policing Athens: Social Control in the Attic Lawsuits, 420–320 B.C.* Princeton, N.J.

Isager, S., and M. H. Hansen. 1975. *Aspects of Athenian Society in the Fourth Century B.C.: A Historical Introduction to and Commentary on the Paragraphe Speeches and the Speech against Dionysiodorus in the Corpus Demosthenicum*. Odense.

Johnstone, S. 1994. "Virtuous Toil, Vicious Work: Xenophon on Aristocratic Style." *CP* 89:219–40.

―――. Forthcoming. *Disputes and Democracy*.

Jones, A. H. M. 1957. *Athenian Democracy*. Oxford.

Jones, J. W. 1956. *The Law and Legal Theory of the Greeks*. Oxford.

Just, R. 1991. *Women in Athenian Law and Life*. London.

Kagan, R. L. 1983. "A Golden Age of Litigation: Castile, 1500–1700." In Bossy (1983) 145–66.

Kennedy, C. R. 1891. "Sycophantes." In *A Dictionary of Greek and Roman Antiquities*, edited by W. Smith. 3d ed. London.

Kennedy, G. 1963. *The Art of Persuasion in Greece*. Princeton, N.J.

―――. 1968. "The Rhetoric of Advocacy in Greece and Rome." *AJP* 89:419–36.
Kerferd, G. B. 1981. *The Sophistic Movement.* Cambridge.
Kinzl, K. H. 1995. *Demokratia: Der Weg zur Demokratie bei den Griechen.* Wege der Forschung, Band 657. Darmstadt.
Kleve, K. 1964. "Ἀπραγμοσύνη and πολυπραγμοσύνη: Two Slogans in Athenian Politics." *SO* 39:83–88.
Knox, R. A. 1985. "'So Mischievous a Beaste'? The Athenian Demos and Its Treatment of Its Politicians." *G&R* 32:132–61.
Koch, C. 1991. *Volksbeschlüsse in Seebundangelegenheiten. Das Verfahrensrecht Athens im Ersten attischen Seebund.* Frankfurt a.M.
―――. 1993. "Die Herrschaft Athens im Ersten Athenischen Seebund: Rechtsvereinheitlichung im Verwaltungsverfahren." *RIDA* 40:139–82.
Konstan, D. 1985. "The Politics of Aristophanes' *Wasps.*" *TAPA* 115:27–46. Revised in *Greek Comedy and Ideology*, 15–28. Oxford, 1995.
―――. 1995. "Patrons and Friends." *CP* 90:328–42.
―――. 1996. "Greek Friendship." *AJP* 117:71–94.
―――. 1997. "Philosophy, Friendship, and Cultural History." In Golden and Toohey (1997) 66–78.
Konstan, D., and M. Dillon. 1981. "The Ideology of Aristophanes' *Wealth.*" *AJP* 102:371–94.
Krentz, P. 1982. *The Thirty at Athens.* Ithaca, N.Y.
Kroll, J. H. 1972. *Athenian Bronze Allotment Plates.* Cambridge, Mass.
Kurke, L. 1992. "The Politics of ἁβροσύνη in Archaic Greece." *CA* 11: 91–120.
Kurz, D. 1970. Ἀκρίβεια. *Das Ideal der Exaktheit bei den Griechen bis Aristoteles.* Göppinger Akademische Beiträge 8. Goppingen.
Lacey, W. K. 1968. *The Family in Classical Greece.* Ithaca, N.Y.
Lang, M. 1995. "Pinakia." In Boegehold (1995) 59–64.
Lateiner, D. 1981. "An Analysis of Lysias' Political Defense Speeches." *RS* 11:147–60.
―――. 1982. "'The Man Who Does not Meddle in Politics': A *Topos* in Lysias." *CW* 76:1–12.
Latte, K. 1931a. "Συκοφάντης." *RE*, 2d ser., 4.A.1. 1028–31.
―――. 1931b. "Beiträge zum griechischen Strafrecht, I: Die Entstehung der Popularklagen." *Hermes* 66:30–48. Reprinted in Berneker (1968) 263–82.
Lavency, M. 1964. *Aspects de la logographie judiciaire attique.* Louvain.
Lee, E. N., A. P. D. Mourelatos, and R. M. Rorty, eds. 1973. *Exegesis and Argument: Studies in Greek Philosophy Presented to Gregory Vlastos.* Assen.
Lee, T. R. 1990. "The Standing of *Qui Tam* Relators under the False Claims Act." *University of Chicago Law Review* 57:543–71.
Leisi, E. 1908. *Der Zeuge im attischen Recht.* Frauenfeld.

Lewis, D. M. 1966. "After the Profanation of the Mysteries." In Badian (1966) 177–91.
———. 1990. "Public Property in the City." In Murray and Price (1990) 245–63.
———. 1993. "Oligarchic Thinking in the Late Fifth Century." In Rosen and Farrell (1993) 207–11.
Lieberman, J. K. 1981. *The Litigious Society.* New York.
Link, S. 1994. "Zur archaischen Gesetzgebung in Katane und im epizephyrischen Lokroi." In Gehrke (1994) 165–177.
Lipsius, J. H. 1905–15. *Das attische Recht und Rechtsverfahren.* 3 vols. in 4. Leipzig.
Lofberg, J. O. 1917. *Sycophancy in Athens.* Chicago.
———. 1920. "The Sycophant-Parasite." *CP* 15:61–72.
Loraux, N. 1986. *The Invention of Athens: The Funeral Oration in the Classical City.* Translated by A. Sheridan. Cambridge, Mass.
Macaulay, S. 1989. "Popular Legal Culture: An Introduction." *Yale Law Journal* 98:1545–58.
MacDowell, D. M., ed. 1962. *Andokides: On the Mysteries.* Oxford.
———. 1963. *Athenian Homicide Law in the Age of the Orators.* Manchester.
———. 1971a. "The Chronology of Athenian Speeches and Legal Innovations in 401–398 B.C." *RIDA* 18:267–73.
———, ed. 1971b. *Aristophanes: Wasps.* Oxford.
———. 1975. "Law-Making at Athens in the Fourth Century B.C." *JHS* 95:62–74.
———. 1976. Review of E. Cohen (1973). *CR* 26:84–85.
———. 1978. *The Law in Classical Athens.* Ithaca, N.Y.
———. 1983. "Athenian Laws about Bribery." *RIDA* 30:57–78.
———. 1985. "The Length of the Speeches on the Assessment of the Penalty in Athenian Courts." *CQ*, n.s., 35:525–26.
———. 1986. *Spartan Law.* Edinburgh.
———. 1990a. "Foreign Birth and Athenian Citizenship in Aristophanes." In Sommerstein, Halliwell, Henderson, and Zimmermann (1990) 359–71.
———, ed. 1990b. *Demosthenes Against Meidias (Oration 21).* Oxford.
———. 1991. "The Athenian Procedure of *Phasis*." In Gagarin (1991) 187–98.
———. 1994. "The Case of the Rude Soldier (Lysias 9)." In Thür (1994) 153–63.
Maffi, A. 1988. "Écriture et pratique juridique dans la Grèce classique." In Détienne (1988) 188–210.
Maine, H. S. 1861. *Ancient Law.* London.
Maio, D. P. 1983. "*Politeia* and Adjudication in Fourth-Century B.C. Athens." *American Journal of Jurisprudence* 28:16–45.

Manning, B. 1977. "Hyperlexis: Our National Disease." *Northwestern University Law Review* 71:767–82.
Manuwald, B. 1995. "Zur rechtlichen Problematik von Antiphon, or. 5." *RhM* 138:41–59.
Manville, P. B. 1990. *The Origins of Citizenship in Ancient Athens*. Princeton, N.J.
Markesinis, B. S. 1990. "Litigation-Mania in England, Germany and the U.S.A.: Are We So Very Different?" *Cambridge Law Journal* 49:233–76.
Markle, M. M. 1985. "Jury Pay and Assembly Pay at Athens." In Cartledge and Harvey (1985) 265–97.
———. 1990. "Participation of Farmers in Athenian Juries and Assemblies." *AS* 21:149–65.
Marr, J. L. 1983. "Notes on the Pseudo-Xenophontic *Athenaion Politeia*." *C&M* 34:45–53.
———. 1993. "Ephialtes the Moderate?" *G&R* 40:11–19.
Mastromarco, G. 1989. "L'eroe e il mostro (Aristofane *Vespe* 1029–44)." *RFIC* 117:410–23.
McGlew, J. 1997. "After Irony: Aristophanes' *Wealth* and Its Modern Interpreters." *AJP* 118:35–53.
Meiggs, R. 1972. *The Athenian Empire*. Oxford.
Meikle, S. 1996. "Aristotle on Business." *CQ*, n.s., 46:138–51.
Meyer-Laurin, H. 1965. *Gesetz und Billigkeit im attischen Prozess*. Graezistische Abhandlungen 1. Weimar.
Michelini, A. N. 1994. "Political Themes in Euripides' *Suppliants*." *AJP* 115:219–52.
Millett, P. 1989. "Patronage and Its Avoidance in Classical Athens." In Wallace-Hadrill (1989) 15–47.
———. 1991. *Lending and Borrowing in Ancient Athens*. Cambridge.
Mirhady, D. 1991a. "The Oath-Challenge in Athens." *CQ*, n.s., 41:78–83.
———. 1991b. "Non-Technical *Pisteis* in Aristotle and Anaximenes." *AJP* 112:5–28.
———. 1996. "Torture and Rhetoric in Athens." *JHS* 116:119–31.
Mitchell, L. G., and P. J. Rhodes. 1996. "Friends and Enemies in Athenian Politics." *G&R* 43:11–30.
Morris, I. 1994. "The Athenian Economy Twenty Years after *The Ancient Economy*." *CP* 89:351–66.
Mossé, C. 1983. "The 'World of the *Emporium*' in the Private Speeches of Demosthenes." In Garnsey, Hopkins, and Whittaker (1983) 53–63.
Murphy, T. M. 1992. "Lysias 25 and the Intractable Democratic Abuses." *AJP* 113:543–58.
Murray, O. 1990. "The Affair of the Mysteries: Democracy and the Drinking Group." In Murray, ed., *Sympotica: A Symposium on the Symposion*, 149–61. Oxford.

Murray, O., and S. R. F. Price, eds. 1990. *The Greek City: From Homer to Alexander.* Oxford.

Nader, L., and H. F. Todd, eds. 1978. *The Disputing Process: Law in Ten Societies.* New York.

Nelson, R. L. 1988. "Ideology, Scholarship, and Sociolegal Change: Lessons from Galanter and the 'Litigation Crisis.'" *Law and Society Review* 21:677–93.

Nesselrath, H.-G. 1985. *Lukians Parasitendialog.* Berlin.

Nestle, W. 1927. "Ἀπραγμοσύνη (Zu Thukydides II 63.)." *Philologus,* n.s., 35: 129–40.

Ober, J. 1989. *Mass and Elite in Democratic Athens: Rhetoric, Ideology, and the Power of the People.* Princeton, N.J.

———. 1994a. "Power and Oratory in Democratic Athens: Demosthenes 21, Against Meidias." In Worthington (1994) 85–108.

———. 1994b. "How to Criticize Democracy in Late Fifth- and Fourth-Century Athens." In Euben, Wallach, and Ober (1994) 149–71.

Ober, J., and C. Hedrick, eds. 1996. *Dēmokratia: A Conversation on Democracies, Ancient and Modern.* Princeton, N.J.

Ober, J., and B. S. Strauss. 1990. "Drama, Political Rhetoric, and the Discourse of Athenian Democracy." In Winkler and Zeitlin (1990) 237–70.

Olck, F. 1909. "Feige." *RE* 6.2. 2100–2151.

Olson, S. D. 1990a. "Economics and Ideology in Aristophanes' *Wealth.*" *HSCP* 93:223–42.

———. 1990b. "The New Demos of Aristophanes' *Knights.*" *Eranos* 88: 60–63.

———. 1991. "Dicaeopolis' Motivations in Aristophanes' *Acharnians.*" *JHS* 111:200–203.

———. 1992. "Names and Naming in Aristophanic Comedy." *CQ,* n.s., 42:304–19.

———. 1996. "Politics and Poetry in Aristophanes' *Wasps.*" *TAPA* 126: 129–50.

Olson, W. K. 1991. *The Litigation Explosion.* New York.

Osborne, R. 1985a. *Demos: The Discovery of Classical Attika.* Cambridge.

———. 1985b. "Law in Action in Classical Athens." *JHS* 105:40–58.

———. 1990. "Vexatious Litigation in Classical Athens: Sykophancy and the Sykophant." In Cartledge, Millett, and Todd (1990) 83–102.

Osborne, R., and S. Hornblower, eds. 1994. *Ritual, Finance, Politics: Athenian Democratic Accounts Presented to David Lewis.* Oxford.

Ostwald, M. 1973. "Was There a Concept ἄγραφος νόμος in Classical Greece?" In Lee, Mourelatos, and Rorty (1973) 70–104.

———. 1986. *From Popular Sovereignty to the Sovereignty of Law: Law, Society, and Politics in Fifth-Century Athens.* Berkeley.

Park, V. R. 1991. "The False Claims Act, *Qui Tam* Relators, and the Govern-

ment: Which Is the Real Party to the Action?" *Stanford Law Review* 43:1061–93.
Parker, R. 1983. *Miasma: Pollution and Purification in Early Greek Religion.* Oxford.
Patterson, C. B. 1981. *Pericles' Citizenship Law of 451–50 B.C.* New York.
Pickard-Cambridge, A. W. 1968. *The Dramatic Festivals of Athens.* 2d ed. Oxford.
Piérart, M., ed. 1993. *Aristote et Athènes.* Paris.
Pomeroy, S., ed. 1994. *Xenophon, Oeconomicus: A Social and Historical Commentary.* Oxford.
Pringsheim, F. 1955. "The Transition from Witnessed to Written Transactions in Athens." In *Aequitas und Bona Fides: Festgabe A. Simonius,* 287–97. Basel. Reprinted in Pringsheim, *Gesammelte Abhandlungen,* 2.401–9. Heidelberg, 1961.
Pritchett, W. K. 1971–91. *The Greek State at War.* 5 vols. Berkeley.
Raaflaub, K., ed. 1986. *Social Struggles in Archaic Rome: New Perspectives on the Conflict of the Orders.* Berkeley.
———. 1989. "Contemporary Perceptions of Democracy in Fifth-Century Athens." *C&M* 40:33–70.
———. 1992. "Politisches Denken und Krise der Polis: Athen im Verfassungskonflikt des späten 5. Jahrhunderts v. Chr." *HZ* 225:1–59.
———. 1995. "Einleitung und Bilanz: Kleisthenes, Ephialtes und die Begründung der Demokratie." In Kinzl (1995) 1–54.
———. 1996. "Equalities and Inequalities in Athenian Democracy." In Ober and Hedrick (1996) 139–74.
Reden, S., von. 1995. "The Piraeus—A World Apart." *G&R* 42:24–37.
Reidinger, P. 1996. "Fraud Doctors." *ABA Journal* 82:50–54.
Rhodes, P. J. 1972. *The Athenian Boule.* Oxford.
———. 1981. *A Commentary on the Aristotelian Athenaion Politeia.* Oxford.
———. 1984. "*Nomothesia* in Fourth-Century Athens." *CQ,* n.s., 35:55–60.
———. 1985. *The Athenian Empire. G&R* New Surveys in the Classics 17. Oxford.
———. 1988. *Thucydides History II.* Warminster.
———. 1991. "The Athenian Code of Laws, 410–399 B.C." *JHS* 111:87–100.
———. 1993. "'Alles eitel gold'? The Sixth and Fifth Centuries in Fourth-Century Athens." In Piérart (1993) 53–64.
———. 1995. "Judicial Procedures in Fourth-Century Athens: Improvement or Simply Change?" In Eder (1995) 303–19.
Rihll, T. E. 1995. "Democracy Denied: Why Ephialtes Attacked the Areiopagus." *JHS* 115:87–98.
Robb, K. 1994. *Literacy and Paideia in Ancient Greece.* Oxford.

Roberts, J. T. 1982. *Accountability in Athenian Government.* Madison, Wis.
———. 1994. *Athens on Trial: The Antidemocratic Tradition in Western Thought.* Princeton, N.J.
Roberts, S. 1983. "The Study of Dispute: Anthropological Perspectives." In Bossy (1983) 1–24.
Robertson, N. 1990. "The Laws of Athens, 410–399 B.C.: The Evidence for Review and Publication." *JHS* 110:43–75.
Romilly, J. de. 1971. *La loi dans la pensée Grecque.* Paris.
———. 1979. *La douceur dans la pensée Grecque.* Paris.
———. 1992. *The Great Sophists in Periclean Athens.* Translated by J. Lloyd. Oxford.
Rosen, R. M., and J. Farrell, eds. 1993. *Nomodeiktes: Greek Studies in Honor of Martin Ostwald.* Ann Arbor, Mich.
Rosivach, V. J. 1991. "Some Athenian Presuppositions about 'the Poor.'" *G&R* 38:189–98.
Rubinstein, L. 1993. *Adoption in IV. Century Athens.* Copenhagen.
Ruschenbusch, E. 1966. Σόλωνος νόμοι: *Die Fragmente des solonischen Gesetzeswerkes mit einer Text- und Überlieferungsgeschichte.* Historia Einzelschriften 9. Wiesbaden.
———. 1968. *Untersuchungen zur Geschichte des athenischen Strafrechts.* Cologne and Graz.
Sagan, E. 1991. *The Honey and the Hemlock: Democracy and Paranoia in Ancient Athens and Modern America.* Princeton, N.J.
Ste. Croix, G. E. M. de. 1961. "Notes on Jurisdiction in the Athenian Empire." *CQ,* n.s., 11:94–112, 268–80.
———. 1972. *Origins of the Peloponnesian War.* Ithaca, N.Y.
———. 1974. "Ancient Greek and Roman Maritime Loans." In Edey and Yamey (1974) 41–59.
Scafuro, A. C. 1994. "Witnessing and False Witnessing: Proving Citizenship and Kin Identity in Fourth-Century Athens." In Boegehold and Scafuro (1994) 156–98.
———. 1997. *The Forensic Stage: Settling Disputes in Graeco-Roman New Comedy.* Cambridge.
Schneider, J. 1977. "Zum Nachleben von συκοφάντης im Lateinischen." *ZAnt* 27:43–50.
Schuller, W., ed. 1982. *Korruption im Altertum.* Munich and Vienna.
Schulz, B. J. 1981. "Bezeichnungen und Selbstbezeichnungen der Aristokraten und Oligarchen in der griechischen Literatur von Homer bis Aristoteles." In Welskopf (1981) 3.67–155.
Sealey, R. 1960. "Who Was Aristogeiton?" *BICS* 7:33–43.
———. 1982. "On the Athenian Concept of Law." *CJ* 77:289–302.
———. 1987. *The Athenian Republic: Democracy or the Rule of Law?* Philadelphia.

---. 1990. *Women and Law in Classical Greece.* Chapel Hill, N.C.
---. 1993. *Demosthenes and His Time: A Study in Defeat.* Oxford.
---. 1994. *The Justice of the Greeks.* Ann Arbor, Mich.
Sharpe, J. A. 1983. "'Such Disagreement betwyx Neighbours': Litigation and Human Relations in Early Modern England." In Bossy (1983) 167–87.
Sickinger, J. P. 1994. "Inscriptions and Archives in Classical Athens." *Historia* 43:286–96.
Sinclair, R. K. 1988. *Democracy and Participation in Athens.* Cambridge.
Slater, N. W. 1996. "Literacy and Old Comedy." In Worthington (1996) 99–112.
Smith, R. M. 1995. "A New Look at the Canon of the Ten Attic Orators." *Mnemosyne* 48:66–79.
Sommerstein, A. H. 1980–96. *The Comedies of Aristophanes.* Vols. 1–9. Warminster. (*Acharnians* [1980]; *Knights* [1981]; *Clouds* [1981]; *Wasps* [1983]; *Peace* [1985]; *Birds* [1987]; *Lysistrata* [1990]; *Thesmophoriazusae* [1994]; *Frogs* [1996]).
---. 1984. "Aristophanes and the Demon Poverty." *CQ*, n.s., 34: 314–33.
---. 1996. "How to Avoid Being a *Komodoumenos.*" *CQ*, n.s., 46: 327–56.
Sommerstein, A. H., S. Halliwell, J. Henderson, and B. Zimmermann, eds. 1990. *Tragedy, Comedy and the Polis.* Bari.
Stadter, P. A. 1989. *A Commentary on Plutarch's Pericles.* Chapel Hill, N.C.
Stanley, P. V. 1993. "Release from Liturgical Service in Athens." *Laverna* 4:26–44.
Starr, J., and J. F. Collier, eds. 1989. *History and Power in the Study of Law: New Directions in Legal Anthropology.* Ithaca, N.Y.
Stockton, D. 1990. *The Classical Athenian Democracy.* Oxford.
Stone, L. M. 1981. *Costume in Aristophanic Comedy.* New York.
Strauss, B. S. 1985. "The Cultural Significance of Bribery and Embezzlement in Athenian Politics: The Evidence of the Period 403–386 B.C." *AW* 11:67–74.
---. 1993. *Fathers and Sons in Athens.* Princeton, N.J.
Stroud, R. S. 1968. *Drakon's Law on Homicide.* Berkeley.
Sutton, D. F. 1993. *Ancient Comedy: The War of the Generations.* New York.
Svenbro, J. 1993. *Phrasikleia. An Anthropology of Reading in Ancient Greece.* Translated by J. Lloyd. Ithaca, N.Y.
Szegedy-Maszak, A. 1978. "Legends of the Greek Lawgivers." *GRBS* 19:199–209.
---. 1981. *The Nomoi of Theophrastus.* New York.
Taillardat, J. 1965. *Les images d'Aristophane.* Paris.
Tammaro, V. 1973–74. "Note ad Eupoli." *MC* 8–9:180–90.

Bibliography

Thomas, R. 1989. *Oral Tradition and Written Record in Classical Athens.* Cambridge Studies in Oral and Literate Culture 18. Cambridge.

———. 1994a. "Literacy and the City-State in Archaic and Classical Greece." In Bowman and Woolf (1994) 33–50.

———. 1994b. "Law and the Lawgiver in the Athenian Democracy." In Osborne and Hornblower (1994) 119–33.

———. 1996. "Written in Stone? Liberty, Equality, Orality and the Codification of Law." In Foxhall and Lewis (1996) 9–31.

Thompson, W. E. 1981. "Athenian Attitudes towards Wills." *Prudentia* 13:13–23.

Thür, G. 1977. *Beweisführung vor den Schwurgerichtshöfen Athens: Die Proklesis zur Basanos.* Vienna.

———, ed. 1994. *Symposion 1993: Vorträge zur griechischen und hellenistischen Rechtsgeschichte.* Cologne, Weimar, and Vienna.

———. 1996. "Reply to D. C. Mirhady, 'Torture and Rhetoric in Athens.'" *JHS* 116:132–34.

Todd, H. F. 1978. "Litigious Marginals: Character and Disputing in a Bavarian Village." In Nader and Todd (1978) 86–121.

Todd, S. C. 1990a. "The Purpose of Evidence in Athenian Courts." In Cartledge, Millett, and Todd (1990) 19–39.

———. 1990b. "Lady Chatterly's Lover and the Attic Orators." *JHS* 110:146–73.

———. 1993. *The Shape of Athenian Law.* Oxford.

———. 1996. "Lysias against Nikomachos: The Fate of the Expert in Athenian Law." In Foxhall and Lewis (1996) 101–31.

Too, Y. L. 1995. *The Rhetoric of Identity in Isocrates: Text, Power, Pedagogy.* Cambridge.

Trede, M. 1983. "Ἀκρίβεια chez Thucydide." In *Mélanges Edouard Delebecque,* 407–15. Aix-en-Provence.

Trevett, J. 1991. "The Date of [Demosthenes] 49: A Re-examination." *Phoenix* 45:21–27.

———. 1992. *Apollodorus the Son of Pasion.* Oxford.

———. 1996. "Aristotle's Knowledge of Athenian Oratory." *CQ,* n.s., 46:371–79.

Triantaphyllopoulos, J. 1985. *Das Rechtsdenken der Griechen.* Munich.

Turner, E. G. 1946. "φιλοδικεῖν δοκοῦμεν (Thuc. 1.77)." *CR* 60:5–7.

Usher, S. 1976. "Lysias and His Clients." *GRBS* 17:31–40.

Vannier, F. 1988. *Finances publiques et richesses privées dans le discours Athénien aux Ve et IVe siècles.* Annales littéraires de l'Université de Besançon 362. Paris.

Versnel, H. S. 1991. "Beyond Cursing: The Appeal to Justice in Judicial Prayers." In Faraone and Obbink (1991) 60–106.

Voegelin, W. 1943. *Die Diabole bei Lysias.* Basel.

Wallace, R. W. 1989. *The Areopagus Council, to 307 B.C.* Baltimore.
———. 1993. "Personal Conduct and Legal Sanction in the Democracy of Classical Athens." In *Questions de responsabilité*. XLVème Session de la Société Internationale "Fernand de Visscher" pour l'Histoire des Droits de l'Antiquité, 397–413. Miskolc-Eger, Hungary.
———. 1994. "Private Lives and Public Enemies: Freedom of Thought in Classical Athens." In Boegehold and Scafuro (1994) 127–55.
Wallace-Hadrill, A., ed. 1989. *Patronage in Ancient Society*. London.
Walters, K. R. 1980. "Rhetoric as Ritual: The Semiotics of the Attic Funeral Oration." *Florilegium* 2:1–27.
———. 1983. "Perikles' Citizenship Law." *CA* 2:314–36.
Wankel, H. 1976. *Rede für Ktesiphon über den Kranz*. 2 vols. Heidelberg.
———. 1982. "Die Korruption in der rednerischen Topik und in der Realität des klassischen Athen." In Schuller (1982) 29–53.
Weissenberger, M. 1987. *Die Dokimasiereden des Lysias (orr. 16, 25, 26, 31)*. Beiträge zur klassischen Philologie 182. Frankfurt a.M.
Welskopf, E. C., ed. 1981. *Soziale Typenbegriffe im alten Griechenland und ihr Fortleben in den Sprachen der Welt*. 7 vols. Berlin.
West, W. C. 1989. "The Public Archives in Fourth-Century Athens." *GRBS* 30:529–43.
Whitehead, D. 1983. "Competitive Outlay and Community Profit: φιλοτιμία in Democratic Athens." *C&M* 34:55–74.
———. 1986. *The Demes of Attica, 508/7–ca. 250 B.C.: A Political and Social Study*. Princeton, N.J.
———. 1993. "Cardinal Virtues: The Language of Public Approbation in Democratic Athens." *C&M* 44:37–75.
Williams, B. 1993. *Shame and Necessity*. Berkeley.
Wilson, P. J. 1991. "Demosthenes 21 (*Against Meidias*): Democratic Abuse." *PCPS*, n.s., 37:164–95.
Winkel, L. C. 1982. "Quelques remarques sur l'accusation publique en droit grec et romain." *RIDA* 29:281–94.
Winkler, J. 1990. "Laying Down the Law: The Oversight of Men's Sexual Behavior in Classical Athens." In Halperin, Winkler, and Zeitlin (1990) 171–209.
Winkler, J., and F. Zeitlin, eds. 1990. *Nothing to Do with Dionysus? Athenian Drama in Its Social Context*. Princeton, N.J.
Wolff, H. J. 1966. *Die attische Paragraphe*. Graezistische Abhandlungen 2. Weimar.
———. 1970. "'Normenkontrolle' und Gesetzesbegriff in der attischen Demokratie: Untersuchung zur Graphe Paranomon*. Heidelberg.
———, ed. 1975. *Symposion 1971: Vorträge zur griechischen und hellenistischen Rechtsgeschichte*. Cologne and Vienna.

Wood, E. M. 1988. *Peasant-Citizen and Slave: The Foundations of Athenian Democracy*. London.

Worthington, I. 1989. "The Duration of an Athenian Political Trial." *JHS* 109:204–7.

———. 1991. "Greek Oratory, Revision of Speeches and the Problem of Historical Reliability." *C&M* 42:55–74.

———. 1993. "Once More, The Client/*Logographos* Relationship." *CQ*, n.s., 43:67–72.

———. 1994. "The Canon of the Ten Attic Orators." In Worthington (1994) 244–63.

———, ed. 1994. *Persuasion: Greek Rhetoric in Action*. London.

———, ed. 1996. *Voice into Text: Orality and Literacy in Ancient Greece*. Leiden.

Wyse, W., ed. 1904. *The Speeches of Isaeus*. Cambridge.

Yngvesson, B. 1989. "Inventing Law in Local Settings: Rethinking Popular Legal Culture." *Yale Law Journal* 98:1689–1709.

Yunis, H. 1988. "Law, Politics, and the *Graphe Paranomon* in Fourth-Century Athens." *GRBS* 29:361–82.

———. 1996. *Taming Democracy: Models of Political Rhetoric in Classical Athens*. Ithaca, N.Y.

Ziebarth, E. 1897. "Popularklagen mit Delatorienprämien nach griechischem Recht." *Hermes* 32:609–28.

Ziolkowski, J. E. 1981. *Thucydides and the Tradition of Funeral Speeches at Athens*. New York.

Index of Ancient Citations

Aelian (Ael.)
 Varia Historia (VH): 13.24.1–5, 76
Aeschines (Aesch.)
 1: 1.1, 136, 151; 1.1–2, 262 n. 122; 1.2, 148, 155; 1.20, 95; 1.59, 268 n. 98 bis; 1.105, 96, 264 n. 16; 1.107, 98, 135, 249 n. 17, 250 n. 19; 1.114–15, 260 n. 91; 1.193, 38
 2: 246 n. 79; 2.5, 244 n. 34; 2.66, 201; 2.89, 197; 2.99, 96; 2.124, 243 n. 30; 2.145, 98, 243 n. 24; 2.148, 250 n. 21; 2.165, 240 n. 145; 2.170, 127; 2.182, 136, 151, 260 n. 91; 2.183, 243 n. 23
 3: 246 n. 79; 3.1, 149; 3.7, 149, 269 n. 8; 3.15, 201; 3.16, 201; 3.20, 272 n. 55; 3.22, 201; 3.28, 198; 3.30, 201; 3.35, 198 bis; 3.37, 198, 202; 3.38–40, 21; 3.52, 132; 3.75, 197; 3.172, 243 nn. 23, 28; 3.173, 240 n. 145; 3.192, 207; 3.194, 137; 3.199–200, 195, 198, 208; 3.226, 98; 3.235, 249 n. 3; 3.255, 129; 3.255–56, 95, 96

Aeschylus (A.)
 Prometheus Bound (Pr.): 326, 240 n. 170
Alexis (Alex.)
 fr. 187 K-A: 245 n. 64
Anaximenes. See Ps.-Aristotle
Andocides (And.)
 1: 1.17, 19, 234 n. 44; 1.74, 32 bis; 1.84, 199; 1.85–87, 196; 1.99, 96, 247 n. 86; 1.100, 96; 1.104, 263 n. 137; 1.105, 93, 97, 98, 249 n. 17; 1.132, 37, 66; 1.150, 236 n. 86
 4: 4.1, 261 n. 111
Antiphanes (Antiph.)
 fr. 157.11–12 K-A: 182
 fr. 177 K-A: 105, 245 n. 64, 251 n. 43
 fr. 194.13–14 K-A: 238 n. 122
 fr. 202 K-A: 251 n. 49
 fr. 281 K-A: 251 n. 45, 271 n. 43
Antiphon (Ant.)
 1: 272 n. 58; 1.2, 265 n. 40 bis; 1.3–4, 173; 1.17, 168
 2: 2.1.5–8, 36; 2.2.12, 247 n. 86, 252 n. 71, 253 n. 85

Index of Ancient Citations

Antiphon (Ant.) (cont.)
  3: 3.2.1, 166; 3.2.1–2, 204; 3.3.3, 200, 204; 3.4.1, 39; 3.4.2, 204, 270 n. 32, 272 n. 58
  4: 4.2.2, 192; 4.4.6, 192
  5: 5.8, 211; 5.8–19, 211; 5.18, 211; 5.25, 37, 66; 5.78, 91; 5.80, 91, 93, 98, 249 n. 17; 5.85–96, 211; 5.86, 195
  6: 272 n. 58; 6.12, 153; 6.35, 148, 153; 6.43, 243 n. 29, 258 n. 54; 6.49–50, 153
  Fragments (Gernet): fr. III.1, 249 n. 1; fr. V.1, 156
Apollodorus Carystius or Gelous (Apollod. Car. or Gel.)
  fr. 1 K-A: 252 n. 55
  fr. 13 K-A: 96, 245 n. 57
  fr. 13.12 K-A: 247 n. 90
Aristophanes (Ar.)
  Acharnians (Ach.): 17–22, 40; 212–13, 110; 325–36, 110; 377–82, 113; 515–19, 68, 248 n. 105; 517, 62; 517–19, 53, 243 n. 23; 517–22, 141 bis; 530–38, 248 n. 108; 541–43, 141; 685, 109, 152; 687, 109; 688, 109, 243 n. 29 bis, 245 n. 59; 691, 110, 112; 693–702, 112; 698–701, 110, 112, 251 n. 40; 698–718, 112; 702–7, 110; 703–12, 110 bis, 245 n. 48; 703–18, 245 n. 52; 707, 243 n. 29; 713–16, 245 n. 48; 713–18, 110; 725–26, 53, 110, 243 n. 23, 245 n. 64; 818, 62, 246 n. 65; 818–29, 53 bis, 112, 141, 248 n. 105; 825, 246 n. 65; 829, 62, 105, 246 n. 65; 846–47, 245 n. 48; 898–905, 2; 903–4, 251 n. 39; 903–5, 105; 904–5, 54; 906, 254 n. 112; 908, 244 n. 43; 908–58, 53, 141, 248 n. 105; 910, 62; 926, 54; 926–28, 54; 926–58, 54; 927, 54; 934, 244 n. 34; 936–39, 54, 258 n. 54; 938, 141; 939, 243 n. 29; 944–45, 54; 952, 54; 956, 244 n. 34; 957–58, 254 n. 112

Birds (Av.): 33–41, 105, 113; 109–11, 105, 113; 145–47, 248 n. 104; 285–86, 113; 935–51, 61; 1054, 270 n. 24; 1286–89, 198–99; 1410, 62; 1410–11, 246 n. 69; 1410–69, 53, 248 n. 104; 1411, 62; 1412, 62; 1415, 62; 1416–17, 61; 1416–21, 111; 1420, 62; 1421, 61; 1422–24, 62; 1423, 53, 65, 246 n. 70, 247 n. 86; 1425, 54; 1430, 247 n. 86 bis; 1430–31, 53; 1430–35, 53, 65; 1431, 255 n. 117; 1432, 112; 1433–35, 247 n. 86; 1450, 65, 247 n. 86; 1451–52, 65, 247 n. 86; 1451–61, 53; 1455–56, 54; 1459, 54; 1460–61, 54; 1461–65, 54; 1468, 54, 244 n. 31; 1694, 245 n. 64; 1694–1705, 242 n. 17; 1697–99, 247 n. 89; 1699, 245 n. 64; 1699–1701, 243 n. 23
Clouds (Nu.): 112–15, 16; 206–8, 2, 105; 320, 270 n. 32; 434, 244 n. 31; 448, 271 n. 40; 553–56, 108; 757–83, 242 n. 17; 759–74, 270 n. 26; 776, 244 n. 31; 874–76, 245 n. 48; 1003–4, 255 n. 117; 1218–19, 178; 1455, 244 n. 31; 1483, 247 n. 90; 1496, 270 n. 32
Ecclesiazusae (Ec.): 560, 264 n. 16; 561–62, 242 n. 16; 562–63, 247 n. 86; 655–61, 265 n. 27
Frogs (Ra.): 420–25, 252 n. 61; 422, 252 n. 61; 718–37, 248 n. 108
Knights (Eq.): 59, 251 n. 50; 63–70, 55; 66, 243 n. 29; 223–24, 112; 235–36, 254 n. 107; 235–39, 112; 251, 243 n. 29 bis; 255–56, 106; 257, 254 n. 107; 259, 245 n. 64, 254 n. 95; 259–60, 258 n. 54; 259–65, 55, 108, 112, 113, 249 n. 17; 260, 255 n. 130; 261, 56; 264–65, 255 n. 130; 275–81, 252 n. 55; 278–79, 254 n. 107; 288, 112; 300–302, 141; 308, 243 n. 29; 313, 254 n. 110; 326, 113; 326–27, 254 n. 110;

298

358, 243 n. 29, 255 n. 131; *361*, 254 n. 110; *435–44*, 252 n. 55; *437*, 55; *438*, 254 n. 110; *438–39*, 250 n. 21; *452*, 254 n. 107; *465–67*, 254 n. 107; *476–79*, 254 n. 107; *529*, 245 n. 64, 251 n. 48; *626–29*, 254 n. 107; *733–35*, 107; *773–76*, 112; *775*, 55, 245 n. 52; *797–804*, 107; *799*, 251 n. 50; *801–2*, 254 n. 110; *824–26*, 55, 113, 258 n. 54; *830–35*, 107; *832–35*, 254 n. 110; *836–40*, 107; *837–40*, 248 n. 104; *840*, 243 n. 29 bis; *862–67*, 254 n. 107; *866*, 243 n. 29; *867*, 243 n. 29; *973–85*, 106; *974–76*, 254 n. 110; *1017–34*, 262 n. 116; *1034*, 254 n. 110; *1070–71*, 254 n. 110; *1121–30*, 115; *1139–40*, 113; *1196–98*, 254 n. 110; *1254–56*, 108; *1261*, 251 n. 50; *1317*, 105; *1331–63*, 251 n. 40; *1356–63*, 245 n. 48; *1357–63*, 115; *1359–61*, 106; *1359–63*, 152; *1397–1401*, 55; *1405*, 55; *1407–8*, 254 n. 110; *1408*, 248 n. 104

Peace (*Pax*): *107–8*, 55; *190–91*, 247 n. 89; *191*, 64, 243 n. 28; *505*, 1, 105; *632–48*, 107; *639*, 243 n. 29; *639–40*, 113, 248 n. 104; *639–43*, 249 n. 17, 254 n. 107; *639–48*, 254 n. 110; *641*, 245 n. 59; *654*, 243 n. 29 bis; *684*, 147

Wasps (*V.*): *85–135*, 229 n. 3; *100–102*, 258 n. 55; *145*, 245 n. 64; *197*, 106; *230–47*, 40; *240–44*, 114; *344–45*, 254 n. 107; *464–65*, 254 n. 107; *481–83*, 254 n. 107; *488–89*, 254 n. 107; *505*, 40, 106; *506–7*, 254 n. 107; *548–58*, 43; *553–54*, 106, 258 n. 55; *554*, 114; *564–65*, 106, 109; *570–71*, 258 n. 55; *583–86*, 223; *587*, 20; *592–93*, 255 n. 118; *605–12*, 109; *619–20*, 43; *620–30*, 85; *625–26*, 43; *626–28*, 106;

650–51, 107; *669–77*, 254 n. 110; *673–74*, 106; *673–79*, 92, 107; *687–91*, 255 n. 117; *717–18*, 15; *718*, 112, 260 n. 90; *764–1008*, 1, 86; *836–38*, 114; *894f.*, 262 n. 116; *897*, 245 n. 64; *953*, 254 n. 107; *1030*, 114; *1037–42*, 56, 107, 110, 255 n. 117; *1043*, 56, 114, 244 n. 35; *1095–97*, 109, 251 n. 40; *1112–13*, 109; *1205–7*, 255 n. 119; *1285*, 243 n. 29; *1332–34*, 114; *1335–41*, 114; *1392–93*, 114; *1408*, 243 n. 17; *1443–45*, 114; *1457–58*, 115

Wealth (*Pl.*): *30–31*, 55, 94, 111, 243 n. 23, 246 n. 72; *460–65*, 246 n. 73; *555–56*, 110; *567–69*, 246 n. 72; *567–70*, 94, 111; *850–958*, 53; *858–59*, 55, 62; *862*, 62, 248 n. 108; *864–65*, 146; *864–66*, 62; *869*, 62, 261 n. 101; *870*, 54; *870–71*, 62; *870–95*, 146; *873*, 62; *877–79*, 243 n. 24, 248 n. 105; *878*, 146; *881–82*, 246 n. 69; *885*, 146; *890–95*, 62; *893*, 54; *897*, 244 n. 46, 246 n. 72; *900*, 145; *900–901*, 112, 150; *900–925*, 114; *901–25*, 146; *902–6*, 53; *903*, 247 n. 89; *903–5*, 112; *905*, 247 n. 86; *906*, 247 n. 91; *909*, 261 n. 101; *913*, 53, 243 n. 28; *913–15*, 150; *920*, 112; *926–34*, 54; *935*, 54; *938*, 54; *939*, 261 n. 101; *943*, 54; *945–50*, 53, 146, 246 n. 73; *946*, 245 n. 64; *957*, 62, 248 n. 108; *1178*, 246 n. 73

Fragments (K-A): *205*, 152, 245 n. 48; *226*, 15; *228*, 51, 85, 242 n. 7, 243 n. 29, 246 nn. 65, 70; *237*, 260 n. 90; *424*, 112, 245 n. 48, 255 nn. 118, 123; *552*, 111, 243 n. 17; *581*, 251 n. 43; *Olkades t. iv*, 245 n. 51

Life of Aristophanes (*Vita*): *1.19*, 260 n. 90; *1.19–31*, 113

Index of Ancient Citations

Aristotle (Arist.)
  Eudemian Ethics (EE): 1236a33–35, 267 n. 68
  Nicomachean Ethics (EN): 1137a31–1138a3, 25; 1137b29–31, 272 n. 63; 1137b34–1138a2, 271 n. 43; 1156a10, 267 n. 68; 1157b36, 266 n. 57
  Politics (Pol.): 1274a8–9, 14; 1274b5–7, 244 n. 39; 1274b7–9, 235 n. 63; 1282b1–6, 24; 1286a35–40, 24; 1304b19–24, 81, 254 n. 96
  Problems (Pr.): 950b5–8, 223
  Rhetoric (Rh.): 1354a32–b1, 24; 1372a11–14, 239 n. 126; 1375a22–25, 195; 1375b16–18, 194; 1376b2–5, 220; 1376b7–10, 219; 1376b11–14, 220; 1376b15–17, 219; 1382a7, 70, 243 n. 24, 247 n. 84; 1400a32–36, 270 n. 24; 1413b8–9, 271 n. 42
  Fragments (Rose): 611.18, 82; 667, 82, 83, 245 n. 64
Ps.-Aristotle ([Arist.])
  Constitution of Athens (AP): 9.1, 120, 121 bis, 234 n. 50; 9.1–2, 118; 9.2, 24; 16.5, 236 n. 81; 26.3, 236 n. 81; 27.3–5, 14; 29.4, 249 n. 1; 31.1, 249 n. 1; 35.2, 72, 197, 223, 249 n. 4; 35.3, 52, 72, 81; 35.4, 249 n. 3; 43.5, 31, 32, 62; 45.3, 262 n. 125; 53.1, 236 n. 81; 53.2–3, 27; 53.6, 238 n. 111; 55–59, 18; 56.6, 122, 128; 59.3, 28, 31, 32; 67.1, 28, 33; 67.2, 33; 68.4, 30
  Rhetoric to Alexander (Rh. Al.): 1422a3–4, 219; 1424a31–32, 81, 247 n. 86; 1424b10–14, 251 n. 39; 1443a23–28, 195; 1444a18–28, 38, 271 n. 38; 1444a30–32, 248 n. 107; 1444a35–b3, 257 n. 26; 1444b3–7, 38
Athenaeus (Ath.)
  Deipnosophistae: 407c, 198; 509b, 243 n. 17, 255 n. 125

Comica Adespota (Com. Adesp.)
  fr. 526 K-A: 237 n. 95
Cratinus (Cratin.)
  fr. 70 K-A: 242 n. 7, 245 n. 64, 251 n. 48
  fr. 81 K-A: 114
  fr. 82 K-A: 255 n. 118
  fr. 128 K-A: 199
  fr. 171.58–76 K-A: 246 n. 69
  fr. 227 K-A: 242 n. 12
  fr. 251 K-A: 260 n. 90
  fr. 300 K-A: 270 n. 24
Critias (Crit.)
  fr. 88 B 22 D-K: 245 n. 57, 272 n. 48

Demades (Demad.)
  fr. 79 de Falco: 244 n. 31
Demosthenes (Dem.)
  5: 5.6, 263 n. 137
  12: 12.19, 103, 248 n. 105, 251 nn. 39, 53
  13: 13.16–17, 262 n. 114
  15: 15.33, 262 n. 119
  18: 246 n. 79; 18.13, 157; 18.111, 200, 208, 243 n. 29, 245 n. 57; 18.112, 157; 18.118, 157, 246 n. 74; 18.121, 66, 157 bis, 198; 18.123, 157 bis; 18.138, 98; 18.141, 157; 18.143, 157; 18.210, 274 n. 92; 18.212, 243 n. 22, 244 n. 34; 18.235, 251 n. 39; 18.242, 244 n. 34; 18.249–50, 137, 258 n. 54; 18.250, 259 n. 62; 18.251, 137; 18.275, 243 n. 22; 18.278, 157; 18.279, 157; 18.283, 157; 18.289, 244 n. 34; 18.308, 153
  19: 246 n. 79; 19.102, 205, 273 n. 65; 19.129, 197; 19.179, 195; 19.188, 153; 19.222, 154; 19.223, 153; 19.240, 194; 19.250, 272 n. 59; 19.257, 153
  20: 20.93, 24, 199, 203; 20.152, 152, 247 n. 86
  21: 130, 132, 163, 239 n. 125; 21.1, 164; 21.5–7, 132; 21.7–8, 133; 21.13–18, 163; 21.21, 133; 21.27, 209; 21.28, 132; 21.29, 133, 163,

263 n. 137; *21.31–34*, 133; *21.45*, 132; *21.46*, 201; *21.47*, 133, 241 n. 181; *21.74*, 133; *21.83*, 97, 125, 248 n. 99; *21.83–101*, 125 bis; *21.86*, 238 n. 111; *21.91*, 244 n. 31, 245 n. 57; *21.103*, 38, 66, 244 n. 34; *21.106*, 132; *21.112*, 34, 38, 239 n. 126, 257 n. 26; *21.116*, 246 n. 74; *21.123–24*, 98, 126, 164, 192; *21.141*, 98, 126, 132; *21.142*, 133; *21.180*, 163, 164; *21.224*, 23, 200

22: *22.1–3*, 155; *22.25–27*, 26, 124; *22.25–30*, 120; *22.28*, 209; *22.35*, 66

23: *23.1*, 148, 158; *23.5*, 151; *23.22–62*, 206; *23.31*, 206; *23.61*, 195, 207; *23.96–97*, 195; *23.97*, 202; *23.190*, 148, 158, 164; *23.201*, 253 n. 77; *23.206*, 236 n. 86

24: *24.3*, 137, 148, 154, 261 n. 95; *24.6*, 150; *24.8*, 148, 155; *24.14*, 137; *24.17*, 207; *24.18*, 207; *24.19–72*, 207; *24.24*, 196; *24.32*, 207; *24.34*, 195; *24.61*, 207; *24.66*, 137, 205, 207; *24.80*, 20; *24.142*, 197; *24.149–51*, 194; *24.173*, 153; *24.191*, 198, 201; *24.192–93*, 164; *24.193*, 196, 207; *24.210*, 3; *24.212–14*, 120

25: *25.7*, 92; *25.8*, 68; *25.9*, 264 n. 16; *25.12*, 92; *25.13*, 152, 262 n. 124, 263 n. 139; *25.16*, 219; *25.19*, 68, 243 n. 29; *25.28*, 57; *25.32*, 57; *25.36*, 244 n. 32; *25.37*, 152, 258 n. 54, 263 n. 139; *25.38*, 97, 125; *25.38–41*, 262 n. 129; *25.40*, 57, 149, 243 n. 22; *25.41*, 244 n. 34; *25.42*, 243 n. 29; *25.46*, 95; *25.47*, 57; *25.48*, 245 n. 64, 251 n. 43; *25.49*, 57, 85, 244 n. 32; *25.49–50*, 98, 250 n. 20; *25.50*, 57, 58, 98, 243 n. 29, 244 n. 32, 245 n. 59, 258 n. 54; *25.51*, 57, 95, 247 n. 86; *25.52*, 57 bis, 244 n. 34, 264 n. 18; *25.53*, 244 n. 34; *25.54–55*, 57; *25.58*, 59, 126, 244 n. 34; *25.60–62*, 58; *25.62*, 58; *25.63*, 58, 59, 63 bis, 243 n. 22, 244 nn. 34 bis, 35; *25.74*, 243 n. 26; *25.74–75*, 57; *25.78*, 143, 252 n. 71, 260 n. 92; *25.82*, 57 bis, 95, 243 n. 24, 244 n. 34, 247 n. 86, 247 n. 89; *25.83*, 243 n. 22; *25.83–84*, 58; *25.84*, 243 n. 22; *25.85–86*, 56; *25.85–87*, 174, 196; *25.85–91*, 29; *25.87*, 57; *25.87–88*, 174; *25.87–90*, 57; *25.90*, 57; *25.94*, 57, 244 n. 32; *25.95*, 59, 229 n. 3; *25.96*, 57; *25.97*, 82, 264 n. 16

26: *26.4*, 164, 207; *26.15*, 272 n. 44; *26.22*, 145, 149; *26.24*, 31, 199

27: *27.65*, 169

28: *28.1*, 270 n. 29; *28.20*, 173

29: *29.28*, 38

30: 129; *30.3*, 38

31: 129

32: 186, 268 n. 85, 274 n. 87; *32.1–2*, 218; *32.10*, 247 n. 86; *32.23*, 268 n. 91

33: 274 n. 87; *33.2*, 216, 261 n. 100; *33.4*, 268 n. 83; *33.16*, 246 n. 74; *33.16–18*, 220; *33.27*, 212, 217, 274 n. 93; *33.36*, 219 bis; *33.37*, 242 n. 16; *33.38*, 247 n. 86

34: 186, 268 n. 85, 274 n. 87; *34.2*, 162; *34.3–4*, 188, 218; *34.4*, 216, 272 n. 45, 273 n. 77; *34.50–52*, 268 n. 91

35: 186, 268 n. 85, 274 nn. 87, 96; *35.1*, 220, 274 n. 92; *35.1–2*, 188, 189, 219; *35.2*, 216, 243 n. 17; *35.3–4*, 188; *35.5*, 189; *35.10–13*, 220; *35.11*, 189; *35.15*, 202, 243 n. 17; *35.15–16*, 188; *35.17*, 220; *35.17–25*, 189; *35.18–25*, 220; *35.22*, 219; *35.25*, 219, 220; *35.26*, 188; *35.27*, 37; *35.37*, 220; *35.38–42*, 243 n. 17;

Demosthenes (Dem.) (*cont.*)
  35.43, 219; 35.45, 189; 35.46,
  237 n. 105; 35.50, 189; 35.50–
  54, 189; 35.51, 200, 268 n. 90;
  35.51–52, 205, 219; 35.52, 220;
  35.54, 189, 274 n. 92; 35.54–56,
  221; 35.56, 189
36: 274 n. 87; 36.2, 217; 36.2–3,
  216; 36.3, 217, 246 n. 74; 36.24,
  217; 36.25, 217; 36.26–27, 217;
  36.52, 51; 36.53–54, 262 n. 120;
  36.54, 243 n. 27; 36.58, 93, 97,
  244 n. 34
37: 268 n. 81, 274 n. 87; 37.1, 218;
  37.3, 246 n. 74; 37.4, 185; 37.5,
  185; 37.6–8, 185; 37.10, 185;
  37.15, 185 bis; 37.21, 218; 37.26,
  185; 37.35, 185; 37.39, 247
  n. 86; 37.46, 128; 37.49–50, 185;
  37.54, 185
38: 274 n. 87; 38.3, 129; 38.17,
  217, 257 n. 34; 38.20, 129;
  38.23, 257 n. 32
39: 39.1, 164; 39.2, 243 n. 28, 247
  n. 86; 39.6, 162, 265 n. 39;
  39.14, 260 n. 92; 39.17, 241
  n. 184; 39.34, 266 n. 49
40: 40.1–2, 265 n. 40 bis; 40.9, 38,
  247 n. 86; 40.12, 266 n. 49;
  40.30, 38–39; 40.32, 66; 40.40,
  274 n. 93; 40.47, 266 n. 49
41: 41.1, 166
42: 173, 238 n. 125; 42.15, 201
43: 43.54, 257 n. 37; 43.75, 257
  n. 37
44: 44.3, 257 n. 26; 44.8, 195;
  44.11, 214; 44.15, 39; 44.28, 239
  n. 126; 44.49, 198; 44.57–59,
  213–14
45: 217; 45.3–4, 241 n. 184; 45.4,
  258 n. 41; 45.5–6, 217; 45.6,
  216, 217, 273 n. 77; 45.29, 223;
  45.42, 66; 45.54, 169; 45.57–58,
  270 n. 29; 45.67, 239 n. 126;
  45.84–85, 173
46: 217, 272 n. 60; 46.8, 201;
  46.10, 200, 201 bis; 46.25, 270
  n. 29; 46.26, 30, 127

47: 173, 239 n. 125; 47.34–38, 31;
  47.45, 31; 47.64, 29, 30
48: 48.1, 169, 171 bis, 265 n. 40;
  48.1–2, 265 n. 40; 48.3, 172;
  48.6, 171, 172; 48.7, 172; 48.8,
  172; 48.8–11, 172; 48.20, 172;
  48.29–32, 172; 48.36, 257 n. 26;
  48.40, 172; 48.46, 169; 48.53,
  172; 48.53–55, 172; 48.56, 1;
  48.58, 172
49: 267 n. 77; 49.1, 184; 49.2, 184;
  49.2–3, 184; 49.3, 184; 49.4, 184
  bis; 49.5, 184; 49.17, 184; 49.19,
  270 n. 29; 49.27, 184; 49.43,
  184; 49.50, 184; 49.54, 184;
  49.59, 184; 49.64, 184; 49.65–68,
  184; 49.66–67, 260 n. 90
51: 51.11, 239 n. 126; 51.16, 50
52: 52.12, 66; 52.23, 267 n. 75;
  52.28, 178; 52.33, 246 n. 75, 252
  n. 71
53: 266 n. 55; 53.1, 64, 148; 53.1–
  2, 140, 154; 53.1–3, 122; 53.2,
  138; 53.4, 122, 176, 177; 53.4–
  18, 155; 53.7, 176; 53.7–13, 177;
  53.8, 176; 53.8–12, 267 n. 78;
  53.12, 176; 53.13, 177; 53.14,
  177; 53.14–15, 177; 53.15–16,
  177; 53.16, 192; 53.17, 130, 177,
  257 n. 18, 266 n. 56, 268 n. 98,
  269 n. 98; 53.18, 266 n. 56;
  53.19–29, 266 n. 56
54: 173; 54.1, 131, 204; 54.3–6,
  164; 54.5, 268 n. 98; 54.7–9,
  164, 268 n. 98; 54.13, 131;
  54.17, 203; 54.17–19, 192, 204,
  264 n. 9; 54.18, 204; 54.27, 270
  n. 29; 54.31, 270 n. 29; 54.42,
  131
55: 55.1, 166, 175; 55.1–2, 175;
  55.2, 246 n. 74; 55.3–12, 175;
  55.9, 176; 55.20, 175; 55.22, 175;
  55.23, 175; 55.24–25, 175; 55.26,
  246 n. 74; 55.28, 175, 246 n. 74;
  55.29, 175; 55.30, 1; 55.31–35,
  175; 55.35, 176, 243 n. 30
56: 186, 268 n. 85, 274 n. 96; 56.1–2,
  190; 56.1–3, 274 n. 92; 56.2, 190,

219; 56.4, 190, 237 n. 105; 56.6–7, 221; 56.8, 190; 56.11, 66, 219, 221; 56.14, 221; 56.16, 190; 56.18, 190; 56.43, 190; 56.48, 190, 219; 56.48–50, 221
57: 260 n. 91, 267 n. 63; 57.2, 179; 57.5, 200, 205; 57.6, 179, 263 n. 137; 57.7, 179; 57.8, 179; 57.9–13, 179; 57.17, 179; 57.32, 97, 247 n. 91; 57.32–34, 97; 57.33, 243 n. 26, 247 n. 86; 57.36, 97; 57.48, 179; 57.49, 263 n. 137; 57.56, 180; 57.57, 179; 57.58–60, 179; 57.63, 179, 194, 261 n. 111; 57.64, 270 n. 24
58: 263 n. 136; 58.1–3, 123; 58.2, 97, 125; 58.5–13, 97, 141; 58.10–11, 238 n. 117; 58.10–13, 142; 58.12, 244 n. 34; 58.13, 142; 58.15, 200; 58.19, 204, 206, 240 n. 145; 58.23, 97; 58.24, 200 bis, 204, 211; 58.29, 85, 153, 243 n. 26; 58.30, 150; 58.30–34, 128, 257 n. 19; 58.32, 250 n. 20; 58.34, 96, 148, 250 n. 20; 58.35–36, 97; 58.38, 91; 58.41, 204; 58.43, 29; 58.45, 143, 244 n. 32, 260 n. 92; 58.45–46, 148; 58.48, 211; 58.52, 211; 58.55, 91, 92; 58.59, 151; 58.59–60, 148; 58.61, 195, 201, 204 bis; 58.62–63, 251–52 n. 53; 58.63, 91, 92, 94, 247 nn. 84, 86, 262 n. 114; 58.65, 66, 95–96, 98, 242 n. 16, 247 n. 86
59: 142, 260 n. 83; 59.1–14, 155; 59.8, 155; 59.9, 155; 59.12, 162; 59.13, 155; 59.15, 206 bis; 59.16, 138, 206; 59.39, 96; 59.41, 96; 59.43, 95, 137, 143, 260 n. 92; 59.52, 138, 206; 59.53, 142; 59.64–70, 130; 59.64–71, 258 n. 39; 59.65, 96; 59.66, 31; 59.68, 96; 59.87, 206; 59.88, 234 n. 50
60: 60.11, 119
Dinarchus (Din.)
1: 1.41–45, 270 n. 23; 1.55, 196; 1.114, 149

2: 2.9–10, 245 n. 60
3: 3.15, 152
Fragments (Conomis): IX.3, 198; LXXXVII, 261 n. 111
Diodorus Siculus (D.S.)
11.87, 251 n. 39; 12.10, 52; 12.12.2, 52, 60, 251 n. 39; 18.18.2, 238 n. 122
Diogenes Laertius (D.L.)
Lives of the Philosophers: 1.59.7–8, 121; 9.50, 244 n. 39
Diphilus (Diph.)
fr. 31.10–17 K-A: 247 n. 91
fr. 31.12–17 K-A: 243 n. 23, 244 n. 35, 247 n. 84
fr. 31.16–17 K-A: 242 n. 16

Ephippus (Ephipp.)
fr. 14 K-A ap. Ath. 509b: 243 n. 17, 255 n. 125
Ephorus (Ephor.)
FGrH 70 F 139: 235 n. 62, 251 n. 39
FGrH 70 F 139.11–14: 244 n. 40
Eubulus
fr. 74 K-A: 60–61, 251 n. 43
fr. 74.6 K-A: 270 n. 23
Eupolis (Eup.)
fr. 80 K-A: 252 n. 61
fr. 89 K-A: 108
fr. 99.79–120 K-A: 111, 251 n. 40
fr. 99.86–89 K-A: 111, 114, 248 n. 105
fr. 99.103–11 K-A: 111
fr. 99.104–5 K-A: 111
fr. 99.112 K-A: 111
fr. 193 K-A: 108, 245 n. 48, 254 n. 107, 255 n. 131
fr. 193 K-A ap. Plu. Nic. 4.3: 253 n. 87
fr. 220 K-A: 262 n. 116
fr. 245 K-A: 248 n. 104
Euripides (E.)
Suppliant Women (Supp.): 433–34, 34; 433–37, 199

Gorgias
fr. 82 B 6.12–14 D-K: 200

Index of Ancient Citations

Harpocration (Harp.)
  Lexicon: 167.12–13 Dindorf, 128
Heraclides Criticus (Heracl. Crit.)
  fr. 1.4 Pfister: 243 nn. 26, 28, 29,
  248 n. 105
Herodotus (Hdt.)
  4.68, 260 n. 93
Hesiod (Hes.)
  Works and Days (Op.): 27–34, 247
  n. 88; *276–80,* 245 n. 59; *346,*
  174
Homer (Hom.)
  Iliad (Il.): 4.35, 58
  Odyssey (Od.): 7.120–21, 83
Homeric Hymn to Hermes (Hom. h.
  Merc.)
  264, 260 n. 94
Hyperides (Hyp.)
  1: 1. fr. 3a, 210; *1.2,* 243 nn. 26, 27,
  248 n. 101; *1.8,* 210; *1.10,* 127;
  1.12, 136, 210, 261 n. 110
  2: 2.12, 32
  3: 3.8, 221, 222, 271 n. 41; *3.9,*
  222, 274 n. 99; *3.10,* 222 bis;
  3.12, 221, 222 bis, 271 n. 41;
  3.13, 203, 219 bis, 222 bis; *3.13–
  17,* 201; *3.13–18,* 222; *3.18,* 221,
  222 bis; *3.21–22,* 201, 222; *3.22,*
  195; *3.25,* 221; *3.25–26,* 247
  n. 89; *3.31,* 219 bis, 222
  4: 4.1–10, 209; *4.4,* 209, 274 n. 93;
  4.9, 262 n. 129; *4.11,* 127; *4.12,*
  236 n. 86; *4.13,* 127; *4.27,* 209;
  4.27–28, 262 n. 129; *4.30,* 209;
  4.32, 41, *92–93,* 259 n. 81; *4.32–
  35,* 143; *4.32–36,* 93; *4.36–37,*
  93
  5: 5.25–26, 135
  fr. 245 Jensen: 265 n. 39

Isaeus (Is.)
  1: 1.3, 274 n. 93; *1.5–8,* 169; *1.6,*
  265 n. 40; *1.8,* 169; *1.18,* 274
  n. 93; *1.26,* 223; *1.35,* 223
  2: 274 n. 85
  3: 274 n. 85; *3.46–47,* 128; *3.47,*
  128

5: 5.9–10, 169; *5.17–18,* 266 n. 48;
  5.29, 169, 266 n. 48
6: 6.3, 215; *6.3–4,* 273 n. 77; *6.4,*
  214, 215; *6.43,* 273 n. 77; *6.52,*
  215, 273 n. 77; *6.59,* 273 n. 77
7: 7.2, 223; *7.3,* 215, 273 n. 77;
  7.6–7, 129
8: 8.30, 205; *8.41,* 258 n. 41
9: 9.2, 223; *9.25,* 169; *9.26,* 37;
  9.27–31, 223
11: 128, 129; *11.4,* 198, 244 n. 31,
  246 n. 74; *11.13,* 264 n. 16;
  11.31, 85, 136, 210 bis, 261
  n. 110; *11.32,* 210; *11.34–35,*
  210; *11.35,* 195, 210 bis; *11.36,*
  66, 198, 210
12: 260 n. 91, 267 n. 63; *12.8,* 263
  n. 137, 267 n. 64; *12.10–12,* 267
  n. 64
Fragments (Thalheim): 2, 223; *4,*
  179; *22,* 169, 265 n. 40; *32,* 131

Isocrates (Isoc.)
  1: 1.36, 251 n. 50
  4: 4.39–40, 3; 4.45, 174; *4.78,* 235
  n. 62
  7: 7.38, 272 n. 55; *7.39–42,* 82, 235
  n. 62; *7.51,* 17, 46, 82; *7.67,* 240
  n. 172, 249 n. 3
  8: 8.129–30, 101, 103, 238 n. 116,
  247 n. 84; *8.133,* 100, 253 n. 90
  12: 12.12–13, 253 n. 90; *12.139–42,*
  253 n. 90; *12.144,* 235 n. 62
  15: 15.4–5, 101; *15.21,* 102, 194;
  15.23, 102; *15.24,* 76; *15.99,* 260
  n. 92; *15.164,* 102, 247 n. 86;
  15.224, 102, 253 n. 94; *15.230,*
  243 n. 28; *15.237,* 64, 243 n. 28;
  15.237–38, 243 n. 17; *15.238,*
  251 n. 45; *15.288,* 247 n. 84;
  15.299–301, 69, 102, 243 n. 24;
  15.300, 59; *15.308,* 103; *15.313–
  14,* 31; *15.313–15,* 46, 82, 103;
  15.314, 247 n. 86; *15.315,* 243
  n. 22; *15.315–19,* 253 n. 90;
  15.316, 264 n. 16; *15.317,* 264
  n. 16; *15.318,* 103, 249 n. 2
  16: 16.3, 41

17: 267 n. 74; 17.1, 182; 17.2, 182
   bis; 17.4, 182, 183; 17.6, 183;
   17.42, 141; 17.47, 183
18: 274 n. 87; 18.1, 274 n. 88;
   18.1–3, 274 n. 88; 18.2–3, 216;
   18.9–10, 36, 75; 18.10, 75, 250
   n. 20; 18.11, 198; 18.14, 250
   n. 20; 18.22, 264 n. 16; 18.27–
   28, 220; 18.34, 195; 18.43, 243
   n. 29; 18.52–54, 63, 246 n. 76;
   18.54, 64; 18.55, 63 bis; 18.55–
   56, 50; 18.64, 252 n. 71
19: 19.16, 195
20: 20.2–5, 131; 20.11, 249 n. 3;
   20.14, 60; 20.19–20, 239 n. 126
21: 21.5, 94; 21.7, 241 n. 184
fr. 11 Mathieu: 82
Istros
   FGrH 334 F 12: 49

Lycurgus (Lyc.)
   1: 1.3, 148 ter, 149, 150 bis, 243
   n. 28; 1.3–5, 144; 1.5–6, 157,
   262 n. 122; 1.8–9, 195, 196; 1.9,
   272 n. 63; 1.33, 196; 1.66, 198;
   1.114–25, 206; 1.124, 206;
   1.124–26, 64; 1.129, 195, 206;
   1.138, 257 n. 26; 1.146, 145, 194
   Fragments (Conomis): VI.1, 132; X–
   XI.2, 262 n. 122
Lysias (Lys.)
   1: 1.2, 195, 205; 1.15–16, 155; 1.16,
   66; 1.23–28, 268 n. 98; 1.28, 66;
   1.30, 201; 1.31, 201; 1.36, 234
   n. 50; 1.44, 36; 1.49, 205, 222
   2: 2.12, 119; 2.14, 119; 2.18–19, 3;
   2.22, 119
   3: 205; 3.6–9, 268 n. 98; 3.7, 257
   n. 18; 3.12–13, 269 n. 98; 3.44,
   274 n. 98; 3.45, 164
   4: 205
   6: 6.10, 196, 269 n. 15; 6.14, 272
   n. 55
   7: 7.1, 96–97, 102, 243 n. 30, 249
   n. 17, 250 n. 19; 7.21, 76; 7.40–
   41, 243 n. 30
   8: 8.18, 126

9: 259 n. 80; 9.7, 139; 9.10, 139;
   9.16, 139; 9.17, 139; 9.22, 139,
   263 n. 137
10: 10.1–2, 31; 10.1–3, 164; 10.6–
   20, 198; 10.7, 196; 10.13, 200,
   205; 10.15, 205; 10.15–20, 21,
   234 n. 40
12: 12.2, 156, 263 n. 135; 12.3,
   150; 12.5, 52, 72 bis, 244 n. 35;
   12.16–34, 156
13: 13.1–3, 156; 13.8–12, 249 n. 5;
   13.18–22, 249 n. 5; 13.41–42, 123;
   13.65, 260 n. 92; 13.85, 274 n. 93
14: 14.1, 148; 14.1–2, 148, 156;
   14.25, 88, 252 n. 61
17: 17.3, 241 n. 184
18: 18.1, 196; 18.9, 91, 243 n. 30;
   18.16, 140
19: 19.9, 140, 252 n. 71; 19.11, 92,
   140; 19.53, 196
20: 20.7, 250 n. 19; 20.10, 250
   n. 19; 20.12, 247 n. 89
21: 21.17, 252 n. 71
22: 22.3, 148, 151; 22.4, 152
23: 23.13, 273 n. 79
24: 24.1–3, 263 n. 137; 24.2, 157;
   24.17, 76
25: 25.1, 150; 25.2, 99; 25.3, 247
   n. 86, 249 n. 17; 25.6, 100; 25.8,
   100; 25.14, 99; 25.18, 99; 25.19,
   99, 243 n. 24, 248 n. 104, 249
   n. 2; 25.24, 100; 25.24–25, 100;
   25.26, 94, 99, 243 n. 30; 25.27,
   99, 100, 254 n. 96; 25.28, 100;
   25.29–30, 100; 25.30, 94, 111
26: 26.15, 263 n. 138
27: 27.1, 41, 92; 27.1–2, 92; 27.2,
   250 n. 19; 27.6, 250 n. 21; 27.12,
   178; 27.14, 250 n. 21; 27.14–15,
   153, 258 n. 55
28: 28.3, 254 n. 95; 28.5, 91; 28.6–
   7, 91
29: 29.1, 140, 153, 250 n. 21; 29.6,
   250 n. 21
30: 30.2, 197; 30.5, 197; 30.22, 92,
   259 n. 81; 30.34–35, 153, 258
   n. 55

Index of Ancient Citations

Lysias (Lys.) (cont.)
   31: 31.2, 152, 263 n. 138; 31.18–19, 125; 31.27, 196; 31.32, 153
   32: 266 n. 44; 32.1, 169, 170; 32.2, 170, 171; 32.4–5, 170; 32.9–10, 129; 32.10, 169; 32.11, 171; 32.11–18, 170; 32.12, 171, 266 n. 45; 32.12–17, 171; 32.17, 169; 32.18, 171; 32.19, 171; 32.22, 163
   Fragments (Thalheim): 1, 243 n. 17; 26a, 260 n. 92, 264 n. 16; 43, 129; 75, 268 n. 98 bis

Menander (Men.)
   Epikleros Test. K-T: 86
   Georgos (Georg.) fr. 1 Sandbach: 59, 112
   Monostichoi (Mon.) (Jaekel): 382, 271 n. 43; 603, 243 n. 22
   Theophoroumene (Theoph.) fr. 1.16–17 Sandbach: 242 n. 12
   fr. 545 K-T: 193, 200, 245 n. 64

Nicolaus Comicus (Nicol. Com.)
   fr. 1.1–2 K-A: 247 n. 84

Philemo Junior (Philem. Jun.)
   fr. 3 K-A: 152
Philippides (Philippid.)
   fr. 30 K-A: 243 n. 22
Philochorus (Philoch.)
   FGrH 328 F 119: 15
Phrynicus Comicus (Phryn. Com.)
   fr. 62 K-A: 255 n. 131
Plato (Pl.)
   Apology (Ap.): 22e6–23a2, 263 n. 137; 23e2–24a1, 263 n. 137
   Crito (Cri.): 44e–45a, 250 n. 22, 252 n. 66; 45a6–9, 250 n. 20; 50a5–54d1, 219
   Gorgias (Grg.): 515e2–7, 235 n. 61
   Laws (Lg.): 768a1–2, 133; 769d1–e2, 25; 858b2–c1, 235 n. 63; 875e2–876a6, 24; 876b1–c3, 24; 876b3–5, 63; 937d6–938c5, 50; 938a7–c5, 82

   Republic (R.): 235 n. 64; 340d1–341a9, 49, 242 n. 17; 405b6–c6, 83; 405c1–3, 244 n. 31; 545a2–3, 17, 162; 549c2–6, 161; 549d6–550a2, 162; 550b6–7, 162; 565b5–c4, 81, 254 n. 96; 575b7–8, 242 n. 16
   Theaetetus (Tht.): 172c3–173b3, 84
Plato Comicus (Pl. Com.)
   fr. 21 K-A: 199, 234 n. 38
   fr. 109 K-A: 255 n. 118
   fr. 110 K-A: 38
   fr. 239 K-A: 234 n. 38
Plutarch (Plu.)
   Comparison of Nicias and Crassus (Comp. Nic. et Crass.): 1.3, 76
   Life of Aristides (Arist.): 26.1, 250 n. 37, 251 n. 43
   Life of Cimon (Cim.): 10.8–9, 248 n. 105, 252 n. 65
   Life of Demosthenes (Dem.): 23.5, 149
   Life of Nicias (Nic.): 4.3, 253 n. 87; 4.5, 108; 4–5, 255 n. 131
   Life of Pericles (Per.): 37.3–4, 15
   Life of Solon (Sol.): 5.2, 239 n. 126; 18.5, 120, 121
   Life of Timoleon (Tim.): 37.1, 251 n. 39
   Moralia (Mor.): 154d11–e2, 121; 519b, 251 n. 39; 519b8–10, 244 n. 40; 541f2–6, 76
Ps.-Plutarch ([Plu.])
   Moralia (Mor.): 842a7–b2, 76
Pollux (Poll.)
   Onomasticon: 8.38, 29; 8.46, 238 n. 115; 8.47, 238 n. 117; 8.53, 136

Scholia
   VAld Ar. V. 191, 263 n. 1
Solon
   fr. 36 West: 121
   fr. 40b Ruschenbusch: 120
Sophocles (S.)
   Antigone (Ant.): 453–55, 232 n. 8; 454–55, 269 n. 15

Strabo
  6.1.8.37–40, 229 n. 3
Suda
  θ368.1–3, 243 n. 22, 251 n. 41

Teleclides (Telecl.)
  fr. 2 K-A: 243n. 29, 245n. 59
  fr. 44 K-A: 255n. 131
Theophrastus (Thphr.)
  Characters (Char.): 6.8, 38, 271
    n. 38; 26.5, 82; 26.5–7, 251
    n. 48; 29.4a, 149
  Laws (Lg.): fr. 4 a, b Sz-M, 82
Theopompus (Theopomp. Hist.)
  FGrH 115 F 110: 50, 52, 242 n. 16,
    251 n. 39
  FGrH 115 F 281: 67, 105, 242
    nn. 12, 16, 243 n. 23, 244 n. 38,
    250 n. 34
Thucydides (Th.)
  1.77.1, 17, 68, 248 nn. 104, 107;
  2.37.3, 119, 256 n. 4, 269 n. 15;
  2.39.4, 23; 2.40.2, 248 n. 99;
  2.60.5, 153, 263 n. 131; 2.63.2,
  248 n. 99; 3.46.4, 272 n. 44;
  5.90, 272 n. 44; 6.53, 254 n. 107;
  6.53.2, 250 n. 37; 8.1, 254
  n. 107

Xenophon (X.)
  Hellenica (HG): 1.7.2, 88 bis; 2.3.11,
    81; 2.3.11–12, 249 n. 4; 2.3.12,
    52, 59, 72, 80–81, 99, 247 n. 86;
    2.3.22, 72; 2.3.38, 81; 2.4.8–10,
    249 n. 5; 2.4.19, 85
  Memorabilia (Mem.): 2.9.1, 82, 243
    n. 28, 249 n. 17; 2.9.1–2, 243
    n. 22; 2.9.1–8, 84, 86–87; 2.9.2,
    262 n. 116; 2.9.4, 252 n. 53;
    2.9.5, 252 n. 58; 2.9.7, 262
    n. 116; 2.9.8, 242 n. 12; 3.5.16–
    17, 17, 83; 3.7, 85; 4.4.11, 243
    n. 17
  Oeconomicus (Oec.): 11.21, 85;
    11.21–25, 84; 11.23–24, 86;
    11.25, 86
  Symposium (Smp.): 3.9, 84; 4.29, 84;
    4.29–33, 84 bis; 4.30, 84; 4.31,
    84 bis, 85 bis; 4.32, 84 bis, 85
    bis; 4.33, 85 bis
Ps.-Xenophon ([X.])
  Constitution of Athens (Ath.): 1.9, 79;
    1.10, 45; 1.13, 79, 85; 1.14, 80,
    90, 242 n. 7, 248 nn. 104, 106;
    1.16, 29, 80; 1.17, 80; 1.18, 80,
    84; 2.10, 79; 2.18, 112; 3.1, 45;
    3.2, 45, 105; 3.6, 45

General Index

actions, legal: barring, 212–18; choice of, 26, 130, 131, 209; with financial rewards, 138–43; against legal abuse, 30–32; private vs. public, 26–30, 33. *See also under specific actions*
Adeimantus, 161–62
adultery, 237 n. 110
Aeschines, 150–51, 153, 157, 207–8
Aeschines the Socratic, 242–43 n. 17
agents, legal, 38
aggression, 4, 145, 161–66, 191–92
agōn, 35, 163, 213
agora, 21, 44, 143, 164, 198
akindunos, 128, 134, 136, 210, 258 n. 43, 261 n. 110
akribeia, 25, 200, 204, 207, 219, 235 n. 62, 271 nn. 42, 43, 272 nn. 44, 58
Alcibiades, 198, 245 n. 48
Alcibiades, the younger, 88, 147
altruism, 120, 121–22, 124, 257 n. 18
amateurism, legal, 37–38, 203–24; and contracts, 218–22; before homicide courts, 205; *idiōtai* and, 203–5; and legal research, 203–4; and literacy, 200, 204; and procedural arguments, 208–18; *rhētores* and, 205–8; and wills, 222
Amnesty of 403 B.C., 258 n. 50
anakrisis, 27, 30, 213, 236 nn. 82, 84
Androcles, 187–89
anthropology, legal, 8–12, 263 n. 3
antidosis, 46, 75, 79, 101, 238–39 n. 125
apagōgē, 122, 211, 238 n. 117
apographē, 29, 138, 139–40, 142–43, 260 n. 92
Apollodorus, 96, 140, 155, 173, 176–77, 183–84, 192, 206, 216–17, 260 n. 83
apophasis, 233 n. 30
apragmōn, 55, 66, 88, 95, 97, 108, 113, 150, 165–66, 192, 248 n. 99, 253 n. 87
arbitration: private, 27, 165, 170, 172; public, 27, 45, 46, 165, 198, 241 n. 178
Archedemus, 87–89, 252 n. 64
archives. *See* laws: archiving of
archons, 18
Ardettos Hill, 269 n. 6
Areopagus, Council of, 14, 20, 82, 96, 205, 211, 233 n. 30, 272 nn. 55, 58

General Index

Arethusius, 177, 266 n. 56
Arginusae, battle of, 88
Aristides, 111
Aristocrates, 151, 158
aristocrats, 35, 82–90, 122
Aristogeiton, 56–59, 63, 68, 92, 95, 97, 143, 149, 152, 245 n. 60, 263 n. 139, 264 n. 18
Ariston, 131, 204
Aristophanes, 4, 5, 16, 53–56, 61–62, 63, 145–47
Aristophon of Azenia, 137
Aristotle, 4, 77; on *epieikeia*, 25; on juries, 24; on laws and law making, 24–25
Artemo, 187
ass, shadow of an, 160
Assembly, 3, 15, 16, 31, 45, 90, 137, 152, 194, 209; composition of, 18; as court, 21; payment for attendance at, 40; and popular courts, 20–21; powers of, 18; quorum at, 21
Athenogenes, 221–22
atimia, 26, 28, 29, 32, 35, 134, 135, 137, 143, 237 nn. 98, 101, 238 n. 122
autarkeia, 83, 84, 252 n. 57

Baker, R., 2
bankers, 168, 180–84, 186, 267 n. 69
barring actions, 212–18
Bdelycleon, 107, 109, 112, 114
bios, 65
blackmail, legal, 37, 50, 51, 55, 62, 75–77, 96, 108, 135, 142, 143, 154
Boeotia, 251 n. 39
boētheia, 132, 148, 149
Bonner, R., and G. Smith, 139
Bosporus, 182
boulē, 18. *See also* Council
boulomenos, ho, 34, 118, 120, 122, 261 n. 102
bribery, 31, 76, 92, 135
Burkert, W., 51

Callias, 85, 113, 114
Callicles, 175–76
Callimachus, 63
Carion, 54, 62
Carter, L., 66
Cephalus, 137
Chairephon, 111, 242–43 n. 17
charis, 41, 74, 87, 89, 93, 101, 167, 177, 184, 185, 240 n. 162, 252 nn. 65, 71, 264 n. 18
Charmides, son of Aristoteles, 251 n. 51
Charmides, son of Glaukon, 84–85, 86, 88, 89, 251 n. 51
Charondas, 52, 244 n. 39
Chersonese, 113
children, legal status of, 25, 123, 128. *See also* orphans
chorēgia, 33, 125, 133, 238–39 n. 125
citizenship: guarding of, 31, 74, 134, 138, 139, 155, 179–80; law of 451/0 B.C., 15; models of, 68–69. *See also atimia*
civic identity, 48, 59, 67–71, 74
class: conflict, 72–73; Greek terminology of, 74, 78; labor and, 95–96; leisure, 73, 74; middle, 74; and politics, 4, 74; tension, 73, 74, 78, 106, 109, 116. *See also* elite, the
Cleisthenes, 14, 18, 118, 178
Cleon, 55, 106, 107, 108, 111, 112, 113, 115, 149
Clytemnestra, 168
Cohen, D., 24, 25, 162, 191
community, ideals of, 161, 167, 190–91
Comon, 171
competition, 4, 35. *See also agōn*
conspiracy, legal, 37, 38–39
contentiousness, 8, 17, 46, 157, 161–66, 191
contracts, 186–90, 213, 218–22, 274 n. 92
cooperation, 160–66, 167, 191–92
Council, 16, 31, 45, 152, 153, 194, 262 n. 125; composition of, 18; as court, 21; powers of, 18; under the Thirty, 81, 99
councilmen, 15, 18–19, 152–53, 262 n. 125

General Index

countersuit, 273 n. 73
court buildings, 44
court capacity, 44–46
court days, 19, 44
court fees, 28–29, 33
court secretary, 200–201
courts, homicide, 20, 205, 272 n. 58. *See also* Areopagus, Council of
courts, popular, 2, 19–21; and Assembly, 20–21; composition of, 19; and the elite, 17–18, 34, 75–77, 83–84; jurisdiction of, 15, 20; and law making, 20, 21–22; and politics, 42–43; and sykophancy, 68, 78–81, 90–94, 100, 101, 102, 106–11, 114; the Thirty and, 72. *See also* juries; jurors
criminals, 20
Crito, 86–89, 252 n. 66
cross-examination, 28, 236 n. 88
Ctesiphon, 157, 207–8
curse tablets, 36
Cyrene, 82

Dareius, 189–90
decrees, 15, 21–22. *See also graphē paranomōn*
defendants, 26, 28
Delphinion, 205
demarch, 178, 179
deme, 178
deme judges, 27, 33, 45, 164, 236 n. 82
demesmen, 168, 178–80
democracy, Athenian: critics of, 4, 6–7, 17, 24–25, 69, 78, 79–82; principles of, 24–25 (*see also* egalitarianism; freedom; ideology, democratic); and sykophancy, 7–8, 67–68, 78–90, 105, 242 n. 11, 251 n. 39
demography, Athenian, 18
dēmos, 14, 78, 104, 105, 250 n. 29; and laws, 22; and popular courts, 20, 34. *See also* courts, popular; jurors
Demos, 115

Demosthenes, 56–59, 125–26, 131–33, 152, 153, 157, 192, 207–8
desertion, 134, 147
diadikasia, 168, 213, 214, 215
diallagē, 172
diamarturia, 212–16, 273 nn. 77, 80, 274 nn. 83, 85
diapsēphisis of 346/5 B.C., 142, 179, 260 n. 91, 267 n. 63
dikaia, ta, 41, 195, 208, 210, 215, 218, 219, 275 n. 104
dikai emmēnoi, 45–46
Dikaiopolis, 54, 68, 110, 141
Dikaios, 54, 62, 145–47
dikastēria, 14. *See also* courts, popular
dikastēs, 19, 20, 234 n. 32. *See also* jurors
dikē, 26, 209, 210
dikē aikeias, 31, 45, 131
dikē blabēs, 268 n. 85, 274 n. 97
dikē emporikē, 30, 45, 186, 187, 190, 213, 220, 241, 268 n. 85
dikē epitropēs, 128–29, 257 n. 34
dikē exoulēs, 28
dikē kakēgorias, 31
dikē kakotechniōn, 30
dikē lipomarturiou, 30
dikē phonou, 211
dikē pseudomarturiōn, 30, 214, 217
dikorrhaphein, 65
Diodorus, 207
Diogeiton, 170
Dionysodorus, 189
disfranchisement. *See atimia*
disputes, 167, 264 n. 19
disputing behavior, 17, 36–39, 75–76, 162–66, 191–92, 268 n. 97
dokimasia, 19, 98, 134–35, 137, 150, 152, 258 n. 49, 262 n. 125, 263 n. 137
Dover, K. J., 122
dowries, 168
Draco, 21, 256 n. 6

echinos, 27, 198, 236 n. 84, 270 n. 29, 271 n. 38
egalitarianism, 34, 144, 193, 199, 239 n. 127

General Index

Egypt, 189, 190
eisangelia, 26, 90, 122, 127, 137, 143, 144, 209, 259 n. 81; as *akindunos*, 128, 136–37; against arbitrators, 238 n. 111; against generals, 19, 134, 136–37; on behalf of heiresses, 122, 257 n. 37; on behalf of orphans, 122, 128, 129, 210, 257 n. 37; against *rhētores*, 209, 238 n. 116; against sykophants, 31
eisphora, 41, 73, 75, 104, 254 n. 95
ekklēsia, 18. See also Assembly
Eleven, the, 20
elite, the: circumvention of courts by, 76, 93–94; legal advantages of, 33–34, 38, 76–77, 193; as leisure class, 73; as litigants, 32–34, 199–200; as litigating class, 33, 238 n. 123; litigation concerns of, 75–76; and liturgies, 33, 39, 73, 74, 75, 93, 238–39 n. 125; political diversity of, 74, 89, 116; and popular courts, 17–18, 34, 75–77, 83–84; as readers, 77, 78, 116; as victims of sykophancy, 7–8, 75–77, 78, 81, 82–90; and wealth, 39, 73, 75, 183
empire, Athenian: and class relations, 74; rising litigation under, 14–15; and sykophancy, 53, 68, 79–80, 106, 107–8, 249 n. 2, 254 nn. 107, 110
endeixis, 30, 56, 122, 204, 211 bis, 238 n. 117, 262 n. 124
Engel, D., 9, 11
enmity, 124, 148, 154–59, 162–63, 179, 183, 184, 263 n. 137
envy, 36, 77, 78, 157, 180, 263 n. 137
ephetai, 233 n. 30
Ephialtes, 14, 82
Epichares, 91, 97, 128, 141, 142, 148, 150, 201, 204, 211, 263 n. 136
Epicrates, 92
Epidaurus, 111, 114
epieikeia, 25, 271 n. 43
epiklēroi, 129, 168
epimelētēs, 146, 150
epōbelia, 29, 30, 129, 237 n. 99
eranos, 126

Erasinides, 88
Eratosthenes, 156
ergastēria, 65
Ergocles, 90–91
ergon, 65
erōtēsis, 28, 236 n. 88
Euathlus, 109, 110, 245 n. 48, 255 n. 123
euergetēs, 147
Euergus, 185
eunoia, 132
Eupolis, 108, 110–11
euthudikia, 213, 215 bis, 216, 273 n. 77
euthunai, 19, 55, 91, 98, 134, 135–36, 137, 141, 151, 152, 153, 156, 258 n. 52
Euthycles, 151, 158
Euxenippus, 92–93, 209–10
Euxitheus: Athenian, 97, 179; Mytilenean, 211–12
expertise, legal, 37, 193; and education, 202; and laws, 24, 197–202; and literacy, 199–200. See also amateurism, legal

fairness. See *dikaia, ta*; justice
family, litigation within, 168–73
feuding, 163
fig, 49, 52, 55, 60–61, 83, 113
foreigners, 180; legal status of, 25; sykophancy against, 68
forensic oratory. See oratory, forensic
Forer, L., 1
forgery: of documents, 37, 223; of laws, 197, 199
Four Hundred, the, 22, 74, 99, 249 n. 1
fraud, 186–90
freedom: personal, 23; of speech, 98–103, 105
Friedman, L., 2
friendship. See *philia*
funeral oratory, 68, 69, 70, 200

Galanter, M., 8–9, 11
generals, 19; subject to *eisangelia*, 19, 134, 136–37; and popular courts, 42, 43

311

General Index

Gorgias, 242–43 n. 17
gossip, 23
grain, 15, 45, 186, 189, 190
graphē, 26, 151, 210, 211, 257–58 n. 39, 262 n. 121
graphē adikōs heirchthēnai, 31, 122, 130
graphē dōroxenias, 31
graphē hubreōs, 122, 130, 131–33, 177, 241 n. 181
graphē nomon mē epitēdeion theinai, 22, 206
graphē paranomōn, 19, 22, 134, 137–38, 151, 206–8
graphē pseudengraphēs, 122
graphē pseudoklēteias, 30, 32, 122, 130, 266 n. 56
graphē sukophantias, 31, 32, 238 n. 115
graphē xenēs enguēs, 138, 142
graphē xenias, 31, 138, 139, 142, 260 n. 83
Greenhouse, C., 9–10, 11, 17
guardians, 128–29, 168, 170, 257 n. 34

Harpalus, 152
Harris, E., 195
Harrison, A. R. W., 29, 216
Harvey, D., 49, 50, 67, 139
Hedrick, C., 199
Hegemon of Thasos, 198
Heliastic oath, 40, 194–95, 201–2
Henderson, J., 105, 115
Herman, G., 191
hēsuchia, 82, 87
hetaireia, 96
homicide. See courts, homicide
homosexuality, 23, 96
honor, 34–36, 154, 161–63
hubris, 35. See also graphē hubreōs
Hunter, V., 69
Hyperbolus, 108, 245 n. 48

ideology, democratic, 104, 105. See also civic identity
idiōtēs, 153, 203–5, 207, 208
impeachment. See eisangelia

impiety, 43
indictment. See graphē
informers, 143
inheritance, 33, 72, 168, 212–16, 222–23. See also diadikasia; diamarturia
Ischomachus, 85–86, 89
ischurizesthai, 209, 219 bis, 222, 274 n. 93
Isocrates, 4, 31–32, 46, 69–70, 77, 79, 100–103, 111, 242–43 n. 17
isonomia, 14, 34

juries: selection of, 19; size of, 19, 26; social composition of, 20, 36, 233 n. 28
jurors: bribery of, 31, 238 n. 112; and charis, 41 (see also charis); and envy, 36, 77, 78, 180; and euthunai, 20; and Heliastic oath, 40, 194–95, 201–2; identification plaques of, 3; and laws, 40–41, 198–202; and norms, 41, 42–43, 194–96, 270 n. 19; payment of, 14, 19, 29, 40, 46, 85; and politicians, 46, 137; as poor men, 106; power of, 43; qualifications of, 19; roles of, 39–43; and thorubos, 42. See also courts, popular
justice, 43, 194–96, 201–2. See also dikaia, ta

kairos, 271 n. 43
kanōn, 195, 208, 272 n. 63
kathairō, 51, 56
kerdos, 83, 140, 181
kinaidos, 96, 248 n. 110
kindunos, 35, 36, 76, 144, 148, 215
klepsudra, 27, 61
knights, 107–8
kolax, 87, 242 n. 12
kukaō, 51
kurbis, 271 n. 40
kurios: contract as, 219; demos as, 234 n. 50; law as, 22, 195; master of household as, 23, 168

Laches, 114
Lacritus, 187–88, 220–21

General Index

lambanō, 251–52, n. 53
law making, 21–22
laws: accretive nature of, 23; archiving of, 21, 197–98, 199, 220, 271 nn. 35, 39; citation of, 30–31, 200, 203, 271 n. 39; common, 195, 207; confidence in, 197–98; and contracts, 189, 218–20, 274 n. 92; and decrees, 21–22; evolution of, 18; as footholds for litigation, 15; in forensic oratory, 5, 40–41, 195–96, 198, 200–218; forgery of, 197, 199; and Heliastic oath, 194–95, 201–2; and justice, 194–96, 201–2; and the lawgiver, 196; and law making, 21–22; and legal expertise, 24, 197–202; and norms, 41, 196; as partisan instruments, 198, 201; and politics, 42–43; preciseness of (*see akribeia*); and private sphere, 23; reforms of, in 410–399 B.C., 21–22; and rhetoric, 200–202; and "rule of law," 22–23, 195–96; and sexual behavior, 23; unwritten, 196, 269 n. 15; vagueness of, 23–24, 196; and writing, 197–98, 198–200
legal excess and abuse, 3, 6, 12, 225–26; and civic identity, 48–71; class and perception of, 73–78; in elite writers, 78–90; and legal expertise, 193–224; measures against, 28–32; and private suits, 160–92; in public discourse, 90–117; and public suits, 134–59. See also litigiousness; sykophancy
legalities, 208–18
legality, 40, 195, 269 n. 11
legal system, 2
Leocrates, 144, 157
leptos, 199, 204, 270 n. 32
Lewis, D., 138
literacy, 77, 199–200, 204, 222, 271 n. 38
litigation: and aristocratic values, 82–90; and Athenian empire, 14–15; changes in, during fifth century, 2–3, 14–18; and class conflict, 72–117; and community ideals, 160–92; as contest, 35, 163; dirty tricks in, 36–39; and disputes, 167, 264 n. 19; and the elite, 32–34, 75–77 (*see also* elite, the); gamesmanship in, 36–39; ideals and realities of, 37–39; in practice, 32–47 (*see also* disputing behavior); rules of, 18, 25–32; and social relations, 17, 167–92; as status competition, 35–36; as theater, 39–40; and urbanization, 232 n. 14; and the weak, 119–30
litigation levels, 8; in Athens, 14–18, 43–47, 241 n. 184; in modern Western democracies, 231 n. 43
litigiousness, 1–13, 227, 231 n. 39; anthropologists on, 8–12; as cultural self-representation, 10, 11; outsiders and, 8, 9–10; a problematic term, 12, 231–32 n. 47; in the U.S., 1–2, 8–12. See also legal excess and abuse; sykophancy
liturgies, 33, 41, 73, 74, 75, 104, 163, 173, 238–39 n. 125; avoidance of, 39, 75, 76, 93, 183. See also *antidosis*; *chorēgia*; *eisphora*; trierarchy
loans: maritime, 181, 186–90, 220–21, 267 n. 69; personal, 126, 177, 181, 183–84
Lofberg, J. O., 6–7, 36, 42, 139, 140
logistai, 135
logographers, 5, 16, 27, 33, 38, 202, 203, 226
loidoria, 157
Lycophron, 210
Lycurgus, 76, 144, 150, 157
Lysias, 156

MacDowell, D., 146
magistrates, 15, 18–19, 134; as conveners of courts, 20; as receivers of complaints, 27
Maine, H. S., 42
manliness, 35, 123, 160–66, 264 n. 16. See also honor
Marathōnomachai, 109, 110, 112
Maricas, 108
masses, 74

313

General Index

mēchanaomai, 66
meddlesomeness, 53, 124, 145, 150–53, 155, 161. See also *polupragmōn*
Megara, 68, 112, 141, 160, 248 n. 108
Meidias, 23, 38, 97–98, 125–26, 131–33, 192, 209
mēnutēs, 143, 144, 145
mēnutron, 260 n. 94
metics, 180, 189; legal status of, 25, 123, 256 n. 16; as sykophants, 32, 56, 245 n. 53
Metroön, 21, 197–98, 199, 200, 271 nn. 35, 39
Micon, 97, 141
Miltiades, 111
misthophora, 92
misthos, 89, 95
moicheia, 237 n. 110
moneylenders, 184–86
monthly suits, 45–46, 186, 241 n. 180
Mytilene, 211

Nausicrates, 187
Neaira, 96, 155, 162, 206
neighbors, 165, 168, 174–77, 178
Nicias, 108, 113
Nicobulus, 185–86
Nicostratus, 176–77, 266 n. 56
nomothetai, 21, 22

oath challenge, 264 n. 11
Ober, J., 22, 74, 101, 103–4
Odeion, 44
oikeiotēs, 167, 176, 183, 265 n. 24
oikos, 170
Old Oligarch, 44–45, 77, 79–80, 81, 90, 105
oligarchs, 91, 99, 100, 103, 196. See also democracy, Athenian: critics of; Four Hundred, the; Thirty, the
Olympiodorus, 171
orator. See *rhētōr, rhētores*
oratory, forensic, 4–6, 16, 34; character in, 41, 196; contracts in, 218–22; extralegal arguments in, 40–43; facts in, 40; financial relations in, 167, 180–81; hearsay in, 28; laws in, 5, 40–41, 195–96, 198, 200–218; metalegal concerns in, 39, 227, 240 n. 147; procedural arguments in, 208–18; social relations in, 167; social types in, 66; witness testimony in, 41, 203
oratory, funeral, 68, 69, 70, 200
orphans, 127–30, 173, 210, 257 nn. 32, 34, 37
Osborne, R., 7, 50, 64–65, 128, 139, 142
outsiders: and Athenian civic identity, 59, 67; and litigiousness, 8, 9–10; and the popular courts, 60, 187–89. See also *under* sykophant(s)

Palladion, 272 n. 58
Pamphilus, 189
Pantainetus, 185
paragraphē, 30, 187, 188, 212–13, 216–18, 220, 237 n. 99, 268 nn. 81, 85, 273 n. 77, 274 nn. 83, 87–89
parakatabolē, 30
parasitos, 242 n. 12
paraskeuē, 38–39, 66, 149
parastasis, 28, 32, 237 n. 95
Parker, R., 52
Parmeniscus, 189
Pasicles, 173
Pasio, 180, 182–83, 183–84
patronage, legal, 122, 122–23, 129–30
Peisetairos, 54, 62, 65, 113
Peloponnesian War, 74, 85, 91, 111, 141
penalties: imposed on defendants, 26, 28; imposed on prosecutors, 26, 29–30, 64, 136–37, 143, 208, 237 n. 98
Pericles, 14, 15, 19, 111
Pericles, the younger, 82
periergos, 51
Persian Wars, 109, 110, 111, 251 n. 40
Phaeacia, 83
pharmakos, 51, 55

General Index

Phaselis, 187, 188
phasis, 53, 138, 139, 140–42, 142–43, 238 n. 117, 244 n. 44, 257 n. 32, 260 nn. 86, 92
philanthrōpia, 57, 144, 196
philia, 89, 126, 127, 150, 167, 169, 171, 173–87 passim, 190, 264 n. 18, 264–65 n. 21
Philip of Macedon, 52, 154
Philo, 152
Philocleon, 106, 109, 114
philodēmos, 150
philodikos, 68, 164, 221, 248 n. 107
philonikia, 157, 162. *See also* contentiousness
philopolis, 144, 145, 147, 150, 263 n. 131
philopragmōn, 144
philotimia, 162
Phokides, 97
Phormio, 93, 97, 173, 216–17
piezō, 102, 254 n. 95
pinakia, 3, 229 n. 10
Piraeus, 80, 98, 189
pistis, 181, 182, 183, 187. *See also* trust
plaintiff, 26
Plato, 4, 77, 242–43 n. 17; on juries, 24; on law making, 24–25; on legal abuse, 81–82; on payment of jurors, 235 n. 61
plattō, 66
politicians, 15, 42, 43, 46. *See also* generals; *rhētōr, rhētores*
politics, 34, 114, 137–38; and law, 42–43
poludikein, 81, 82
polupragmōn, 51, 66, 146, 147, 243 n. 28
Polyeuctus, 209
Polyeuktes, 128
Poneropolis, 52
ponēros. *See under* sykophant(s)
popular courts. *See* courts, popular
Posner, R., 10
praotēs, 92, 196
prayers, judicial, 36
pretrial procedures, 26–27

privacy, 23, 165, 170, 172
private sphere, 23, 25, 165, 171, 172, 173
private suits, 26–30, 33, 160–92
probolē, 209; against hubris, 132; against sykophants, 31, 32, 238 nn. 115, 118
professionalism, legal. *See* expertise, legal
prosecution, volunteer, 26; outside Athens, 118, 260 n. 93; on behalf of the city, 133–59; and egalitarianism, 144, 261 n. 98; enmity in, 154–59, 263 n. 137; financial rewards of, 138–43, 153–54; growth of, under democracy, 15, 118; motivations for, 139, 147–59; origins of, 256 n. 6; and politics, 137–38; and the public interest, 121, 131, 133, 256 n. 7; scope of, 119; under Solon, 120–22; and third-party suits, 119–30; vengeance in, 154–59; by victims, 130–33
prosecutor, volunteer: as aggressor, 144, 145; as *apragmōn*, 150; as avenger, 151, 154–57; concerns about, 143–59; councilman as, 152–53; as friend of the demos, 150; as meddler, 124, 145, 150–53, 155; as neutral agent, 157–59; officeholder as, 151–53; as patriot, 148–50; subject to penalties (*see under* penalties); *rhētōr* as, 153, 158; self-justification of, 143–59; as soldier, 148–49; *sunēgoros* (state prosecutor) as, 152; as sykophant, 50, 53, 114; as venal, 153–54, 155; as watchdog, 15, 88, 149, 159. *See also under* sykophant(s)
prostatēs: as civic leader, 146, 147, 150, 262 n. 117; as patron of metic, 123, 256 n. 16
prostitution, 23, 39, 96
Protagoras, 244 n. 39
proxenoi, 237
prutaneia, 28–29, 80, 237 n. 96
public discourse, 77

315

General Index

public suits, 26–30, 33, 118–59. *See also* prosecution, volunteer
Pythodorus, 183

quarrelsomeness, 161, 164. *See also* contentiousness
qui tam prosecutions, 230 n. 22, 260 n. 93, 261 n. 96

reconciliation, 172–73, 266 n. 48
reputation, 34–36, 41, 161, 182
research, legal, 203–4
rhētōr, rhētores, 140, 164, 204, 261 n. 99, 262 n. 119; subject to *eisangelia,* 209, 238 n. 116; subject to *graphē paranomōn,* 19, 134, 137–38, 206–8; as legal amateur, 203, 205–8; as legislator, 197; number of, 19; and *phasis,* 143; as sykophant, 55, 56, 67, 95, 99, 101, 238 n. 116, 246 n. 72; as volunteer prosecutor, 153, 158
rhetoric, 200–202. *See also* oratory, forensic
Rhodes, 189, 190

sanides, 64, 197
Sausage-seller, 55, 107, 108, 111
seiō, 51
self-help, legal, 2, 26, 30, 31, 33, 36
sexual behavior, 23, 39, 96, 237 n. 110
shame, 35
Sinclair, R., 139
slander, 31, 35, 39, 50, 55, 91
slaves, 80, 85; legal status of, 25; public, 20; torture of, 25
Socrates, 43, 83, 85, 86, 87, 102, 161, 242–43 n. 17, 252 n. 66
Solon, 21, 31, 111, 120–22, 124
Sopaeus, son of, 182–83
sophists, 16, 50, 202
sources, ancient, 4–6, 39, 77–78
Sparta, 17, 23, 69, 162, 206
speech writers. *See* logographers
status, 34, 35, 122, 123
statute of limitation, 217
Stephanus, 96, 143, 155, 162
Stoa Poikilē, 144
stratēgos, 19. *See also* generals

Strato, 97, 98, 125–26
strephō, 51, 54
summons, 26, 30, 60
sunēgoros, 255–56 n. 2; as state prosecutor, 118, 135, 148–49, 152, 263 n. 139; as supporting speaker, 27, 30, 37, 38, 50, 92, 93, 97, 126–27, 129, 151, 155, 170, 207, 217, 236 n. 86, 257 n. 25
sungnōmē, 196
sykophancy, 3, 12, 48–71; activities associated with, 50; and Athenian empire, 53, 68, 79–80, 106, 107–8, 249 n. 2, 254 nn. 107, 110; and civic identity, 48, 67–71, 117; and class conflict, 72–117; in comedy, 53–56, 61–62, 104–16, 145–47; and democracy, 7–8, 67–68, 78–90, 105, 242 n. 11, 251 n. 39; against the elite, 7–8, 75–77, 78, 81, 82–90; in elite writers, 78–90; etymology of term, 49; and financial rewards, 139–43; flexibility of term, 50; against foreigners, 68; legal actions against, 31–32, 64; no legal definition of, 238 n. 114; in oratory, 56–59, 62–63, 90–104; and *phasis,* 140–41; and politics, 114; and popular courts, 68, 78–81, 90–94, 100, 101, 102, 106–11, 114; punning on term, 55, 60–61, 62–63, 113, 245 n. 64, 246 n. 74; and social labeling, 59–63; and the Thirty, 52, 72, 80–81, 99, 223; in Thurii, 52–53; and treason charge, 106, 254 n. 107; victims of, 78–79, 96–98, 112–14; as "work," 51, 57, 65–66, 67, 81, 95–96, 112, 147, 247 nn. 86–91. *See also* legal excess and abuse; litigiousness
sykophant(s), 3; as anti-Athenian, 50–51, 69; and *apragmōn,* 66, 165–66; Aristogeiton as, 56–59; Athenians as, 79–80; as cannibal, 58, 245 n. 59; Cleon as, 55, 106, 107, 112, 113, 115; as a *genos,* 64; metic as, 32, 56, 245 n. 53; as outsider, 48, 50–52, 53, 57–58, 68, 78, 188; as

316

polluted, 51, 54–55, 59; as *ponēros*, 78, 79, 87, 101, 102, 112, 113, 175; as poor man, 61, 94–95; private prosecutor as, 50; as prostitute, 96; as restless force, 51, 54, 57, 62; *rhētōr* as, 55, 56, 67, 95, 99, 101, 238 n. 116, 246 n. 72; as scapegoat, 51–53, 68; as social type, 60, 66, 243 n. 20; sophist as, 50; *sunēgoros* (supporting speaker) as, 50; volunteer prosecutor as, 50, 53, 114; witness as, 50
symposium, 84
Syracuse, 251 n. 39

Taillardat, J., 113
Tanagra, 58
tarattō, 51
taxation. *See eisphora*; liturgies
technē, 65
technicalities, 208–18
Thargelia, 51–52
Thebes, 54
Theocrines, 97, 128, 141, 143, 148, 150, 151, 201, 204, 211, 257 n. 31, 263 n. 136
Theomnestus, 155, 162, 206
Theophrastus, 136
Theopompus, 210
Theramenes, 81
Theseus, 34, 251 n. 41
thesmothetai, 18, 21, 22, 31, 210
third-party suits, 119–30, 148; under the classical democracy, 122–30; on behalf of friends, 126–27; on behalf of heiresses, 122, 129; and legal capacity, 123; on behalf of orphans, 127–30; and the public interest, 121, 256 n. 7; under Solon, 120–22; on behalf of strangers, 124–26; *sunēgoria* as alternative to, 126–27. *See also* prosecution, volunteer
Thirty, the, 22, 74, 77, 85, 98, 116, 156, 197, 241 n. 184, 258 n. 50; and judicial murder, 43; and sykophants, 52, 72, 80–81, 99, 223
thorubos, 42, 63, 240 n. 157
Thucydides, son of Melesias, 110

Thurii, 52–53, 244 nn. 39, 40, 251 n. 39
Timarchus, 96, 135, 155
timē, 35. *See also* honor
timēsis, 28, 35
Timocrates, 207
timōria, 35, 154, 161. *See also* vengeance
Timotheus, 184
Todd, S., 42
trade, 15, 30, 45
traders, 180–81, 186–90
treason, 134, 144; as sykophantic charge, 106, 254 n. 107
trierarchy, 33, 176, 238–39 n. 125
trust, 167, 171, 181, 182, 183, 187, 190

vengeance, 35, 133, 148, 161–63; in third-party suits, 120, 123; in volunteer prosecution for the city, 151, 154–59
verdicts, enforcement of, 28, 29
violence, 36, 192, 268 n. 98. *See also* aggression
volunteer prosecution. *See* prosecution, volunteer
volunteer prosecutor. *See* prosecutor, volunteer

war tax. *See eisphora*
wealth, concealment of, 39, 75, 183
wiliness, 4, 36–39
wills, 222–23
witnesses, 27–28, 32, 37, 38, 41, 50, 60, 64, 203, 212, 220, 240 n. 160. *See also dikē pseudomarturiōn*
women, legal status of, 25, 123, 171
writing: in arbitration, 27, 241 n. 178; and circulation of texts, 77; in complaints, 27; and contracts, 186–87, 213, 218–19; and laws, 197, 198–200; and public records, 168; of speeches, 38, 202, 271 n. 38 (*see also* logographers); verdicts not recorded in, 64; in witness testimony, 27. *See also* forgery; literacy

xenoi, 25. *See also* foreigners
Xenophon, 4, 77, 80–81, 82, 84–89, 99

ANCIENT SOCIETY AND HISTORY

The series Ancient Society and History offers books, relatively brief in compass, on selected topics in the history of ancient Greece and Rome, broadly conceived, with a special emphasis on comparative and other nontraditional approaches and methods. The series, which includes both works of synthesis and works of original scholarship, is aimed at the widest possible range of specialist and nonspecialist readers.

Published in the Series:
Eva Cantarella, *Pandora's Daughters: The Role and Status of Women in Greek and Roman Antiquity*
Alan Watson, *Roman Slave Law*
John E. Stambaugh, *The Ancient Roman City*
Géza Alfödy, *The Social History of Rome*
Giovanni Comotti, *Music in Greek and Roman Culture*
Christian Habicht, *Cicero the Politician*
Mark Golden, *Children and Childhood in Classical Athens*
Thomas Cole, *The Origins of Rhetoric in Ancient Greece*
Maurizio Bettini, *Anthropology and Roman Culture: Kinship, Time, Images of the Soul*
Suzanne Dixon, *The Roman Family*
Stephen L. Dyson, *Community and Society in Roman Italy*
Tim G. Parkin, *Demography and Roman Society*
Alison Burford, *Land and Labor in the Greek World*
Alan Watson, *International Law in Archaic Rome: War and Religion*
Stephen H. Lonsdale, *Dance and Ritual Play in Greek Religion*
J. Donald Hughes, *Pan's Travail: Environmental Problems of the Ancient Greeks and Romans*
C. R. Whittaker, *Frontiers of the Roman Empire: A Social and Economic Study*
Pericles Georges, *Barbarian Asia and the Greek Experience*
Nancy Demand, *Birth, Death, and Motherhood in Classical Greece*
Elaine Fantham, *Roman Literary Culture: From Cicero to Apuleius*
Kenneth W. Harl, *Coinage in the Roman Economy, 300 B.C. to A.D. 700*
Christopher Haas, *Alexandria in Late Antiquity*
James C. Anderson, jr., *Roman Architecture and Society*
Matthew R. Christ, *The Litigious Athenian*

Library of Congress Cataloging-in-Publication Data
Christ, Matthew R., 1960–
    The litigious Athenian : Matthew R. Christ.
      p. cm. — (Ancient society and history)
    Includes bibliographical references and index.
    ISBN 0-8018-5863-1 (alk. paper)
      1. Adversary system (Law)—Greece—Athens—
History. 2. Justice, Administration of—Greece—Athens—
History. I. Title. II. Series.
KL4115.A75C48   1998
347.38'5—dc21   97-52752
                                                                    CIP